Your True Horoscope

(Birth Time Rectification)

Revised and Enlarged

Your True Horoscope
(Birth Time Rectification)
Revised and Enlarged

S.P. Khullar
I.T.S.
G.M. Telecommunications (Rtd.)

Sagar Publications
72, Janpath, Ved Mansion, New Delhi-110001
Tel.: 23320648, 23328245
E-mail: sagarpub@vsnl.com
Website: www.sagarpublications.com

First Edition, 2005
Revised and Enlarged Second Edition, 2011

Published and printed by Saurabh Sagar for Sagar Publications New Delhi-110001 and printed at The Artwaves, A-487, Double Storey, Kalkaji, New Delhi-110019. Ph.: 011-41609709

Acknowledgment

The revised and enlarged edition of the book on "Your True Horoscope" has been written, like my earlier books on Astrology, under the spell of inspiration and guidance of the Supreme Intelligence. The effort has consumed lot of my vitality and affected my health adversely. However, I remained focused in my approach due to sincere and awe-inspiring devotion of my wife, friends and students of True Astrology. I sincerely thank them all. My special thanks to my senior students Mr RS Chani and Mr Roopeshwar Gupta. Both of them had worked on the manuscript with full dedication to ensure that the book is released without any technical error.

I am equally grateful to Mrs Sandy L Crowther of USA and Mr Ron Gaunt of Brisbane, Australia.They have always provided me the required motivation to undertake this work.

Sagar Publications has shown the skill and professionalism they have attained during the years. They have brought the revised and enlarged edition of my book "Your True Horoscope" in amazingly short time without sacrificing quality. I express my sincere thanks to the

S.P. Khullar
I.T.S.

Contents

Introduction

S.P. Khullar

The sacred science of Astrology is based on the doctrine of reincarnation and laws of Karma. It essentially recognizes that the human being consists of body, mind and soul. To the Astrologer the heavens form the Macrocosm and man the Microcosm. Man is an exact copy of the universe, a little world or miniature of the great world around him. Astrology believes in the three great truths as stated by the Author of "The Idyll of the White Soul" as follows:

The Soul of man is immortal.

The principle, which gives life dwell in us and without us, is undying and eternally beneficent.

Each man is his own absolute lawgiver.

The concept of human being as body, mind and Soul has been expressed not only by the Astrologers or the metaphysists but also found expression in the writing of all the evolved souls in the universe. The poet Longfellow has beautifully expressed his belief in the existence of the soul in the famous poem, 'A psalm of life'.

Tell me not, in mournful numbers,

Life is but an empty dream!-

For the soul is dead that slumbers,

And things are not what they seem.

Life is real! Life is earnest!

And the grave is not its goal,

Dust thou art, to dust retunes,

Was not spoken of the soul....

John Greenleaf Whittier has expressed his belief in rebirth in Raphael as under:

The Tissue of the Life to be

We weave with colors of our own,

And in the field of Destiny

We reap as we have sown.

To understand the true purport of Astrology, it is imperative that we should understand how the human being is born. This has been explained in the first chapter. The time that the incarnating soul chooses to take possession of a particular body in a particular family, in particular socio-economic, natural environment based on its past Karmas and Sanskars (tendencies) is called the Astrological Birth Time. It defies the capability of the doctor to note it. **However, it has to be closely linked with the first breath the child takes when it comes out of the womb of the mother.**

It is the responsibility of the Astrologer to fix it and construct the true horoscope of the native. The true horoscope has to be unique for each individual. It should simulate conditions to reflect the native's heredity, individuality, personality, state of health, longevity, name and fame, virtues, capacity to face struggle of life, social, financial, marital, educational, and professional status. It is, therefore, imperative that we need to place the correct degree, minutes and seconds on each of the twelve cuspal positions. How to do this has been explained in this book.

The reader's dedication, devotion and the open-minded approach will bring rewards. However, let us not forget that our success in efforts to construct true horoscope is largely dependant on the accuracy of the software, which we use for the calculation of planetary and cuspal positions. **It may be noted that the author has used True position of Rhau and Ketu in constructing the horoscopes. Programme is set to convert Latitude to geo centric values.**

No doubt blessed ones alone can discover what is hitherto unknown. I have only made a sincere and dedicated attempt to dig out and revive our true concepts of Astrology. The aspiring reader will doubtlessly find the methods of rectification of birth chart elaborated in this book as an exposition of sound techniques based on scientific analysis.

S.P. Khullar
I.T.S.
G.M. Telecommunications (Rtd.)
www.khullarastrologyinstitute.com
info@khullarastrologyinstitute.com

Preface to Second Edition

Two new chapters have been added namely advanced techniques of birth time rectification, and rectification of birth charts of Twins. These chapters are written taking into consideration the research findings of the author regarding the concept of promise for various aspects of life and the execution of promises based on the concept of progression. The concept of progression is based on the philosophy of Vimsottary Dasa progression. Theory of timing events defines clearly that an event happens when Dasa period lords of fruitful significators run, transit supports and the progressed ascendant and progressed chart confirms the event. In addition to the new chapters author has also briefly discussed the views of Varah Mihira and others on the subject of casting horoscopes for those who have no known birth details.

Index has also been added. It may be noted that charts in Chapter V and VI are cast using True Astrology Software Version 4.3 using Khullar (Hourly) Ayanamsa.

S.P. Khullar
I.T.S.
G.M. Telecommunications (Rtd.)
www.khullarastrologyinstitute.com
info@khullarastrologyinstitute.com

Chapter 1

Human Being and Astrology

Every human being is a unique person born with a particular psychophysical constitution. According to modern biology heredity and environment are the two principal factors in the origin and development of an individual. The metaphysists on the other hand recognize the existence of body, mind and soul. According to them each man has his own personal consciousness entrenched in his body and gets into touch with his surroundings only through his body and senses, and the mind using the senses. If Astrology has to be a true science, the horoscope of each individual has to be unique and it must simulate conditions that can account for his heredity and genetical connections, and also what the metaphysists have to say about human birth and cause for individual differences and also the life pattern of each individual.

Modern Gynecologists Opinion of Human Birth

Human body, according to the modern biology, consists of innumerable minute cells that are responsible for its structure and function. As noted by Dr. Ville, "The cell theory includes the concept that the cell is the fundamental unit of both function and structure - the fundamental unit that shows all the characteristics of living things." Each living cell contains a number of component parts, one of which is called protoplasm; in the nucleus of the cell are threads like structures, called chromosomes. There are a definite or fixed number of chromosomes in every cell of a creature and the number of chromosomes in every cell varies from species to species.

For example, every human cell contains forty-six chromosomes. However, the germ cell of every species contains only half the number of chromosomes in any other cell so that when the chromosomes of the male and female germ cells unite, a new cell is formed that contains the correct total number of chromosomes for the species. For example, each germ cell of man and woman, carries twenty-three chromosomes and when those unite, their total number in every cell of a human body becomes forty-six. Further, each one of the chromosomes is composed of a large number of entities, called genes. Each gene is supposed to control some characteristics in the individual.

Embryology of Man

Prof. Otto Grosser in his book "Outline of Human Embryology" has divided embryology of man into three phases:

1. **Progenesis or Primordial Development:** It comprises the maturation of sex cells and the process of fertilization.
2. **Blastogenesis or Embryonic Development:** It comprises the embryonic development from fertilization to the development of primitive organs.
3. **Organogenesis:** It is the development of individual organs in the embryo.

How Conception Takes place?

The reproduction cell in the male body is called the sperm and the reproduction cell in the female body is called the ovum or egg. For the birth of a human being, the fertilization of the ovum and sperm is a pre-requisite. In female just one egg (Ovum) ripens every month and is released from one of the ovaries (alternately from each ovary). This happens in the middle of the menstruation cycle i.e. from 13 to 18 days from the day of menstruation. After the release the Ovum remains alive for 18-24 hrs. The sperm, on the other hand, is contained in the semen released by the male at the time of orgasm. There is about 100-300 million sperms in each ejaculate and only one meet the ovum to cause conception. Fig 1.1 explains how conception takes place.

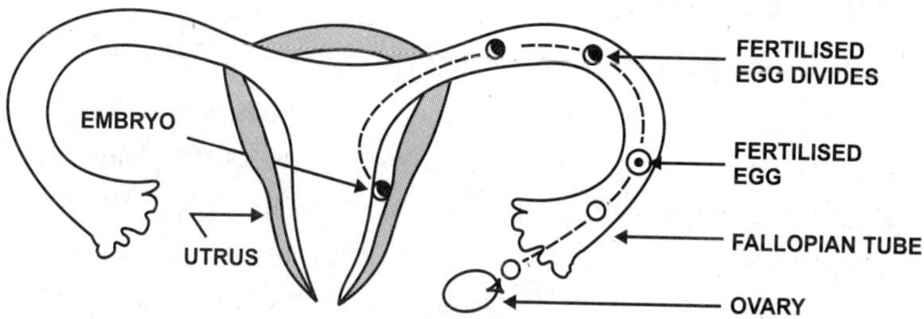

Fig 1.1

After intercourse the sperms ascend the uterus and enter the fallopian tubes to meet the ovum travelling in the opposite direction. The fertilization (meeting of sperm and ovum) has taken place in the left fallopian tube. The fertilization brings about a new cell called zygote, the fertilized egg, which develops into an individual in due course.

Thus, according to current biology the starting point of an individual's life is the zygote produced by the fusion of the nuclei of the male and the female reproduction cell. The fertilized egg contains twenty-three chromosomes from the male parent and twenty-three from the female parent. The heredity units, the genes, of both lies within. The chromosomes and genes function as a single unit. Dobzhansky in his book "The Biology of Ultimate Concern" says, "A child receives one half of the genes of his father and one-half of the maternal ones; which particular maternal and parental genes are transmitted to a given child is a matter of chance. Which mutations occur, and when and where, is also a matter of chance." Julian Huxley supports the theory of chance when he says, "Egg and sperm carry the destiny of generations. The egg realizes one chance combination with millions of pairs of sperms, each one actually different in the combination of cards which it holds". It is, according to him, only a chance that a particular sperm fertilizes the ovum to produce a genius or a moron.

Sex of the Child: According to the biologists, the sex chromosomes in man (sperm) carry x y- chromosomes while in a woman (egg or ovum) it is only x x- chromosomes. The sex of the baby depends upon which sperm fertilizes the egg. When an x-carrying sperm fertilizes the egg, the baby will be x or a girl. And if a y-carrying sperm fertilizes the egg, the baby will be x y or a boy. Since the female only carries x x-chromosomes, it would appear as if the father were the sex determining factor, although it is not impossible that the power of attraction present in the ovum give preference to one or the other. Biologists, however, have no clue and attribute it to a chance factor only.

Critical Review of Biologists Opinion of Human Birth

The biologists opinion is based on the principle that 'like begets like'. As you sow, so shall you reap? Humans are born of human parents. The tendency of the individuals to resemble their progenitors is called heredity. This resemblance, however, does not exclude individual variations. Heredity, in a wide sense, is inclusive of both similarity and divergence. Every creature despite the resemblance it bears to its progenitors retains its individuality. Modern geneticist has not been able to find a satisfactory solution of the problem of variations. **Neither heredity nor environment, not even their interaction, can explain the birth and growth of an individual. This theory also fails to account for the birth of geniuses out of mediocre parents or the birth of morons of normal parents.** The birth of a genius or a prodigy cannot be termed as a chance. The geneticists have, in fact, now come to the conclusion that life cannot be synthesized by the synthesis of genes. Szent-Gyorgi, the Nobel Prize winning chemist, has rightly said, "In search for the secret of life, I ended up with atoms and electrons which have no life at all. Somewhere along the line, life has run out through my fingers. So, in my old age I am now retracing my steps".

Human Being and the viewpoint of Vedanta

The Vedantic concept of human birth is based on the doctrine of reincarnation that is a complement to the doctrine of Karma. According to this philosophy death is not the end of an individual nor is birth the beginning of him. Man is not just a physical, or a biophysical, or a psychophysical being. Man has a body, mind and soul. An individual functions as an organized system because of the co-ordination of these three primal constituents. The real man is the knowing self, the central principal of consciousness, which is the unchanging witness of the changing condition of the body, organs, the mind and the external world. An individual's mind is distinct from the self and the body as well, although closely associated with both. It is the identity of the mind that maintains one's individuality beyond death and rebirth. Hence the child's mind cannot be a fragment of the parental mind. Neither it can arise from either parent's body or self, being different by nature from both. According to this philosophy every individual brings his own mind and develops his own way.

How is an Individual Born?

The Vedantic view of human birth, as already said above, is based on the theory of reincarnation. So birth accordingly is considered only as a rebirth of one of the many individuals who died somewhere some time back. **At death, the self, the real man, leaves the physical body, but retains the subtle and the casual body. The mind with all its content belongs to the subtle body.** In Gita, Lord Krishna explains that manifestation or descent of a soul in a particular body, family and environment depends upon the soul's earlier impressions or predispositions, resulting from its past births. The next life of a being is determined by what resolves he has at the time of its death i.e. according to those impressions (volitional actions, experiences, and thoughts) that become prevalent in the mind of the dying man. **Very fine physical vesture for the subtle and the casual body is formed at the time of his departure from the gross body. This fine garb carries the potencies of the next gross body he assumes.** Through food, he enters the body of the male parent suitable for his purpose. There he gets into the requisite sperm, which turns into potent seed for his development as an individual. This is the seed that being united with the appropriate ovum in the female parent turns into zygote and becomes ready for germination. These are the two specialized male and female reproductive cells that are responsible for the birth of the offspring out of countless sperms and ova that are brought into play in sexual reproduction. In other words, we say that led by its Karma the transmigrating soul gets into the requisite sperm and ovum out of countless reproductive cells. The fusion of the sperm and the ovum required for its physical body is by no means a matter of chance. It is, as a matter of fact based on the law of cause and effect in the form of the law of Karma.

Heredity cannot logically explain the difference in the inborn aptitudes of the individuals. The doctrine of reincarnation, sequence to the law of Karma, alone provides the satisfactory explanation of the inequalities of life. An individual's weakness and excellences, knowledge and ignorance, rise and fall depend primarily on his own past thoughts and deeds. No external agency, parentage or divine dispensation, chance or fate, is responsible for them. It is the interplay of the body, the mind, and the self (soul) in human personality that accounts for the development of the individual. **According to Vedanta, the development means unfoldment of inherent potency. What lies latent in the cause becomes manifest as the effect. Heredity and genetical connections account only for the physical aspects of the individual like colour, shape, and resistance to various diseases etc.**

Human Being and Astrology

Astrology is based on the doctrine of reincarnation and law of Karma as declared by the metaphysists. It recognizes that the human being essentially consist of body, mind and soul. Our ancients found that the planets & the zodiac accounts for the reincarnation of the soul, its selection of the body and environment and its evolution in the material universe. The ancients declared the significations of the planets, the zodiacal degrees and the houses of the horoscope on the basis of the three cosmic principles viz law of polarity, law of elements and law of mode of action. It is believed that **"The universe proceeds from the tattvas; it goes into the tattvas; it vanishes into the tattvas".** The zodiac as a limiting circle of the earth's aura is the field and storehouse of all that was, is, and is to be. It is the battlefield of Arjuna, the playground of the Logos, and the stage upon which the great drama of life is enacted. The planetary spirits are the players, and the principal actors in the drama. Even the minutest part of the zodiac represents firstly a particular state of matter, secondly a characteristic mode of motion and thirdly a coordinated type of consciousness or self. These three, the matter, the motion and the consciousness, correspond and agree. They are connected with the fundamental classification of Self, Not-self, and the relation between them. The creative life proceeds from the self and runs through the other two, and upon this fact all the laws of Astrology are based.

Astrological Explanation of Human Birth

At the time of death, the Astral Body (The Etheric Double) leaves the physical vehicle and returns to a condition more similar to its own nature but carries with it its wishes, choices and aspirations. Human being is a "Divine Fragment", a center within the universal divine consciousness, inseparably united with every other center, and all blended in one ultimately by the universal life and consciousness in which they are centered. When the spiritual impulse towards fresh experience and unfoldment becomes potent once more, then it will descend into a body at a time when the celestial conditions resemble itself, its wishes, choice and aspirations. The soul brings its various faculties with it when it is born upon this earth, but its possibility of using them effectively depends upon the kind of body that is given to it; and because character determines fate to a very large extent, the type of body decides what the man's career will be, his good and evil fortune, his success and failures. The plan of body, therefore, varies according to the kind of character to be expressed by the soul and the kind of experience it is destined to pass through during its lifetime in the body. Lords of karmas decide the plan of the body and the environment into which it will be born. **It may be remembered that the casual body is the only vehicle that is permanent**

throughout the whole cycle of the human pilgrimage. It continues life after life and contains all the seeds, good and bad, of each earthly existence, and upon the entry into each new physical life these seeds awaken out of latency and give forth their vibratory powers, aroused into activity by the stimulation of the Ego. Astrology, the sacred science, takes this into consideration and offer the satisfactory explanation of human birth.

Selection of Time of Conception

Astrology treats the problem of conception and maternity both in the light of modern gynecological knowledge and the metaphysists view of human birth. Led by its Karma the transmigrating soul gets into the requisite sperm and ovum out of countless reproductive cells. The fusion of the sperm and ovum required for its physical body is by no means a matter of chance. **The time of fertilization of the egg, the selection of sperm and ovum has to account for the plan of body that the soul has to use as its vehicle.** Conception takes place at a time represented by the most minute division of the rising sign at the place of conception and the planets co-ruling this minute division of the rising sign accounts for the seed cast in the cosmic soil or Ether to unfold its latent qualities, of which the individual then born is supposed to absorb more or less according to the powers of response and stage of soul-evolution. The selection of the time of the epoch is controlled by the planets as per their position in the zodiac to simulate the plan for the body as per the lords of Karma. What the planets represent are indicated below:

i) The planet Sun symbolizes cosmic life or consciousness or spark of divinity (self), which afterwards becomes the separated life of body, mind and soul. It supplies Prana or vital force.

ii) The planet Moon represents the Not-self. It represents in the body the lower part of the brain, the spinal cord and the sympathetic system and is closely connected with the senses. It denotes the interaction between thought and feeling, or the psychic nature with all its rapid and fluctuating moods and changes of consciousness. In its Sub-influence under Jupiter, it represents the Etheric Aura. Moon governs the whole of personality and the etheric double of the physical body and may be said to act as the vehicle for influence handed down from the astral and mental planes. Moon rules over the Water tattva that affects the Etheric double upon which the physical cells are built.

iii) The planet Jupiter is called the seed planet of the physical plane. When the physical body is dropped at death, all that is latent in the earthy signs is preserved in the influence of the planet Jupiter and carried upward to the next vehicle of manifestation, so that on the astral plane we have the influence of its own triplicity plus that of Jupiter.

iv) Mercury represents the cerebral-spinal nervous system.

v) The planet Saturn is called the Antha Karana. The whole fate of an incarnation depends on whether Antha Karana (Saturn) will be able to restrain the Kama-Manas (Mars) or not. Saturn rules over the tattva Vayu that is often spoken of as the Auric Egg, the preserver of every Karmic record. This Auric Egg itself, regarded as vehicle, is under the dominant influence of Jupiter.

vi) Mars governs the personal feelings, the animal soul, and the consciousness of our emotional body as the sum total of all our varying moods, sensations and feelings.

vii) Venus is often linked with Kama -Rupa, which is the vehicle of desires and passions.

The element ruling at the moment of conception decides the sex of the child as per the wishes of the incarnating Soul.

Development of Embryo

It is believed that the soul does not enter into the fertilized egg but remains in touch with it unconsciously and various currents of energy flowing down the soul that plays a part in the shaping of the body or what we call the development of Embryo. **Thus the moment of epoch truly speaking is the moment at which the Ego is prepared to enter into this world.** During the period of Gestation only the plastic forces, the etheric body, are active in the body in a state of development. During this development, there are three factors at work upon the embryo. These are:

A. The forces of heredity, contained in the fertilized ovum.

B. The plan given by the lords of Karma in accordance with which the artificial elemental builds the body.

C. The influence of the incoming soul, generally exercised unconsciously.

Gestation and Planetary Influence

The average length of human gestation is 40 weeks (280 days), but a good deal of variation from this is possible. A week is one quarter of the Moon's revolution. The birth of human being is regulated by Moon. The following synodical revolutions, if taken in simple proportions, measure close to the period of gestation, 280 days.

Planet	Synodical Revolution	Proportion	Days
Moon	29.530 days	9 ½	281
Mercury	115.877 days	2 ½	290
Venus	583.920 days	½	292
Earth	365.256 days	¾	274
Mars	779.936 days	1/3	260
Jupiter	398.867 days	¾	299
Saturn	378.090 days	¾	284
Uranus	369.656 days	¾	277
Neptune	367.488 days	¾	276
	The average of the whole		281

A synodical revolution is the time intervening between two conjunctions with the Sun, or the time that elapses before the return to the same relative position in the zodiac with regard to Sun, as seen from the earth. The table shows that 9 ½ mean synodical revolutions of the Moon measure 281 (280.54 days exactly) or within one day of the normal period of gestation. 2 ½ synodical revolutions of the Mercury measures 290 days. Half the period of Venus gives 292 days. The other planets give either a little more or little less than normal; the average of the whole being 281 days, a very close approach to the 280 days demanded by medical science.

If the column headed "Synodical Revolution" is added up and an average taken, it will amount to 376.514 days. Three fourth of this average is 282.386 days, which is again a very close approach to the average of 280 given by medical men. The fact speaks loudly of the close connection between heavenly bodies and the period of gestation.

Role of planets in Gestation Period

The planets that control the period of gestation or pregnancy are indicated below:

First Month: Venus rules it. The embryo continues to be in a fluid state.

Second Month: Mars governs it. Embryo solidifies.

Third Month: Jupiter rules over it. Limbs are formed.

Fourth Month: Sun governs it. Bones are formed.

Fifth Month: Moon supplies the skin.

Sixth Month: Saturn allows hairs to grow.

Seventh Month: Mercury develops nervous system.

Eight Month: Lord of the Epoch Ascendant rules over it. Umbilical cord takes food to the Child.

Ninth Month: Sun governs it. Fetus feels thirst and hunger.

Tenth Month: Moon rules it. Ready for delivery.

From the above, it should be clear that the development of the embryo into the child is under the influence of planets, which alone according to their position in the zodiac at the time of epoch will account for the normal or defective growth.

Astrological Birth Time and Formation of Horoscope

The Astrological moment of birth is that moment at which the soul takes possession of the body. It is difficult to measure but is closely related to the first breath the child takes after coming out of the mother's womb. The selection of the time of birth is controlled by the life giving planet

Sun (Self) and Moon (Not-self) and the position of planets in the various but specified degrees of the zodiac. As Varahamihir said, "The planets offer a lawful channel for the outward operations of cause-effect equilibrium that man has set into motion in the past as a free agent." **Corresponding to the birth time a particular degree, minutes and seconds will rise in the eastern horizon at the place of birth. This we call as Ascendant.** Based on the zodiacal degree of the Ascendant and the latitude and longitude of the place of birth, other Cuspal positions are formed. The planets occupy specific positions in the Zodiac as they ought to occupy according to the predetermined plan based on lords of Karma and under the guidance of Supreme Intelligence. Our soul or inner mind is carrier of our Karmas, both past and present but it is our body, which is responsible for the execution of Karma or bear the fruits of our past and present Karmas. The formation of the horoscope has to be such that it explains completely the pattern of unfoldment of the incarnated soul in the material universe. The zodiac represents the storehouse of cosmic energy. The planets according to their position in the zodiac attain the necessary energy content and their linkages through Star, Sub & Sub-Sub etc.with the various cuspal positions in the horoscope indicate the manner in which they are going to provide results as per the lords of Karma. Cuspal positions that are formed corresponding to the position of the Ascendant are the concrete expressions of mundane affairs of life in the physical body. The houses may be equated to matter-the body-which operates under the law of ultimate dissolution and the zodiacal degrees rising on the Ascendant and other cuspal positions may be equated to represent the real man. **The concept of Destiny or Fate is based on the fact that the birth of human beings takes place according to the theory of incarnation.** There has been ample proof for this concept of incarnation. However, we safely forget that the theory of incarnation has also an inbuilt and latent element. This element specifies that each new incarnation is step forward in the evolution of the soul. If we were to enjoy the fruits of past Karmas alone then how could evolution take place?

The record of past karmas is contained in the physical-etheric nucleus called "permanent particle' by Charles Leadbeater and Annie Besant. It is analogous to DNA in the bio-molecular body. The physical-etheric body provides an electromagnetic matrix which plays a critical role in the morphogenessis of the physical bio-molecular body. The physical-etheric nucleus enables the transfer of information from one body to another body during the death process.

Unfortunately in the recent past the emphasis in astrology has been based only on the physical concept of human being. We know that human being is a composite being of spirit(Purusha,the spark of Divinity,a part of Universal consciousness, soul or causal body).the subtle body (Antakaran,the etheric double and astral body),the gross physical body. It has been discovered by Prof.Czizivyeski of Moscow **that surrounding our physical body there is an electro-structure which is called as the etheric double e.t.c. The subtle bodies are as much a part of our reality as are the physical ones. The subtle body, in fact, is in the real sense our functional body.** It is electrical in nature and has lines of force which act as channels for the flow of energy received from the causal body to the physical body.

The laws of true Astrology were based on this concept of human being. This theory if studied in detail clearly points out the role of past karmas and future dispositions. The quantum and quality of energy apportioned to the native at the time of incarnation is indicated by the zodiacal degree rising at the Ascdt. Its channelizing is indicated by the linkages established by the

SSL of the various cuspal positions. The nature of the SSLs as modified by the signs in which they are placed in the chart indicates the limiting factors for the growth of the native. Let me refer to James Hillman "*Acorn Theory*".

Hillman's central thesis, illustrated by several fine biographical sketches, is that "remarkable" peopie, ranging from serial killers to renowned artists, are born, not made. This flies in the face of conventional psychological wisdom which says that early childhood conditioning is the greatest determinant of what a person will make of himself years down the road. To the contrary, Hillman asserts that it is "neither nature nor nurture" (neither genetics nor environment) that dictates the outcome of a life. Rather, it is an innate quality possessed by each person, the spark of individuality that, like a master code for a person's life, determines the direction in which he will pursue his destiny.

Hillman favors the Greek term daimon as a substitute for the complementary notions of "guardian angel", spirit, or soul, all of which imply an over-arching intelligence that provides a road map for the life. This is the "soul's code". Thanks to the daimon, the adult's true fate is already known to the child, and it is this knowledge that guides the child unerringly, despite all the obstacles imposed by parental and societal norms, in the inevitable direction of its fate.

Hillman calls this his "acorn theory", which proposes that each life is animated by a particular image that calls it to its destiny. Plant an acorn in a corn field; it produces an oak, not a corn stalk. Let mother encourage or discourage, it makes no matter, the little child-soul knows where it's going and will have its way in time. The daimon is in the driver's seat.

Readers with an appreciation for astrology might well wonder whether the "soul's code", this animating image conferred by fate, could be an academic euphemism for the astrological birth chart. Although Hillman never gives his readers an explicit nod in this direction, his occasional references to astrology encourage us to believe that he is familiar with its basic principles and practices. He is perhaps even sympathetic when he says, "There is in each of us a longing to see beyond what our usual sight tells us. A revelation of the invisible in an intelligible form leads us to the astrologer." That the soul's code is indeed locked in the chakra of the birth chart

The physical Constitution (structure and size) and colour of a person is controlled by one's genes. The selection of one's genes is the prerogative of one's soul (casual body). But unfortunately some Astrologers put too much emphasis on the Ascendant to declare the physical aspects of the native like colour etc. This has been my concern. The colour, size and structure of the body are under the control of DNA theory. DNA and hereditary, however, play role in the formation of the horoscope too. How could we predict about the diseases due to genetical disorder or what we call hereditary diseases? **The casual body first creates the Astral and etheric body as per karmic code. This etheric body is implant in the womb of the selected mother. The development of the child in the womb of the mother and also after birth is as per the quality of this etheric body. The etheric body, in fact, is our real functioning body.** The modern scientist has explained it by the concept of electro-structure surrounding the physical body of each living organism. Its function is best explained by the concept of Chakras or psycho spiritual centers. **There are seven chakras and each chakra is linked to a particular endocrine gland. Any imbalance in any chakra creates an impact on the functioning of a particular gland and these results in the malfunctioning of a particular system in the**

body. In the horoscope each cuspal position represents certain aspects of the individual's life. The Ascendant stands for one's individuality, personality, temperament, physical body, state of health, longevity, name and fame, virtues, capacity to face struggles of life, direction and aspects of life in which the native will channelise his energies; proneness to accidents or untoward happenings. Ascendant, in other words, reflects the quality and quantum of energy apportioned to the native according to which he executes the Karma or bears the fruits of the Karma. In Astrology energy content is a concept that defies qualitative or quantitative measurement as is understood by a student of Physics. To understand this concept one needs to understand the theory of Human birth based on the Theory of Incarnation. Horoscope is a map which depicts the Karmic potential of the soul that incarnates. **Monad** (single celled micro organism) contains information of previous lives of the soul that incarnates in an electromagnetic matrix. Karmic potential is the balance sheet of native's past karmas and future dispositions. This is what we mean by energy content. To an Astrologer its measure is nothing but the sum total of the static and dynamic significations of the Planets that co-rule the Ascdt. Nature of Planets is studied against the backdrop of the Zodiac.

Planets play the role of actors according to the script written by Supreme Intelligence and under the direction of the Divinity within him. The innate quality of these Actors i.e. Planets is defined by their zodiacal degree positions and the nature of their role is as per their house significations. Study of the Ascendant, therefore, is the study of the whole horoscope in brevity.

In the horoscope, the houses 1, 4, 7 and 10 are called Angular houses. These are directly connected with the physical and external world, and represent outgoing activities originating in the Self but affecting the Not-Self very directly. They generally show the nature of things that must be openly expressed, and therefore denote the name, reputation, public position, and general activities more clearly and definitely then any of the other houses.

The houses 2, 5, 8 and 11 are called the Succedent houses. These are connected with desire, feeling, and emotion and with the guna Tamas. Experiences and characteristics based upon planets linked to these houses tend to continue unchanged or with the minimum of alteration for long periods, sometimes all through the life.

The houses 3, 6, 9 and 12 are called Cadent or Mental houses. These houses show how thought guides and directs both action and desire.

Each incarnated soul has its own secret. It stands revealed only by the minute divisions of the Zodiac that rise on each of the twelve cuspal positions and the minute divisions of the Zodiac, which influence each planet. The horoscope cast and analysed on cuspal interlinks basis will simulate and reveal conditions to represent the unique life pattern of the individual.

Chapter 2

Theories of Rectification of Birth Time

Birth time is the foundation of any radical (natal) chart. No matter how correctly a given birth time has been stated by a doctor, it is no guarantee for the exact astrological moment of birth of the native. The horoscope of the native has to be a unique portrait that should clearly simulate the conditions to represent the native's individuality, personality, temperament, state of health, longevity, field of education, professional activities, genetical connections etc. Since each individual is unique, the Astrological moment of birth has to be fixed to produce a unique horoscope. **This moment may be intimately related to the physical moment of birth (the first breath), but is of a spiritual nature that determines the quality and quantum of energy apportioned to the native according to which he executes the Karma or bears the fruits of the Karma.** To fix the Astrological moment of birth forms a primary and essential process in the field of astrology. It is a vexed problem and defies easy solution. Astrologers have used various theories to fix the correct birth time. Some of the important theories are:

1. Tattva Sidhant or Nadi Theory of Rectification
2. Pre-Natal Epoch Theory of Rectification
3. Varaha Mahira's Views on Lost Horoscopes
4. The Ruling Planets and Construction of Horoscope

5. Rectification to Match genetical connections, Promise of each cusp and Dasa and Transit potential of planets to justify events

In this chapter we will explain Nadi Theory of Rectification, PNE Theory of Rectification and Varaha Mihira's Views on Lost Horoscopes. Theories at Sl. Nos.4 and 5 are dealt in detail in chapter III and chapter IV respectively.

Tattva Sidhant or Nadi Theory of Rectification

This Theory is based on the following fundamental concepts:

1. The regular intervals of time in any weekday from Sunrise are governed by the one or the other five Tattvas (Elements) viz. Earth, Water, Fire, Air and Akash. These Tattvas follow a definite and pre-ordained order dependent upon the weekday and the time of Sunrise.
2. The sex of the child is dependent on the inherent nature of the particular Tattva governing the moment of birth.
3. The moment of birth is related to Moon's Star at the time of birth, the nature of the Ascending Sign as Moveable, Fixed or Common; and the weekday.

Human births take place by the Soli-Lunar energy coupled with the planet ruling the weekday.In other words, this theory postulates that the Sun sends at regular intervals of time from the moment of Sun rise cosmic energy that contains Gama-Rays, X-Rays, Ultra Violet Rays and other rays which are necessary for birth, growth and development and evolution of human beings. In astrological language we say that Sun represents the spark of Divinity or the life force. Moon while passing over a Nakshatra each day receives this energy and transforms it into a medium, the embryo, which later on develops into a physical body. The Tattva of the planets ruling the particular moment on a day determines the sex of the embryo and even accounts for his genetical connections and heredity.

Tattvas Duration and Cyclic Order:

The five Tattvas follow a definite cyclic order. They repeat the order after every 90 minutes starting with the Tattva at Sunrise in accordance with the weekday lord. The following Table shows the cyclic order, duration of each Tattva and the Planets ruling the Tattva.

Tattva

Tattva	Duration	Planet Ruler ship	Week Day	Sex
Earth	6 Minutes	Mercury	Wednesday	Male
Water	12 Minutes	Moon & Venus	Mon & Fri	Female
Fire	18 Minutes	Sun & Mars	Sun & Tuesday	Male
Air	24 Minutes	Saturn	Saturday	Female
Akash	30 Minutes	Jupiter	Thursday	Male

The Astrologers following the hints from the Upanishads believed that each Tattva, in fact, includes the characteristics of other Tattvas also. As such they divided each Tattva into Antara Tattva or Sub Tattva in the same proportion as they are allotted in the complete cycle of 90 minutes. The complete Table of Antara Tattva is shown below:

Earth 6			Water 12			Fire 18			Air 24			Akash 30		
Min	Sec	Sex	Min	Sec	Sex	Min	Sec	Sex	Min	Sec	Sex	Min	Sec	Sex
0	24	M	1	36	F	3	36	M	6	24	F	10	0	M
0	48	F	2	24	M	4	48	F	8	0	M	2	0	M
1	12	M	3	12	F	6	0	M	1	36	M	4	0	F
1	36	F	4	0	M	1	12	M	3	12	F	6	0	M
2	0	M	0	48	F	2	24	F	4	48	M	8	0	F

Application of Tattva Sidhant or Nadi Rectification.

The application of this theory for correctly fixing the Birth time requires the use of Table A and Table B. In Table A, the Star lord in place of the Star is used. The data required for rectification is listed below:

1. Date, place and noted time of birth.
2. The time of Sunrise on the day and place of birth.
3. Day of birth (From Sunrise to Sunrise).
4. Ascendant in the chart under consideration.
5. Moon's Star at the time of birth.

Table A

A.M.	A.M.	P.M.	P.M.	A.M.	A.M.	Aries Cancer Libra Capri.	Taurus Leo Scor. Aqu.	Gemini Virgo Sagi. Pisces	S No.
603	1033	303	733	1203	433	Sun	Mars	Jupiter	1
606	1036	306	736	1206	436	Moon	Rahu	Saturn	2
609	1039	309	739	1209	439	Mars	Jupiter	Mercury	3
612	1042	312	742	1212	442	Rahu	Saturn	Ketu	4
615	1045	315	745	1215	445	Jupiter	Mercury	Venus	5
618	1048	318	748	1218	448	Saturn	Ketu	Sun	6
621	1051	321	751	1221	451	Mercury	Venus	Moon	7
624	1054	324	754	1224	454	Ketu	Sun	Mars	8
627	1057	327	757	1227	457	Venus	Moon	Rahu	9
630	1100	330	800	1230	500	Sun	Mars	Jupiter	10
633	1103	333	803	1233	503	Moon	Rahu	Saturn	11
636	1106	336	806	1236	506	Mars	Jupiter	Mercury	12
639	1109	339	809	1239	509	Rahu	Saturn	Ketu	13

Contd......

Table A

A.M.	A.M.	P.M.	P.M.	A.M.	A.M.	Aries Cancer Libra Capri.	Taurus Leo Scor. Aqu.	Gemini Virgo Sagi. Pisces	S No.
642	1112	342	812	1242	512	Jupiter	Mercury	Venus	14
645	1115	345	815	1245	515	Saturn	Ketu	Sun	15
648	1118	348	818	1248	518	Mercury	Venus	Moon	16
651	1121	351	821	1251	521	Ketu	Sun	Mars	17
654	1124	354	824	1254	524	Venus	Moon	Rahu	18
657	1127	357	827	1257	527	Sun	Mars	Jupiter	19
700	1130	400	830	100	530	Moon	Rahu	Saturn	20
703	1133	403	833	103	533	Mars	Jupiter	Mercury	21
706	1136	406	836	106	536	Rahu	Saturn	Ketu	22
709	1139	409	839	109	539	Jupiter	Mercury	Venus	23
712	1142	412	842	112	542	Saturn	Ketu	Sun	24
715	1145	415	845	115	545	Mercury	Venus	Moon	25
718	1148	418	848	118	548	Ketu	Sun	Mars	26
721	1151	421	851	121	551	Venus	Moon	Rahu	27
724	1154	424	854	124	554	Sun	Mars	Jupiter	28
727	1157	427	857	127	557	Moon	Rahu	Saturn	29
730	1200	430	900	130	600	Mars	Jupiter	Mercury	30
733	1203	433	903	133		Rahu	Saturn	Ketu	31
736	1206	436	906	136		Jupiter	Mercury	Venus	32
739	1209	439	909	139		Saturn	Ketu	Sun	33
742	1212	442	912	142		Mercury	Venus	Moon	34
745	1215	445	915	145		Ketu	Sun	Mars	35
748	1218	448	918	148		Venus	Moon	Rahu	36
751	1221	451	921	151		Sun	Mars	Jupiter	37
754	1224	454	924	154		Moon	Rahu	Saturn	38
757	1227	457	927	157		Mars	Jupiter	Mercury	39

Contd......

Table A

A.M.	A.M.	P.M.	P.M.	A.M.	A.M.	Aries Cancer Libra Capri.	Taurus Leo Scor. Aqu.	Gemini Virgo Sagi. Pisces	S No.
800	1230	500	930	200		Rahu	Saturn	Ketu	40
803	1233	503	933	203		Jupiter	Mercury	Venus	41
806	1236	506	936	206		Saturn	Ketu	Sun	42
809	1239	509	939	209		Mercury	Venus	Moon	43
812	1242	512	942	212		Ketu	Sun	Mars	44
815	1245	515	945	215		Venus	Moon	Rahu	45
818	1248	518	948	218		Sun	Mars	Jupiter	46
821	1251	521	951	221		Moon	Rahu	Saturn	47
824	1254	524	954	224		Mars	Jupiter	Mercury	48
827	1257	527	957	227		Rahu	Saturn	Ketu	49
830	100	530	1000	230		Jupiter	Mercury	Venus	50
833	103	533	1003	233		Saturn	Ketu	Sun	51
836	106	536	1006	236		Mercury	Venus	Moon	52
839	109	539	1009	239		Ketu	Sun	Mars	53
842	112	542	1012	242		Venus	Moon	Rahu	54
845	115	545	1015	245		Sun	Mars	Jupiter	55
848	118	548	1018	248		Moon	Rahu	Saturn	56
851	121	551	1021	251		Mars	Jupiter	Mercury	57
854	124	554	1024	254		Rahu	Saturn	Ketu	58
857	127	557	1027	257		Jupiter	Mercury	Venus	59
900	130	600	1030	300		Saturn	Ketu	Sun	60
903	133	603	1033	303		Mercury	Venus	Moon	61
906	136	606	1036	306		Ketu	Sun	Mars	62
909	139	609	1039	309		Venus	Moon	Rahu	63
912	142	612	1042	312		Sun	Mars	Jupiter	64
915	145	615	1045	315		Moon	Rahu	Saturn	65

Contd......

Table A

A.M.	A.M.	P.M.	P.M.	A.M.	A.M.	Aries Cancer Libra Capri.	Taurus Leo Scor. Aqu.	Gemini Virgo Sagi. Pisces	S No.
918	148	618	1048	318		Mars	Jupiter	Mercury	66
921	151	621	1051	321		Rahu	Saturn	Ketu	67
924	154	624	1054	324		Jupiter	Mercury	Venus	68
927	157	627	1057	327		Saturn	Ketu	Sun	69
930	200	630	1100	330		Mercury	Venus	Moon	70
933	203	633	1103	333		Ketu	Sun	Mars	71
936	206	636	1106	336		Venus	Moon	Rahu	72
939	209	639	1109	339		Sun	Mars	Jupiter	73
942	212	642	1112	342		Moon	Rahu	Saturn	74
945	215	645	1115	345		Mars	Jupiter	Mercury	75
948	218	648	1118	348		Rahu	Saturn	Ketu	76
951	221	651	1121	351		Jupiter	Mercury	Venus	77
954	224	654	1124	354		Saturn	Ketu	Sun	78
957	227	657	1127	357		Mercury	Venus	Moon	79
1000	230	700	1130	400		Ketu	Sun	Mars	80
1003	233	703	1133	403		Venus	Moon	Rahu	81
1006	236	706	1136	406		Sun	Mars	Jupiter	82
1009	239	709	1139	409		Moon	Rahu	Saturn	83
1012	242	712	1142	412		Mars	Jupiter	Mercury	84
1015	245	715	1145	415		Rahu	Saturn	Ketu	85
1018	248	718	1148	418		Jupiter	Mercury	Venus	86
1021	251	721	1151	421		Saturn	Ketu	Sun	87
1024	254	724	1154	424		Mercury	Venus	Moon	88
1027	257	727	1157	427		Ketu	Sun	Mars	89
1030	300	730	1200	430		Venus	Moon	Rahu	90

Table B

No.	SUN.	MON.	TUE.	WED.	THU.	FRI.	SAT.
1	Male	Female	Male	Male	Male	Female	Female
2	Male	Female	Male	Male	Male	Female	Female
3	Male	Female	Male	Female	Male	Female	Female
4	Male	Female	Male	Female	Male	Female	Female
5	Male	Male	Male	Female	Male	Male	Female
6	Male	Male	Male	Female	Male	Male	Female
7	Female	Male	Female	Male	Male	Male	Female
8	Female	Male	Female	Male	Male	Male	Female
9	Female	Male	Female	Male	Male	Male	Male
10	Female	Male	Female	Male	Male	Male	Male
11	Female	Female	Female	Male	Male	Female	Male
12	Female	Female	Female	Male	Male	Female	Male
13	Female	Female	Female	Female	Female	Female	Male
14	Female	Female	Female	Female	Female	Female	Male
15	Male	Female	Male	Female	Female	Female	Male
16	Male	Female	Male	Female	Female	Female	Male
17	Male	Female	Male	Female	Male	Female	Male
18	Male	Female	Male	Female	Male	Female	Male
19	Male	Male	Male	Female	Male	Male	Male
20	Male	Male	Male	Female	Male	Male	Male
21	Male	Male	Male	Male	Male	Male	Female
22	Male	Male	Male	Male	Male	Male	Female
23	Male	Male	Male	Male	Female	Male	Female
24	Male	Male	Male	Male	Female	Male	Female
25	Male	Male	Male	Male	Female	Male	Male
26	Male	Male	Male	Male	Female	Male	Male
27	Female	Male	Female	Male	Female	Male	Male
28	Female	Male	Female	Male	Female	Male	Male

Contd.....

Table B

No.	SUN.	MON.	TUE.	WED.	THU.	FRI.	SAT.
29	Female	Male	Female	Male	Female	Male	Male
30	Female	Male	Female	Male	Female	Male	Male
31	Male	Female	Male	Male	Male	Female	Female
32	Male	Female	Male	Male	Male	Female	Female
33	Male	Female	Male	Female	Male	Female	Female
34	Male	Female	Male	Female	Male	Female	Female
35	Male	Male	Male	Female	Male	Male	Female
36	Male	Male	Male	Female	Male	Male	Female
37	Female	Male	Female	Male	Male	Male	Female
38	Female	Male	Female	Male	Male	Male	Female
39	Female	Male	Female	Male	Male	Male	Male
40	Female	Male	Female	Male	Male	Male	Male
41	Female	Female	Female	Male	Male	Female	Male
42	Female	Female	Female	Male	Male	Female	Male
43	Female	Female	Female	Female	Female	Female	Male
44	Female	Female	Female	Female	Female	Female	Male
45	Male	Female	Male	Female	Female	Female	Male
46	Male	Female	Male	Female	Female	Female	Male
47	Male	Female	Male	Female	Male	Female	Male
48	Male	Female	Male	Female	Male	Female	Male
49	Male	Male	Male	Female	Male	Male	Male
50	Male	Male	Male	Female	Male	Male	Male
51	Male	Male	Male	Male	Male	Male	Female
52	Male	Male	Male	Male	Male	Male	Female
53	Male	Male	Male	Male	Female	Male	Female
54	Male	Male	Male	Male	Female	Male	Female
55	Male	Male	Male	Male	Female	Male	Male
56	Male	Male	Male	Male	Female	Male	Male

Contd.....

Table B

No.	SUN.	MON.	TUE.	WED.	THU.	FRI.	SAT.
57	Female	Male	Female	Male	Female	Male	Male
58	Female	Male	Female	Male	Female	Male	Male
59	Female	Male	Female	Male	Female	Male	Male
60	Female	Male	Female	Male	Female	Male	Male
61	Male	Female	Male	Male	Male	Female	Female
62	Male	Female	Male	Male	Male	Female	Female
63	Male	Female	Male	Female	Male	Female	Female
64	Male	Female	Male	Female	Male	Female	Female
65	Male	Male	Male	Female	Male	Male	Female
66	Male	Male	Male	Female	Male	Male	Female
67	Female	Male	Female	Male	Male	Male	Female
68	Female	Male	Female	Male	Male	Male	Female
69	Female	Male	Female	Male	Male	Male	Male
70	Female	Male	Female	Male	Male	Male	Male
71	Female	Female	Female	Male	Male	Female	Male
72	Female	Female	Female	Male	Male	Female	Male
73	Female	Female	Female	Female	Female	Female	Male
74	Female	Female	Female	Female	Female	Female	Male
75	Male	Female	Male	Female	Female	Female	Male
76	Male	Female	Male	Female	Female	Female	Male
77	Male	Female	Male	Female	Male	Female	Male
78	Male	Female	Male	Female	Male	Female	Male
79	Male	Male	Male	Female	Male	Male	Male
80	Male	Male	Male	Female	Male	Male	Male
81	Male	Male	Male	Male	Male	Male	Female
82	Male	Male	Male	Male	Male	Male	Female
83	Male	Male	Male	Male	Female	Male	Female
84	Male	Male	Male	Male	Female	Male	Female

Contd.....

Table B

No.	SUN.	MON.	TUE.	WED.	THU.	FRI.	SAT.
85	Male	Male	Male	Male	Female	Male	Male
86	Male	Male	Male	Male	Female	Male	Male
87	Female	Male	Female	Male	Female	Male	Male
88	Female	Male	Female	Male	Female	Male	Male
89	Female	Male	Female	Male	Female	Male	Male
90	Female	Male	Female	Male	Female	Male	Male

Procedure: Note the interval of time between Sunrise on the day of birth and 6.00 A.M. If the Sunrise is before 6.00 A.M. add the difference to the noted time of birth. If the Sunrise is after 6.00 A.M. subtract the difference from the noted time of birth. This will give us the Derived Time.

Match the Derived Time, Ascendant rising, Moon's Star, Weekday and sex of the child in Table A & Table B to determine the correct birth time. It is explained through an example below:

Example:

Date of Birth: 7.9.1972, Sex: Male,

Noted Time: 8.50 P.M Day: Thursday,

Sunrise: 06.7.18 A.M, Ascendant: Aries,

Star Lord: Venus.

Since Sunrise is 7 minutes 18 seconds after 6.00 A.M, our derived time comes as 8.50-7.18 = 8.42.42 P.M. We find that this derived time matches data at Sl. No. 27 corresponding to which the time is 8.51 P.M. This is one minute ahead of our derived time. Therefore the corrected birth time will be 8.51 P.M.

Critical Review of the Theory: The tables only afford to correct the time within a few minutes only. Matching the birth time with the sex of the native causes serious doubt about the truthfulness of its application. The sex of the native is decided right at the time of conception. It does not depend on the time of delivery. Since the Nakshatra repeats only after 27 minutes in the table, the corrected time may vary significantly from the noted time. This poses a serious problem.

The Pre-Natal Epoch Theory: Epoch means the moment of conception when fecundation takes place in the mother's womb. This generally happens, in normal cases, about nine months before the moment of birth, depending on the Moon and Lunar rhythm. We find reference to Epoch in the 51st Centiloquy of the Tetrabiblos as translated by J. M. Ashmad as under:

"Make the sign occupied by the Moon at the time of birth the ascending sign at the conception, and consider that in which she may be posited at the conception, or the opposite one, as the sign ascending at birth."

This rule, said Pegius (1570), can be traced back to the legendary Hermes Trismegistus of Egypt, and is generally known as the Trutina Hermetis. According to this theory, for the epoch,

1. take the radical Moon for the Ascendant of the epoch, and
2. take the Moon at the time of the epoch for the radical Ascendant or Descendant.

Middle Epoch: It is believed that the Moon transits over its radical position nine months before the birth. The day of this transit is called the middle epoch.

According to this theory, the day of the epoch, it self depends on the position of the Moon with respect to the horizon, but not on its position with respect to the Sun. The complete rule for deciding the day of the epoch is stated below:

"If the radical Moon is above the horizon, it will have to travel in a forward direction from its middle epoch position to reach the position of the radical ascendant."

Should the radical Moon (i.e. Moon in the Rashi chart at the time of birth) be below the horizon, then it has already transited over the radical ascendant and we must count backward in order to find the day of the epoch.

Thus, according to this theory, on the day of the epoch we take the radical Moon

i) For the ascendant of the epoch, or

ii) For the descendant of the epoch.

Having fixed this position, we have to note the exact position of Moon at that time on the epoch day. This position of Moon has to be put as the Ascendant degree, minutes and seconds for the correct horoscope.

Amendment of Trutina Hermetis Theory:

A German Astrologer Chiwa, in his book 'Die Epoche' has stated on the basis of his research that 75% of births in 500 cases studied took place between the 9th and 10th lunation; in the remaining number of cases pregnancy lasted for a longer or shorter period. Chiwa has amended the rules governing the epoch as found in the Trutina Hermetis.

He states:

"The duration of the epoch is x lunations plus y days, the epoch representing the period which the Moon requires to return to its radical position."

He came to the conclusion that the radical Moon could be

a) the Ascendant of the epoch; or

b) the Descendant of the epoch.

There is a possibility that the radical Moon may become

c) the radical M.C. or

d) the radical I.C.

Sepharial's Pre-Natal Epoch Theory:

Towards the end of the 19th century, the late Sepharial expounded the theory that the rules laid down by Hermes Trismegistis had a close affinity to the principles of Hindu Astrology relating to lunar mansions. Sepharial believed that

1. The general period of intra-uterine life is 9 solar, or 10 lunar months.
2. This period is subject to an increase or decrease, according to the position of the Moon in regard to the Sun, and the horizon of the place of birth.

We may put Sepharial's theory in a succinct form as follows:

1. When the Moon at birth is increasing in light, and above the earth, or decreasing, and below earth, the period is less than the lunar revolutions by one day for every 12 degrees of the Moon's distance from the horizon to which it next comes

after birth. But, when the Moon at birth is increasing and below the earth, or decreasing and above the earth, the period is by the same measure more than ten lunar revolutions counted backward from the day of birth.

2. When the Moon at birth is increasing in light, its place will be the Ascendant at the epoch, and the Moon's place at the epoch will be the ascendant at birth. But, when the Moon at birth is decreasing in light, then its place will be setting at the epoch, and the Moon's place at the epoch will be the descendant at birth.

Sepharial also indicated how to decide the sex of the child. According to him the sex of the child is determined as follows:

1. If the Ascendant of the epoch be in a male degree the sex of the birth will be male, and vice versa.
2. If the Moon be in a critical degree and the Ascendant not in a critical degree at all, then the Moon's position controls the sex, according to whether its degree of longitude is male or female.
3. When both the Ascendant and Moon are in critical degrees of the same sex, the birth will be of that sex.
4. When neither the Moon nor Ascendant is in a critical degree, then the quadrant the Moon occupies will determine the sex.
5. When the Ascendant and the Moon are in critical degrees of opposite sexes, the quadrant the Moon occupies will determine the sex.

The critical degrees and the quadrants are given in the following diagrammatic table C for ready reference.

Sex of Child

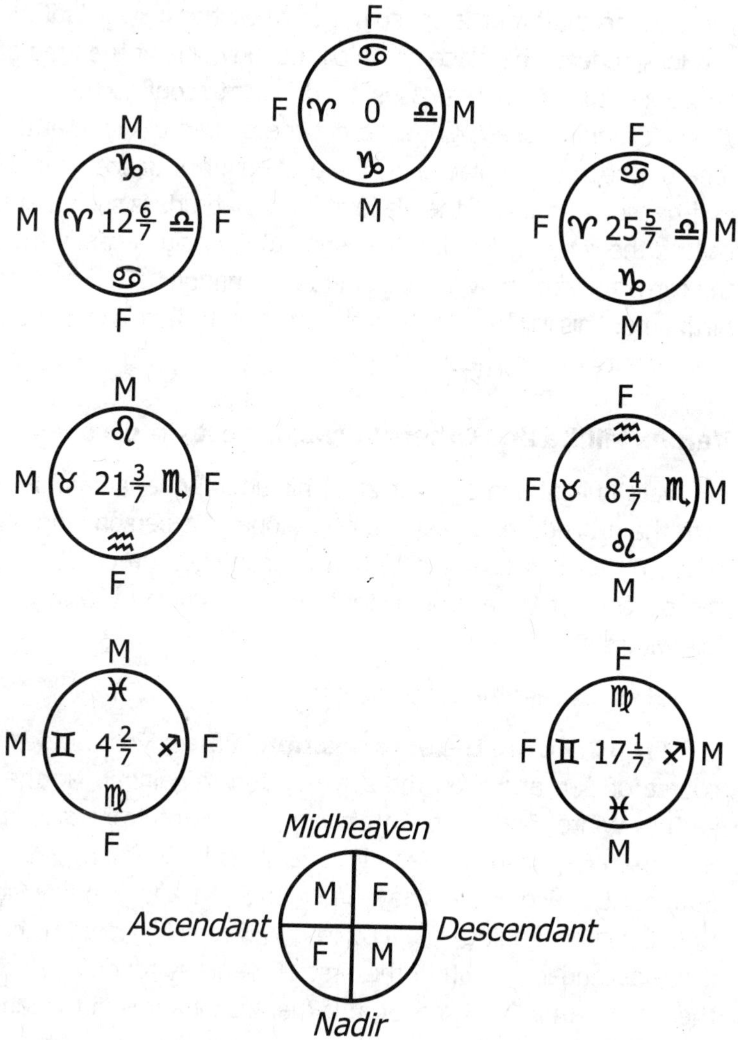

Table C

This theory appears to be based on the sound cosmic laws. Its application, however, does not often give accurate results because the chart for the epoch has to be cast as per the latitude and longitude of the place at which the lady was at the time of the epoch. In most of the cases it is difficult to confirm this. This theory expects the astrologer to put the degree of Moon at the time of epoch to be placed on the ascendant or descendant or mid-heaven or nadir. If the place of birth's latitude is such that it causes the time of rising of the Signs to vary significantly then the corrected time may show significant variation from the noted birth time. This raises a doubt in the mind of the Astrologer about the veracity of the theory.

Varaha Mihira and Others Views on Lost Horoscopes

Varaha Mihira in chapter 26 of his book Brihajjatkam deals with the procedure to cast the horoscope of a person who has no birth details. According to him we can cast the chart using the concept of Horary or Instant (Prasna) chart by using the following steps.

Step 1: Cast the Horary chart.

Step 2: Fixing the Sign position of Sun: First decide the course of Sun and then the season. Sun remains in Northern Path or Winter Solstice or Uttarayana when Sun transits in any Sign from Capricorn to Gemini; it remains in Southern Path or Summer Solstice or Daksinayana when Sun transits in any Sign from Cancer to Sagittarius. According to Varaha Mihira and others if the ascendant is within the first 15 degrees range of Rashi, then the birth is in Uttarayana. If the Ascendant is in the latter half of the Sign that rises in the Ascendant then the birth is in Daksinayana.

There are six seasons in a year. The winter season (15th January to 15th March) when the Sun transits in Capricorn and

Aquarius, the Spring Season (15th March to 15th May) when Sun transits in Pisces and Aries, the Summer Season (from 15th May to 15th July) when Sun transits in Taurus and Gemini, the Rainy Season (from 15th July to 15th September) when Sun transits in Cancer and Leo, the Autumn (from 15th Sep to 15th November) when Sun transits in Virgo and Libra, the Cold Season (from 15th Nov to 15th January) when Sun transits in Scorpio and Sagittarius. According to Varaha Mihira the strongest Planet placed in the Ascendant in the Horary Chart decides the season. If no Planet is placed in the Ascendant the ruler of the rising Decanate decides the season.

Sun rules the hot summer season when it transits in Taurus and Gemini; Saturn rules the winter season; Venus indicates the spring; Mars rules the summer; Moon indicates the Rainy season; Mercury rules autumn; and Jupiter indicates the Cold season.

Suppose the Horary Chart rises in 15 degree 26 minutes in Gemini. Since the Ascendant is in the second half of the Sign Sun will be in Sothern Path that is in signs from Cancer to Sagittarius.

Since the second Dacanate rises in the Ascendant we need to take 5th sign from Gemini to decide the lord of the Dacanate. It is Libra and as such Venus rules it. Suppose Venus in the chart rises in second Dacanate of Pisces then its ruler will be Cancer that is Moon. Here we will say that Moon decides the season which is rainy season when Sun transits in Cancer or Leo. To decide between Cancer and Leo we need to note whether the degree rising in the ascendant is in first half or second half of the Decanate. Here in this example the rising degree indicates the second half and as such Sun should be in Leo.

Note: If the ascendant degree indicates Northern Path but the planet placed in the ascendant indicates a season which occurs only when Sun is in Southern Path then Moon, Mercury and Jupiter should be respectively exchanged by Venus, Mars and

Saturn. Take an example when the horary ascendant rises in Leo 25 degree and 18 minutes. Here the longitude of ascendant is in excess of 15 degrees suggesting birth in Summer Solstice or Daksinayana. Third Decanate of Leo falls in Aries whose lord is Mars indicating summer season at birth. Daksinayana and summer season cannot coincide and hence the season of Mars should be replaced by the season of Mercury. As such autumn season should have prevailed at birth. In this example since the second part of Decanate prevails, the birth should have been in the second month of autumn that is when Sun will be in Libra.

Step 3: Fixing the Sign Position of Jupiter: Some authors feel that the position of Sign occupied by Jupiter at birth is determined by the lord of the rising Decanate in the Horary Chart. If the first Decanate rises Jupiter will be in the same Sign as the ascendant Sign. Second Decanate means fifth and third Decanate means 9th sign from the ascendant sign. Other authors say that Jupiter's sign position should be fixed by multiplying the longitude of the rising sign by 2 and then dividing it by 5. The quotient will represent the Jupiter's natal position. For example let the ascendant longitude be 8 degrees 33 minutes and 36 seconds in Libra. If we multiply the longitude of the ascendant by 2 and divide the product by 5 it gives a quotient of 3 and 1 as remainder. This means that the sign of Jupiter at birth will be 4th from Libra. Age of the person can then be ascertained from the appearance of the person. Suppose Jupiter Sign comes to be Virgo (6) then the age of the person could be 6 or 18 or 30 or 42 or 54 like that.

Step 4: Fixing the Lunar Day of Birth: According to Varaha Mihira, the ruling Tithi at birth would be equal to the longitude obtained by the Sun in the sign occupied by him in the horary chart. Suppose Sun occupies 6 degree 30 minutes in a Sign then it is indicative of Saptami Tithi (of Shukla Paksha).

The lunar month commences from the first lunar day of the bright fortnight. Suppose the Sun to occupy18th degree of the sign Capricorn at the time of birth. The lunar day or Tithi during birth is the 18th day that is 3rd day of the dark fortnight.

Another method of calculating the lunar day is from the proportion of semi-Decanate that has risen above the Horizon. Semi Decanate is of 5 degrees representing 30 days; so that 10 minutes of the rising Decanate represent a lunar day. Suppose the ascendant rises in Libra 8 degrees 33 minutes and 36 seconds. Reduce 5 from the longitude of ascendant and we get 3 degrees 33 minutes and 36 seconds which should be multiplied by 60 and divided by 30. We will get a quotient of 7 with remainder 3 degrees 36 which indicates that 7 tithis have passed at birth. This means Astami tithi.

Step 5: Fixing the Ascendant: If the Day Sign (Leo, Virgo, Libra, Scorpio, Aquarius and Pisces) rises in the ascendant then it should be expected that the birth had taken place at night. If the Night Sign (Aries, Taurus, Gemini, Cancer, Sagittarius and Capricorn) rises in the ascendant it indicates that the birth should have taken place in day time. Knowing the length of the day or night from the rising sign we can fix the time of birth for fixing the ascendant position by the proportion of the degrees that have already risen in the horary chart. Suppose the length of the day is of 30 ghatikas and the portion of the sign risen above is 5 degrees then the birth time will be 5 ghatikas from the morning.

According to some authors the rising Navamsa in horary chart will be the ascendant that has risen at birth. Or note the total number of Decanates between the rising one and the one occupied by the Sun. So many Decanates counted from the Sun will the natal ascendant be.

The birth time can be ascertained by another method also. Find out the duration of the day and that of night for the day the query is raised. The duration (of the day or the night as the case may be) should be multiplied by the longitude of the horary ascendant and divided by 30. The quotient thus obtained represents the duration passed in the night or day at birth as the case may be. If the ascendant rises in Libra 8 degrees33 minutes and 36 seconds then since Libra is a day sign the birth would have taken place at night. Let Day duration be 32 ghatis and night duration be 28 ghatis. If the Longitude of ascendant be multiplied by 28 and the product then is divided by 30 we will get the resultant figure as 7-56 which means 7 ghatis and 56 vighatis have passed in the night at the time of birth.

Step 6: Fixing the Sign Position of Moon: The sign occupied by Moon at the time of birth will be the same sign that rises in the horary ascendant or 5th from there or 9th from there whichever is most powerful.

According to some authors the other method to fix the Moon sign is by ascertaining how far horary Moon is away from the horary ascendant. So much will be the distance of natal Moon, counted from horary Moon. If however the horary ascendant is in Pisces, then the natal Moon will also be in Pisces.

Step 7: Fixing the Date of Birth: Once the season is ascertained, its actual duration must be known, for a season is not exactly sixty days as a rule. We may look into the Ephemeris and find out how long Sun actually remains in the two signs of the season. The sum of the two should be used to work out the date of birth by the semi-Decanate proportion. For simple explanation we may assume that the duration is 60 days. One Decanate is of 10 degrees. Thus each degree will be equal to 6 days. If the rising Ascendant longitude is in the second part of the Decanate it would mean that Sun will be in the second sign of the season and Sun's entry in the sign will be after the number of days calculated by multiplying the degrees of the portion of the Decanate. Suppose the longitude of the ascendant is 7 degrees and 30 minutes then Sun's entry in the sign would be after 15 days from the time Sun enters in the beginning of the Sign.

From the above data we may cast the horoscope of the native.

Chapter 3

The Ruling Planets and Construction of Horoscope

Astrology, says Mr. Astrologer, is not only for the blessed ones whose parent sincerely kept records of their birth time. Astrologer is a friend and a counselor of humanity! So am I told? He possesses the Jupiterian optimism and foresight; he is always under the Saturnian's spell that provides him caution, calculative and meditative skills. Mr. Astrologer is; thus, always ready to construct the horoscope for all those who do not possess correct birth data. His venture is based on certain sound techniques of Astrology.

The edifice on which astrology is based is time personified. There is continuum between past, present and future. Even Albert Einstein in his Theory of Relativity amply makes this clear. It is an accepted belief that no event happens in the life of the native unless Sun and Moon occupy particular positions in the Zodiac. Moon knows no rest and every moment it occupies a different degree, minute and second in the Zodiac. An observer on earth finds every moment a different Zodiacal Arc rising in the Eastern horizon. Planets co-ruling the Moon's position and the ascendant i.e. the degree rising in the eastern horizon at the moment of judgement are called the ruling planets. It is believed that the ruling planets at the moment of judgement are the ruling planets at the fructification of the event in past or future. This belief is based on the spiritual concept of Time continuum that is Past,

Present and future co-exist. Astrologers make use of this dictum to construct horoscope for an individual who has doubt about:

1. Date, Month, Year of birth
2. Time of birth

Ruling Planets and Schools of Thought

There are two schools of thought. The followers of one school of thought were inspired, probably, by the Nadi theory of birth rectification using Tattva Sidhanta. According to this theory human births take place only at certain intervals and the sex of the child is dependent on the inherent nature of the element governing that moment. The birth time is inviolably interrelated to the star of the Moon on any given day and to the nature of the ascendant sign and the day lord. Accordingly this school of thought declared that the following planets should be used as ruling planets to construct the horoscope:

1. Day lord.
2. Ascendant sign and star lord.
3. Moon sign and star lord.

The followers of second school of thought probably had their conviction based on the philosophy of Adhana Lagna for birth rectification as pronounced by the Indian sages or the philosophy of Pre- Natal Epoch formulated by Ptolemy and later on developed by Speherial in the 19th century. Both these theories clearly emphasize **that the position of Moon at the moment of Epoch represents the degree, minutes and seconds to be put on the ascendant at the time of birth. The position of the ascendant at the time of Epoch takes the position of Moon at the time of birth.** With this view the followers of this school of thought declared that:

i) The planets co-ruling the ascendant at the moment of judgement should be used to fix the position of Moon or any planet in the horoscope about which there is a doubt.

ii) The position of Moon at the moment of judgement should be used to correct the position of ascendant or any cusp about which there is a doubt.

Application of Ruling Planets and Construction of Horoscope

First School of Thought: According to the followers of first school of thought, a horoscope can be constructed or rectified by using the principle that the ruling planets at the moment of judgement should be the ruling planets at the time of birth. If any ruling planet at the time of birth does not agree directly with the ruling planets at the moment of judgement, that planet may at the time of judgement be transiting in the star or sub of one of the ruling planets at the moment of judgement. **That is any planet can be taken as the ruling planet if it is in the star or sub of a ruling planet.** Ascendant sign star, sub and sub-sub lords of the horoscope under consideration should agree with the ruling planets at the time of judgement.

However, late Mr. Krishnamurthy, one of the pioneers who used this theory of ruling planets to construct or rectify horoscope declared that we should reject the ruling planet, which is in the star or sub of a planet that is retrograde at the time of judgement. It is not clear why a person who believed that retrogression of planets play no part in the predictive techniques as used for Natal chart analysis could make such a decision. Moreover, in the recent past the followers of this school have realized the importance of sub lord or Kalamsa lord of the ascendant and Moon and have thus included them in the list of ruling planets. But the confusion about retrogression is still prevalent among them. **I am sure planets do not make choices for their behaviour as per natal chart or horary chart. They behave according to their longitudinal position only**. The followers of this school include Rahu and Ketu in the list of ruling planets if they happen to represent any ruling planet. This technique of rectification can be explained as follows:

Suppose, an astrologer is presented a horoscope of a person born on Sunday when Capricorn 12 degree 25 minutes was rising in the eastern horizon and the Moon was in Pisces at 21 degree 49 minutes. The ruling planets of this horoscope are Sun, Saturn, Moon, Jupiter and Mercury. If the Astrologer wants to check the correctness of the horoscope, he has to cast the chart for the moment of judgement. Let us say, he does it on Monday when the ascendant Virgo 8 degree 41 minutes rises and Moon is in Cancer 9 degree 58 minutes. Therefore the ruling planets at the time of judgement are Moon, Mercury, Sun, and Saturn. Let us say, at the time of judgement Rahu is in Aquarius and Ketu is in Leo. Therefore, Rahu and Ketu will also become the ruling planets at the moment of judgement.

If we examine the ruling planets at the time of birth and at the time of judgement, all agree except Jupiter. Now, if Jupiter at the time of judgement is in the star of any of the ruling planet, the chart is taken as correct. That is any planet is as good as a ruling planet if it is in the star or sub of a ruling planet.

We can also check the correctness of the planets co-ruling the ascendant at the time of birth. Here, the ascendant Capricorn 12 degree 25 minutes is co-ruled by Saturn-Moon-Rahu-Jupiter as sign, star, sub and sub-sub lord respectively. All these planets as stated above agree with the ruling planets at the time of judgement. The horoscope is thus taken to be correct.

In a horoscope, there may be doubt about time, day or year and let us try to understand the use of this technique to construct or rectify charts through following examples:

Example 1: Doubt about time - A young lady comes to Mr. Astrologer and requests for the construction of an accurate horoscope for the following birth data.

D.O.Birth - 21.3.1979

P.O. Birth - Agra (India).

T.O.Birth - Between 16 hrs to 16.30 hrs.

Mr. Astrologer took up the job for the construction of the horoscope on 30.1.2002 at 08.29 AM. The planetary and cuspal positions at the time of judgement are shown in Figure 3.1.

Fig. 3.1

Name	Fig. 3.1	Place of Birth	Noida
Sex	Male	Latitude	028.20.N
Date of Birth	30/01/2002	Longitude	077.20.E
Day of Birth	Wednesday	Local Birth Time	08:08: 20
Time of Birth	08:29:00	Local Birth Date	30/01/2002
Sidereal Time	16:45:2	Lunar Tithi	2
Bal. of Dasha	Ket 5Y 7M 30D	K.P. (New) Ayanamsa	23:54:56
Lagan	Aquarius	Lagan Lord	Saturn
Sign	Leo	Sign Lord	Sun
Nakshatra	Magha	Nakshatra Lord	Ketu

Fig. 3.1 Contd......

Nirayana Cusps

Bhav No.	Sign	Degree	Star Lord	Sub Lord	Sub-Sub Lord
1	Aquarius	10: 01' 30"	Rah	Jup	Mon
2	Pisces	20: 34' 28"	Mer	Ven	Jup
3	Aries	22: 57' 58"	Ven	Sat	Ven
4	Taurus	18: 50' 08"	Mon	Mer	Rah
5	Gemini	12: 23' 02"	Rah	Sat	Jup
6	Cancer	07: 43' 44"	Sat	Ket	Rah
7	Leo	10: 01' 30"	Ket	Sat	Ket
8	Virgo	20: 34' 28"	Mon	Ven	Ven
9	Libra	22: 57' 58"	Jup	Sat	Sun
10	Scorpio	18: 50' 08"	Mer	Ket	Mar
11	Sagittarius	12: 23' 02"	Ket	Mer	Mon
12	Capricorn	07: 43' 44"	Sun	Ket	Mer

Planetary Position

Planet	Sign	Degree	Star Lord	Sub Lord	Sub-Sub Lord
Sun	Capricorn	16: 10' 16"	Mon	Sat	Mer
Mon	Leo	02: 32' 47"	Ket	Ven	Sat
Mar	Pisces	14: 15' 22"	Sat	Rah	Ven
Mer (R)	Capricorn	10: 52' 49"	Mon	Mon	Ven
Jup (R)	Gemini	13: 15' 17"	Rah	Mer	Sun
Ven	Capricorn	19: 55' 25"	Mon	Ket	Mon
Sat (R)	Taurus	14: 14' 11"	Mon	Jup	Sat
Rah (R)	Gemini	02: 30' 23"	Mar	Ket	Sat
Ket (R)	Sagittarius	02: 30' 23"	Ket	Ven	Sat
Ura	Aquarius	00: 07' 05"	Mar	Mer	Mer
Nep	Capricorn	14: 39' 25"	Mon	Jup	Mer
Plu	Scorpio	23: 05' 01"	Mer	Mon	Ket
Fortuna	Leo	26: 24' 01"	Ven	Ket	Jup

The ruling planets at the time of judgement were:

Day lord = Mercury (Wednesday)

Ascendant = Aquarius 10 degree 1 minutes 30 seconds. Saturn-Rahu and Jup rule that sign, star and sub-lord respectively.

Moon = Leo 2 degree 32 minutes 47 seconds that is ruled by Sun, Ketu and Venus as sign, star and sub Lord respectively.

Procedure to Rectify the Chart: The astrologer cast the chart as per the given data using the mid position of the time period given by the native. He then confirms what Planet position in the ascendant is prone to change during the time period. He is assured that the sign and star lord of the ascendant is not showing any proneness to change. As such he is not bothered whether these are the RPs at the time of judgement or not.

The emphasis of the Astrologer is to fix the sub and sub-sub lord of the ascendant using the Planets from the RPs. The astrologer found that at 16.16 hrs on 21.3.1979 at Agra the ascendant is ruled by Sun-Ketu-Jup-Sat. All these planets of the ascendant agree with the ruling planets at the time of judgement. Correspondingly, the Moon position is also ruled by all the ruling planets at the time of judgement. The Astrologer thus fixes the time of birth as 16.16 hrs. The corrected horoscope of the Lady is shown in Fig. 3.2.

Fig. 3.2

Name	Fig. 3.2	Place of Birth	AGRA
Sex	Female	Latitude	027.12.N
Date of Birth	21/03/1979	Longitude	078.00.E
Day of Birth	Wednesday	Local Birth Time	15:58:00
Time of Birth	16:16:00	Local Birth Date	21/03/1979
Sidereal Time	3:51:25	Lunar Tithi	8
Bal. of Dasha	Ket 3Y 8M 1D	K.P. (New) Ayanamsa	23:33:18
Lagan	Leo	Lagan Lord	Sun
Sign	Sagittarius	Sign Lord	Jupiter
Nakshatra	Mula	Nakshatra Lord	Ketu

Lagna Chart

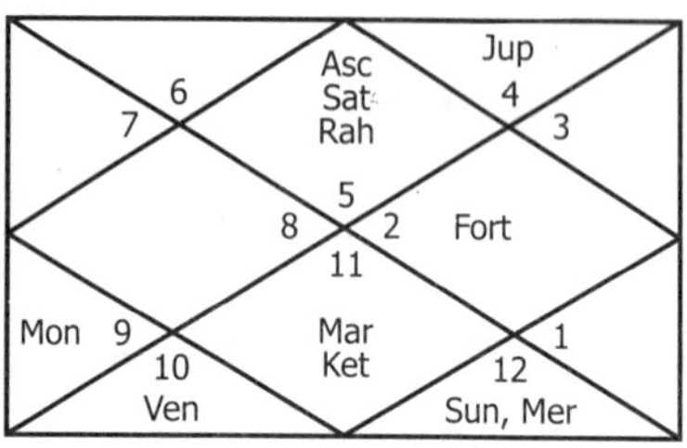

Bhava Chart

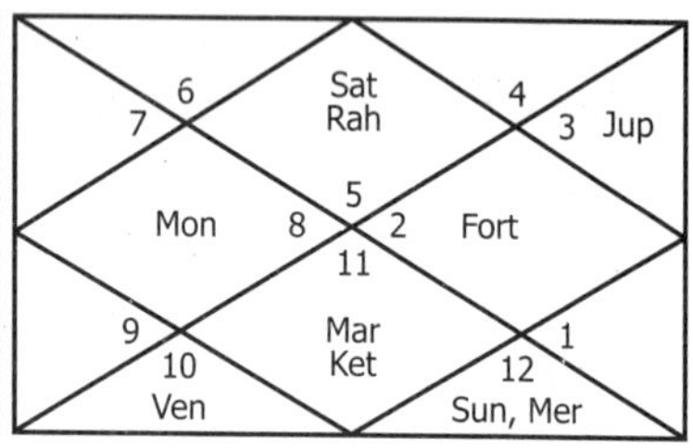

Cusp Chart

Mer 12:22:4 Sun 6:40:28 VIII 4:24:25	IX 4:26:19	X 6:28:46 Fort 7:36:28	XI 8:23:5
Ket 23:50:58 Mar 23:28:7 VII 7:56:36			Jup 5:29:5 XII 9:0:3
Ven 27:18:32 VI 9:0:3			I 7:56:36 Sat 15:27:54 Rah 23:50:58
V 8:23:5 Mon 6:20:20	IV 6:28:46	III 4:26:19	II 4:24:25

Fig. 3.2 Contd......

Nirayana Cusps

Bhav No.	Sign	Degree	Star Lord	Sub Lord	Sub-Sub Lord
1	Leo	07: 56' 36"	Ket	Jup	Sat
2	Virgo	04: 24' 25"	Sun	Sat	Mar
3	Libra	04: 26' 19"	Mar	Ven	Sat
4	Scorpio	06: 28' 46"	Sat	Mer	Mar
5	Sagittarius	08: 23' 05"	Ket	Jup	Ket
6	Capricorn	09: 00' 03"	Sun	Ven	Jup
7	Aquarius	07: 56' 36"	Rah	Rah	Ket
8	Pisces	04: 24' 25"	Sat	Sat	Ven
9	Aries	04: 26' 19"	Ket	Mon	Mer
10	Taurus	06: 28' 46"	Sun	Mer	Jup
11	Gemini	08: 23' 05"	Rah	Rah	Mon
12	Cancer	09: 00' 03"	Sat	Ven	Rah

Planetary Position

Planet	Sign	Degree	Star Lord	Sub Lord	Sub-Sub Lord
Sun	Pisces	06: 40' 28"	Sat	Mer	Rah
Mon	Sagittarius	06: 20' 20"	Ket	Rah	Sat
Mar	Aquarius	23: 28' 07"	Jup	Sat	Rah
Mer (R)	Pisces	12: 22' 04"	Sat	Mar	Jup
Jup (R)	Cancer	05: 29' 05"	Sat	Mer	Mer
Ven	Capricorn	27: 18' 32"	Mar	Jup	Sun
Sat (R)	Leo	15: 27' 54"	Ven	Ven	Ket
Rah (R)	Leo	23: 50' 58"	Ven	Sat	Jup
Ket (R)	Aquarius	23: 50' 58"	Jup	Sat	Jup
Ura (R)	Libra	27: 10' 15"	Jup	Ven	Mon
Nep	Scorpio	26: 56' 32"	Mer	Jup	Ket
Plu (R)	Virgo	24: 47' 09"	Mar	Rah	Sat
Fortuna	Taurus	07: 36' 28"	Sun	Ket	Sat

Doubt about Morning or Evening: The Astrologer may have to construct the horoscope of a person who is sure of the date of birth but says that the time of birth is between a certain period of the day may be in the morning or evening. In such cases the Astrologer fixes firstly, the Moon position as per the ruling planets at the time of judgement that corresponds to the vicinity of the time period and then fixes the ascendant to match the ruling planets.

Example 2:

A young man gave the following particulars and wanted that his correct horoscope should be drawn:

D.O. Birth: 22.1.1974

T.O. Birth: Between 02.30hrs to 04.00hrs.

P.O. Birth: Jalandhar city (India)

The Astrologer on 5.10.2004 took up the Job at 16.30.11 hrs at Noida (India). The planetary and cuspal positions at the time of judgement are shown in Fig. 3.3. The ruling planets at the time of judgement were as follows:

Day Lord: Mars (Tuesday)

Ascendant: Aquarius 17 degree 34 minutes 37 seconds. It is ruled by Saturn-Rahu-Sun as sign, star and sub lord respectively.

Moon: Gemini 8 degree 6 minutes 25 seconds. It is ruled by Mercury-Rahu-Rahu as sign, star and sub lord respectively. Rahu being in Aries represents Mars.

Fig. 3.3

Name	Fig. 3.3	Place of Birth	Noida
Sex	Male	Latitude	028.20.N
Date of Birth	05/10/2004	Longitude	077.20.E
Day of Birth	Tuesday	Local Birth Time	16:09:31
Time of Birth	16:30:11	Local Birth Date	05/10/2004
Sidereal Time	17:7:20	Lunar Tithi	7
Bal. of Dasha	Rah 16Y 0M 21D	K.P. (New) Ayanamsa	23:54:42
Lagan	Aquarius	Lagan Lord	Saturn
Sign	Gemini	Sign Lord	Mercury
Nakshatra	Ardra	Nakshatra Lord	Rahu

Fig. 3.3 Contd......

Nirayana Cusps

Bhav No.	Sign	Degree	Star Lord	Sub Lord	Sub-Sub Lord
1	Aquarius	17: 34' 37"	Rah	Sun	Rah
2	Pisces	27: 33' 51"	Mer	Jup	Mar
3	Aries	28: 45' 14"	Sun	Mar	Sat
4	Taurus	23: 58' 28"	Mar	Mar	Ven
5	Gemini	17: 33' 12"	Rah	Sun	Mar
6	Cancer	13: 40' 57"	Sat	Rah	Sat
7	Leo	17: 34' 37"	Ven	Mar	Jup
8	Virgo	27: 33' 51"	Mar	Jup	Mar
9	Libra	28: 45' 14"	Jup	Ven	Ket
10	Scorpio	23: 58' 28"	Mer	Mar	Ven
11	Sagittarius	17: 33' 12"	Ven	Mar	Jup
12	Capricorn	13: 40' 57"	Mon	Rah	Mon

Planetary Position

Planet	Sign	Degree	Star Lord	Sub Lord	Sub-Sub Lord
Sun	Virgo	18: 38' 13"	Mon	Mer	Mon
Mon	Gemini	08: 06' 25"	Rah	Rah	Ven
Mar	Virgo	11: 58' 19"	Mon	Rah	Rah
Mer	Virgo	18: 24' 24"	Mon	Mer	Ven
Jup	Virgo	08: 19' 20"	Sun	Ven	Mon
Ven	Leo	08: 06' 49"	Ket	Jup	Mer
Sat	Cancer	02: 23' 36"	Jup	Rah	Mer
Rah (R)	Aries	08: 23' 06"	Ket	Jup	Ket
Ket (R)	Libra	08: 23' 06"	Rah	Rah	Mon
Ura	Aquarius	09: 30' 52"	Rah	Jup	Ket
Nep	Capricorn	18: 47' 43"	Mon	Mer	Mar
Plu	Scorpio	25: 58' 29"	Mer	Rah	Mon
Fortuna	Scorpio	07: 02' 49"	Sat	Mer	Sat

At 02.30 hrs on 22.1.1974 at Jalandhar City, Moon's position is in Sagittarius in Venus star, Jupiter sub and Mercury sub-sub. The Jupiter sub remains during the time period that the native has given. As such the Astrologer has to fix the sub-sub of Moon. Moon is in the sub-sub of Mercury at this time. Mercury is a ruling planet. But corresponding to this position of Moon, ascendant rises in Libra and Jupiter star. Both Venus and Jupiter are not the direct ruling planets. The earliest sub-sub, which the Astrologer can thus choose from the ruling planets at the time of judgement, is Sun, which occurs at 03.23.04 hrs. Corresponding to this position of Moon, the ascendant rises in the sign of Mars, star of Saturn but sub of Venus. Mars and Saturn are the ruling planets at the time of judgement but Venus is not the ruling planet. The next sub is Sun which is a ruling planet corresponding to birth time 03.25.11hrs.The birth time of the native is thus fixed as 03.25.11hrs.The corrected horoscope of the native as per this Astrologer, is shown in Figure. 3.4.

Fig. 3.4

Name	Fig. 3.4	Place of Birth	Jullundur
Sex	Male	Latitude	031.18.N
Date of Birth	22/01/1974	Longitude	075.36.E
Day of Birth	Tuesday	Local Birth Time	02:57:35
Time of Birth	03:25:11	Local Birth Date	22/01/1974
Sidereal Time	11:1:3	Lunar Tithi	14
Bal. of Dasha	Ven 8Y 0M 18D	K.P. (New) Ayanamsa	23:28:59
Lagan	Scorpio	Lagan Lord	Mars
Sign	Sagittarius	Sign Lord	Jupiter
Nakshatra	P.Asadha	Nakshatra Lord	Venus

Lagna Chart

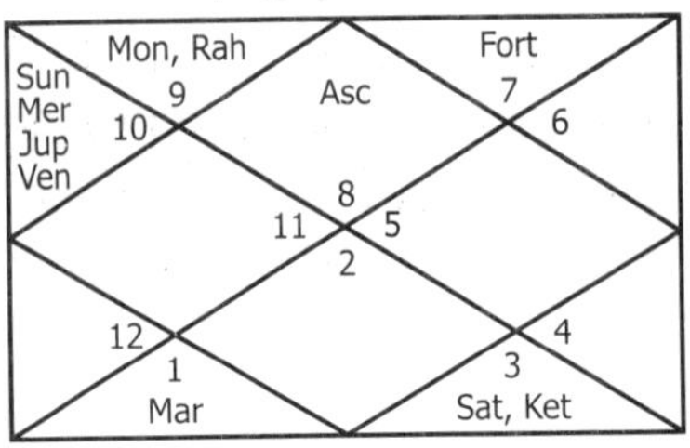

Bhava Chart

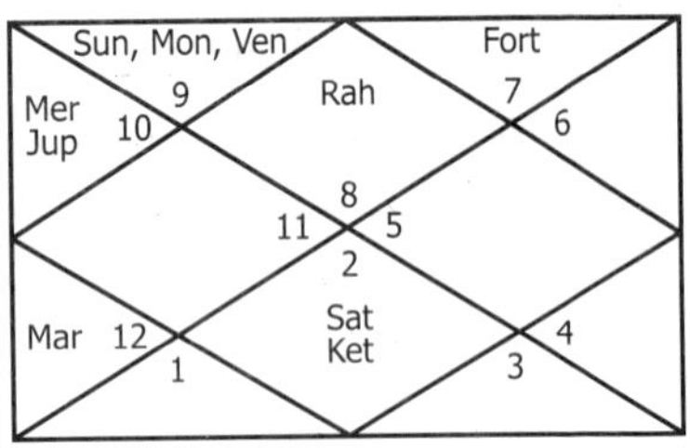

Cusp Chart

V 21:46:20	Mar 17:44:30 VI 17:53:43	VII 10:25:22	Ket 4:54:35 Sat 5:31:7 VIII 11:16:30
IV 20:31:9			IX 15:34:31
Jup 25:40:30 Mer 16:19:2 III 15:34:31 Ven 11:13:30 Sun 8:0:29			X 20:31:9
Mon 21:17:56 II 11:16:30 Rah 4:54:35	I 10:25:22	Fort 23:42:49 XII 17:53:43	XI 21:46:20

Fig. 3.4 Contd......

Nirayana Cusps

Bhav No.	Sign	Degree	Star Lord	Sub Lord	Sub-Sub Lord
1	Scorpio	10: 25' 22"	Sat	Sun	Mar
2	Sagittarius	11: 16' 30"	Ket	Sat	Jup
3	Capricorn	15: 34' 31"	Mon	Jup	Rah
4	Aquarius	20: 31' 09"	Jup	Jup	Mer
5	Pisces	21: 46' 20"	Mer	Sun	Rah
6	Aries	17: 53' 43"	Ven	Mar	Ven
7	Taurus	10: 25' 22"	Mon	Mon	Jup
8	Gemini	11: 16' 30"	Rah	Sat	Ven
9	Cancer	15: 34' 31"	Sat	Jup	Mer
10	Leo	20: 31' 09"	Ven	Jup	Sat
11	Virgo	21: 46' 20"	Mon	Ven	Jup
12	Libra	17: 53' 43"	Rah	Sun	Mer

Planetary Position

Planet	Sign	Degree	Star Lord	Sub Lord	Sub-Sub Lord
Sun	Capricorn	08: 00' 29"	Sun	Ven	Ven
Mon	Sagittarius	21: 17' 56"	Ven	Jup	Sun
Mar	Aries	17: 44' 30"	Ven	Mar	Mer
Mer	Capricorn	16: 19' 02"	Mon	Sat	Ket
Jup	Capricorn	25: 40' 30"	Mar	Rah	Ven
Ven (R)	Capricorn	11: 13' 30"	Mon	Mar	Rah
Sat (R)	Gemini	05: 31' 07"	Mar	Sun	Ven
Rah (R)	Sagittarius	04: 54' 35"	Ket	Mar	Rah
Ket (R)	Gemini	04: 54' 35"	Mar	Sun	Sun
Ura	Libra	04: 14' 39"	Mar	Ven	Sat
Nep	Scorpio	15: 28' 27"	Sat	Jup	Mer
Plu (R)	Virgo	13: 17' 30"	Mon	Rah	Ven
Fortuna	Libra	23: 42' 49"	Jup	Sat	Jup

Example 3:

Doubt about Date: A gentle man requested an Astrologer to confirm his date of birth. He gave the following data:

D.O.Birth: 03 or 04.9.1959

P.O Birth: Moradabad, India.

T.O. Birth: 07.29 AM

When there is a doubt about the date, the astrologer has to match the position of Moon on the respective dates with the ruling planets at the moment of judgement.

The astrologer took up the job at 20.06 hrs on 5.10.2004 at Noida. The planetary and cuspal positions at the time of judgement are shown in Fig. 3.5. The ruling planets were as under:

Day lord: Mars (Tuesday)

Ascendant: Aries 29 degree 51 minutes 27 seconds. It is ruled by Mars-Sun-Rahu as sign, star and sub Lord respectively.

Moon: Gemini 09 degree 53 minutes 06 seconds. It is ruled by Mer-Rahu-Jup as sign, star and sub Lord. Rahu being in Aries represent Mars.

Fig. 3.5

Name	Fig. 3.5	Place of Birth	Noida
Sex	Male	Latitude	028.20.N
Date of Birth	05/10/2004	Longitude	077.20.E
Day of Birth	Tuesday	Local Birth Time	19:45:20
Time of Birth	20:06:00	Local Birth Date	05/10/2004
Sidereal Time	20:43:44	Lunar Tithi	7
Bal. of Dasha	Rah 13Y 7M 27D	K.P. (New) Ayanamsa	23:54:42
Lagan	Aries	Lagan Lord	Mars
Sign	Gemini	Sign Lord	Mercury
Nakshatra	Ardra	Nakshatra Lord	Rahu

Fig. 3.5 Contd......

Nirayana Cusps

Bhav No.	Sign	Degree	Star Lord	Sub Lord	Sub-Sub Lord
1	Aries	29: 51' 27"	Sun	Rah	Sat
2	Taurus	26: 39' 34"	Mar	Jup	Mer
3	Gemini	20: 07' 56"	Jup	Jup	Jup
4	Cancer	14: 35' 56"	Sat	Rah	Sun
5	Leo	13: 46' 47"	Ven	Ven	Sun
6	Virgo	20: 07' 30"	Mon	Ket	Jup
7	Libra	29: 51' 27"	Jup	Mon	Jup
8	Scorpio	26: 39' 34"	Mer	Jup	Mer
9	Sagittarius	20: 07' 56"	Ven	Jup	Jup
10	Capricorn	14: 35' 56"	Mon	Jup	Mer
11	Aquarius	13: 46' 47"	Rah	Mer	Rah
12	Pisces	20: 07' 30"	Mer	Ven	Mar

Planetary Position

Planet	Sign	Degree	Star Lord	Sub Lord	Sub-Sub Lord
Sun	Virgo	18: 47' 05"	Mon	Mer	Mar
Mon	Gemini	09: 53' 06"	Rah	Jup	Sun
Mar	Virgo	12: 04' 09"	Mon	Rah	Rah
Mer	Virgo	18: 40' 08"	Mon	Mer	Mon
Jup	Virgo	08: 21' 16"	Sun	Ven	Mon
Ven	Leo	08: 17' 17"	Ket	Jup	Mer
Sat	Cancer	02: 24' 08"	Jup	Rah	Mer
Rah (R)	Aries	08: 23' 13"	Ket	Jup	Ket
Ket (R)	Libra	08: 23' 13"	Rah	Rah	Mon
Ura	Aquarius	09: 30' 36"	Rah	Jup	Ket
Nep	Capricorn	18: 47' 38"	Mon	Mer	Mar
Plu	Scorpio	25: 58' 39"	Mer	Rah	Mon
Fortuna	Capricorn	20: 57' 28"	Mon	Ven	Mon

Now on 03.9.1959 Moon is in Venus star and on 4.9.1959 it is in Sun star at 07.29 hrs. Venus is not the ruling planet and as such the astrologer declares that the correct date of the gentleman is 4-9-1959. The position of Moon at 07.29hrs on 4.9.1959 is Mer-Sun-Rahu that completely matches with the ruling planets at the moment of judgement. The corrected horoscope as per this astrologer is shown in Figure 3.6 as under:

Fig. 3.6

Name	Fig. 3.6	Place of Birth	Moradabad
Sex	Male	Latitude	028.48.N
Date of Birth	04/09/1959	Longitude	078.48.E
Day of Birth	Friday	Local Birth Time	07:14:12
Time of Birth	07:29:00	Local Birth Date	04/09/1959
Sidereal Time	6:3:58	Lunar Tithi	2
Bal. of Dasha	Sun 4Y 4M 2D	K.P. (New) Ayanamsa	23:16:56
Lagan	Virgo	Lagan Lord	Mercury
Sign	Virgo	Sign Lord	Mercury
Nakshatra	U.Phalguni	Nakshatra Lord	Sun

Lagna Chart

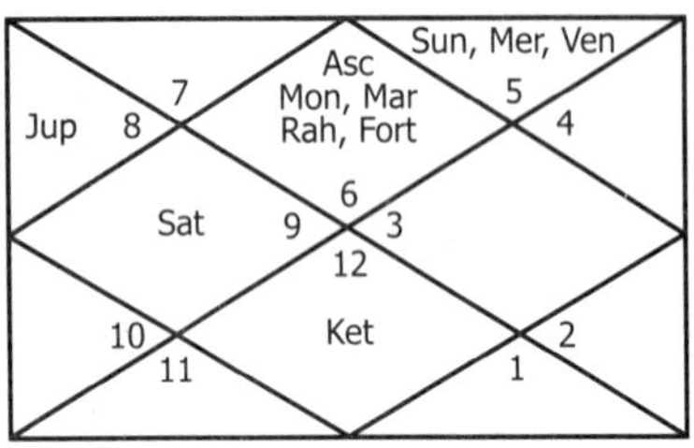

Bhava Chart

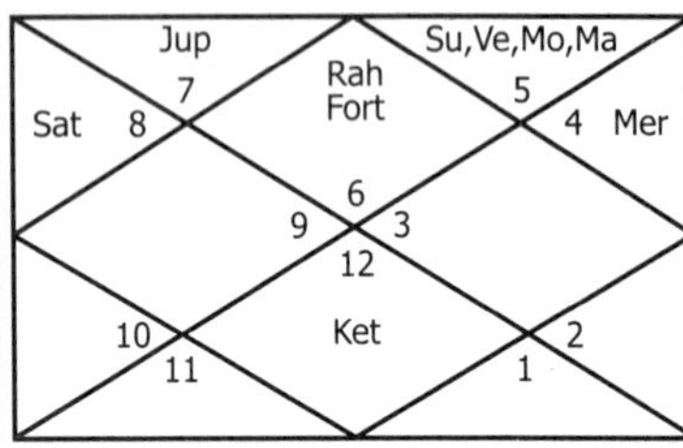

Cusp Chart

Ket 10:45:57 VII 7:35:32	VIII 5:39:8	IX 6:5:31	X 7:37:42
VI 9:36:38			XI 9:10:35
V 9:10:35			Mer 4:50:47 XII 9:36:38 Ven 13:3:36 Sun 17:31:32
IV 7:37:42 Sat 7:10:33	III 6:5:31 Jup 1:50:6	II 5:39:8	Mon 0:21:1 Mar 5:31:22 I 7:35:32 Rah 10:45:57 Fort 20:25:1

Fig. 3.6 Contd......

Nirayana Cusps

Bhav No.	Sign	Degree	Star Lord	Sub Lord	Sub-Sub Lord
1	Virgo	07: 35' 32"	Sun	Ket	Sat
2	Libra	05: 39' 08"	Mar	Mon	Mar
3	Scorpio	06: 05' 31"	Sat	Mer	Ven
4	Sagittarius	07: 37' 42"	Ket	Jup	Jup
5	Capricorn	09: 10' 35"	Sun	Ven	Jup
6	Aquarius	09: 36' 38"	Rah	Jup	Ven
7	Pisces	07: 35' 32"	Sat	Ket	Mon
8	Aries	05: 39' 08"	Ket	Rah	Rah
9	Taurus	06: 05' 31"	Sun	Mer	Mar
10	Gemini	07: 37' 42"	Rah	Rah	Mer
11	Cancer	09: 10' 35"	Sat	Ven	Rah
12	Leo	09: 36' 38"	Ket	Sat	Sat

Planetary Position

Planet	Sign	Degree	Star Lord	Sub Lord	Sub-Sub Lord
Sun	Leo	17: 31' 32"	Ven	Mar	Jup
Mon	Virgo	00: 21' 01"	Sun	Rah	Mer
Mar	Virgo	05: 31' 22"	Sun	Mer	Ven
Mer	Leo	04: 50' 47"	Ket	Mar	Rah
Jup	Scorpio	01: 50' 06"	Jup	Rah	Jup
Ven (R)	Leo	13: 03' 36"	Ket	Mer	Sat
Sat	Sagittarius	07: 10' 33"	Ket	Rah	Sun
Rah (R)	Virgo	10: 45' 57"	Mon	Mon	Mer
Ket (R)	Pisces	10: 45' 57"	Sat	Sun	Mer
Ura	Cancer	24: 56' 04"	Mer	Rah	Sat
Nep	Libra	11: 32' 27"	Rah	Sat	Ven
Plu	Leo	10: 53' 37"	Ket	Sat	Rah
Fortuna	Virgo	20: 25' 01"	Mon	Ket	Mer

Doubt about Year: Similarly this method can be used to check the correctness of the month or the year of birth by matching the ruling planets with the position of Sun or Jupiter respectively.

Second School of Thought: The followers of 2nd school of thought divide the ruling planets in two parts as follows:

1. **R.P. (Ascendant):** The planets co-ruling the ascendant at the time of judgement. That is sign, star, sub and sub-sub Lords.

2. **R.P. (Moon):** The sign, star, sub and sub-sub lord of Moon at the time of judgement.

R.P. (Ascendant) series is used to rectify the position of planets and R.P. (Moon) series is used to correct the Cuspal positions.

Followers of this school of thought have rightly decided not to use seven day week lord as an RP.

The *planetary week*, came in vogue as early as the 2nd century BC. It is ostensibly of Mesopotamian or Syrian origin. The days of the week, in most of the Indo-European languages, have names associated with the planets: Mon-day (day of the Moon) ... through Sun-day (day of the Sun). Even though this "astrological" legacy may be firmly anchored in our vocabulary and culture, these attributions have no strict astrological value, since they occurred through a simple arithmetic process without any physical foundation. The science of astrology has its origin much before 2nd century BC. The ancient sages were of the firm opinion that any event in the life of the native happens in accordance with the promise of that event in the native's chart and at a time when Moon transits in a particular Nakshatra and its minute divisions. In other words the day of happening of the event is related to the Moon's star lord. There was no concept of the planetary week in vogue at that time.

Calculation of Moon's Period in a Day

Before we use this technique to construct or rectify charts on the basis of doubtful birth data, let us try to understand how to calculate **Moon's Period in a Day.**

If we observe the movement of Moon on daily basis, we find that Moon covers a Nakshatra, on an average, in about 24 hrs. The movement of Moon in a particular Nakshatra can be divided into sub and sub–sub periods on 24 hr basis in the same proportion as it is done in calculating sub and sub-sub periods in Vimsottari Dasa.

Let us assume that Moon enters in Poorvashada Nakshatra at a particular time on a particular day. It takes approximately 24 hrs 2 minutes to complete its movement in Poorvashada. Now we want to know when Moon will complete its movement in Venus sub, Sun sub etc. It is calculated as follows:

Venus Sub in

Poorvashada	= 20/120 x 24 hrs 2 mins.	= 4 hrs 0 mt 20 sec
Sun Sub	= 06/120 x 24 hrs 2 mins.	= 1hr 12mins 06 sec
Moon Sub	= 10/120 x 24 hrs 2 mins.	= 2 hrs 0 min 10 sec
Mars Sub	= 07/120 x 24 hrs 2 mins.	= 1 hrs 24 mins 07 sec
Rahu Sub	= 18/120 x 24 hrs 2 mins.	= 3 hrs 36 mins 18 sec
Jup Sub	= 16/120 x 24 hrs 2 mins.	= 3 hrs 12 mins. 16 sec.
Sat Sub	= 19/120 x 24 hrs 2 mins.	= 3 hrs 48 mins. 19 sec.
Mer Sub	= 17/120 x 24 hrs 2 mins.	= 3 hrs 24 mins. 17 sec.
Ketu Sub	= 7/120 x 24 hrs 2 mins.	= 1 hr 24 mins. 07 sec.

Similarly we can calculate the sub-sub periods in various sub periods when Moon is transiting in Poorvashada. For example,

Rahu sub-sub period in Rahu sub can be calculated as follows:

Rahu Sub-Sub period = 18/120 x 3 hrs 36 minutes 18 seconds

= 32 minutes 24 seconds approximately

The following examples illustrate the use of RPs as followed by many astrologers. However the detailed procedure and philosophy of Birth Time Rectification as practiced by the author is explained in the next chapter.

We may use the ruling planets as per second school of thought to construct or rectify horoscope from doubtful data. This is explained through examples as follows:

Example 1:

Doubt about Time of Birth - Suppose a person is sure about the date of birth and there is a slight doubt about the time, may be of a few minutes only. In such cases, we need only to match the ascendant of the native with the planets co-ruling the Moon position at the time of judgement. For example, a young girl came to Mr. Astrologer and asked to correct her horoscope. She gave the following birth data:

Date of Birth: 26.07.1981

Place of Birth: Jaipur. (India).

Time of Birth: 15.20 hrs to 15.30 hrs.

Mr. Astrologer took the job at 17 hrs 39 minutes 52 seconds on 10.1.2005 at Noida (U.P) India. The planetary and cuspal positions at the time judgement are shown in Fig. 3.7 as under:

Fig. 3.7

Name	Fig. 3.7	Place of Birth	Noida
Sex	Male	Latitude	028.20.N
Date of Birth	10/01/2005	Longitude	077.20.E
Day of Birth	Monday	Local Birth Time	17:19:12
Time of Birth	17:39:52	Local Birth Date	10/01/2005
Sidereal Time	0:39:38	Lunar Tithi	1
Bal. of Dasha	Ven 0Y 3M 1D	K.P. (New) Ayanamsa	23:54:55
Lagan	Gemini	Lagan Lord	Mercury
Sign	Sagittarius	Sign Lord	Jupiter
Nakshatra	P.Asadha	Nakshatra Lord	Venus

Fig. 3.7 Contd......

Nirayana Cusps

Bhav No.	Sign	Degree	Star Lord	Sub Lord	Sub-Sub Lord
1	Gemini	26: 43' 07"	Jup	Ven	Ven
2	Cancer	19: 42' 22"	Mer	Ven	Sun
3	Leo	15: 52' 01"	Ven	Sun	Jup
4	Virgo	16: 51' 55"	Mon	Sat	Sun
5	Libra	21: 29' 36"	Jup	Jup	Mar
6	Scorpio	25: 40' 50"	Mer	Rah	Ven
7	Sagittarius	26: 43' 07"	Sun	Sun	Mon
8	Capricorn	19: 42' 22"	Mon	Ket	Ket
9	Aquarius	15: 52' 01"	Rah	Ven	Mon
10	Pisces	16: 51' 55"	Mer	Mer	Mer
11	Aries	21: 29' 36"	Ven	Jup	Mon
12	Taurus	25: 40' 50"	Mar	Rah	Ven

Planetary Position

Planet	Sign	Degree	Star Lord	Sub Lord	Sub-Sub Lord
Sun	Sagittarius	26: 26' 55"	Ven	Ket	Sat
Mon	Sagittarius	26: 30' 03"	Ven	Ket	Sat
Mar	Scorpio	17: 00' 54"	Mer	Mer	Ket
Mer	Sagittarius	06: 33' 16"	Ket	Rah	Mer
Jup	Virgo	24: 09' 31"	Mar	Rah	Rah
Ven	Sagittarius	07: 06' 03"	Ket	Rah	Ven
Sat (R)	Cancer	00: 14' 46"	Jup	Mon	Mer
Rah (R)	Aries	04: 20' 55"	Ket	Mon	Mer
Ket (R)	Libra	04: 20' 55"	Mar	Ven	Sat
Ura	Aquarius	10: 24' 21"	Rah	Jup	Rah
Nep	Capricorn	20: 15' 55"	Mon	Ket	Sat
Plu	Scorpio	29: 08' 45"	Mer	Sat	Mon
Fortuna	Gemini	26: 46' 15"	Jup	Ven	Ven

The ruling planets at this time were

		Sign		Star		Sub		Sub-Sub
RP (Ascdt)	=	Mer	-	Jup	-	Ven	-	Ven
RP (Moon)	=	Jup	-	Ven	-	Ket	-	Sat.

Mr. Astrologer fixed the birth time at 15 hrs 27 minutes 36 seconds when the ascendant position was Scorpio 15 degree 39 minutes 47 seconds. The planets co-ruling the ascendant were Mars-Sat-Jup-Ket as sign, star, sub, and sub-sub lord. Since the doubt was only of a few minutes, changing the ascendant sign was not needed. The corrected horoscope of the native is shown in Figure 3.8.

Fig. 3.8

Name	Fig. 3.8	Place of Birth	Jaipur
Sex	Female	Latitude	026.55.N
Date of Birth	26/07/1981	Longitude	075.49.E
Day of Birth	Sunday	Local Birth Time	15:00:52
Time of Birth	15:27:36	Local Birth Date	26/07/1981
Sidereal Time	11:16:53	Lunar Tithi	10
Bal. of Dasha	Sun 1Y 6M 16D	K.P. (New) Ayanamsa	23:35:16
Lagan	Scorpio	Lagan Lord	Mars
Sign	Taurus	Sign Lord	Venus
Nakshatra	Krittika	Nakshatra Lord	Sun

Lagna Chart

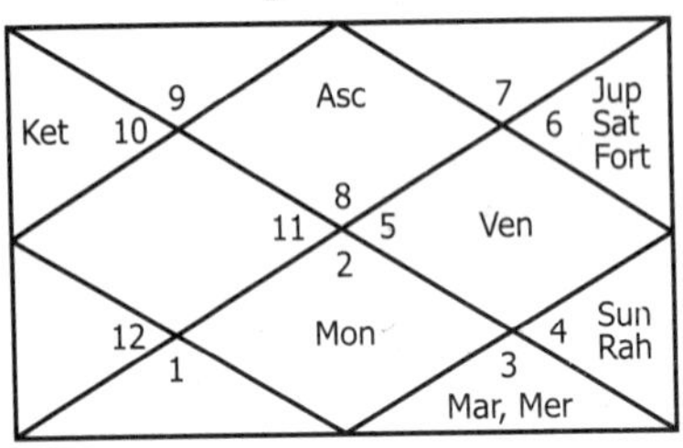

Bhava Chart

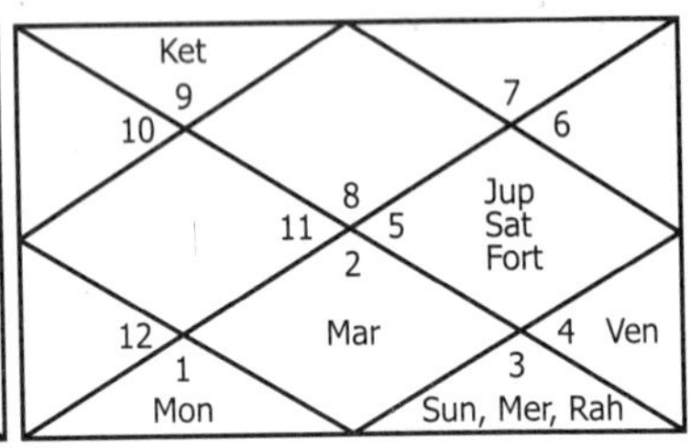

Cusp Chart

V 25:50:43	VI 22:20:8	Mon 6:33:41 VII 15:39:47	Mar 11:50:9 VIII 16:29:9 Mer 24:11:10
IV 24:41:30			Rah 8:6:40 Sun 9:44:10 IX 20:16:25
III 20:16:25 Ket 8:6:40			Ven 8:37:57 X 24:41:30
II 16:29:9	I 15:39:47	XII 22:20:8	Sat 11:31:32 Jup 11:40:54 Fort 12:29:18 XI 25:50:43

Fig. 3.8 Contd......

Nirayana Cusps

Bhav No.	Sign	Degree	Star Lord	Sub Lord	Sub-Sub Lord
1	Scorpio	15: 39' 47"	Sat	Jup	Ket
2	Sagittarius	16: 29' 09"	Ven	Mon	Rah
3	Capricorn	20: 16' 25"	Mon	Ket	Sat
4	Aquarius	24: 41' 30"	Jup	Mer	Mon
5	Pisces	25: 50' 43"	Mer	Rah	Mon
6	Aries	22: 20' 08"	Ven	Sat	Mer
7	Taurus	15: 39' 47"	Mon	Jup	Rah
8	Gemini	16: 29' 09"	Rah	Ven	Jup
9	Cancer	20: 16' 25"	Mer	Ven	Rah
10	Leo	24: 41' 30"	Ven	Mer	Ven
11	Virgo	25: 50' 43"	Mar	Rah	Mon
12	Libra	22: 20' 08"	Jup	Sat	Mer

Planetary Position

Planet	Sign	Degree	Star Lord	Sub Lord	Sub-Sub Lord
Sun	Cancer	09: 44' 10"	Sat	Ven	Sat
Mon	Taurus	06: 33' 41"	Sun	Mer	Jup
Mar	Gemini	11: 50' 09"	Rah	Sat	Mar
Mer	Gemini	24: 11' 10"	Jup	Mer	Ket
Jup	Virgo	11: 40' 54"	Mon	Mar	Ven
Ven	Leo	08: 37' 57"	Ket	Jup	Ven
Sat	Virgo	11: 31' 32"	Mon	Mar	Mer
Rah (R)	Cancer	08: 06' 40"	Sat	Ven	Ven
Ket (R)	Capricorn	08: 06' 40"	Sun	Ven	Ven
Ura (R)	Scorpio	02: 30' 06"	Jup	Rah	Ket
Nep (R)	Scorpio	28: 53' 10"	Mer	Sat	Ven
Plu	Virgo	28: 07' 16"	Mar	Sat	Sat
Fortuna	Virgo	12: 29' 18"	Mon	Rah	Sat

Example 2: A young lady came to Mr. Astrologer and wanted her horoscope to be constructed as per the following data:

Date of Birth: 18.10.1971

Place of Birth: Madurai (India)

Time of Birth: Between 16 hrs and 18.30 hrs.

In such cases when the native has no doubt about the date but the doubt about the time period of birth is significant, the following procedure should be adopted.

Step 1: Prepare the horoscope as per the date of birth and place of birth at time midway the time period. Check if the Moon star at that time is likely to change during the time period or not.

Step 2: If the star Lord of Moon is not likely to change in the vicinity of the time period, then we need not bother to change it to match the RP (Ascendant) series of planets. If the star lord changes in the given time period, then the star lord also has to be fixed in accordance with the planets co-ruling RP (Ascendant)

Step 3: Having decided the star lord of Moon, we need to fix sub and sub-sub lords of Moon using the planets co-ruling RP (Ascendant).

Step 4: After fixing the Moon's star, sub and sub-sub, we need to fix the ascendant to match the planets co-ruling the RP (Moon).

In this example, Moon star on 18.10.1971 during the period 16 hrs to 18.30 hrs remains Moon only. Hence we need only to fix the sub and sub-sub of Moon.

Mr. Astrologer took up the job on 3.2.2002 (Sunday) at 12.25 hrs at Noida (U.P), India. The planetary and cuspal positions at the time of judgement are shown in Fig. 3.9.

Fig. 3.9

Name	Fig. 3.9	Place of Birth	Noida
Sex	Male	Latitude	028.20.N
Date of Birth	03/02/2002	Longitude	077.20.E
Day of Birth	Sunday	Local Birth Time	12:04:20
Time of Birth	12:25:00	Local Birth Date	03/02/2002
Sidereal Time	20:57:27	Lunar Tithi	7
Bal. of Dasha	Mar 1Y 5M 3D	K.P. (New) Ayanamsa	23:52:27
Lagan	Taurus	Lagan Lord	Venus
Sign	Libra	Sign Lord	Venus
Nakshatra	Chitra	Nakshatra Lord	Mars

Fig. 3.9 Contd......

Nirayana Cusps

Bhav No.	Sign	Degree	Star Lord	Sub Lord	Sub-Sub Lord
1	Taurus	03: 46' 30"	Sun	Sat	Ven
2	Taurus	29: 55' 46"	Mar	Sat	Jup
3	Gemini	23: 17' 08"	Jup	Sat	Mar
4	Cancer	18: 01' 40"	Mer	Mer	Jup
5	Leo	17: 46' 21"	Ven	Mar	Mer
6	Virgo	24: 30' 10"	Mar	Rah	Jup
7	Scorpio	03: 46' 30"	Sat	Sat	Mer
8	Scorpio	29: 55' 46"	Mer	Sat	Jup
9	Sagittarius	23: 17' 08"	Ven	Sat	Mar
10	Capricorn	18: 01' 40"	Mon	Mer	Mer
11	Aquarius	17: 46' 21"	Rah	Sun	Sat
12	Pisces	24: 30' 10"	Mer	Rah	Jup

Planetary Position

Planet	Sign	Degree	Star Lord	Sub Lord	Sub-Sub Lord
Sun	Capricorn	20: 23' 45"	Mon	Ket	Mer
Mon	Libra	03: 57' 35"	Mar	Ven	Jup
Mar	Pisces	17: 16' 08"	Mer	Mer	Ven
Mer (R)	Capricorn	06: 44' 01"	Sun	Mer	Sat
Jup (R)	Gemini	12: 52' 58"	Rah	Mer	Ket
Ven	Capricorn	25: 08' 57"	Mar	Rah	Mer
Sat (R)	Taurus	14: 10' 58"	Mon	Jup	Sat
Rah (R)	Gemini	02: 07' 04"	Mar	Ket	Mon
Ket (R)	Sagittarius	02: 07' 04"	Ket	Ven	Jup
Ura	Aquarius	00: 21' 17"	Mar	Mer	Ket
Nep	Capricorn	14: 48' 53"	Mon	Jup	Ven
Plu	Scorpio	23: 11' 19"	Mer	Mon	Ven
Fortuna	Capricorn	17: 20' 20"	Mon	Sat	Rah

The ruling planets were as follows:

	Sign	Star	Sub	Sub-Sub
RP (Ascdt):	Ven	Sun	Sat	Ven
RP (Moon):	Ven	Mars	Ven	Jup.

At the time of judgement Ketu was in Sagittarius sign and hence represented Jupiter.

At 16.00 hrs on 18.10.1971, Moon is in Moon star, Ven sub and Mars sub-sub. Mars, Ra, Jup do not appear in RP (Ascdt) series. Thus we need to fix the sub-sub of Moon as Sat which occurs at 17 hrs 22 minutes and lasts up to 18 hrs 4 minutes. Corresponding to this position of Moon, we have to set the ascendant that matches the planets co-ruling the RP (Moon). At 17 hrs 22 minutes, Pisces 21 degree 6 minutes 49 seconds rises in the ascendant. That is the star lord of ascendant comes as Mercury, which does not appear in RP (Moon) series. Moreover, Mercury is also not in the star or sub of a planet that appears in RP (Moon) on the date of judgement. Hence the native's ascendant as Pisces is ruled out. The correct ascendant for the native has to be fixed as Aries 0 degree 4 minutes 52 sec, which occurs at 17 hrs 53 minutes. The planets co-ruling the ascendant of the native will be Mars-Ket-Ket-Ven as sign, star, sub and sub-sub lords. The Moon position corresponding to this time of birth is Moon star Ven sub, Sat sub-sub and Rahu sub-sub-sub. Rahu does not appear in RP (ascendant) series. But Rahu is in Mercury sign and Mars star in RP chart. Mercury is in Sun star who is RP (ascendant series). Thus Rahu qualifies to be Ruling planet and can come as sub-sub-sub lord. The correct horoscope of the native is shown in Fig. 3.10.

Fig. 3.10

Name	Fig. 3.10	Place of Birth	Madurai
Sex	Male	Latitude	009.54.N
Date of Birth	18/10/1971	Longitude	078.06.E
Day of Birth	Monday	Local Birth Time	17:35:24
Time of Birth	17:53:00	Local Birth Date	18/10/1971
Sidereal Time	19:20:43	Lunar Tithi	15
Bal. of Dasha	Mon 0Y10M25D	K.P. (New) Ayanamsa	23:27:05
Lagan	Aries	Lagan Lord	Mars
Sign	Virgo	Sign Lord	Mercury
Nakshatra	Hasta	Nakshatra Lord	Moon

Lagna Chart

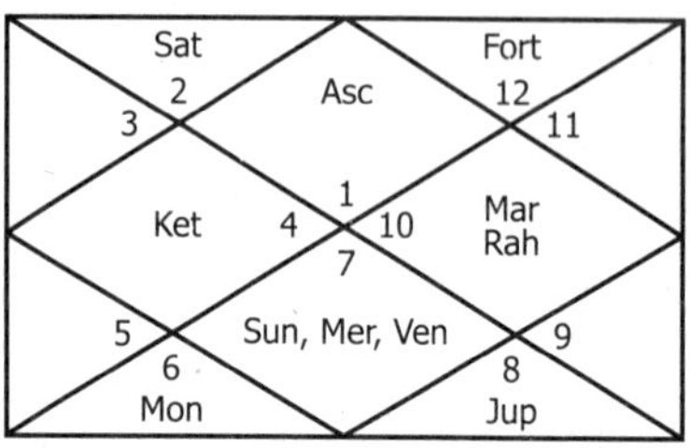

Bhava Chart

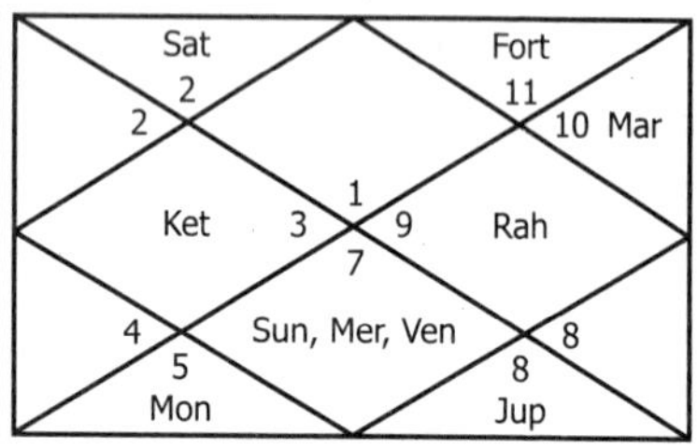

Cusp Chart

Fort 21:11:41	I 0:4:52	II 1:21:47 Sat 12:18:21 III 28:50:7	IV 25:10:58
XII 25:18:25			Ket 18:17:39 V 23:20:16
Mar 27:29:6 XI 23:20:16 Rah 18:17:39			VI 25:18:25
X 25:10:58	IX 28:50:7 Jup 12:39:6 VIII 1:21:47	Ven 14:44:35 Mer 7:48:47 Sun 1:1:0 VII 0:4:52	Mon 22:7:49

Fig. 3.10 Contd......

Nirayana Cusps

Bhav No.	Sign	Degree	Star Lord	Sub Lord	Sub-Sub Lord
1	Aries	00: 04' 52"	Ket	Ket	Ven
2	Taurus	01: 21' 47"	Sun	Jup	Jup
3	Taurus	28: 50' 07"	Mar	Sat	Ven
4	Gemini	25: 10' 58"	Jup	Mer	Rah
5	Cancer	23: 20' 16"	Mer	Mar	Mar
6	Leo	25: 18' 25"	Ven	Mer	Rah
7	Libra	00: 04' 52"	Mar	Mer	Mer
8	Scorpio	01: 21' 47"	Jup	Rah	Rah
9	Scorpio	28: 50' 07"	Mer	Sat	Ven
10	Sagittarius	25: 10' 58"	Ven	Mer	Rah
11	Capricorn	23: 20' 16"	Mar	Mar	Mar
12	Aquarius	25: 18' 25"	Jup	Mer	Jup

Planetary Position

Planet	Sign	Degree	Star Lord	Sub Lord	Sub-Sub Lord
Sun	Libra	01: 01' 00"	Mar	Mer	Mar
Mon	Virgo	22: 07' 49"	Mon	Ven	Sat
Mar	Capricorn	27: 29' 06"	Mar	Jup	Mon
Mer	Libra	07: 48' 47"	Rah	Rah	Mer
Jup	Scorpio	12: 39' 06"	Sat	Mar	Ket
Ven	Libra	14: 44' 35"	Rah	Ket	Mar
Sat (R)	Taurus	12: 18' 21"	Mon	Rah	Jup
Rah (R)	Capricorn	18: 17' 39"	Mon	Mer	Ven
Ket (R)	Cancer	18: 17' 39"	Mer	Mer	Sat
Ura	Virgo	21: 10' 27"	Mon	Ven	Mar
Nep	Scorpio	07: 59' 35"	Sat	Ket	Sat
Plu	Virgo	07: 01' 32"	Sun	Ket	Ket
Fortuna	Pisces	21: 11' 41"	Mer	Ven	Mer

Example 3:

Doubt about both Date and Time of Birth - We may construct the horoscope of a person who has doubt both about date as well as time of birth by using the procedure indicated in the following steps.

Step 1: Match the Moon position on the respective dates and approximate time of birth with the planets co-ruling the RP (Ascendant) at the time of judgement. The date for which the Moon position matches with the planets co-ruling the RP (Ascendant) should be taken as the correct date of birth.

Step 2: Having fixed the Moon star, fix its sub and sub-sub using planets co-ruling RP (Ascendant).

Step 3: As per this Moon position, fix the ascendant to match the planets co-ruling RP (Moon).

A gentleman came to Mr. Astrologer and wanted his horoscope to be constructed. He gave the following birth data.

Date of Birth: 4 or 5.9.1959

Time of Birth: Morning between 6 to 8 AM.

Place of Birth: Moradabad

Mr. Astrologer took up the job on 11.1.2005, Tuesday at 07.49.19 AM at Noida. The planetary and cuspal positions of RP chart are indicated in Figure 3.11.

Fig. 3.11

Name	Fig. 3.11	Place of Birth	Noida
Sex	Male	Latitude	028.20.N
Date of Birth	11/01/2005	Longitude	077.20.E
Day of Birth	Tuesday	Local Birth Time	07:28:39
Time of Birth	07:49:19	Local Birth Date	11/01/2005
Sidereal Time	14:51:24	Lunar Tithi	1
Bal. of Dasha	Sun 1Y 11M 29D	K.P. (New) Ayanamsa	23:54:55
Lagan	Capricorn	Lagan Lord	Saturn
Sign	Capricorn	Sign Lord	Saturn
Nakshatra	U.Asadha	Nakshatra Lord	Sun

Fig. 3.11 Contd......

Nirayana Cusps

Bhav No.	Sign	Degree	Star Lord	Sub Lord	Sub-Sub Lord
1	Capricorn	05: 21' 34"	Sun	Mer	Mer
2	Aquarius	14: 13' 03"	Rah	Mer	Sat
3	Pisces	21: 12' 09"	Mer	Ven	Mer
4	Aries	21: 24' 11"	Ven	Jup	Mon
5	Taurus	16: 23' 30"	Mon	Sat	Ket
6	Gemini	09: 41' 08"	Rah	Jup	Ven
7	Cancer	05: 21' 34"	Sat	Sat	Jup
8	Leo	14: 13' 03"	Ven	Ven	Rah
9	Virgo	21: 12' 09"	Mon	Ven	Mar
10	Libra	21: 24' 11"	Jup	Jup	Mon
11	Scorpio	16: 23' 30"	Sat	Jup	Mar
12	Sagittarius	09: 41' 08"	Ket	Sat	Mer

Planetary Position

Planet	Sign	Degree	Star Lord	Sub Lord	Sub-Sub Lord
Sun	Sagittarius	27: 03' 00"	Sun	Sun	Sat
Mon	Capricorn	05: 33' 58"	Sun	Mer	Ven
Mar	Scorpio	17: 25' 26"	Mer	Mer	Sun
Mer	Sagittarius	07: 22' 10"	Ket	Rah	Mon
Jup	Virgo	24: 11' 55"	Mar	Rah	Rah
Ven	Sagittarius	07: 50' 24"	Ket	Jup	Sat
Sat (R)	Cancer	00: 11' 51"	Jup	Mon	Mer
Rah (R)	Aries	04: 14' 01"	Ket	Mon	Sat
Ket (R)	Libra	04: 14' 01"	Mar	Ven	Sat
Ura	Aquarius	10: 25' 57"	Rah	Jup	Rah
Nep	Capricorn	20: 17' 10"	Mon	Ket	Sat
Plu	Scorpio	29: 09' 57"	Mer	Sat	Mon
Fortuna	Capricorn	13: 52' 32"	Mon	Rah	Mar

Mr. Astrologer compared the Moon position on 4.9.1959 at 6 Am and found that it is in Mer sign, Sun star and Rahu sub. Since Rahu on the date of Judgement represents Mars, the position of Moon in the star of Sun and sub of Rahu are taken as correct. The sub-sub of Moon could be Saturn or Mercury. It is found that when we keep Saturn as the sub-sub of Moon we are not able to match the planets co-ruling the ascendant with the RP (Moon) series. Keeping the sub-sub of Moon as Mercury we are able to fix the position of the ascendant at Virgo 3 degree 41 minutes 22 seconds. The sub-sub lord of the ascendant is fixed as Ketu that represents Venus. The planets co-ruling the ascendant are Mer- Sun-Sat- Ket that totally agrees with the planets co-ruling the RP (Moon) position. The planetary and cuspal positions of the corrected chart are indicated in figure 3.12.

Fig. 3.12

Name	Fig. 3.12	Place of Birth	Moradabad
Sex	Male	Latitude	028.48.N
Date of Birth	04/09/1959	Longitude	078.48.E
Day of Birth	Friday	Local Birth Time	06:56:32
Time of Birth	07:11:20	Local Birth Date	04/09/1959
Sidereal Time	5:46:15	Lunar Tithi	2
Bal. of Dasha	Sun 4Y 4M 30D	K.P. (New) Ayanamsa	23:16:56
Lagan	Virgo	Lagan Lord	Mercury
Sign	Virgo	Sign Lord	Mercury
Nakshatra	U.Phalguni	Nakshatra Lord	Sun

Lagna Chart

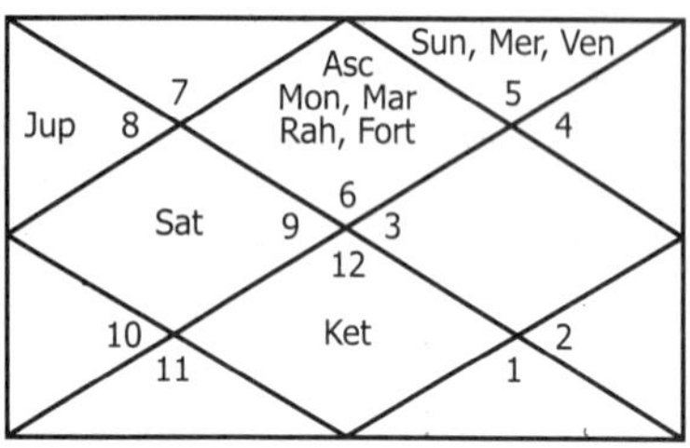

Bhava Chart

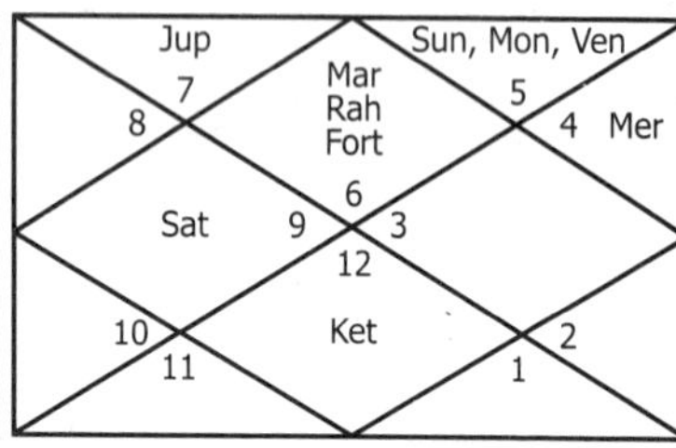

Cusp Chart

Ket 10:45:57 VII 3:41:22	VIII 1:34:8	IX 1:59:41	X 3:33:52
VI 5:32:24			XI 5:5:40
V 5:5:40			Mer 4:49:26 XII 5:32:24 Ven 13:4:3 Sun 17:30:49
Sat 7:10:33 IV 3:33:52	III 1:59:41 Jup 1:50:1	II 1:34:8	Mon 0:10:48 I 3:41:22 Mar 5:30:54 Rah 10:45:57 Fort 16:21:21

Fig. 3.12 Contd......

Nirayana Cusps

Bhav No.	Sign	Degree	Star Lord	Sub Lord	Sub-Sub Lord
1	Virgo	03: 41' 22"	Sun	Sat	Ket
2	Libra	01: 34' 08"	Mar	Mer	Jup
3	Scorpio	01: 59' 41"	Jup	Rah	Sat
4	Sagittarius	03: 33' 52"	Ket	Sun	Ven
5	Capricorn	05: 05' 40"	Sun	Sat	Jup
6	Aquarius	05: 32' 24"	Mar	Sun	Ven
7	Pisces	03: 41' 22"	Sat	Sat	Mer
8	Aries	01: 34' 08"	Ket	Ven	Mar
9	Taurus	01: 59' 41"	Sun	Jup	Ket
10	Gemini	03: 33' 52"	Mar	Ven	Rah
11	Cancer	05: 05' 40"	Sat	Sat	Rah
12	Leo	05: 32' 24"	Ket	Mar	Mon

Planetary Position

Planet	Sign	Degree	Star Lord	Sub Lord	Sub-Sub Lord
Sun	Leo	17: 30' 49"	Ven	Mar	Jup
Mon	Virgo	00: 10' 48"	Sun	Rah	Mer
Mar	Virgo	05: 30' 54"	Sun	Mer	Ven
Mer	Leo	04: 49' 26"	Ket	Mar	Rah
Jup	Scorpio	01: 50' 01"	Jup	Rah	Jup
Ven (R)	Leo	13: 04' 03"	Ket	Mer	Sat
Sat	Sagittarius	07: 10' 33"	Ket	Rah	Sun
Rah (R)	Virgo	10: 45' 57"	Mon	Mon	Mer
Ket (R)	Pisces	10: 45' 57"	Sat	Sun	Mer
Ura	Cancer	24: 56' 02"	Mer	Rah	Sat
Nep	Libra	11: 32' 26"	Rah	Sat	Ven
Plu	Leo	10: 53' 36"	Ket	Sat	Rah
Fortuna	Virgo	16: 21' 21"	Mon	Sat	Ket

Example 4:

Doubt about Month and Time of Birth - Let us consider the case for constructing the horoscope when the native has a doubt about the month of birth as well as time of birth. The gentleman gave the following data:

Date of Birth: 29.8.1948 or 29.9.1948

Place of Birth: Delhi (India)

Time of Birth: 15.00 hrs to 17.00 hrs.

The astrologer took the job on 11.1.2005 (Tuesday), at 12.45 hrs. The planetary and Cuspal positions of RP chart are indicated in Fig. 3.13.

Fig. 3.13

Name	3.13	Place of Birth	Noida
Sex	Male	Latitude	028.20.N
Date of Birth	11/01/2005	Longitude	077.20.E
Day of Birth	Tuesday	Local Birth Time	12:24:20
Time of Birth	12:45:00	Local Birth Date	11/01/2005
Sidereal Time	19:47:54	Lunar Tithi	1
Bal. of Dasha	Sun 0Y 7M 0D	K.P. (New) Ayanamsa	23:54:58
Lagan	Aries	Lagan Lord	Mars
Sign	Capricorn	Sign Lord	Saturn
Nakshatra	U.Asadha	Nakshatra Lord	Sun

Fig. 3.13 Contd......

Nirayana Cusps

Bhav No.	Sign	Degree	Star Lord	Sub Lord	Sub-Sub Lord
1	Aries	12: 57' 52"	Ket	Mer	Jup
2	Taurus	12: 59' 54"	Mon	Rah	Mer
3	Gemini	07: 24' 57"	Rah	Rah	Sat
4	Cancer	01: 07' 04"	Jup	Mar	Ven
5	Cancer	28: 06' 19"	Mer	Sat	Sat
6	Virgo	02: 11' 15"	Sun	Jup	Ven
7	Libra	12: 57' 52"	Rah	Mer	Ven
8	Scorpio	12: 59' 54"	Sat	Rah	Rah
9	Sagittarius	07: 24' 57"	Ket	Rah	Mon
10	Capricorn	01: 07' 04"	Sun	Rah	Mar
11	Capricorn	28: 06' 19"	Mar	Sat	Sat
12	Pisces	02: 11' 15"	Jup	Rah	Sat

Planetary Position

Planet	Sign	Degree	Star Lord	Sub Lord	Sub-Sub Lord
Sun	Sagittarius	27: 15' 33"	Sun	Sun	Ven
Mon	Capricorn	08: 42' 49"	Sun	Ven	Rah
Mar	Scorpio	17: 33' 59"	Mer	Mer	Mon
Mer	Sagittarius	07: 39' 16"	Ket	Jup	Jup
Jup	Virgo	24: 12' 44"	Mar	Rah	Rah
Ven	Sagittarius	08: 05' 50"	Ket	Jup	Mer
Sat (R)	Cancer	00: 10' 50"	Jup	Mon	Mer
Rah (R)	Aries	04: 11' 40"	Ket	Mon	Sat
Ket (R)	Libra	04: 11' 40"	Mar	Ven	Sat
Ura	Aquarius	10: 26' 31"	Rah	Jup	Rah
Nep	Capricorn	20: 17' 36"	Mon	Ket	Sat
Plu	Scorpio	29: 10' 22"	Mer	Sat	Mon
Fortuna	Aries	24: 25' 08"	Ven	Mer	Ven

Step 1: Since there is a doubt about the month of birth, we need to match the planets co-ruling the RP (Ascdt) with the planets co-ruling the position of Sun on 29.8.1948 and 29.9.1948 .The Planets co-ruling the RP (Ascdt) are Mars-Ket-Mer-Jup. The planets co-ruling the position of Sun on 29.8.1948 at 15.00hrs are Sun-Ket-Mer-Jup and the planets co-ruling the position of Sun on 29.9.1948 at 15.00 hrs are Mer-Mo-Ra-Ket. This clearly establishes that the date of birth of the gentleman has to be 29.8.1948.

Step 2: Having fixed the date of birth, we have to fix the position of Moon and Ascdt as we did in example 3. The corrected horoscope of the native is shown in fig. 3.14.

Fig. 3.14

Name	Fig. 3.14	Place of Birth	Delhi
Sex	Male	Latitude	028.39.N
Date of Birth	29/08/1948	Longitude	077.13.E
Day of Birth	Sunday	Local Birth Time	16:00:46
Time of Birth	16:21:54	Local Birth Date	29/08/1948
Sidereal Time	14:30:57	Lunar Tithi	10
Bal. of Dasha	Mar 1Y 7M 14D	K.P. (New) Ayanamsa	23:07:43
Lagan	Capricorn	Lagan Lord	Saturn
Sign	Gemini	Sign Lord	Mercury
Nakshatra	Mrigasira	Nakshatra Lord	Mars

Lagna Chart

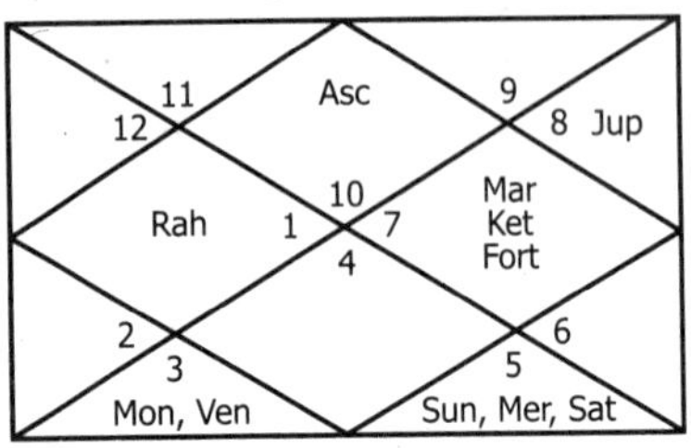

Bhava Chart

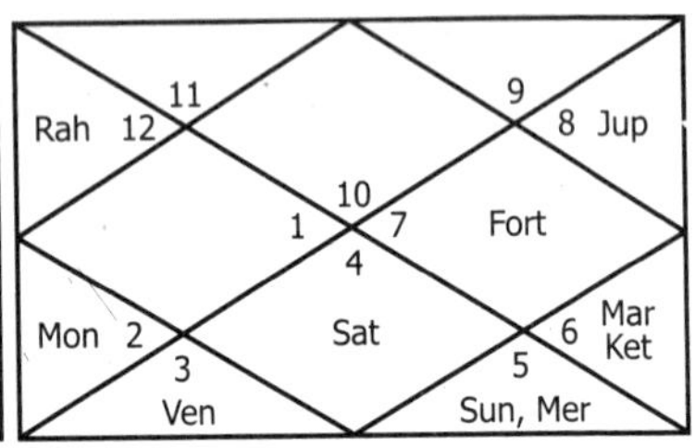

Cusp Chart

III 16:0:39	RAh 13:50:38 IV 17:1:26	V 12:27:42	Mon 3:35:4 VI 5:38:53 Ven 27:5:54
II 8:37:11			VII 0:28:43
I 0:28:43			Sat 4:19:22 VIII 8:37:11 Sun 12:51:53 Mer 28:32:29
XII 5:38:53	Jup 26:15:10 XI 12:27:42	Fort 21:11:54 X 17:1:26 Ket 13:50:38 Mar 3:31:33	IX 16:0:39

Fig. 3.14 Contd......

Nirayana Cusps

Bhav No.	Sign	Degree	Star Lord	Sub Lord	Sub-Sub Lord
1	Capricorn	00: 28' 43"	Sun	Rah	Ket
2	Aquarius	08: 37' 11"	Rah	Rah	Mar
3	Pisces	16: 00' 39"	Sat	Jup	Ven
4	Aries	17: 01' 26"	Ven	Mon	Mer
5	Taurus	12: 27' 42"	Mon	Rah	Sat
6	Gemini	05: 38' 53"	Mar	Mon	Mar
7	Cancer	00: 28' 43"	Jup	Mon	Ven
8	Leo	08: 37' 11"	Ket	Jup	Ven
9	Virgo	16: 00' 39"	Mon	Sat	Mer
10	Libra	17: 01' 26"	Rah	Ven	Mer
11	Scorpio	12: 27' 42"	Sat	Mar	Sat
12	Sagittarius	05: 38' 53"	Ket	Rah	Rah

Planetary Position

Planet	Sign	Degree	Star Lord	Sub Lord	Sub-Sub Lord
Sun	Leo	12: 51' 53"	Ket	Mer	Jup
Mon	Gemini	03: 35' 04"	Mar	Ven	Rah
Mar	Libra	03: 31' 33"	Mar	Ven	Rah
Mer	Leo	28: 32' 29"	Sun	Mar	Rah
Jup	Scorpio	26: 15' 10"	Mer	Jup	Jup
Ven	Gemini	27: 05' 54"	Jup	Ven	Mon
Sat	Leo	04: 19' 22"	Ket	Mon	Mer
Rah (R)	Aries	13: 50' 38"	Ven	Ven	Mon
Ket (R)	Libra	13: 50' 38"	Rah	Mer	Rah
Ura	Gemini	06: 50' 24"	Rah	Rah	Rah
Nep	Virgo	18: 16' 56"	Mon	Mer	Ven
Plu	Cancer	22: 06' 09"	Mer	Sun	Ket
Fortuna	Libra	21: 11' 54"	Jup	Jup	Sun

Special Cases: Sometimes the native is sure of the date of birth and time of birth, but not sure whether the time is before Noon or after Noon. Taking the Ruling planets can solve this problem. The sign in which the star of the sub-sub lord of the RP (Ascendant) is deposited provides the clue as per below:

Star Lord of S-S lord deposited in	Time Period
Moveable Sign	0 to 8 hrs
Fixed Sign	8 to 16 hrs.
Common Sign	16 to 24 hrs.

We may sometime check the day lord, Moon Rashi lord and Moon star lord by noting the sub-sub lord of RP (Ascendant), its star lord and the lord of the sign in which the star lord is deposited. These three planets will indicate the Day lord, star lord and Rashi lord.

Important Note: Rectification of a horoscope by using Ruling Planets whether as per first school of thought or as per second school of thought can at best provide an approximately correct horoscope? For absolute rectification of the horoscope, we need not only to place the correct degree on the ascendant but also on all the cuspal positions. This is explained in next chapter. **We may also remember that the accuracy of the ruling planets and as such of the horoscope depends upon the accuracy of the software that you use for constructing the horoscopes.**

Chapter 4

Construction of True Horoscope

The true horoscope of a native is a simulation of the total life pattern of the individual. It recognizes the fact that each human being consists of body, mind and soul which are unique for each individual i.e. each person has his own personal consciousness entrenched in his body. The true horoscope has, therefore, to reflect the quality and quantum of energy that has been apportioned to the incarnated soul. The interplay of body, mind and soul sets the pace for the development of the native's life pattern. In other words, the true horoscope has to be a true portrait of the native that should clearly reveal all facets of his life i.e. his individuality, personality, temperament, state of health, longevity, name and fame, virtues, capacity to face struggles of life, social, financial, marital, educational, and the professional status. It is, therefore, imperative that we need to place the correct degree, minutes and seconds on each of the twelve cuspal positions. This chapter explains the various techniques to correct all the cuspal positions of the native's horoscope.

Philosophy behind Theory of Birth Time Rectification

Why the soul has chosen a particular moment of time on a particular day, month and year to incarnate in the form of a human being? It is so because this particular moment or the ascendant has to reflect the very being of the individual. The person's nature, his capacity to enjoy the pleasures and struggles of life; his /her style of functioning; what is destined for him in this incarnation as per the wisdom acquired from earlier lives is depicted by the significations of planets co-ruling the ascendant. We know that other cuspal positions are set, using a particular house formation system, in accordance with the degree, minutes and seconds that rise in the ascendant at the time and place of birth. Ascendant, in fact is the epitome of the whole horoscope. The native experiences only those events in life that are promised by the dynamic significations of the planets that co-rule the ascendant.

The birth of a human being is an event in the life of a person who has fathered the native. And we know that the fundamental postulate of Astrology is that no event takes place unless Sun and Moon occupy particular positions in the Zodiac. The planets that co-rule these positions have to be significators of the houses that take part in enacting the event. The formation of the ascendant, therefore, has to have a close relationship with the Sun and Moon's position at the time of birth. We also know that each human being has specific fatherhood and motherhood. Mother is represented by the fourth house and father by the 9th house in the horoscope. The sub sub lord of these cusps should establish relationship with their Moon stars respectively. We must remember that heredity plays significant role in the formation of the horoscope.

The 9th house in the chart represents father. The ascendant is the 5th house from the 9th house. The birth of an individual will take place only when the Sun and Moon's position are closely linked with 2, 5 and 11 houses from the 9th house i.e. the planets co-ruling the positions of Sun and Moon at the time of birth has to be linked with 10th, 1st and 7th house in the native's chart. We need to remember that the native's chart, in fact, is an event or transit chart for father. Planets co-ruling ascendant have to be significators of houses 2(addition in the family), 5(Progeny) and 11 (fulfillment of desire or successful completion of the event) as per the theory of transit as explained in my Books Kalamsa and Cuspal Interlinks and Key to Learn.

Since the birth is only at a particular moment, we have, taking into consideration the limitations of the software's, selected the sub-sub lord of the ascendant to represent the moment of birth. As such, the sub-sub lord of the ascendant has to be fixed so as to clearly reflect Moon's star lord. This can happen in the following three ways:

1. The sub-sub lord of the ascendant itself may be the Moon's star lord. The sub-sub lord may or may not have the positional status. If the sub-sub lord of the ascendant does not have the positional status, it only means that this sub-sub lord is not contributing to the significations of the ascendant but during its dasa period, it provides the results of the houses linked through its star iord by the conscious efforts of the native.

2. The star lord, the sub lord or the sub-sub lord of the sub-sub lord of the ascendant can be the star lord of Moon. That is the sub sub lord of the ascendant may be a planet whose star or sub or sub sub lord is the same planet as the star lord of the moon. If Moon itself comes as the sub sub lord of the ascendant then it always establishes relationship.

3. The star lord of Moon can be in the star or sub or sub-sub of the sub-sub lord of the ascendant. If X is the star lord of Moon in a horoscope in which Y is the sub sub lord of the ascendant then if X is in the star of y or sub of y or sub sub of Y we say that the relationship is established?

4. In a similar way we verify the relationship of 4th cusp sub sub lord with Moon star of Mother and the 9th cusp sub sub lord with the Moon star of Father.

These three ways of checking the Moon's star lord's relationship with the sub-sub lord of the ascendant have been derived from the following principles:

A. A planet during its transit gives the result of the houses to which it is linked through its star lord.

B. The star lord of the planet may itself appear in the relevant cusps that take part in enacting the event.

C. The planet's star lord may be responsible for giving the results of the relevant cusps that take part in enacting the event.

Let us try to check the veracity of the ways we have declared to fix the sub-sub lord of the ascendant for a correct horoscope through examples.

Example 1: Figure 4.1 is the chart of a child born on 23.09.2004 at 10.30.35 hrs at Noida, U.P (India).

Fig. 4.1

Name	Fig. 4.1	Place of Birth	Noida
Sex	Female	Latitude	028.20.N
Date of Birth	23/09/2004	Longitude	077.20.E
Day of Birth	Thursday	Local Birth Time	10:09:55
Time of Birth	10:30:35	Local Birth Date	23/09/2004
Sidereal Time	10:19:26	Lunar Tithi	10
Bal. of Dasha	Sun 5Y 9M 24D	K.P. (New) Ayanamsa	23:54:40
Lagan	Scorpio	Lagan Lord	Mars
Sign	Sagittarius	Sign Lord	Jupiter
Nakshatra	U.Asadha	Nakshatra Lord	Sun

Lagna Chart

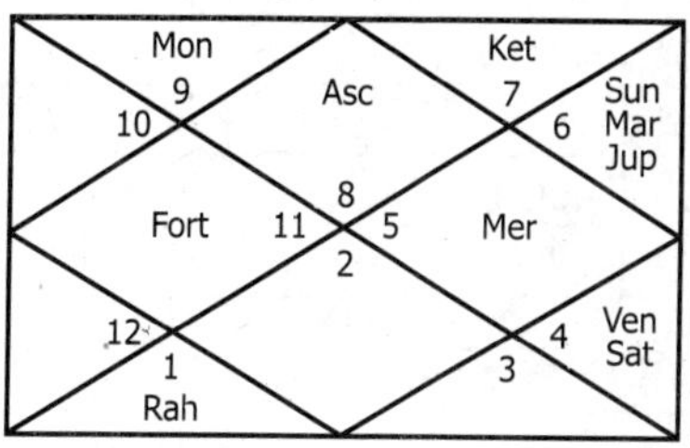

Bhava Chart

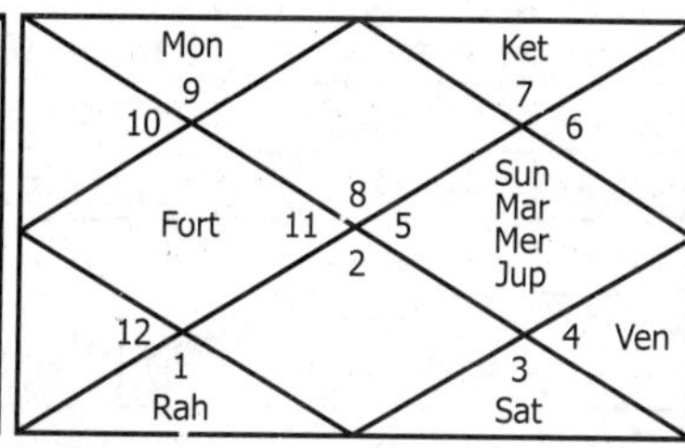

Cusp Chart

V 11:0:11	VI 8:39:1 Rah 8:39:30	VII 2:25:44	VIII 2:21:17
Fort 22:54:4 IV 8:59:56			Sat 1:32:53 IX 4:59:18 Ven 24:3:27
III 4:59:18			X 8:59:56 Mer 26:14:35
Mon 27:4:43 II 2:21:17	I 2:25:44	Ket 8:39:30 XII 8:39:1	Mar 4:3:5 Jup 5:40:53 Sun 6:36:23 XI 11:0:11

Fig. 4.1 Contd......

Nirayana Cusps

Bhav No.	Sign	Degree	Star Lord	Sub Lord	Sub-Sub Lord
1	Scorpio	02: 25' 44"	Jup	Rah	Mer
2	Sagittarius	02: 21' 17"	Ket	Ven	Sat
3	Capricorn	04: 59' 18"	Sun	Sat	Jup
4	Aquarius	08: 59' 56"	Rah	Jup	Sat
5	Pisces	11: 00' 11"	Sat	Mon	Mon
6	Aries	08: 39' 01"	Ket	Jup	Ven
7	Taurus	02: 25' 44"	Sun	Jup	Sun
8	Gemini	02: 21' 17"	Mar	Ket	Jup
9	Cancer	04: 59' 18"	Sat	Sat	Rah
10	Leo	08: 59' 56"	Ket	Jup	Mar
11	Virgo	11: 00' 11"	Mon	Mon	Ven
12	Libra	08: 39' 01"	Rah	Rah	Mar

Planetary Position

Planet	Sign	Degree	Star Lord	Sub Lord	Sub-Sub Lord
Sun	Virgo	06: 36' 23"	Sun	Mer	Jup
Mon	Sagittarius	27: 04' 43"	Sun	Sun	Sat
Mar	Virgo	04: 03' 05"	Sun	Sat	Ven
Mer	Leo	26: 14' 35"	Ven	Ket	Rah
Jup	Virgo	05: 40' 53"	Sun	Mer	Ven
Ven	Cancer	24: 03' 27"	Mer	Mar	Mon
Sat	Cancer	01: 32' 53"	Jup	Rah	Rah
Rah (R)	Aries	08: 39' 30"	Ket	Jup	Ven
Ket (R)	Libra	08: 39' 30"	Rah	Rah	Mar
Ura (R)	Aquarius	09: 53' 51"	Rah	Jup	Sun
Nep (R)	Capricorn	18: 57' 24"	Mon	Mer	Rah
Plu	Scorpio	25: 46' 55"	Mer	Rah	Sun
Fortuna	Aquarius	22: 54' 04"	Jup	Sat	Sun

In this chart, we find that the sub-sub lord of the ascendant is Mercury, and the Moon's star lord is Sun. Since Sun in the chart is in the sub of Mercury, we assume that the sub-sub lord of the ascendant bears the relationship with the Moon's star lord.

The Moon at the time of birth of the child is moving in Jupiter Sign, Sun star, and Sun sub, Sat sub-sub, Jupiter sub-sub-sub, and Sat sub-sub-sub-sub lord. All these planets per force have to bear relationship with the cuspal positions 2, 5, 11 from the 9th cusp or 10th, 1st and 7th cusps in the chart.

Jupiter the sign lord of Moon itself is the star lord of 1st, sub lord of 7th and 10th cusps. Moreover Jupiter is in the star of Sun, which is the star lord and the sub-sub lord of the 7th cusp. Jupiter is in Mercury sub that has appeared as the sub-sub lord of the ascendant.

The star lord and sub-lord of the Moon is Sun that itself is in its own star and appears as the star lord and sub-sub lord of the 7th cusp. Sun is in the sub of Mercury that is the sub-sub of the ascendant. Sun is in the sub-sub of Jupiter that appears in cusps 1, 7 and 10.

The sub-sub and the sub-sub-sub-sub lord of the Moon is Saturn. It is in Jupiter star that appears in cusps 1,7 & 10. The sub lord and sub-sub lord of Saturn is Rahu that appears as sub lord of the ascendant. Since Rahu represents Venus (being in Ketu star that represents Venus); it is linked with 7th and 10th cusps also.

Jupiter the sub-sub-sub lord of Moon at the moment of birth is linked with cusps 1,7 and 10 because Jupiter is in Sun star that appears as star lord and sub-sub lord of 7th cusps; it itself is the star lord of the ascendant and sub lord of the 7th & 10th cusps.

The above clearly reveals that the planets co-ruling the Moon's position have to establish relationship with the relevant cusps that take part in enacting an event.

Similarly we know that the exact moment of happening of an event is reflected by the ascendant at that moment. The planets co-ruling the ascendant should also be the planets that can cause that event. Hence the planets co-ruling the ascendant of the native should also bear the relationship with 1st, 7th and 10th houses i.e. 2, 5, 11 from the 9th house. Here the ascendant sign lord is Mars. Mars in the chart is in the star of Sun that appears as the star lord and sub-sub lord of the 7th cusp and is resident of 10th house. Jupiter appears as the star lord and Rahu as the sub lord of the ascendant. We have seen above that they are linked with the relevant cusps. The sub-sub lord of the ascendant is Mercury that is in Venus star, Ketu sub and Rahu sub-sub. All these planets appear in relevant cusps 7, 10 and 1.

From the above discussion, it should not be concluded that the planets co-ruling the ascendant will and should only be linked with 1, 7 and 10. The ascendant represents the total being of the native and the linkages of the planets co-ruling the ascendant fixes the destiny of the native and as such will have other linkages too.

Formation of other Cuspal Positions

Having fixed the ascendant position up to sub-sub lord, we have to play around the time, may be in seconds to fix the sub-sub lords of other cuspal positions so that the horoscope clearly reveals the following:

A. Genetical connections of the Native. This means that the sub sub lords of cusps representing father, mother, younger and elder co-borns, and children should establish relationship with their Moon stars.

B. The promise in respect of all 12 cuspal positions i.e. the sub-sub lords of all the cuspal positions should justify what is destined for the native in respect of all facets of his life viz.

1. Mental characteristics, health, vitality and vigour, habit of thinking, success or failure in attempts, longevity, general, social, financial, administrative status.

2. Money matters, fortune & favours, capability to express, vision & right eye, voice & tongue, nose, teeth, cheeks & jaws.

3. Communication, writings, documents & agreements, courage, fairness, short travel, accounting, mathematics, telephone, journalism, change of residence, contracts.

4. Mother, education, property, inheritance, vehicle, domestic environment, rare articles.

5. Progeny, intelligence, sports, game, fine arts, drawing, creative pursuit, gambling, lottery, shares.

6. Service, servants, pet animals, loans, debts, success, disease.

7. Marriage, business partners, socialization, litigation, opponents, divorce, reputation & influence in foreign Nations.

8. Mode of death, delays, accidents, false allegation, unexpected gain/loss, unearthed money, dejections, sorrow & strife etc.

9. Fortune, law and justice, father, higher education, second marriage, long journey.

10. Status and prestige through profession, honour, dignity and public esteem, name & fame, authority.

11. Wealth, fortune, influence, society, accumulation of money, fulfillment of desires, litigation, speculation.

12. Loss and impediments, research, foreign travel, investments, imprisonment, deception, secrecy, secret enemies.

C. We know that a promised event happens in the life of the native during the joint period of planets those are fruitful significators of the Primary and Supporting cusps that enact the event. At the same time dasa period lords, Jupiter, Moon and Sun should in transit also justify the happening of the event. Thus dasa period lords and transit potential of each planet should justify all events that happen in the Native's life.

But we also know that each event happens only at a specified time as destined. Destiny enfoldment is indicated by the progressed position of the ascendant. That is when the progressed ascendant is co-ruled by planets those are strong significator of the event.

Each cusp and each planet progresses from its position at the time of birth as per Vimsottari dasa rules. At the time of happening of the event the progressed chart should also justify the event. True Astrology Software developed by Mr Mukesh Gupta has the provision to calculate the progressed chart.

Thus we need to be sure that the rectified chart meets these requirements also.

Rectification of Cuspal Positions to reflect Genetical Connections.

By genetical connections we mean that the relevant cusps that represent the native's father, mother, younger and elder co-born, and children should reveal their Moon's star lord as well as ascendant. Relationship is checked in the same way as described above for the sub sub lord of the ascendant.

Let us explain this through an example. Figure 4.2 is the chart of a young man born on 13.01.1983 at 15.46.20 hrs at Delhi, RML Hospital.

Figure 4.3 and Figure 4.4 represent the chart of his father and mother respectively.

Step I: The ascendant of the young man is correctly fixed with Jupiter as the sub-sub lord because it establishes the relationship with the Native's Moon star Venus, because Jupiter is in Venus sub.

Step II: Let us check the genetical connection with father from the 9th cusp. The Moon's star of the father (Ref. Figure 4.3) is Mars. In the chart of the young man Mars is in the sub of Venus that is sub as well as the sub-sub lord of the 9th cusp. Now for complete genetical connection, the ascendant of the father should also be ruled by the planets co-ruling the 9th cusp of the young man or by the planets that are in the star or sub or sub-sub of the planets co-ruling the 9th cusp of the young man. Planets Mars-Sat-Ven-Jup rules the ascendant of the father as seen from Figure 4.3. The planets co-ruling the 9th cusp of the young man are Sat-Moon-Ven-Ven. It can be seen that Sat and Venus appears in the ascendant of the father directly. Now Mars and Jupiter can appear only in the ascendant of the father to confirm fatherhood if these planets are in the star, sub or sub-sub of the planets co-ruling the 9th cusp of the young man. Now we find that Mars in the chart of the young man is in the sub of Venus and Jupiter is in the star of Saturn and sub of Venus. Thus we assume that there is a complete genetical connection between the father and the child.

We can also check the genetical connection between the father and the child from the 5th cusp of the father's chart. The sub-sub lord of the 5th cusp in the Figure 4.3 is Mercury that is in Venus star. The Moon's star of the young man is Venus. The planets Jup-Mer-Ket-Mer rule the 5th cusp. The ascendant of the young man (Ref. Figure 4.2) is ruled by Mer-Mars-Ven-Jupiter. In the father's horoscope, Mars and Venus are both in the sub of Jupiter. Hence we assume that the planets as per the 5th cusp of the father's horoscope rightly represent the ascendant of the young man.

Step III: We may now check the genetical connection of the young man with his mother from the 4th cusp in the chart. The sub-sub lord of the 4th cusp is Jupiter that is the Moon's star lord in the mother's chart (Refer Figure 4.4). Now the 4th cusp in the young man's chart is ruled by Sun-Venus-Rahu-Jup.

The ascendant of the mother is Mercury-Moon-Mars-Rahu. Now Mercury in the young man's chart is in the star of Sun, and Moon and Mars are in the star or the sub of Venus. As such we assume the planets co-ruling the ascendant of mother are related to the planets co-ruling the 4th cusp of the young man.

In the same way, we may check the correction of the horoscope for genetical connections with the younger or the elder co-born.

Fig. 4.2

Name	Fig 4.2	Place of Birth	Delhi
Sex	Male	Latitude	028.39.N
Date of Birth	13/01/1983	Longitude	077.13.E
Day of Birth	Thursday	Local Birth Time	15:25:12
Time of Birth	15:46:20	Local Birth Date	13/01/1983
Sidereal Time	22:54:30	Lunar Tithi	15
Bal. of Dasha	Ven 9Y 1M 18D	K.P. (New) Ayanamsa	23:36.30
Lagan	Gemini	Lagan Lord	Mercury
Sign	Sagittarius	Sign Lord	Jupiter
Nakshatra	P.Asadha	Nakshatra Lord	Venus

Lagna Chart

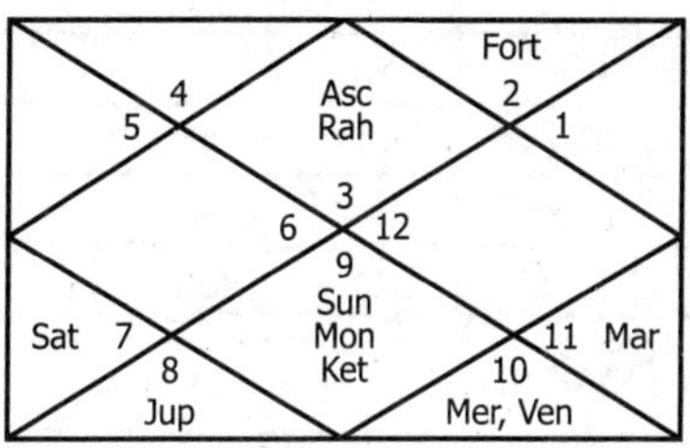

Bhava Chart

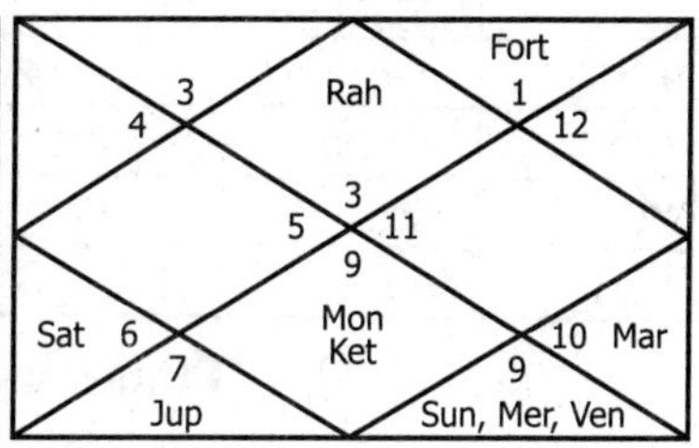

Cusp Chart

XI 22:25:41	XII 29:24:4	Fort 25:21:37	I 3:50:27 Rah 10:41:34 II 26:45:18
X 18:38:3 Mar 3:10:2			III 20:38:45
IX 20:38:45 Ven 16:1:47 Mer 5:11:35			IV 18:38:3
Sun 29:3:29 VII 26:45:18 Mon 20:34:39 Ket 10:41:34 VII 3:50:27	Jup 9:54:43	VI 29:24:4 Sat 10:3:13	V 22:25:41

Fig. 4.2 Contd......

Nirayana Cusps

Bhav No.	Sign	Degree	Star Lord	Sub Lord	Sub-Sub Lord
1	Gemini	03: 50' 27"	Mar	Ven	Jup
2	Gemini	26: 45' 18"	Jup	Ven	Ven
3	Cancer	20: 38' 45"	Mer	Ven	Jup
4	Leo	18: 38' 03"	Ven	Rah	Jup
5	Virgo	22: 25' 41"	Mon	Ven	Mer
6	Libra	29: 24' 04"	Jup	Sun	Ven
7	Sagittarius	03: 50' 27"	Ket	Mon	Rah
8	Sagittarius	26: 45' 18"	Sun	Sun	Mon
9	Capricorn	20: 38' 45"	Mon	Ven	Ven
10	Aquarius	18: 38' 03"	Rah	Mon	Sat
11	Pisces	22: 25' 41"	Mer	Mon	Rah
12	Aries	29: 24' 04"	Sun	Rah	Rah

Planetary Position

Planet	Sign	Degree	Star Lord	Sub Lord	Sub-Sub Lord
Sun	Sagittarius	29: 03' 29"	Sun	Mar	Ven
Mon	Sagittarius	20: 34' 39"	Ven	Jup	Sat
Mar	Aquarius	03: 10' 02"	Mar	Ven	Mon
Mer (R)	Capricorn	05: 11' 35"	Sun	Mer	Mer
Jup	Scorpio	09: 54' 43"	Sat	Ven	Mer
Ven	Capricorn	16: 01' 47"	Mon	Sat	Mer
Sat	Libra	10: 03' 13"	Rah	Jup	Mon
Rah (R)	Gemini	10: 41' 34"	Rah	Sat	Sat
Ket (R)	Sagittarius	10: 41' 34"	Ket	Sat	Mon
Ura	Scorpio	13: 58' 15"	Sat	Rah	Mer
Nep	Sagittarius	04: 05' 55"	Ket	Mon	Jup
Plu	Libra	05: 49' 04"	Mar	Mon	Rah
Fortuna	Taurus	25: 21' 37"	Mar	Rah	Ket

Fig. 4.3

Name	Fig 4.3	Place of Birth	Delhi
Sex	Male	Latitude	028.39.N
Date of Birth	25/05/1952	Longitude	077.13.E
Day of Birth	Sunday	Local Birth Time	18:37:20
Time of Birth	18:58:28	Local Birth Date	25/05/1952
Sidereal Time	10:49:35	Lunar Tithi	2
Bal. of Dasha	Mar 2Y 9M 9D	K.P. (New) Ayanamsa	23:10.51
Lagan	Scorpio	Lagan Lord	Mars
Sign	Gemini	Sign Lord	Mercury
Nakshatra	Mrigasira	Nakshatra Lord	Mars

Lagna Chart

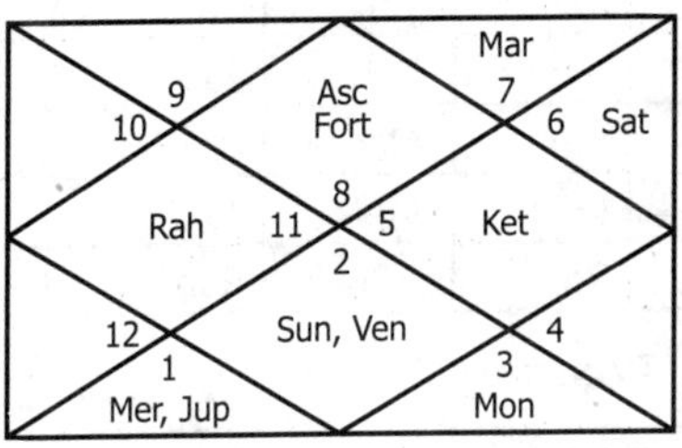

Bhava Chart

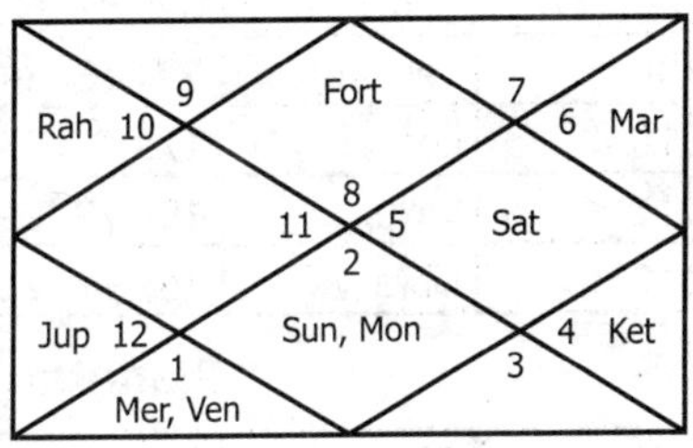

Cusp Chart

V 19:19:24	Jup 13:3:28 VI 16:11:21 Mer 24:55:7	Ven 2:50:49 VII 9:27:9 Sun 11:5:3	Mon 1:22:14 VIII 9:52:55
IV 17:44:33 Rah 1:47:8			IX 13:18:34
III 13:18:34			Ket 1:47:8 X 17:44:33
II 9:52:55	Fort 29:44:20 I 9:27:9	XII 16:11:21 Mar 9:37:14	Sat 15:13:16 XI 19:19:24

Fig. 4.3 Contd......

Nirayana Cusps

Bhav No.	Sign	Degree	Star Lord	Sub Lord	Sub-Sub Lord
1	Scorpio	09: 27' 09"	Sat	Ven	Jup
2	Sagittarius	09: 52' 55"	Ket	Sat	Mer
3	Capricorn	13: 18' 34"	Mon	Rah	Ven
4	Aquarius	17: 44' 33"	Rah	Sun	Jup
5	Pisces	19: 19' 24"	Mer	Ket	Mer
6	Aries	16: 11' 21"	Ven	Sun	Ven
7	Taurus	09: 27' 09"	Sun	Ven	Sat
8	Gemini	09: 52' 55"	Rah	Jup	Sun
9	Cancer	13: 18' 34"	Sat	Rah	Jup
10	Leo	17: 44' 33"	Ven	Mar	Mer
11	Virgo	19: 19' 24"	Mon	Mer	Jup
12	Libra	16: 11' 21"	Rah	Ven	Rah

Planetary Position

Planet	Sign	Degree	Star Lord	Sub Lord	Sub-Sub Lord
Sun	Taurus	11: 05' 03"	Mon	Mon	Sun
Mon	Gemini	01: 22' 14"	Mar	Mer	Jup
Mar (R)	Libra	09: 37' 14"	Rah	Jup	Ven
Mer	Aries	24: 55' 07"	Ven	Mer	Mon
Jup	Aries	13: 03' 28"	Ket	Mer	Sat
Ven	Taurus	02: 50' 49"	Sun	Jup	Rah
Sat (R)	Virgo	15: 13' 16"	Mon	Jup	Mon
Rah (R)	Aquarius	01: 47' 08"	Mar	Mer	Sat
Ket (R)	Leo	01: 47' 08"	Ket	Ven	Rah
Ura	Gemini	18: 38' 12"	Rah	Mon	Sat
Nep (R)	Virgo	26: 04' 18"	Mar	Rah	Mar
Plu	Cancer	26: 02' 56"	Mer	Rah	Mar
Fortuna	Scorpio	29: 44' 20"	Mer	Sat	Jup

Fig. 4.4

Name	Fig 4.4	Place of Birth	Jammu
Sex	Female	Latitude	032.42.N
Date of Birth	02/02/1958	Longitude	074.54.E
Day of Birth	Sunday	Local Birth Time	21:31:26
Time of Birth	22:01:50	Local Birth Date	02/02/1958
Sidereal Time	6:20:50	Lunar Tithi	14
Bal. of Dasha	Jup 6Y 9M 29D	K.P. (New) Ayanamsa	23:15.37
Lagan	Virgo	Lagan Lord	Mercury
Sign	Gemini	Sign Lord	Mercury
Nakshatra	Punarvasu	Nakshatra Lord	Jupiter

Lagna Chart

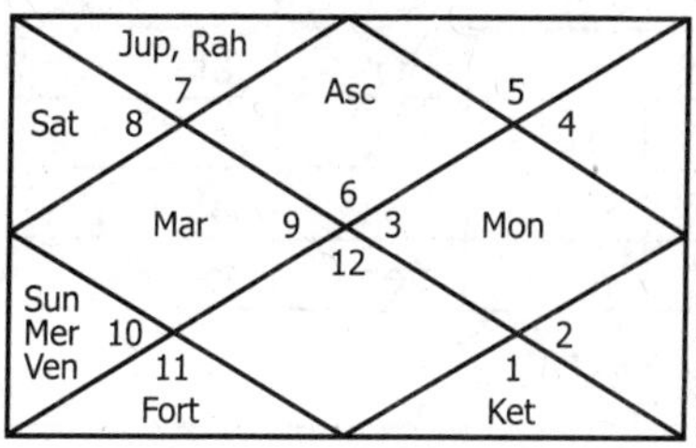

Bhava Chart

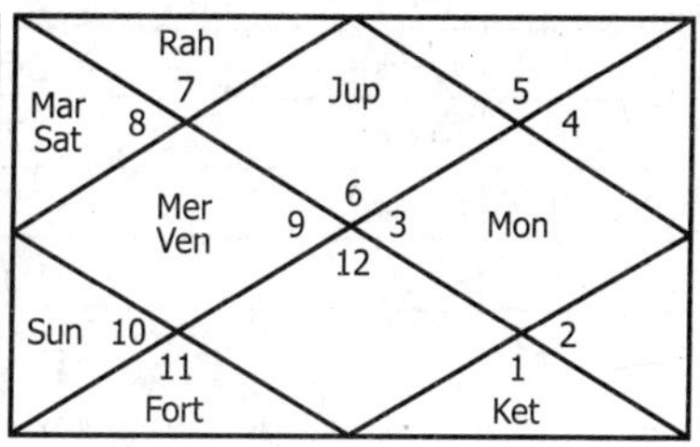

Cusp Chart

VII 11:11:10	VIII 8:50:29 Ket 11:56:12	IX 9:22:4	X 11:31:13 Mon 27:38:41
Fort 18:44:56 VI 14:2:7			XI 13:40:7
Sun 20:4:55 V 13:40:7 Ven 12:12:47 Mer 0:52:47			XII 14:2:7
IV 11:31:13 Mar 5:57:36	Sat 29:32:19 III 9:22:4	Rah 11:56:12 II 8:50:29 Jup 8:8:24	I 11:11:10

Fig. 4.4 Contd......

Nirayana Cusps

Bhav No.	Sign	Degree	Star Lord	Sub Lord	Sub-Sub Lord
1	Virgo	11: 11' 10"	Mon	Mar	Rah
2	Libra	08: 50' 29"	Rah	Jup	Jup
3	Scorpio	09: 22' 04"	Sat	Ven	Jup
4	Sagittarius	11: 31' 13"	Ket	Mer	Mer
5	Capricorn	13: 40' 07"	Mon	Rah	Mon
6	Aquarius	14: 02' 07"	Rah	Mer	Jup
7	Pisces	11: 11' 10"	Sat	Mon	Rah
8	Aries	08: 50' 29"	Ket	Jup	Mon
9	Taurus	09: 22' 04"	Sun	Ven	Sat
10	Gemini	11: 31' 13"	Rah	Sat	Ven
11	Cancer	13: 40' 07"	Sat	Rah	Sat
12	Leo	14: 02' 07"	Ven	Ven	Mar

Planetary Position

Planet	Sign	Degree	Star Lord	Sub Lord	Sub-Sub Lord
Sun	Capricorn	20: 04' 55"	Mon	Ket	Rah
Mon	Gemini	27: 38' 41"	Jup	Ven	Rah
Mar	Sagittarius	05: 57' 36"	Ket	Rah	Jup
Mer	Capricorn	00: 52' 47"	Sun	Rah	Sun
Jup	Libra	08: 08' 24"	Rah	Rah	Ven
Ven (R)	Capricorn	12: 12' 47"	Mon	Rah	Jup
Sat	Scorpio	29: 32' 19"	Mer	Sat	Rah
Rah (R)	Libra	11: 56' 12"	Rah	Sat	Mar
Ket (R)	Aries	11: 56' 12"	Ket	Mer	Ven
Ura (R)	Cancer	16: 11' 30"	Sat	Jup	Mon
Nep	Libra	11: 30' 53"	Rah	Sat	Ven
Plu (R)	Leo	08: 14' 54"	Ket	Jup	Mer
Fortuna	Aquarius	18: 44' 56"	Rah	Mon	Sat

Composite Approach to Rectification of Chart without use of Progression Concept

We have already explained that for constructing a true horoscope we need to correct all the 12 cuspal positions to justify the genetical connections, the promise of each cusp and also the dasa potential of each planet to justify events in the life of the native. We will discuss this approach through examples.

Example 1: Figure 4.5 is the chart of a business man who gave the following birth data:

D.O Birth: 04.01.1954

T.O Birth: 09.30 A.M

P.O Birth: Jaipur, (India)

Figure 4.5

Name	Fig. 4.5	Place of Birth	Jaipur
Sex	Male	Latitude	026.55.N
Date of Birth	04/01/1954	Longitude	075.49.E
Day of Birth	Monday	Local Birth Time	09:03:16
Time of Birth	09:30:00	Local Birth Date	04/01/1954
Sidereal Time	15:56:9	Lunar Tithi	15
Bal. of Dasha	Ket 2Y 6M 1D	K.P. (New) Ayanamsa	23:12:12:
Lagan	Capricorn	Lagan Lord	Saturn
Sign	Sagittarius	Sign Lord	Jupiter
Nakshatra	Mula	Nakshatra Lord	Ketu

Lagna Chart

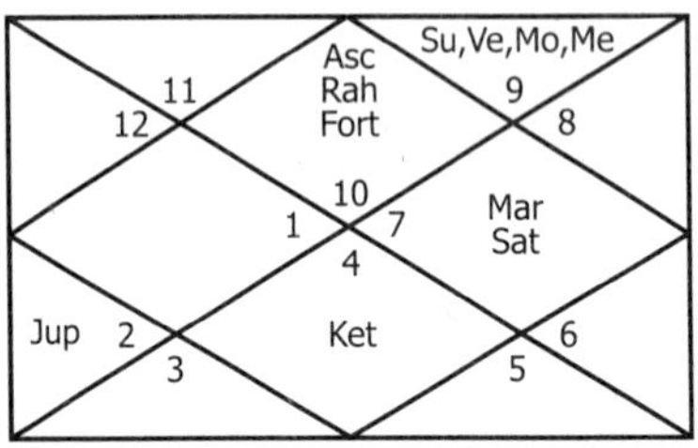

Bhava Chart

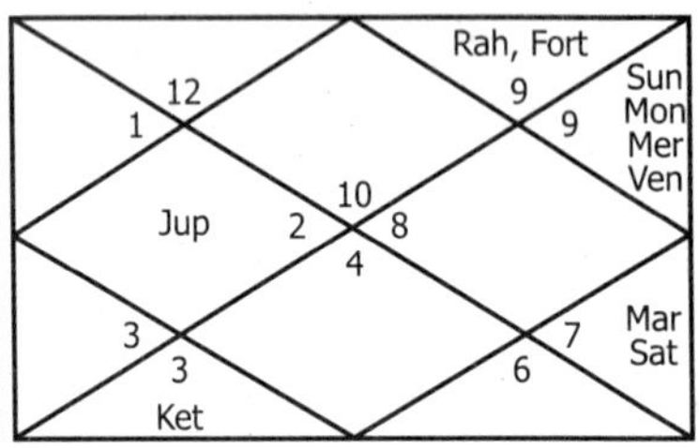

Cusp Chart

II 5:34:8	III 10:13:59	IV 7:58:1 Jup 25:26:25	V 2:3:52 VI 26:22:45
			Ket 0:46:27 VII 25:31:7
I 25:31:7 Fort 14:1:40 Rah 0:46:27			
XII 26:22:45 Sun 20:3:57 Ven 13:53:16 Mer 13:46:5 Mon 8:34:30 XI 2:3:52	X 7:58:1	Mar 15:36:30 Sat 14:30:32 IX 10:13:59	VIII 5:34:8

Fig. 4.5 Contd......

Nirayana Cusps

Bhav No.	Sign	Degree	Star Lord	Sub Lord	Sub-Sub Lord
1	Capricorn	25: 31' 07"	Mar	Rah	Ven
2	Pisces	05: 34' 08"	Sat	Mer	Mer
3	Aries	10: 13' 59"	Ket	Sat	Ven
4	Taurus	07: 58' 01"	Sun	Ven	Ven
5	Gemini	02: 03' 52"	Mar	Ket	Sun
6	Gemini	26: 22' 45"	Jup	Ket	Sat
7	Cancer	25: 31' 07"	Mer	Rah	Ven
8	Virgo	05: 34' 08"	Sun	Mer	Ven
9	Libra	10: 13' 59"	Rah	Jup	Rah
10	Scorpio	07: 58' 01"	Sat	Ket	Sat
11	Sagittarius	02: 03' 52"	Ket	Ven	Jup
12	Sagittarius	26: 22' 45"	Ven	Ket	Jup

Planetary Position

Planet	Sign	Degree	Star Lord	Sub Lord	Sub-Sub Lord
Sun	Sagittarius	20: 03' 57"	Ven	Rah	Mar
Mon	Sagittarius	08: 34' 30"	Ket	Jup	Ven
Mar	Libra	15: 36' 30"	Rah	Ven	Sun
Mer	Sagittarius	13: 46' 05"	Ven	Ven	Sun
Jup (R)	Taurus	25: 26' 25"	Mar	Rah	Ven
Ven	Sagittarius	13: 53' 16"	Ven	Ven	Mon
Sat	Libra	14: 30' 32"	Rah	Ket	Ven
Rah (R)	Capricorn	00: 46' 27"	Sun	Rah	Ven
Ket (R)	Cancer	00: 46' 27"	Jup	Mar	Jup
Ura (R)	Gemini	28: 10' 52"	Jup	Ven	Sat
Nep	Libra	02: 42' 14"	Mar	Ven	Ven
Plu (R)	Leo	01: 28' 02"	Ket	Ven	Mar
Fortuna	Capricorn	14: 01' 40"	Mon	Jup	Jup

The gentleman also gave the following important events of his life and requested that his chart should be rectified if needed.

S.No.		Date and Time
1.	Marriage	20.6.1978
2.	1st Female Issue	11.07.1979 (Fig. 4.6) 06.46.25hrs
3.	Death of Father	5.3.1991 04.00 AM approximately.
4.	Death of Wife	27.5.1994
5.	Date of 2nd Marriage	11.2.1997.

Let us first check the correctness of the chart constructed as per the recorded time.

Step I: For a horoscope to be correct, the ascendant sub-sub lord should reveal the Moon's star lord. In this chart the sub-sub lord of the ascendant is Venus and the Moon's star in the chart is Ketu that does not represent Venus. There appears no relationship of Venus with Ketu directly. However if we take Ketu to represent Moon and Jup, we do find that there is a relationship between the Moon's star and the sub-sub lord of the ascendant.

Step II: **Verification of the Event of Marriage:** Generally the Vedic Astrologers consider the 7th house as the primary house for marriage. The other relevant houses are taken as:

Second House: It is the house of family. Marriage is taken as an addition in the family. Here I would like to suggest to the reader to ponder a little bit. The marriage may be an addition in the family if the marriage partner joins the family. Moreover, the 2nd house is in fact, a house of danger, and death to the 7th house.

Fifth House: It is the house of magnetic attractions, socially accepted forms of courtship, romantic affairs and progeny.

Eleventh House: It is the house of fulfillment of one's desires and personal needs. It is also the fifth house from the 7th House.

Twelfth House: It is considered as the house of pleasures of bed. How far we need to take 12th house to analyse marriage is a question for debate. One can enjoy bed comforts outside wedlock. This house is the house of self-undoing and is generally regarded as a house of loss.

Fourth House: No doubt it is considered as the house of domestic happiness but why should it need to take part in enacting marriage is questionable. This house being 12th to the 5th house can detail for disturbed married life.

From the above discussion it is clear that the houses that should take part in enacting marriage are 5, 7 and 11.

The promise or denial of marriage should be decided as follows:

1. Marriage is promised if:
   a) The sub-sub lord of the ascendant is linked directly or indirectly with the 7th cusp.
   b) The sub-sub lord of the 7th cusp is linked with 7th cusp directly or indirectly.

   Direct linkage means the star lord of the sub sub is in the primary cusp and its sub lord comes in the supporting cusp. Indirect linkage means that the star lord of the sub sub lord appears in one of the supporting cusps and its sub lord appears in the primary cusp.
2. Marriage is denied if both the following conditions exist in the horoscope.

a) The sub-sub lord of the ascendant is linked to 4, 6, 10 and 12 without involving 5 or 7 or 11 cusps or the sub sub lord involves 7th cusp and commits to only 2, 4, 6, 10 without committing to 5 or 7 or 11.

b) The sub-sub lord of the 7th cusp is linked to 2, 4, 6, 10, & 12 cusps through its star lord without being linked to 5 or 11 or 7th cusp sub sub lord involves 7th cusp and commits only to 2, 4, 6, or10 and does not commit to 5 or 11.

The native of this chart got married on 20.6.1978 in the joint period of Sun-Ra-Mo-Sat-Ven as D|B|A|S|P lords.

The sub-sub lords of the ascendant and the 7th cusp show promise of marriage. Here Venus is the sub-sub lord of both the ascendant as well as the 7th cusp. It is in its own star and sub and sub sub Moon. Moon is placed in the 11th Bhava. The chart thus clearly promises marriage.

Now Marriage takes place only in a specific Bhukti in a dasa which is either favourable for marriage or at least is neutral to the relevant cusps that take part in marriage. The specific Bhukti has to meet one of the following conditions:

1. The Bhukti lord may appear as one of the planets co-ruling the 7th cusp and has positional status but should not be in the sub that appears in the 6th cusp.

2. If the Bhukti lord that appears in the 7th cusp has no positional status then its star lord should appear in 5 or 7 or 11 and sub lord should appear in the 7th cusp.

3. The Bhukti lord's star lord may appear in 5th or 11th cusp and sub lord should appear in 7th cusp.

   a) The sub-sub lord of the Bhukti lord should preferably be connected to 5 or 7 or 11 or neutral houses.

b) Here in this chart the Bhukti lord appears as the sub lord of the 7th cusp but has no positional status because Mars and Saturn are in its star. But Rahu is in Sun's star that appears in 5th cusp as sub-sub lord and Rahu being in its own sub, the Bhukti lord meets the relevant condition. More over Rahu is in Venus sub-sub that is the sub-sub lord of the 7th cusp.

Similarly we can check whether all the planets that have taken part in enacting the event of marriage have the right to do so or not. Antara, Sookshma and Prana lords are both strongly linked with favourable as well as unfavorable houses. The Sookshma lord Saturn has the positional status and is appearing as the sub-sub lord of the 6th and 10th cusp and as such causes a doubt whether it can enact marriage or not especially when through its star and sub also it is linked with 6th and 12th cusps. Saturn's transit in Ketu star on the day of marriage further complicates the problem.

Step III: **Birth of Female Child:** The native should be potent and should have the procreative power to produce a child. If the sub-sub lord of the 5th cusp is linked through its star lord with favourable houses with respect to 5th cusp, and also supported by its sub lord and the sub-sub lord, we generally declare that the native is potent. A person lacks potency if the sub-sub lord establishes links with only unfavourable houses like 4th and 12th cusp (i.e. 12th and 8th from 5th) and 10th which is 12th to 11th.

Potency of the native, however, does not ensure child birth. The person is said to be destined to have a child or is said to have the procreative power, if the sub-sub lord of the 5th cusp establishes links, through its star lord and sub lord as shown below:

Star lord in	Sub lord in
5	2
11	2
2	11

The appearance of sub lord in 4 and 12; or 4 or 12 indicates delay in child birth

The sub-sub lord of the sub-sub lord of the 5th cusp should be in cuspal positions, which are favourable to 5th and 2nd cusps.

If the sub lord of the sub-sub lord of the 5th cusp is linked simultaneously to 4th and 12th cusp, it indicates loss of first conception. It is termed as abortion in case of female nativity.

Lack of potency automatically results in lack of procreative power. For the potency and procreative power of the partner we have to analyse the 11th cusp. For child birth, both the partners need to have the procreative power.

Sex of the Child: To be honest, this area needs still much research to provide a foolproof prediction. However, the various methods that are used are listed below:

1. Analyse the planets co-ruling the 5th cusp and the signs in which they appear in various cuspal positions. If the planets are placed in cusps, which rise, in male signs, the chance of getting a male child is more.
2. The sub-sub lord of the sub-sub lord of the 5th cusp if it is in male sign, one gets a male child. In case all the planets are in female signs in a horoscope, we should look to cuspal positions of the sub-sub lord. If it appears in male signs predominantly, we may predict a male child.
3. Another method, which is used by some astrologers, is that if the sub-sub lord of the 5th cusp or its star lord is in Sun hora, one will get a male child.

4. Research minded astrologers could use the Nadi concept of former or later part of the sub-sub lord of the 5th cusp as follows:

Each sub-sub arc is of a particular length. If the sub-sub arc is in1st half of this space in male signs or 2nd half of the space in the female signs, one may get a male child. For example; suppose in a male chart the 5th cusp rises at 12 degree 22 minutes46 seconds in Virgo. Jupiter will rule it. The sub-sub of Jupiter starts from 12 degree 11 minutes 20 seconds and ends at 12 degree 27 minutes 20 seconds. Thus, the sub-sub arc rising on the 5th cusp is in the 2nd part. Virgo being a female sign, the 2nd part indicates male child.

My recommendation is only for the methods explained in para 2 and 4 combined.

Timing Child Birth: If the native is promised progeny, he/ she will get the child during the joint period of the planets that are linked with cusps 2, 5 and 11 through their star lords and supported by their sub lords and sub-sub lords. The transit of dasa periods, Sun and Moon must agree. Simultaneous links of the dasa periods with unfavourable houses indicates problems in pregnancy period. The sub-sub lord of the 5th cusp will indicate the Moon star of the child. The planets co-ruling the 5th cusps or planets in their star, sub or sub-sub will decide the ascendant of the child.

In the chart of the native Figure 4.5 we notice that Sun is the sub sub lord of the 5th cusp. Sun that is in Venus star that appears in 11th cusp and Sun is in Rahu sub that represents Saturn which appears in 2. Thus we find that the native has the procreative power and is capable to produce a child.

The native of this chart got his first female issue on 11.7.1979. The chart of the girl is shown in the Figure 4.6

Fig. 4.6

Name	Fig 4.6	Place of Birth	Jaipur
Sex	Female	Latitude	026.55.N
Date of Birth	11/07/1979	Longitude	075.49.E
Day of Birth	Wednesday	Local Birth Time	06:19:41
Time of Birth	06:46:25	Local Birth Date	11/07/1979
Sidereal Time	1:33:6	Lunar Tithi	2
Bal. of Dasha	Mon 8Y 9M 22D	K.P. (New) Ayanamsa	23:33:34
Lagan	Cancer	Lagan Lord	Moon
Sign	Capricorn	Sign Lord	Saturn
Nakshatra	Sravana	Nakshatra Lord	Moon

Lagna Chart

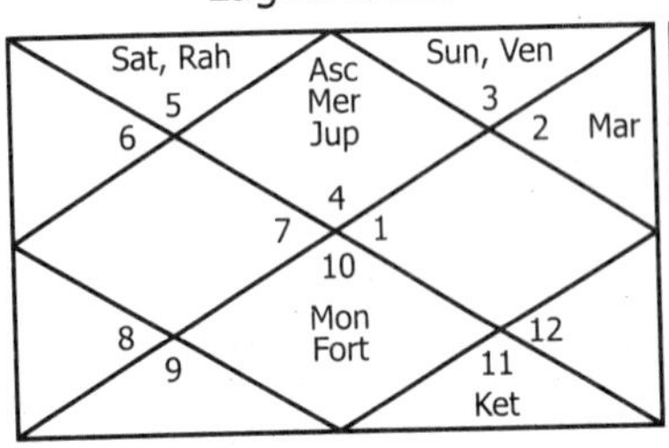

Bhava Chart

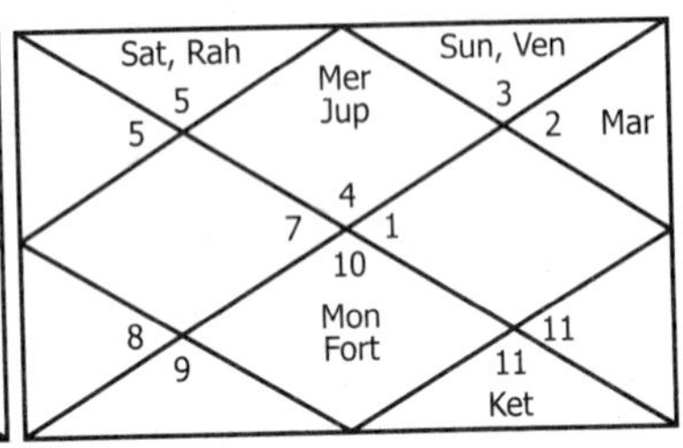

Cusp Chart

	X 1:33:47	XI 5:27:12 Mar 17:0:54	XII 7:59:43 Ven 12:10:17 Sun 24:37:6
IX 29:36:56 Ket 16:0:56 VIII 1:55:9			I 7:57:10 Mer 19:3:2 Jup 19:17:16
Fort 24:55:5 Mon 11:35:1 VII 7:57:10			II 1:55:9 Rah 16:0:56 Sat 16:39:23 III 29:36:56
VI 7:59:43	V 5:27:12	IV 1:33:47	

Fig. 4.6 Contd......

Nirayana Cusps

Bhav No.	Sign	Degree	Star Lord	Sub Lord	Sub-Sub Lord
1	Cancer	07: 57' 10"	Sat	Ket	Sat
2	Leo	01: 55' 09"	Ket	Ven	Jup
3	Leo	29: 36' 56"	Sun	Rah	Jup
4	Libra	01: 33' 47"	Mar	Mer	Jup
5	Scorpio	05: 27' 12"	Sat	Mer	Mer
6	Sagittarius	07: 59' 43"	Ket	Jup	Sat
7	Capricorn	07: 57' 10"	Sun	Ven	Ven
8	Aquarius	01: 55' 09"	Mar	Ket	Ket
9	Aquarius	29: 36' 56"	Jup	Mon	Rah
10	Aries	01: 33' 47"	Ket	Ven	Mar
11	Taurus	05: 27' 12"	Sun	Mer	Ket
12	Gemini	07: 59' 43"	Rah	Rah	Ven

Planetary Position

Planet	Sign	Degree	Star Lord	Sub Lord	Sub-Sub Lord
Sun	Gemini	24: 37' 06"	Jup	Mer	Sun
Mon	Capricorn	11: 35' 01"	Mon	Mar	Mer
Mar	Taurus	17: 00' 54"	Mon	Sat	Mon
Mer	Cancer	19: 03' 02"	Mer	Ket	Jup
Jup	Cancer	19: 17' 16"	Mer	Ket	Mer
Ven	Gemini	12: 10' 17"	Rah	Sat	Rah
Sat	Leo	16: 39' 23"	Ven	Mon	Jup
Rah (R)	Leo	16: 00' 56"	Ven	Sun	Mer
Ket (R)	Aquarius	16: 00' 56"	Rah	Ven	Mar
Ura (R)	Libra	23: 27' 42"	Jup	Sat	Rah
Nep (R)	Scorpio	24: 47' 01"	Mer	Rah	Sat
Plu	Virgo	22: 55' 06"	Mon	Sun	Jup
Fortuna	Capricorn	24: 55' 05"	Mar	Rah	Sat

Let us check the genetical connection of the girl from the 5th cusp of the native (Figure 4.5). The sub-sub lord of the 5th cusp is Sun and the girl's Moon star is Moon. Neither Sun has any connection with Moon nor does Moon have any connection with Sun in Figure 4.5. This indicates that Sun cannot come as the sub-sub lord of the 5th cusp.

Step IV: Death of Father: let us first discuss the Criterion for fixing Markesh Dasa

1. Dasa Lord should be a co-ruling planet in 1st cusp or 8th cusp or Badhaka. Planets placed in 1 or 8 are to be treated as co-ruling planets with PS or no PS.
2. In case of Rahu/Ketu either they themselves should be co-ruling planets in 1 or 8 or the planets they represent should be co-ruling planets.
3. Dasa lord should justify necessary and essential condition for death both as per PS and Stellar status. Dasa lord should be linked with the sub sub lord of the 8th cusp.
4. In case of Rahu or Ketu dasa, Rahu as Rahu or Ketu as Ketu as well as the planets Rahu/Ketu represent all should fulfill necessary & essential conditions for death.

Fixing Transit Position of Sat, Jup, Rahu, Ketu for Timing Death

a. Note the SSL of 8th cusp and the planets placed in 8th house.
b. Note the planets that are in the star of SSL of 8th cusp (planets placed in 8th house may betreated as virtual SSL of 8th cusp)
c. Reject the planets that do not justify death (Both necessary & essential condition)

d. Note the star lord of SSL of the 8th cusp. Note whether it justifies death or not.

e. Reject those planets that do not justify death.

f. Sat will transit in the sign & star of those planets those are strongest significator of death from the above list.

The native lost his father in the joint period of Mo-Ve-Ra-Mo-Ve. Here the Death has taken place in Moon Dasa that does not satisfy the necessary conditions.

Step V: The native lost his wife due to death on 27.5.1994 in the joint period of Mars-Jup-Ket-Jup-Jup. The death of wife takes place in the dasa of a planet that is simultaneously linked with 7th and 2nd cusp. Here the dasa lord Mars appears to have no direct connection with the 2nd cusp. But since Mars is in Rahu star, it is as good as in Saturn's star also because Rahu represents Saturn. Thus dasa lord appears to have connection with 7th and 2nd cusp (because Saturn is the star lord of the 2nd cusp). The other planets that have caused death are Jup and Ketu. Here Ketu represents Jupiter also. Jup is strongly linked with the ascendant i.e. both maraka and badhaka.But both Jupiter and Ketu do not have much connection with the other maraka house i.e. 2nd from the 7th cusp.

Step VI: Second Marriage: The concept of second marriage is subjective. To some it means re-marriage after the death of the first wife or after a legal divorce. Some enjoys the legal or religion sanctity to have a second wife while the first wife is alive and also lives with the native. Astrologers quote a number of planetary combinations or yoga's that cause for second marriage. There are astrologers who believe that the planets Mercury and Jupiter being lords of the dual signs play significant role in causing second marriage. According to them, if the sub lord of the 7th cusp is either Mercury or any planet occupying a dual sign or deposited in the constellation of a planet in a dual sign, there will be more than one marriage. If we seriously apply these rules, we will perforce have to believe that a very large number of persons have to have second marriage.

In Cuspal Interlinks Theory, the problem is analysed as follows:

The ninth house is taken as the house of plurality of sexual relations being 3rd from 7th. It is thus taken as the primary house for second marriage. If the ascendant sub-sub lord maintains relationship with 9th cusp through its star lord and with cusps 5 or 7 or 11 through its sub or sub-sub lord, the native is promised the enjoyment of plurality of sexual relationships. The ascendant sub-sub lord can also establish link with the 9th cusp through its sub lord when it is linked to 11th cusp through its star lord. The sub-sub lord of the 7th cusp if linked with the 9th cusp through its star lord and to cusps 5 or 11 through its sub or sub–sub lord it promises plurality of sexual relations.

If the above two conditions exist and also if the 9th cusp sub-sub lord maintains link with the 7th cusp through its star lord and is supported by its sub and sub-sub lord, or if the star lord of 9th cusp sub sub lord appears in 11 and its sub lord appears in 7 then second marriage can be said to be promised. All about the second marriage and life partner need to be analysed by taking the 9th cusp as the primary cusp.

The second marriage will take place in the Bhukti period of the planet that is strongly linked with 9th cusp.

The native had the second marriage on 11.2.1997. A person can have a second marriage when the following conditions exist in the horoscope.

1. The sub-sub lord of the 7th cusp should be linked through its star lord with the 9th cusp or its star lord may appear in 5th or 11th cusp and sub lord in 9th cusp to indicate plurality in sexual relationship.
2. The sub-sub lord of the 9th cusp should link itself through its star lord with the 7th cusp or its star lord may appear in the 11th cusp and sub lord in the 7th cusp.

Here in the Figure 4.5, the sub-sub lord of the 7th cusp is Venus who is in its own star. Venus appears in 9th cusp. Venus is in the sub of Venus and sub sub of Moon that appears in 7. This promises the possibility of plurality of sexual relationships. Rahu is the sub sub lord of 9th cusp. Rahu is in Sun star that does not appear in 7. Thus it does not promise second marriage.

The above discussion in step I to step VI clearly points out that the horoscope needs rectification.

Rectification of the chart in such cases when the time of birth is recorded as correctly as possible should be done in the following ways so as to justify the life pattern of the individual.

1. Take the RPs at the time of judgement and put the sub-sub lord of Moon as the possible sub-sub lord of the ascendant. Check that this planet bears a relationship with the Moon's star lord in the native's chart. If not try other planets appearing in the RP (Moon) series.
2. Analyse the planetary positions in the native's chart and select the planets that bear relationship with the Moon's star lord. Try those planets one at a time as the sub-sub lord of the ascendant and check the accuracy for various cuspal positions.

Note: In latter examples we will talk about the theory of rectification based on latest research findings.

To rectify the horoscope, the ruling planets were taken on 18.1.2005 at 17.22.27 hrs at Noida, (U.P), India. The RPs was as follows:

Day Lord: Mars

RP (Ascdt): Mer-Jup-Moon-Rahu

RP (Moon): Mars-Ven-Ra Jup.

So Jupiter has come as the sub-sub lord of RP (Moon). From the analysis of the native's chart also we find that Moon's star lord Ketu is in Jupiter star.

Hence it was decided to put Jupiter as the sub-sub lord of the ascendant in the native's chart. The sub-sub arc of Jupiter sub sub in Rahu sub begins at the time 09.26.23 hrs and lasts up to 09.27.15 hrs. So we have to play around this time gap to fix the other cuspal positions to justify all the events and promise of various cusps in the life of the native. The rectified horoscope occurred at 09.27.10 hrs as is shown in Figure 4.7.

Fig. 4.7

Name	Fig 4.7	Place of Birth	Jaipur
Sex	Male	Latitude	026.55.N
Date of Birth	04/01/1954	Longitude	075.49.E
Day of Birth	Monday	Local Birth Time	09:00:26
Time of Birth	09:27:10	Local Birth Date	04/01/1954
Sidereal Time	15:53:18	Lunar Tithi	15
Bal. of Dasha	Ket 2Y 6M 6D	K.P. (New) Ayanamsa	23:12:12
Lagan	Capricorn	Lagan Lord	Saturn
Sign	Sagittarius	Sign Lord	Jupiter
Nakshatra	Mula	Nakshatra Lord	Ketu

Lagna Chart

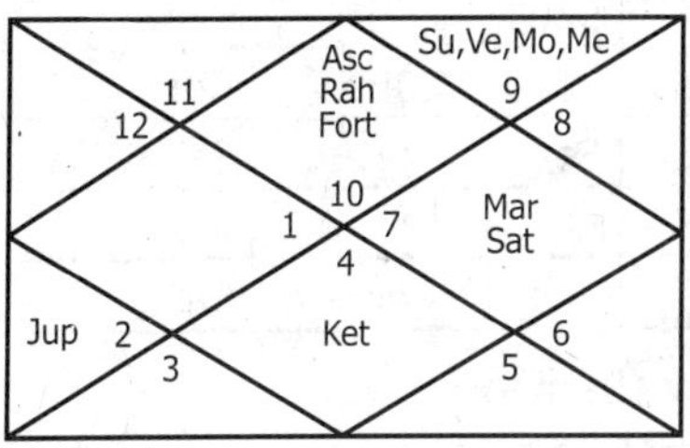

Bhava Chart

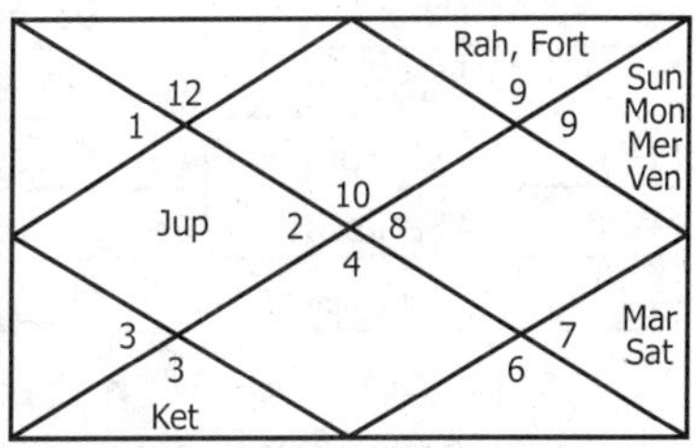

Cusp Chart

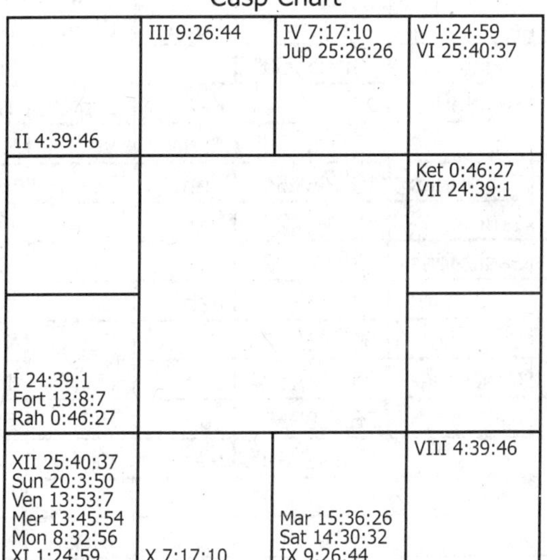

Fig. 4.7 Contd......

Nirayana Cusps

Bhav No.	Sign	Degree	Star Lord	Sub Lord	Sub-Sub Lord
1	Capricorn	24: 39' 01"	Mar	Rah	Jup
2	Pisces	04: 39' 46"	Sat	Sat	Mon
3	Aries	09: 26' 44"	Ket	Sat	Sat
4	Taurus	07: 17' 10"	Sun	Ket	Mar
5	Gemini	01: 24' 59"	Mar	Mer	Jup
6	Gemini	25: 40' 37"	Jup	Mer	Sat
7	Cancer	24: 39' 01"	Mer	Rah	Jup
8	Virgo	04: 39' 46"	Sun	Sat	Rah
9	Libra	09: 26' 44"	Rah	Jup	Ket
10	Scorpio	07: 17' 10"	Sat	Mer	Sat
11	Sagittarius	01: 24' 59"	Ket	Ven	Mon
12	Sagittarius	25: 40' 37"	Ven	Mer	Sat

Planetary Position

Planet	Sign	Degree	Star Lord	Sub Lord	Sub-Sub Lord
Sun	Sagittarius	20: 03' 50"	Ven	Rah	Mar
Mon	Sagittarius	08: 32' 56"	Ket	Jup	Ven
Mar	Libra	15: 36' 26"	Rah	Ven	Sun
Mer	Sagittarius	13: 45' 54"	Ven	Ven	Sun
Jup (R)	Taurus	25: 26' 26"	Mar	Rah	Ven
Ven	Sagittarius	13: 53' 07"	Ven	Ven	Mon
Sat	Libra	14: 30' 32"	Rah	Ket	Ven
Rah (R)	Capricorn	00: 46' 27"	Sun	Rah	Ven
Ket (R)	Cancer	00: 46' 27"	Jup	Mar	Jup
Ura (R)	Gemini	28: 10' 53"	Jup	Ven	Sat
Nep	Libra	02: 42' 14"	Mar	Ven	Ven
Plu (R)	Leo	01: 28' 02"	Ket	Ven	Mar
Fortuna	Capricorn	13: 08' 07"	Mon	Rah	Ket

Verification of the Rectified Chart

Step 1: The sub-sub lord of the ascendant Jupiter is linked with the Moon's star lord Ketu because Ketu is in Jupiter's star. Planets co-ruling ascendant, Moon and Sun establish desired relationship with 1, 7 and 10.

Step 2: Promise of Marriage: Jupiter the sub-sub lord of the ascendant as well as the 7th cusp is in Mars star that appears as the star lord of the 5th cusp. It is in Rahu sub that appears as the sub lord of the 7th cusp. It is in Venus sub-sub that appears as the sub lord of the 11th cusp. Thus marriage is promised. Marriage took place on 20.6.1978 in the joint period of Sun-Ra-Mo-Jup-Sat. Here the Bhukti lord and all other planets are primarily linked with 5, 7 and 11 cusps.

Step 3: Sub sub lord of 5th cusp is Jupiter that is in Mars star that appears in 5. Jupiter is in the sub of Rahu that represents Saturn as sign lord. Saturn appears as star and sub lord of 2. Thus the native is procreative and has the capability to produce a child. Birth of 1st child took place on 11.7.1979 (Ref Figure 4.6). The 5th cusp of the native clearly ensures the genetical connection. The sub-sub lord of the 5th cusp is Jupiter and the Moon's star lord of the child is Moon. Moon in the chart is in Ketu star. Ketu represents Jupiter being in its star. More over Moon is in Jupiter sub.

Step 4: Death of Father – Death of native's father took place on 5.3.1991 in the joint period of Moon-Ven-Ra-Mo-Ra. Now in the rectified chart Moon is in Ketu star that appears as the sub lord of the 4th cusp and sub-sub of the 9th cusp. Thus the dasa lord is simultaneously linked with the ascendant of the father (9th house) and the 8th house from the 9th house i.e. the 4th house. Dasa lord is linked to Jupiter that is placed in the 8th Bhava. Moon is in Ketu star that is the sub sub lord of 9 and sub lord of 4. Moon is in the sub of Jupiter that is the sub sub lord of Badhaka with respect to the 9th house. Dasa period lords are significator of the houses of death with respect to 9th cusp.

Step 5: Loss of Wife - The native lost his wife in the joint period of Mars-Jup-Ket-Mo-Sat. In the rectified chart Mars is in Rahu star that is the sub lord of the 7th cusp and as Rahu represents Saturn, Mars is said to be in Saturn's star. Thus Mars is linked simultaneously with 7th and 2nd cusp. We may check the potential of Jup, Ket, Mo, and Saturn for causing the death of the wife. All are related to death inflicting houses.

Step 6: Second Marriage Promise - The sub-sub lord of the 7th cusp is Jupiter. It is in the Mars star that appears as the star lord of the 5th cusp and is placed in the 9th Bhava. It is in Rahu sub that appears as the star lord of the 9th cusp. Thus it indicates plurality of sexual relationship. The sub-sub lord of the 9th cusp is Ket. It is in Jupiter star that appears as the sub-sub lord of the 7th cusp. Hence 2nd marriage is promised. Now the 2nd marriage takes place in the joint period of the planets that are linked with 5, 9 and 11. The Bhukti lord has to be linked with the primary cusp i.e. 9th for the 2nd marriage in the same way as the Bhukti lord should be linked with the 7th cusp for the 1st marriage. Now the 2nd marriage was held on 11.2.1997 in the joint period of Mars-Ket-Sun-Sat-Mer. Here the Bhukti lord Ket itself appears as the sub-sub lord of the 9th cusp. It is in the Jupiter star that is the sub sub lord of the 5th cusp and sub Lord of 9. Ketu is in Mars sub that appears in 5. Hence the Bhukti lord meets the required condition to enact second marriage. The potential of the planets i.e. Sun, Sat and Mer can also be verified. All are strongly linked with 5, 9 and 11.

Thus the correctness of the chart is verified.

Note: The chart may need microscopic rectification in the light of the author's advanced research techniques of timing events. This will be explained in some examples latter on.

Example 2: Figure 4.8 is the chart of a female. She died on 10.12.1973 at about 18.33 hrs.

Fig. 4.8

Name	Fig 4.8	Place of Birth	General
Sex	Female	Latitude	023.51.N
Date of Birth	19/09/1973	Longitude	072.10.E
Day of Birth	Wednesday	Local Birth Time	07:08:40
Time of Birth	07:50:00	Local Birth Date	19/09/1973
Sidereal Time	7:0:2	Lunar Tithi	7
Bal. of Dasha	Mar 6Y 1M 23D	K.P. (New) Ayanamsa	23:28:42
Lagan	Virgo	Lagan Lord	Mercury
Sign	Taurus	Sign Lord	Venus
Nakshatra	Mrigasira	Nakshatra Lord	Mars

Lagna Chart

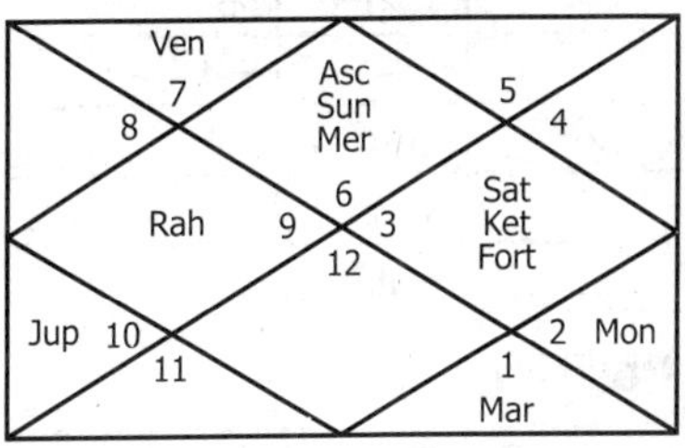

Bhava Chart

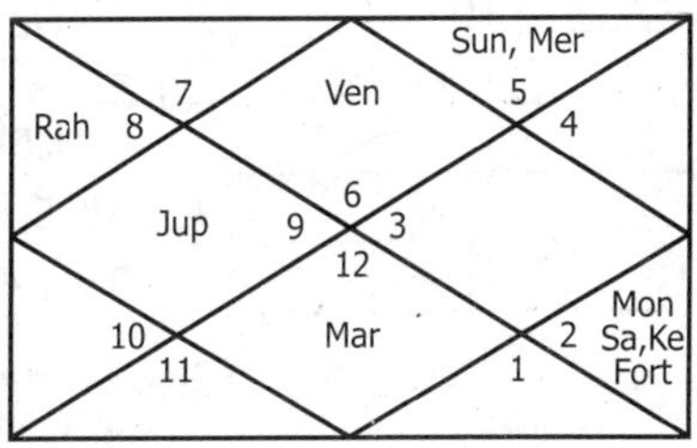

Cusp Chart

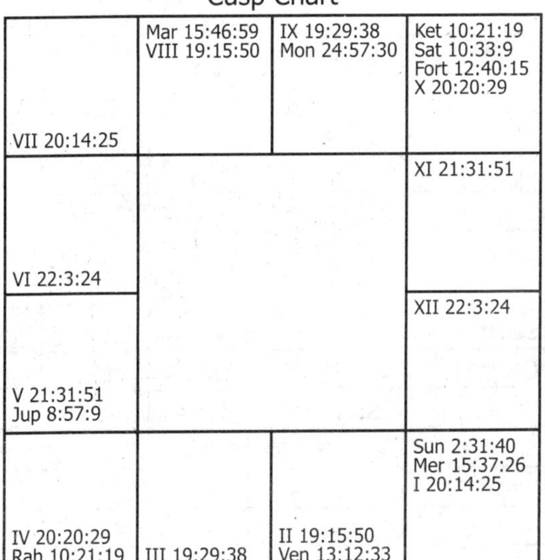

Fig. 4.8 Contd......

Nirayana Cusps

Bhav No.	Sign	Degree	Star Lord	Sub Lord	Sub-Sub Lord
1	Virgo	20: 14' 25"	Mon	Ket	Sat
2	Libra	19: 15' 50"	Rah	Mar	Mar
3	Scorpio	19: 29' 38"	Mer	Ven	Ven
4	Sagittarius	20: 20' 29"	Ven	Jup	Jup
5	Capricorn	21: 31' 51"	Mon	Ven	Rah
6	Aquarius	22: 03' 24"	Jup	Sat	Sat
7	Pisces	20: 14' 25"	Mer	Ven	Rah
8	Aries	19: 15' 50"	Ven	Rah	Mer
9	Taurus	19: 29' 38"	Mon	Mer	Sat
10	Gemini	20: 20' 29"	Jup	Jup	Sat
11	Cancer	21: 31' 51"	Mer	Ven	Ket
12	Leo	22: 03' 24"	Ven	Sat	Sat

Planetary Position

Planet	Sign	Degree	Star Lord	Sub Lord	Sub-Sub Lord
Sun	Virgo	02: 31' 40"	Sun	Jup	Mon
Mon	Taurus	24: 57' 30"	Mar	Rah	Sat
Mar	Aries	15: 46' 59"	Ven	Sun	Rah
Mer	Virgo	15: 37' 26"	Mon	Jup	Rah
Jup (R)	Capricorn	08: 57' 09"	Sun	Ven	Jup
Ven	Libra	13: 12' 33"	Rah	Mer	Ven
Sat	Gemini	10: 33' 09"	Rah	Sat	Sat
Rah (R)	Sagittarius	10: 21' 19"	Ket	Sat	Ven
Ket (R)	Gemini	10: 21' 19"	Rah	Jup	Rah
Ura	Virgo	28: 14' 45"	Mar	Sat	Mer
Nep	Scorpio	11: 29' 18"	Sat	Mon	Sat
Plu	Virgo	10: 28' 45"	Mon	Mon	Sat
Fortuna	Gemini	12: 40' 15"	Rah	Mer	Mer

For such a short life, the sub-sub lord of the ascendant should be strongly linked with Maraka and Badhaka houses through the star lord and its sub lord should not negate the signification of the star lord. Let us verify the chart.

Step 1: The sub-sub lord of the ascendant is Saturn. It has positional status. As such it is a strong significator of the ascendant i.e. the house of longevity. Saturn is in Rahu star which appears in cusps 2, 5, 7, 8 and 3 (resident position of Rahu). Now Rahu represents Jupiter and Ketu. Therefore Saturn is as good as in Jup and Ketu stars also. All those cusps in which Jup and Ketu appear will also be involved. Sat is in its own sub. Since Sat appears in 1st and 6th cusps it negates 2nd and 7th cusp signification of Saturn. The ascendant sub-sub therefore does not promise too short longevity.

Moreover, the sub-sub lord of the ascendant i.e. Saturn also does not establish any relationship with Moon's star lord Mars.

Step 2: The sub-sub lord of 3rd cusp is Venus. It is in Rahu star. Thus Venus, like Saturn, will also be in Jupiter and Ketu star. Venus is in the sub of Mer that appears in 3, 7, 8, 9 and 11 cusps. The significations of 2nd cusp thus stand negated. The sub-sub lord of the 3rd cusp also does not promise too short longevity.

Step 3: The sub-sub lord of the 8th cusp is Mercury that is in Moon star. Moon appears in 1st and 9th cusp as star lord. This also does not promise short longevity.

The above discussion clearly proves that the chart needs rectification. Figure 4.9 shows the rectified chart.

Fig. 4.9

Name	Fig 4.9	Place of Birth	General
Sex	Female	Latitude	023.51.N
Date of Birth	19/09/1973	Longitude	072.10.E
Day of Birth	Wednesday	Local Birth Time	07:07:32
Time of Birth	07:48:52	Local Birth Date	19/09/1973
Sidereal Time	6:58:54	Lunar Tithi	7
Bal. of Dasha	Mar 6Y 1M 25D	K.P. (New) Ayanamsa	23:28:42
Lagan	Virgo	Lagan Lord	Mercury
Sign	Taurus	Sign Lord	Venus
Nakshatra	Mrigasira	Nakshatra Lord	Mars

Lagna Chart

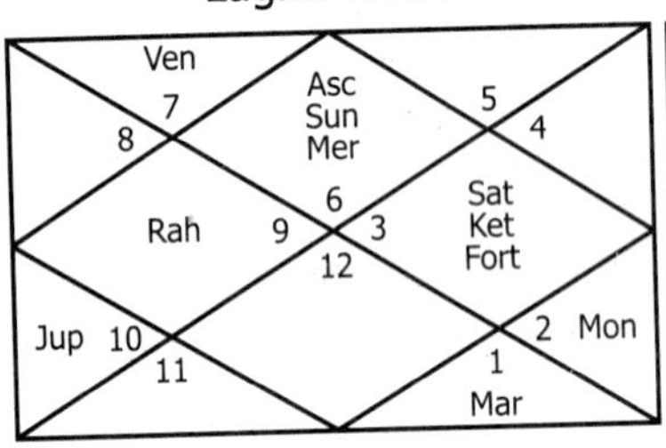

Bhava Chart

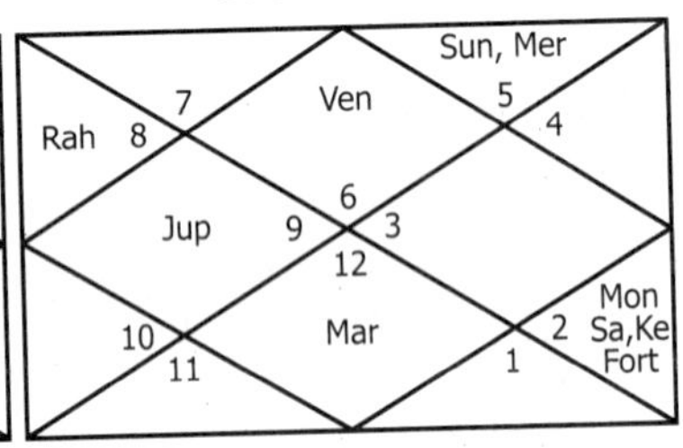

Cusp Chart

VII 19:58:53	Mar 15:46:59 VIII 19:0:8	IX 19:14:4 Mon 24:56:50	Ket 10:21:19 Sat 10:33:9 Fort 12:24:6 X 20:4:40
VI 21:47:2			XI 21:15:31
V 21:15:31 Jup 8:57:9			XII 21:47:2
IV 20:4:40 Rah 10:21:19	III 19:14:4	II 19:0:8 Ven 13:12:29	Sun 2:31:37 Mer 15:37:21 I 19:58:53

Fig. 4.9 Contd......

Nirayana Cusps

Bhav No.	Sign	Degree	Star Lord	Sub Lord	Sub-Sub Lord
1	Virgo	19: 58' 53"	Mon	Ket	Mar
2	Libra	19: 00' 08"	Rah	Mon	Ven
3	Scorpio	19: 14' 04"	Mer	Ket	Mer
4	Sagittarius	20: 04' 40"	Ven	Rah	Mar
5	Capricorn	21: 15' 31"	Mon	Ven	Rah
6	Aquarius	21: 47' 02"	Jup	Sat	Sat
7	Pisces	19: 58' 53"	Mer	Ven	Mon
8	Aries	19: 00' 08"	Ven	Rah	Mer
9	Taurus	19: 14' 04"	Mon	Mer	Jup
10	Gemini	20: 04' 40"	Jup	Jup	Jup
11	Cancer	21: 15' 31"	Mer	Ven	Mer
12	Leo	21: 47' 02"	Ven	Jup	Rah

Planetary Position

Planet	Sign	Degree	Star Lord	Sub Lord	Sub-Sub Lord
Sun	Virgo	02: 31' 37"	Sun	Jup	Mon
Mon	Taurus	24: 56' 50"	Mar	Rah	Sat
Mar	Aries	15: 46' 59"	Ven	Sun	Rah
Mer	Virgo	15: 37' 21"	Mon	Jup	Rah
Jup (R)	Capricorn	08: 57' 09"	Sun	Ven	Jup
Ven	Libra	13: 12' 29"	Rah	Mer	Ven
Sat	Gemini	10: 33' 09"	Rah	Sat	Sat
Rah (R)	Sagittarius	10: 21' 19"	Ket	Sat	Ven
Ket (R)	Gemini	10: 21' 19"	Rah	Jup	Rah
Ura	Virgo	28: 14' 45"	Mar	Sat	Mer
Nep	Scorpio	11: 29' 18"	Sat	Mon	Sat
Plu	Virgo	10: 28' 45"	Mon	Mon	Sat
Fortuna	Gemini	12: 24' 06"	Rah	Sat	Jup

Analysing the planetary positions, it appears that Moon, Mars, Ven, Sun or Rahu can come as the sub-sub lord of the ascendant to establish relationship with Moon's star lord. The first planet that can be tried before Saturn is Rahu. Since Rahu is in Ketu star and Ketu being the resident of the 9th cusp will not cause for short life. Next we can use Mars as the sub sub lord of the ascendant. The horoscope with Mars as the sub-sub lord accounts for short life (Refer Figure 4.9). Mars is in Venus star and Sun sub. Venus appears in 2, 4, 5, 7, 8, 11 and 12. However, it can be seen that Sun the sub lord of Venus does not appear in any cuspal position as star or sub or sub-sub lord but is the resident of 12th house. This negates the 5th house signification being in the 8th house from the 5th house. The significations of 11th and 12th houses are supported by the sub lord Sun. But what does it mean? It only means fulfillment of desire by death because of 12th house commitment. Thus the ascendant sub-sub lord Mars promises short life. Now Mercury appears as the sub-sub lord of the 3rd and the 8th cusp. It is in Moon star and Jupiter sub and Rahu sub-sub. This clearly proves short life.

Death of the native occurred in the joint period of Mar-Ra-Ket-Mer-Mer. Dasa lord appears as the sub-sub lord of ascendant and sign lord of 8. It is in Venus star that appears as the star lord of the 8th cusp and is placed in the ascendant. Thus the dasa lord is simultaneously linked with 1 and 8. Its sub Lord Sun with positional status is placed in the Maraka house 12.The Bhukti lord Rahu itself appears as the sub lord of the 8th cusp and is in Ketu star that appears as the sub lord of the ascendant. Since Ketu is in Rahu star it can be assumed that Rahu is in Rahu star. Thus Rahu has the capability to inflict death.

It may be remembered that if the sub-sub lord of the ascendant promises short life then the joint period of the planets that co-rules the 8th cusp or the ascendant and if these planets have the capability to inflict death, their joint period is dangerous. Her death has taken place in the joint period of the planets Mars, Rahu, Ket and Mercury. Mars, Rahu and Mercury co-rule the 8th cusp directly. Ketu is the sub lord of the ascendant and represents Rahu. As such all the dasa period planets co-rule the 8th cusp and have the capacity to inflict death being significators of Maraka and Badhaka.

Now the question that we need to analyse is why death has not occurred in the Antaras of Saturn and Mercury.

Saturn as discussed above has not the capability to inflict death because it is in its own sub that appears in the 6th cusp.

Mercury Antara runs from 28.9.73 to 20.11.73. Mercury no doubt is linked with 2 and 7 but is also strongly linked with 9th cusp through star lord and is also committed to the 9th cusp by its sub lord Jup.

Here another question arises. Why then Mercury appears as the Sookshma and Prana lord at the time of death. **It should be remembered that for fixing the death we need to fix the Bhukti and Antara lords which are strongly linked with Maraka and Badhaka houses. But the Sookshma and Prana lords are fixed as per the cause of death which is decided by the sub-sub lord of the 8th cusp**. In this chart Mercury is the sub sub lord of the 8th cusp. As such Mercury can appear as Sookshma and Prana lord.

Another doubt that comes in the mind of the reader is why Rahu Bhukti should give death when it is in the sub of Saturn that appears in the 6th cusp. Here we should note that Rahu is in Ketu star that is the sub Lord of ascendant. Since ketu represents Mercury and Rahu is as good as in Mercury star that is the sub sub lord of the 8th cusp. Thus Rahu involves both the ascendant as well as the 8th cusp. Its sub lord does not negate either of the involved houses. More over Rahu is in the sub sub of Venus that appears in 7 and 8.Rahu thus has the full power to enact death of the native.

Thus we may conclude that the horoscope of Figure 4.9 is the true horoscope of the native. The transit of planets at the time of death can be analysed from Figure 4.10.

Fig. 10 Planetary Position

Planet	Sign	Degree	Star Lord	Sub Lord	Sub-Sub Lord
Sun	Scorpio	24: 52' 33"	Mer	Rah	Sat
Mon	Gemini	01: 52' 01"	Mar	Mer	Sat
Mar	Aries	03: 09' 42"	Ket	Sun	Rah
Mer	Scorpio	08: 57' 38"	Sat	Ven	Rah
Jup	Capricorn	16: 32' 26"	Mon	Sat	Ven
Ven	Capricorn	08: 26' 51"	Sun	Ven	Mar
Sat (R)	Gemini	08: 48' 19"	Rah	Jup	Jup
Rah (R)	Sagittarius	05: 05' 13"	Ket	Mar	Sat
Ket (R)	Gemini	05: 05' 13"	Mar	Sun	Rah
Ura	Libra	03: 03' 33"	Mar	Ven	Sun
Nep	Scorpio	14: 05' 44"	Sat	Rah	Ket
Plu	Virgo	13: 05' 27"	Mon	Rah	Ket
Fortuna	Sagittarius	17: 51' 03"	Ven	Mar	Ket

It can be seen that transit agrees with the dasa period to allow the planets to cause death of the native. Saturn transits in Gemini ruled by Mercury that is the sub sub lord of the 8th cusp.

Example 3: A gentleman born on 13.1.1964 at Gwalior (M.P), India at 19.25 hrs. He requested for a true horoscope. He gave the following details:

1. Education: B.E. Electronics.
2. Served as Lecturer in an Engineering college from August 1985 to Jan 1987.
3. Joined NTPC on 18.2.1987.
4. Joined DOT on 20.2.1989 as class I officer.
5. Marriage Engagement on 24.4.1992.
6. Marriage 8.7.1992.
7. 1st Promotion 1.1.1993
8. First female child 5.1.1994 at 04.24.28 hrs.
9. Transfer 7.7.1994
10. Transfer 24.4.1995
11. Transfer 29.9.1995
12. FIR with CBI 11.10.1995
13. Second promotion with transfer 16.12.1997
14. Challan in court 24.1.1999
15. Transfer 29.8.2002
16. Unfavourable court decision 30.7.2003
17. Appeal admission 19.8.2003
18. Suspension 23.9.2003

Figure 4.11 shows the chart of the native as per recorded birth data. Let us analyse the chart for its accuracy.

Fig. 4.11

Name	Fig 4.11	Place of Birth	Gwalior
Sex	Male	Latitude	026.12.N
Date of Birth	13/01/1964	Longitude	078.12.E
Day of Birth	Monday	Local Birth Time	19:07:48
Time of Birth	19:25:00	Local Birth Date	13/01/1964
Sidereal Time	2:36:8	Lunar Tithi	14
Bal. of Dasha	Ven 18Y 1M 17D	K.P. (New) Ayanamsa	23:20:35
Lagan	Cancer	Lagan Lord	Moon
Sign	Sagittarius	Sign Lord	Jupiter
Nakshatra	P.Asadha	Nakshatra Lord	Venus

Lagna Chart

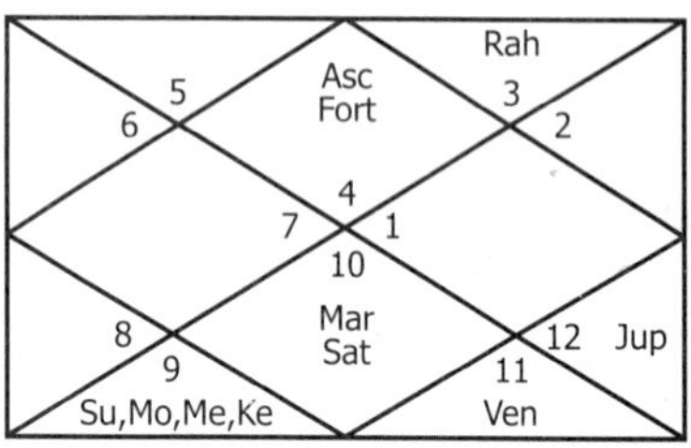

Bhava Chart

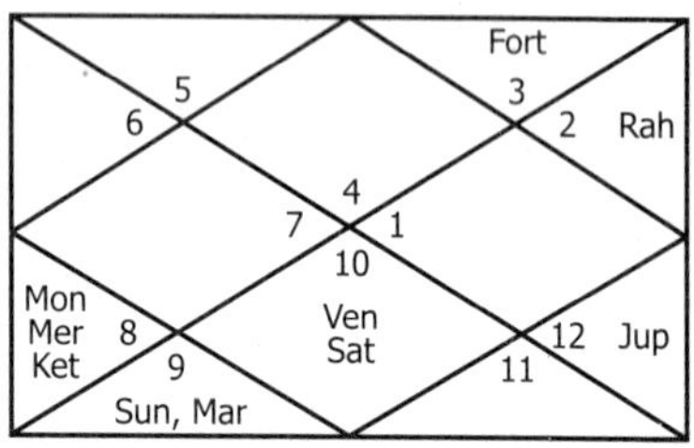

Cusp Chart

Jup 18:44:13 IX 15:50:34	X 18:7:25	XI 20:55:24	Rah 17:54:49 XII 22:10:23
VIII 16:43:5 Ven 2:19:37			Fort 6:59:16 I 21:29:19
Sat 28:25:2 VII 21:29:19 Mar 6:55:21			II 16:43:5
Sun 29:4:45 VI 22:10:23 Ket 17:54:49 Mon 14:34:42 Mer 11:25:36	V 20:55:24	IV 18:7:25	III 15:50:34

Fig. 4.11 Contd......

Nirayana Cusps

Bhav No.	Sign	Degree	Star Lord	Sub Lord	Sub-Sub Lord
1	Cancer	21: 29' 19"	Mer	Ven	Ket
2	Leo	16: 43' 05"	Ven	Mon	Sat
3	Virgo	15: 50' 34"	Mon	Sat	Sat
4	Libra	18: 07' 25"	Rah	Mon	Mon
5	Scorpio	20: 55' 24"	Mer	Ven	Sat
6	Sagittarius	22: 10' 23"	Ven	Sat	Sat
7	Capricorn	21: 29' 19"	Mon	Ven	Rah
8	Aquarius	16: 43' 05"	Rah	Ven	Sat
9	Pisces	15: 50' 34"	Sat	Jup	Ven
10	Aries	18: 07' 25"	Ven	Rah	Rah
11	Taurus	20: 55' 24"	Mon	Ven	Sun
12	Gemini	22: 10' 23"	Jup	Sat	Mer

Planetary Position

Planet	Sign	Degree	Star Lord	Sub Lord	Sub-Sub Lord
Sun	Sagittarius	29: 04' 45"	Sun	Mar	Ven
Mon	Sagittarius	14: 34' 42"	Ven	Ven	Jup
Mar	Capricorn	06: 55' 21"	Sun	Mer	Sat
Mer (R)	Sagittarius	11: 25' 36"	Ket	Sat	Jup
Jup	Pisces	18: 44' 13"	Mer	Ket	Sun
Ven	Aquarius	02: 19' 37"	Mar	Ket	Rah
Sat	Capricorn	28: 25' 02"	Mar	Sat	Mer
Rah (R)	Gemini	17: 54' 49"	Rah	Sun	Mer
Ket (R)	Sagittarius	17: 54' 49"	Ven	Mar	Ven
Ura (R)	Leo	16: 21' 47"	Ven	Mon	Mar
Nep	Libra	24: 08' 09"	Jup	Mer	Mer
Plu (R)	Leo	20: 41' 38"	Ven	Jup	Mer
Fortuna	Cancer	06: 59' 16"	Sat	Mer	Jup

Step I: Check the relationship of the sub-sub lord of the ascendant with Moon's star. Here in this chart the sub-sub lord of the ascendant is Ketu and the Native's Moon star is Venus. Since Ketu in the chart is in Venus star we take it that it establishes relationship with Moon's star lord. More over Venus itself is in Ketu sub. Planets co-ruling ascendant, Moon and Sun also link with houses 1, 7 and 10.

Step II: Check the linkages of the ascendant sub-sub lord for the following:

i. Educational prospects.

ii. Dignified profession in service.

iii. Promise for marriage

iv. Loss of reputation due to CBI case

v. Suspension in service.

Educational Prospects: For achieving qualification by attendance in a school or college the ascendant sub-sub lord should establish relation with 4th or 9th cusp. Here Ketu the sub-sub lord of the ascendant is in Venus star that appears in 4 as well as in 9. Ketu is in sub of Mars that does not appear in any of the houses which are detrimental to the 4th or the 9th house. Thus the chart promises good educational prospect.

Dignified Profession in Service: For a person to achieve excellence in profession, the ascendant sub-sub lord should establish relationship with the 10th cusp either directly through its star lord or its star lord may appear in 1 or 11 and the sub should appear in 10th cusp. In this chart Ketu, the sub-sub lord of the ascendant is directly linked with the 10th cusp through its star lord Venus that appears as the star lord of the 10th cusp. The sub lord of the sub-sub lord of the ascendant is Mars. It appears as the Sign lord of 5th and the 10th cusp and is itself resident of 6th cusp but without PS. Commitment to the 5th cusp causes adverse affects to the house of profession being 8th from it. This indicates that the native will have to face problems in profession. The fact that native was placed under suspension confirms the promise.

Promise for Marriage: The ascendant sub-sub lord Ketu is directly linked with 5, 7, and 11 cusps through its star lord. It clearly promises marriage.

Loss of Reputation due to CBI: First house in the horoscope stands for Status and reputation of the individual. By status we mean the standing of the native in society. Reputation means the views that are generally held about the native or the generally accepted estimation of the native as having particular qualities or attributes. A noble man has a reputation and so does a Don of the underworld. Twelfth house to any house is the house of dissolution of the attributes of the house. Thus twelfth house takes the responsibility of the primary house to reveal the promise of any loss of reputation.

What for a Person Loses Reputation: Broadly speaking a person loses his reputation due to:

1. Imprisonment
2. Raids conducted by investigating agencies like C.B.I, C.I.D, Anti Corruption Bureau, and Revenue Departments.
3. Any type of misconduct.
4. False Allegations.

Let us discuss about Raids by C.B.I. A person suffers trauma due to raid when any investigating agency comes to a conclusion after analyzing preliminary investigation report that a man might have committed an unlawful act. This act may be misappropriation of funds, forgery of document, forgery of negotiable instrument, disproportionate assets, fraudulent sale-purchase of shares, unlawful professional activities like prostitution, gambling, speculation, or criminal acts etc. The trauma due to raid is indicated by the 8th cusp. The person will suffer the trauma as per the cause for which his premises is raided. This is indicated by the linking cuspal position whose sub-sub lord involves the 12th cusp through its star lord and commits to 8th cusp through its sub lord. This is explained below:

Linking Cusps	**Cause for Raid**
1	Involvement in secret activities
2	Non-disclosure of true income, spurious currency
3	Forgery of documents
4	Disproportionate assets.
5	Fraudulent sale-purchase of share, gambling, speculation, entertainment place used for unlawful activities
6	Sale-purchase of stolen goods or spurious drugs.
7	Secret troubles caused by partner.
8	Criminal acts, forgery of father's will, bribe, taxes not paid as per rules etc.
9	Plagiarism in research work, treachery and deception to newly acquainted person
10	Misconduct or misuse of official position to cause loss to the government
11	Misappropriation of funds, criminal acts of elder co-born or friend.
12	Secret activities

Promise of Raid: We need to analyse the chart as follows:

The sub-sub lords of ascendant and 12th cusp should establish linkages through their star lords and sub lords as below to promise raid.

Star lord in	Sub lord in
12	8
1	12

The sub-sub lords of the sub-sub lords of the ascendant and 12th cusp should be in favourable cuspal positions with respect to 12th cusp.

Invariably the raid is conducted by the government agencies. Thus 10th cusp sub-sub lord should also establish linkages through its star lord with 12th cusp and the sub lord of the sub-sub lord will indicate what for the native is put to the trauma of raid. The nature of agency will depend upon the nature of the sub-sub lord of the 10th cusp.

In this chart sub sub lord of the ascendant is Ketu that represents Jupiter and Venus. Ketu is in Venus star does not appear in 12. But it does appear in 1. Ketu is in the sub of Mars that does not appear in 12. Thus we find that the ascendant does not promise loss of reputation. Thus horoscope needs rectification.

Suspension in Service:

In legal terms suspension is not regarded as punishment. It is only a means to disallow a person to do his duty for a period till some investigation is carried out for any misconduct. **In practical life suspension attaches a stigma and the person suffers from trauma due to loss of reputation and also loss of emoluments**.

The person is suspended or may be suspended if the following conditions exist in the natal or horary chart. The sub-sub lords of the ascendant, 10th cusp and 11th cusp should establish linkages as shown below:

Star Lord In	Sub Lord In
12	8
1,12	8

The sub-sub lords of the sub-sub lords should not appear in favourable positions with respect to 10.

In this chart the sub sub lord of ascendant is linked to 10 and 8 simultaneously. It only indicates continuous mental agony.

Step 3: The native achieved the degree of B.E. Electronics. Let us analyse the chart to see whether it promises this qualification or not. For achieving the degree in Electronics Engineering, the native has to first study physics, chemistry and mathematics in his school. For this the planet Sun, Venus, Mercury, Mars and the cusps 2, 3, and 6 should maintain relationship with 4th cusp. In this chart Sun, Venus and Mars do not have any signification of the 4th house. Now let us examine the linkage of 2nd, 3rd and 6th cusp with the 4th cusp. The sub-sub lord of the 2nd cusp, 3rd cusp and 6th cusp is Saturn. It is in Mars star, Saturn sub and Mercury sub-sub. As such none of these cusps are linked to the 4th cusp. This raises serious doubts about the accuracy of the horoscope.

Step 4: Areas of concentration of professional activities: Let us first understand how to determine the nature of profession of a person as per KCIL. This is briefly explained below:

Procedure to determine Profession:

Step 1: Analyse the Ascendant - Natural inclination of the native need to match with the promise of the 10th cusp. If the ascendant sub-sub lord establishes strong relationship i.e. through its star lord with 6th and the 10th house, the person is more likely to be a service person. If the ascendant is strongly connected with 7th and the 10th house, he is likely to adopt business as his profession. Strong connection with 5th and 9th without having any connection with 6, 7, and 10 indicates that the native is likely to live his life without any professional status. For the success in service or business the ascendant sub-sub lord should be linked with cusps 2, 6, 10 and 11 through its star lord and should be supported by its sub and sub-sub lord.

Step 2: Analyse the Tenth House - It is the principle house for analysing profession. It forms the apex of the materialistic triplicity. The other two houses, which we study, are second and sixth. The analysis of the 10th cusp to determine profession is done as follows:

a. Analyse the sign, star, sub, and sub-sub lord rising on the 10th cusp. The sum total of the attributes of the planets co-ruling the cusp will show in general the nature of the Profession of the native.

b. The linkages that the sub-sub lord of the 10th cusp makes with other cusps through its star lord will indicate the promise of the 10th cusp and the area of concentration of activities of profession of the native. The sub and the sub-sub lord of the sub-sub lord of the 10th cusp will **qualify** or **specify** the area minutely. The broad areas where the native will like to concentrate his activities as per the star linkages are shown below:

Linked Area of Professional activities

House	
1	Psychiatrist, a specialist in treating cerebral cases, neuralgia, coma, head injuries, a yoga practitioner, physical instructor, professor of psychology, self-venture, advisor in his own field.
2	Professional in financial institutions, revenue department, economists, accounts department, dental or E.N.T.clinics, acoustics, gastro-entomologist section, jeweller, gems dealer, money lenders.
3	Communication department, print media, information centers, professionals in E.N.T department, news correspondent, physiotherapist, anesthetist, neurology department, commission agencies.
4	Production unit, education institutions, cardiology, lungs or chest specialists, building construction organisation, real estate dealers, agriculture farms, veterinary department, dairy farming, furniture houses.
5	Stock exchange, sports organisations, art and culture, cinema, places of amusement, manufacturing units of toys for children, pediatrics or gynecology department, nuclear science or atomic energy department, clergies.
6	Public health department, chemists, repairing units in a factory, poultry farms, law department, dealers in leather, medical profession, labour oriented jobs, dealers in plastics.

7	Judge in a court of Law, Public relations officer, embassy, marriage bureaus, advocate dealing divorce cases or marital problems, Nephrologists, public administration departments, employment in private companies, brothels, prostitution, sexologists, doctors dealing in venereal diseases, private business.
8	Historians, archaeologists, geologists, personnel's working in insurance, mining, tax collection, Auditing, CID, CBI Departments, pension cells, surgeons, ONGC department, death and estate duty collectors, advocates practicing criminal cases or cases dealing with legacies and wills, urologists.
9	Research organisations, university, religious organisations, honorary posts, export houses, pilot, travel agents, politicians, aeronautical department, space technology organisations, and advocates.
10	Govt. organisations, production houses, politics, self-venture, managers.
11	Computer hardware, general physicians, charitable institution, commercial houses, Journalists.
12	Jail department, hospitals, investigating agents, detectives, research organisations, asylums, foreign countries.

Step 3: The native will carry out the activities of profession as per the influence of other cusps sub-sub lords that maintain relationship through their star lords with the 10th cusp. The sub lord and the sub-sub lord of the linking planet will qualify or specify the nature of profession.

Step 4: Eleventh House - The linkage of the sub-sub lord of this house with ascendant and 10th House through its star lord represents the success of the native in his profession. This linkage can also be established as follows:

a. The sub-sub lord of the 11th cusp can link it-self to the 10th cusp through its star lord and to the 1st cusp through its sub lord.

b. The sub-sub lord of the 11th cusp can link to the ascendant through its star lord and to the 10th cusp through its sub lord.

The native had his first stint in profession as a teacher in an Engineering college. To be in teaching profession the 4th or 9th cusp should maintain relationship with the 10th cusp. Here the sub and sub-sub lord of the 4th cusp is Moon that establishes direct relationship with the 10th cusp and as well as with the 6th cusp through its star lord Venus that appears as the star lord of the 10th cusp and as well as the star lord of the 6th cusp. Later on the native joined Govt. Service. This also can be justified through the sub-sub lord of 10th cusp Rahu that is in its own star and Sun sub.

Step 5: Birth of a daughter: Let us analyse the 5th cusp. The sub-sub lord of the 5th cusp is Saturn. It has positional status and as such causes for the potency of the native. Since Saturn is also the sub-sub lord of the 2nd cusp, it indicates the native has the procreative power. Now Saturn is in the sub-sub of Mercury that occupies a male sign. Moreover the sub-sub arc of Saturn in the 5th cusp rises in Scorpio sign at 20 deg 55 minutes and 24 seconds. The span of the sub-sub arc of Saturn in Venus sub starts at 20 deg 45 minutes and 33 secs and ends at 21 deg 06 minutes and 40 seconds. Thus the sub-sub arc of Saturn in the 5th cusp is in the 2nd half and as such cannot account for the birth of the female child.

Step 6: Genetical Connection -The native got his 1st female child on 5.1.1994 at 04.24.28 hrs on a Moon's star day. Since Moon bears no connection with the sub-sub lord of the 5th cusp, we may assume that the chart shows no genetical connection.

The above discussion reveals that as far as the chart's accuracy in respect of promise of various aspects is concerned, it appears that it needs rectification though in many aspects it justifies accuracy. Let us now examine the accuracy of the chart with respect to dasa potential of planets to justify the events that has happened in the life of the native. We may take first his marriage.

Step 7: The native got married on 8.7.1992 when he was running the joint period of Mo-Sat-Sat-Ve-Mo. Here Saturn has appeared both as the Bhukti lord as well as the Antara lord. This indicates Saturn should be very strongly linked with 5, 7 and 11 under the conditions that we have indicated in example1. Now Saturn has the positional status in this chart. Saturn appears as the Sign lord of the 7th cusp. If a planet has PS we treat the planet as if it is in its own star. Saturn is in its own sub and Mercury sub-sub. We may say that Saturn is in Saturn star, Saturn sub and Mercury sub sub. Mercury appears in 5. Thus we find Saturn has a weak power to enact marriage as per its PS. Let us see what Saturn offers as per its stellar status.

It is in Mars star. Mars appears as sign lord of 5. Saturn is in the sub of Saturn that appears as Sign lord of 7. This involvement and commitment is of relevant cusps but very weak. This type of weak signification of a planet cannot ensure repetition of the planet in dasa period sequence. This further confirms that the chart needs rectification.

Construction of True Chart of the Native

To rectify this chart an Astrologer took ruling planets on 19.1.2005 at 15.23.36 hrs at Noida (U.P.), India.

They were as follows:

Day lord: Mercury (Wednesday)

RP (Ascdt): Mer- Mars-Ven-Sat in Gemini sign.

RP (Moon): Mars-Sun-Ra-Jup in Aries sign.

Astrologer assumed that the time given by the native is a certified time. Thus the astrologer was mainly interested to put the right sub sub lord of the ascendant.

The sub-sub lord of RP Moon is Jupiter. Since the Moon's star lord Venus in the native's chart is in the sub of Ketu that represents Jupiter, it establishes a relationship with the Native's Moon star. More over in the natal chart Jupiter is in the sub of Ketu that represents Venus. He decided to put Jupiter as the sub-sub lord of the ascendant for the rectified chart. Keeping Jupiter as the sub-sub lord of the ascendant, he only decided to play around time in seconds to correctly fix the sub-sub lords of other cusps to justify the promise of each cusp as per the events of the native's life. The true horoscope as rectified by the Astrologer is shown in figure 4.12.

Fig. 4.12

Name	Fig 4.12	Place of Birth	Gwalior
Sex	Male	Latitude	026.12.N
Date of Birth	13/01/1964	Longitude	078.12.E
Day of Birth	Monday	Local Birth Time	19:04:09
Time of Birth	19:21:21	Local Birth Date	13/01/1964
Sidereal Time	2:32:28	Lunar Tithi	14
Bal. of Dasha	Ven 18Y 2M 6D	K.P. (New) Ayanamsa	23:54:59
Lagan	Cancer	Lagan Lord	Moon
Sign	Sagittarius	Sign Lord	Jupiter
Nakshatra	P.Asadha	Nakshatra Lord	Venus

Lagna Chart

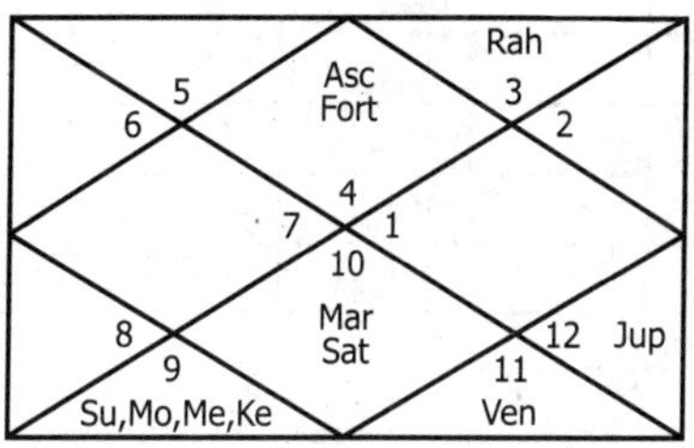

Bhava Chart

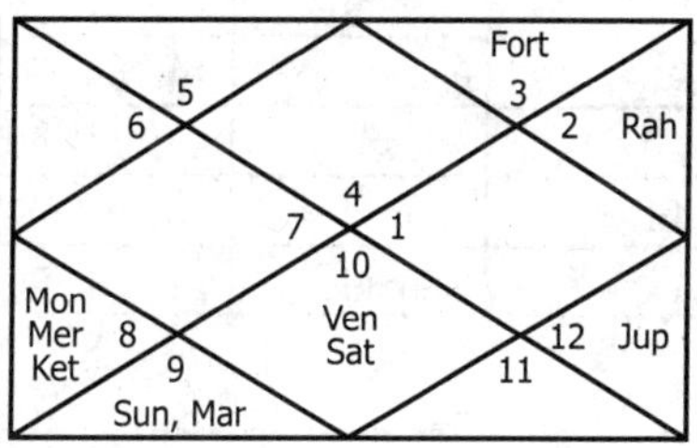

Cusp Chart

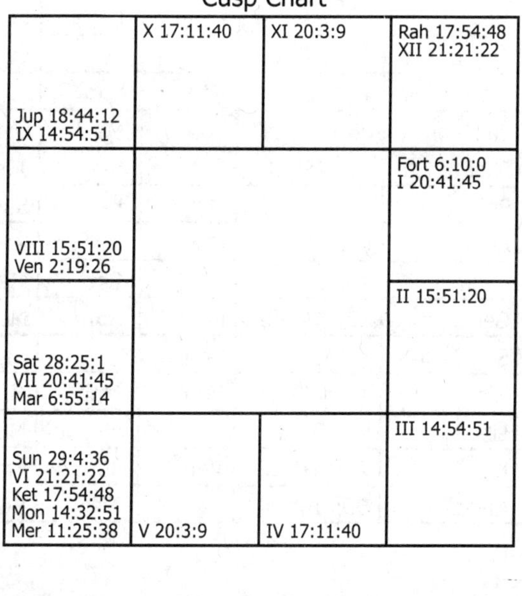

Fig. 4.12 Contd......

Nirayana Cusps

Bhav No.	Sign	Degree	Star Lord	Sub Lord	Sub-Sub Lord
1	Cancer	20: 41' 45"	Mer	Ven	Jup
2	Leo	15: 51' 20"	Ven	Sun	Jup
3	Virgo	14: 54' 51"	Mon	Jup	Ven
4	Libra	17: 11' 40"	Rah	Ven	Mer
5	Scorpio	20: 03' 09"	Mer	Ven	Mar
6	Sagittarius	21: 21' 22"	Ven	Jup	Sun
7	Capricorn	20: 41' 45"	Mon	Ven	Ven
8	Aquarius	15: 51' 20"	Rah	Ven	Mon
9	Pisces	14: 54' 51"	Sat	Jup	Jup
10	Aries	17: 11' 40"	Ven	Mon	Ven
11	Taurus	20: 03' 09"	Mon	Ket	Rah
12	Gemini	21: 21' 22"	Jup	Jup	Mon

Planetary Position

Planet	Sign	Degree	Star Lord	Sub Lord	Sub-Sub Lord
Sun	Sagittarius	29: 04' 36"	Sun	Mar	Ven
Mon	Sagittarius	14: 32' 51"	Ven	Ven	Jup
Mar	Capricorn	06: 55' 14"	Sun	Mer	Sat
Mer (R)	Sagittarius	11: 25' 38"	Ket	Sat	Jup
Jup	Pisces	18: 44' 12"	Mer	Ket	Sun
Ven	Aquarius	02: 19' 26"	Mar	Ket	Rah
Sat	Capricorn	28: 25' 01"	Mar	Sat	Mer
Rah (R)	Gemini	17: 54' 48"	Rah	Sun	Mer
Ket (R)	Sagittarius	17: 54' 48"	Ven	Mar	Ven
Ura (R)	Leo	16: 21' 47"	Ven	Mon	Mar
Nep	Libra	24: 08' 09"	Jup	Mer	Mer
Plu (R)	Leo	20: 41' 38"	Ven	Jup	Mer
Fortuna	Cancer	06: 10' 00"	Sat	Mer	Sun

Let us now verify the corrected chart.

As stated above, the sub-sub lord of the ascendant establishes relationship with the Moon's star lord Venus.

Let us now check the linkages of the ascendant for other aspects.

I. **Educational Prospects**: Jupiter, the sub-sub lord of the ascendant is in Mercury star that appears as the sub-sub lord of the 4th cusp. Jupiter has the positional status and is the sub and sub-sub lord of the 9th cusp. This ensures very good prospects for education.

II. **Dignified Profession in Service:** Jupiter sub-sub lord of the ascendant is in the star of Mercury and sub of Ketu. Mercury is the star lord of the ascendant and Ketu is the sub lord of the 11th cusp. Since Ketu represents Venus, the ascendant sub-sub lord is linked with 10th cusp also because Venus appears as the star and sub-sub lord of the 10th cusp.

III. **Promise for Marriage:** Jupiter, the sub-sub lord of the ascendant is in Mercury star and Ketu sub. Mercury is the star lord of the 5th cusp and Venus (represented by Ketu) is the sub lord and sub-sub lord of the 7th cusp. Ketu itself is the sub lord of the 11th cusp. Thus it clearly promises marriage.

IV. **Loss of Reputation due to CBI case:** Jupiter being in Mercury star and Ketu sub that represents Jupiter and Venus. Thus Jupiter involves ascendant (status) and commits to 12.This indicates that the native by its own conscious efforts will cause for the loss of prestige or reputation. Sub sub lord of 12 is Moon that is in Venus star, Venus sub and Jupiter sub sub. It can be read as that Moon is in Venus star and Jupter sub. Venus appears in 1, 8 and 10(Government) and Jupiter appears in 12. It justifies that the native may lose reputation.

V. **Suspension in Service:** Here the sub-sub lord of the ascendant involves the 1st and 5th cusps through star lord and commits to the 8th as well as the 10th cusp.

Subjects of Study

As stated above, the native achieved the degree of B.E. Electronics. In the rectified chart, we note that the sub sub lord of 2 is Jupiter whose star lord is the sub sub lord of 4.Jupiter is also the sub lord of cusps 3 and 6. The sub sub lord of 3 is strongly linked with 4.

Areas of concentration of Professional activities: Mercury the sub-sub lord of the 4th cusp is in Ketu star that represents Venus that appears in 10. This justifies the native's stint as a lecturer. Since Venus is the sub-sub lord of the 3rd cusp and its star lord appears in 10 this indicates the native will use his knowledge of communication to carry out his professional activities. The native does more than one type of profession if the sub sub lord of the 10th cusp is linked with the 12th cusp directly or indirectly. Here the sub sub lord of 10th cusp is Venus that is placed in 6th Bhava (Service) and 10 (profession) and commits to the 12th cusp through its sub lord Ketu that represents Jupiter.

Birth of Female Child: The sub-sub lord of the 5th cusp is Mars that is in the sub-sub of Saturn. Since Saturn is in Capricorn, it justifies the birth of the female child.

Marriage of the Native: The native got married on 8.7.1992 in the joint period of Mo-Sat-Sat-Mer-Mo. Now the Bhukti lord and the Antara lord possess the necessary capability to cause the event of marriage to happen. Saturn having the positional status is in the 7th cusp and is in the star of Mars that is the sub-sub lord of the 5th cusp. It is in its own sub and sub-sub of Mercury that is the star lord of the 5th cusp. Thus Saturn is strongly linked with the 5th and 7th cusp without having any link with the 6th cusp.

Birth of Daughter: The native got his first child on 5.1.1994 in the joint period of Mo-Sat-Jup-Jup-Mercury. We have already indicated that Sat is linked to the 5th cusp. Now Jupiter has positional status and is in Mercury star that appears as the star lord of the 5th cusp. Jupiter is in the sub of Ketu that is the sub lord of the 11th cusp. Thus Jupiter is simultaneously linked with 2, 5 and 11 cusps and thus has appeared both as Antara and Sookshma lord. The Prana lord Mercury is the star lord of the 5th cusp. It is in Ketu star that is the sub lord of the 11th cusp. Since Ketu represents Venus, which appears as the star lord of the 2nd cusp and sub lord of the 5th cusp, Mercury is linked with the relevant cusps 2, 5 and 11 to ensure the birth of the child. The horoscope of the child is shown in Figure 4.13.

Fig. 4.13

Name	Fig 4.13	Place of Birth	Gwalior
Sex	Female	Latitude	026.12.N
Date of Birth	05/01/1994	Longitude	078.12.E
Day of Birth	Wednesday	Local Birth Time	04:07:16
Time of Birth	04:24:28	Local Birth Date	05/01/1994
Sidereal Time	11:4:29	Lunar Tithi	8
Bal. of Dasha	Mon 2Y 6M 3D	K.P. (New) Ayanamsa	23:45:42
Lagan	Scorpio	Lagan Lord	Mars
Sign	Virgo	Sign Lord	Mercury
Nakshatra	Hasta	Nakshatra Lord	Moon

Lagna Chart

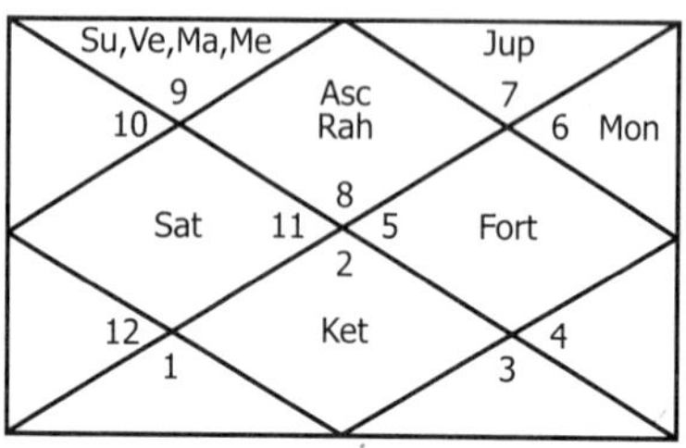

Bhava Chart

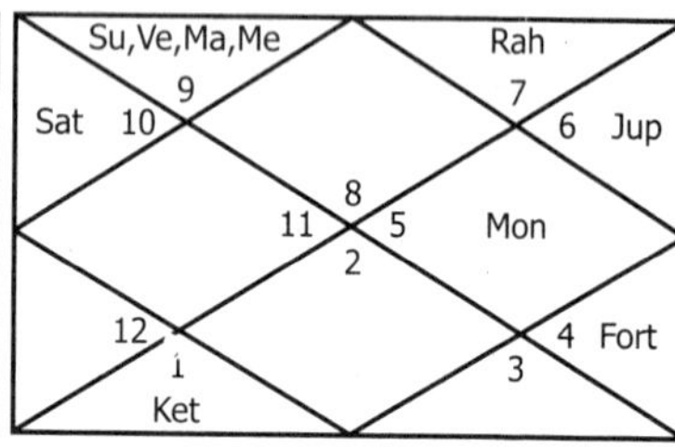

Cusp Chart

V 22:35:38	VI 19:30:23	Ket 8:26:30 VII 13:7:7	VIII 13:37:46
IV 21:10:2 Sat 3:37:34			IX 16:56:39
III 16:56:39			Fort 12:30:22 X 21:10:2
Mer 21:16:38 Sun 20:36:23 Mar 18:19:55 Ven 17:42:52 II 13:37:46	I 13:7:7 Rah 8:26:30	XII 19:30:23 Jup 16:35:28	Mon 19:59:38 XI 22:35:38

Fig. 4.13 Contd......

Nirayana Cusps

Bhav No.	Sign	Degree	Star Lord	Sub Lord	Sub-Sub Lord
1	Scorpio	13: 07' 07"	Sat	Rah	Rah
2	Sagittarius	13: 37' 46"	Ven	Ven	Ven
3	Capricorn	16: 56' 39"	Mon	Sat	Mon
4	Aquarius	21: 10' 02"	Jup	Jup	Ven
5	Pisces	22: 35' 38"	Mer	Mon	Jup
6	Aries	19: 30' 23"	Ven	Rah	Ven
7	Taurus	13: 07' 07"	Mon	Rah	Ket
8	Gemini	13: 37' 46"	Rah	Mer	Rah
9	Cancer	16: 56' 39"	Mer	Mer	Ket
10	Leo	21: 10' 02"	Ven	Jup	Ven
11	Virgo	22: 35' 38"	Mon	Ven	Ket
12	Libra	19: 30' 23"	Rah	Mar	Sat

Planetary Position

Planet	Sign	Degree	Star Lord	Sub Lord	Sub-Sub Lord
Sun	Sagittarius	20: 36' 23"	Ven	Jup	Sat
Mon	Virgo	19: 59' 38"	Mon	Ket	Rah
Mar	Sagittarius	18: 19' 55"	Ven	Rah	Rah
Mer	Sagittarius	21: 16' 38"	Ven	Jup	Ven
Jup	Libra	16: 35' 28"	Rah	Ven	Jup
Ven	Sagittarius	17: 42' 52"	Ven	Mar	Sat
Sat	Aquarius	03: 37' 34"	Mar	Ven	Rah
Rah (R)	Scorpio	08: 26' 30"	Sat	Ven	Ven
Ket (R)	Taurus	08: 26' 30"	Sun	Ven	Mon
Ura	Sagittarius	28: 03' 08"	Sun	Mon	Mer
Nep	Sagittarius	26: 51' 00"	Sun	Sun	Rah
Plu	Scorpio	03: 25' 44"	Sat	Sat	Sat
Fortuna	Leo	12: 30' 22"	Ket	Mer	Rah

The 5th cusp of the native's chart is ruled by Mars-Mer-Ve-Ma. The ascendant of the girl is Mars-Sat-Ra-Ra. Here Mars and Ra that represents Mercury (figure 4.12) have directly appeared and Sat is in the star of Mars in the native's chart. Hence the 5th cusp of the native's chart accounts for the ascendant of the daughter.

Joining First Service: The native joined his first service in August 1985 when he was running Sun dasa, Saturn Bhukti. Now Sun Antara is up to 11.8.1985 and then Moon Antara starts. Since Moon is strongly linked with 2, 6, 10, through its star lord, it is expected that the native should have joined after 11.8.1985.

Leaving the First Job: The native left the job on 31.1.1987 in the joint period of Sun-Ket-Jup-Sat. A person leaves the job in the joint period of planets linked with 1, 5 and 9. Here the Antara lord Jupiter is strongly linked with 1, 5 and 9. Ketu the Sookshma lord is linked with 5 being in Venus star and Mars sub. Ketu represents Jupiter and as such it has to give the result of Jupiter also. Saturn Prana lord is linked with 5 and 9 being in Mars star and its own sub.

Joining Second Job: The native joined the 2nd job on 18.2.1987 in the joint period of Sun-Ket-Sat-Ven-Rahu. A person joins the job in the joint period of planets linked with 2, 6 and 10. The Antara lord Saturn and Sookshma lord Venus being in Mars star that appears as the sub-sub lord of the 5th cusp should not allow the native to join the job. It only is justified because Mars is resident of the 6th cusp and Saturn is the sub-sub lord of the 2nd cusp.

Joining of Third Job: The native joined DOT on 20.2.1989 in the joint period of Mo-Mars-Ra-Ven-Sun. This joining was almost as a promotion. The Antara lord Ra being in its own star and Sun sub is linked with 11th and 2nd cusp. Venus is in Mars star, Ketu sub and Rahu sub-sub. Venus is thus linked with 5, 6, 2, 10 and 11. Sun being in its own star, Mars sub and Venus sub-sub is also linked with 2, 5, 6 and 10 cusps. This justifies leaving the earlier job and joining the new job.

First Promotion: The native got his first promotion in DOT on 1.1.1993 in the joint period of Mo-Sat-Ket-Jup-Ra. The planets are strongly linked with houses 2, 6, 10, and 11 cusps.

Second Promotion: The native was again promoted on 16.12.1997 in the joint period of Mo-Sun-Sat-Sat-Ra. All these planets are strongly linked with 2, 6, 10 and 11 cusps.

Suspension: The native was placed under suspension on 23.9.2003 when he was running the joint period of the planets Mars-Ven-Jup-Sat. The Antara lord Jupiter is, as we have seen earlier, linked with 3, 5, 8 and 9 cusps. Saturn is in the star of Mars and as such is strongly linked with the 5th cusp. It is in the sub of Saturn itself and Saturn appears as the star lord of the 9th cusp. Thus Saturn is linked with the 9th cusp also. The linkage of Saturn with 2 and 6 ensures that the native during suspension do get part of the salary. Saturn has given the result of the 5th and 9th cusps in consonance with the Antara lord Jupiter. The transit of planets on 23.9.2003 is indicated in Figure 4.14. The native received the orders at 16.08 hrs.

Fig. 4.14

Name	Fig 4.14	Place of Birth	Jabalpur
Sex	Male	Latitude	023.12.N
Date of Birth	23/09/2003	Longitude	079.54.E
Day of Birth	Tuesday	Local Birth Time	15:57:36
Time of Birth	16:08:00	Local Birth Date	23/09/2003
Sidereal Time	16:5:3	Lunar Tithi	13
Bal. of Dasha	Ket 6Y 7M 20D	K.P. (New) Ayanamsa	23:53:50
Lagan	Capricorn	Lagan Lord	Saturn
Sign	Leo	Sign Lord	Sun
Nakshatra	Magha	Nakshatra Lord	Ketu

Fig. 4.14 Contd......

Nirayana Cusps

Bhav No.	Sign	Degree	Star Lord	Sub Lord	Sub-Sub Lord
1	Capricorn	28: 58' 46"	Mar	Sat	Ven
2	Pisces	07: 40' 26"	Sat	Ket	Rah
3	Aries	11: 35' 53"	Ket	Mer	Mer
4	Taurus	09: 23' 52"	Sun	Ven	Sat
5	Gemini	04: 00' 44"	Mar	Ven	Jup
6	Gemini	29: 06' 38"	Jup	Sun	Sat
7	Cancer	28: 58' 46"	Mer	Sat	Ven
8	Virgo	07: 40' 26"	Sun	Ket	Mer
9	Libra	11: 35' 53"	Rah	Sat	Sun
10	Scorpio	09: 23' 52"	Sat	Ven	Jup
11	Sagittarius	04: 00' 44"	Ket	Mon	Jup
12	Sagittarius	29: 06' 38"	Sun	Mar	Ven

Planetary Position

Planet	Sign	Degree	Star Lord	Sub Lord	Sub-Sub Lord
Sun	Virgo	06: 06' 19"	Sun	Mer	Mar
Mon	Leo	00: 41' 42"	Ket	Ket	Mer
Mar (R)	Aquarius	06: 19' 36"	Mar	Mon	Mer
Mer	Leo	19: 04' 35"	Ven	Rah	Mer
Jup	Leo	11: 54' 19"	Ket	Mer	Ven
Ven	Virgo	15: 47' 08"	Mon	Sat	Sat
Sat	Gemini	18: 23' 10"	Rah	Mon	Rah
Rah (R)	Aries	27: 54' 35"	Sun	Mon	Sat
Ket (R)	Libra	27: 54' 35"	Jup	Ven	Jup
Ura (R)	Aquarius	05: 49' 03"	Mar	Mon	Rah
Nep (R)	Capricorn	16: 44' 17"	Mon	Sat	Ven
Plu	Scorpio	23: 30' 54"	Mer	Mar	Jup
Fortuna	Sagittarius	23: 34' 09"	Ven	Sat	Rah

The ascendant at the time of receipt of orders is ruled by Sat, Mars, and Venus. All these planets are the joint rulers of dasa periods. Moon at that time was transiting in Ketu star, Ketu sub, Mercury sub-sub, Ven sub-sub-sub and Moon sub-sub-sub-sub. All these planets rule over 3, 5, 8, 10 houses. Sun at that time is in the sub of Mer and sub-sub of Mars. Mercury is the star lord of 5th cusp and Mars is the sub-sub lord of the 5th cusp. Saturn transits in the sub of Moon and the sub-sub of Rahu. Both Moon and Rahu appear in the 8th cusp. Moon also appears in 3 and 12. Jupiter transits in Mercury sub and Venus sub-sub. Thus all the dasa period rulers' transit is related to relevant cusps.

We may conclude that the horoscope of Figure 4.12 may be taken as the correct horoscope.

Example 4: Figure 4.15 is the chart of a gentleman and Figure 4.16 is the chart of his wife as per their recorded times. The couple married on 6.6.1976 but got separated on 25.1.1977. This separation ultimately resulted in divorce on 22.7.1979.

Fig. 4.15

Name	Fig 4.15	Place of Birth	General 1
Sex	Male	Latitude	018.55.N
Date of Birth	27/04/1947	Longitude	072.54.E
Day of Birth	Sunday	Local Birth Time	06:35:36
Time of Birth	07:14:00	Local Birth Date	27/04/1947
Sidereal Time	20:52:25	Lunar Tithi	7
Bal. of Dasha	Jup 2Y 1M 13D	K.P. (New) Ayanamsa	23:06:36
Lagan	Aries	Lagan Lord	Mars
Sign	Cancer	Sign Lord	Moon
Nakshatra	Punarvasu	Nakshatra Lord	Jupiter

Lagna Chart

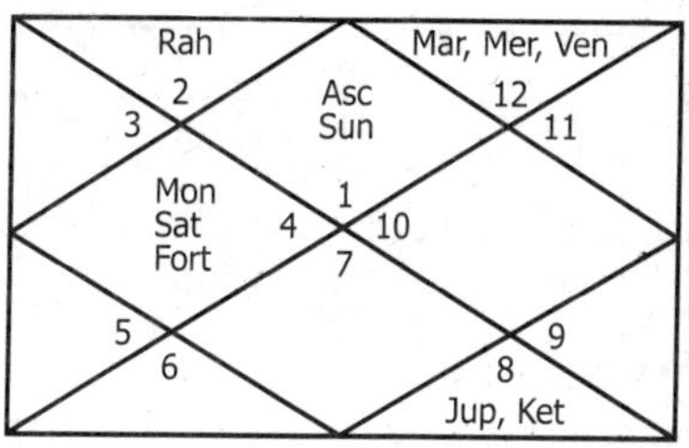

Bhava Chart

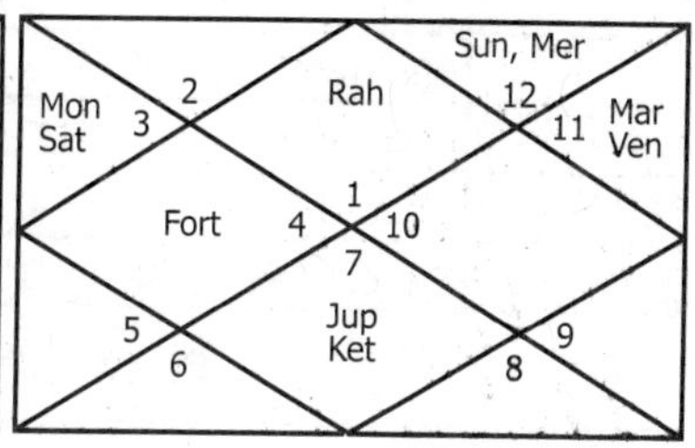

Cusp Chart

Mer 23:50:27 XII 22:39:15 Mar 18:35:40 Ven 9:14:0	Sun 12:52:20 I 28:51:54	Rah 9:41:52 II 26:27:34	III 21:28:8
XI 17:39:4			Mon 1:33:57 Sat 9:20:0 IV 17:32:33 Fort 17:33:31
X 17:32:33			V 17:39:4
IX 21:28:8	VIII 26:27:34 Ket 9:41:52 Jup 1:42:36	VII 28:51:54	VI 22:39:15

Fig. 4.15 Contd......

Nirayana Cusps

Bhav No.	Sign	Degree	Star Lord	Sub Lord	Sub-Sub Lord
1	Aries	28: 51' 54"	Sun	Mar	Mer
2	Taurus	26: 27' 34"	Mar	Jup	Sat
3	Gemini	21: 28' 08"	Jup	Jup	Mar
4	Cancer	17: 32' 33"	Mer	Mer	Mon
5	Leo	17: 39' 04"	Ven	Mar	Sat
6	Virgo	22: 39' 15"	Mon	Ven	Ket
7	Libra	28: 51' 54"	Jup	Sun	Mon
8	Scorpio	26: 27' 34"	Mer	Jup	Sat
9	Sagittarius	21: 28' 08"	Ven	Jup	Mon
10	Capricorn	17: 32' 33"	Mon	Sat	Jup
11	Aquarius	17: 39' 04"	Rah	Sun	Rah
12	Pisces	22: 39' 15"	Mer	Mon	Jup

Planetary Position

Planet	Sign	Degree	Star Lord	Sub Lord	Sub-Sub Lord
Sun	Aries	12: 52' 20"	Ket	Mer	Jup
Mon	Cancer	01: 33' 57"	Jup	Rah	Rah
Mar	Pisces	18: 35' 40"	Mer	Ket	Ket
Mer	Pisces	23: 50' 27"	Mer	Mar	Ket
Jup (R)	Scorpio	01: 42' 36"	Jup	Rah	Jup
Ven	Pisces	09: 14' 00"	Sat	Ven	Rah
Sat	Cancer	09: 20' 00"	Sat	Ven	Jup
Rah (R)	Taurus	09: 41' 52"	Sun	Ven	Mer
Ket (R)	Scorpio	09: 41' 52"	Sat	Ven	Sat
Ura	Taurus	26: 11' 20"	Mar	Jup	Jup
Nep (R)	Virgo	15: 37' 17"	Mon	Jup	Rah
Plu	Cancer	17: 52' 41"	Mer	Mer	Rah
Fortuna	Cancer	17: 33' 31"	Mer	Mer	Mon

Let us analyse charts to see if the chart promise marriage between these and also separation and divorce.

Analysis of Figure 4.15

Step 1: Check the sub-sub lord of the ascendant's relationship with Moon's star. Here the sub-sub lord is Mercury that does not establish any relationship with Moon's star Jupiter.

Step 2: Promise for Marriage - The sub-sub lord of ascendant is Mercury. It is in its own star that does not appear in 5 or 7 or 11. Thus we find ascendant does not promise marriage. The sub-sub lord of the 7th cusp is Moon that has the positional status. It is in Jupiter star that appears as the star lord of the 7th cusp. But Moon is in the sub of Rahu that represents Venus. Venus appears in 5 as well as 6. We may say that the promise of marriage indicated by the sub sub lord of 7 is very weak.

Step 3: Promise for Divorce - Divorce means the ending of a marriage by an official decision in a court of law. In other words it means breaking away from the marriage partner.

Divorce is promised if the following conditions exist in the chart:

The sub- sub lords of the ascendant and 7th cusp should be linked with cusps 4, 6, 10 and 12 through their star lords and the sub lords. The sub-sub lords of the sub-sub lords of these cusps should not appear in cuspal positions which negate these cusps. The other possible linkage that the ascendant and the 7th cusp sub-sub lord can establish for promise of divorce is that their star lords appear in 7th cuspal position/ Bhava and sub lords should appear in 4, 6, 10 and 12.

If the ascendant sub-sub lord does not promise divorce but the 7th sub-sub lord promises, even then the event will not take place. If the ascendant promises but 7th cusp does not promise, even then the event will not take place.

These conditions for divorce are not seen through the sub-sub lords of the ascendant and the 7th cusp in this chart.

Step 4: Check of Compatibility

1. The sub-sub lord of the 7th cusp should reveal the Moon's star lord of the partner. Here the sub-sub lord of the 7th cusp is Moon that does not establish any relationship with Mercury that is the Moon's star in Figure 4.16.
2. The planets co-ruling the 7th cusp should maintain relationship with the planets co-ruling the ascendant of the partner.

7th cusp in Figure 4.15	Ascendant in Figure 4.16
Ven-Jup-Sun-Moon	Mer-Mars-Mer-Ven

If we analyse the planetary positions in Figure 4.15 we find the planet Mercury appearing prominently in the ascendant of Figure 4.16 bears no relationship with the planets appearing in the 7th cusp of the Figure 4.15.

Above all clearly indicates that the sub-sub lords of both ascendant and 7th cusp do not justify the events that have happened in the life of the native of the Figure 4.15.

Let us also check the accuracy of the horoscope as per dasa potential of the planets to cause marriage & separation etc.

The native got married on 6.6.1976 when he was running the period of Mer-Mo-Mer-Sun. Here the Bhukti lord meets all the requirements but the Antara lord Mercury cannot allow the marriage to take place.

This further confirms that the chart of Figure 4.15 needs rectification.

Fig. 4.16

Name	Fig 4.16	Place of Birth	General 2
Sex	Female	Latitude	022.18.N
Date of Birth	21/08/1951	Longitude	070.56.E
Day of Birth	Tuesday	Local Birth Time	00:58:44
Time of Birth	01:45:00	Local Birth Date	21/08/1951
Sidereal Time	22:52:7	Lunar Tithi	5
Bal. of Dasha	Mer 10Y 0M 23D	K.P. (New) Ayanamsa	23:10:13
Lagan	Gemini	Lagan Lord	Mercury
Sign	Pisces	Sign Lord	Jupiter
Nakshatra	Revati	Nakshatra Lord	Mercury

Lagna Chart

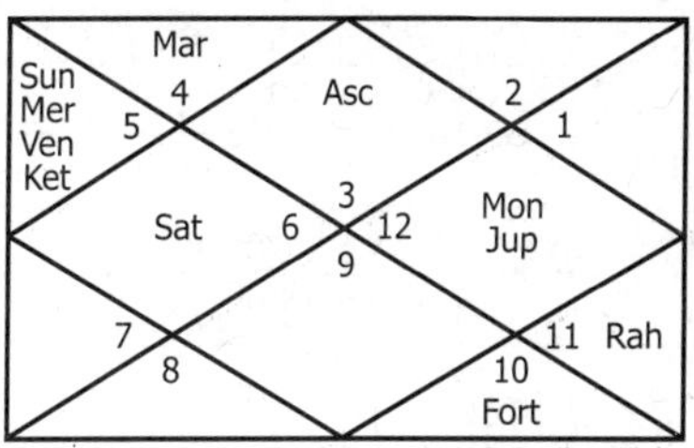

Bhava Chart

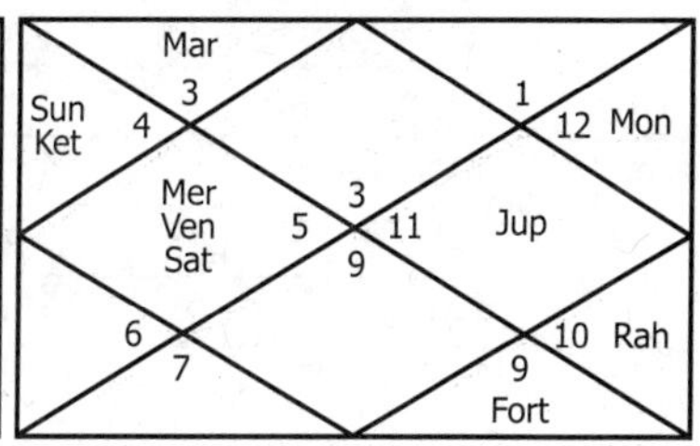

Cusp Chart

Mon 22:6:15 XI 21:51:28 Jup 20:33:23	XII 27:20:5		I 0:31:27 II 24:45:25
X 18:25:53 Rah 16:41:46			Mar 8:22:23 III 19:46:4
IX 19:46:4 Fort 18:48:22			Sun 3:49:20 Ket 16:41:46 IV 18:25:53 Mer 21:28:49 Ven 24:2:41
VIII 24:45:25 VII 0:31:27		VI 27:20:5	Sat 7:35:57 V 21:51:28

Fig. 4.16 Contd......

Nirayana Cusps

Bhav No.	Sign	Degree	Star Lord	Sub Lord	Sub-Sub Lord
1	Gemini	00: 31' 27"	Mar	Mer	Ven
2	Gemini	24: 45' 25"	Jup	Mer	Mon
3	Cancer	19: 46' 04"	Mer	Ven	Sun
4	Leo	18: 25' 53"	Ven	Rah	Jup
5	Virgo	21: 51' 28"	Mon	Ven	Jup
6	Libra	27: 20' 05"	Jup	Ven	Mar
7	Sagittarius	00: 31' 27"	Ket	Ket	Jup
8	Sagittarius	24: 45' 25"	Ven	Mer	Sun
9	Capricorn	19: 46' 04"	Mon	Ket	Ven
10	Aquarius	18: 25' 53"	Rah	Mon	Rah
11	Pisces	21: 51' 28"	Mer	Sun	Jup
12	Aries	27: 20' 05"	Sun	Mon	Mon

Planetary Position

Planet	Sign	Degree	Star Lord	Sub Lord	Sub-Sub Lord
Sun	Leo	03: 49' 20"	Ket	Mon	Mar
Mon	Pisces	22: 06' 15"	Mer	Sun	Ket
Mar	Cancer	08: 22' 33"	Sat	Ven	Ven
Mer (R)	Leo	21: 28' 49"	Ven	Jup	Mon
Jup (R)	Pisces	20: 33' 23"	Mer	Ven	Jup
Ven (R)	Leo	24: 02' 41"	Ven	Mer	Mer
Sat	Virgo	07: 35' 57"	Sun	Ket	Sat
Rah (R)	Aquarius	16: 41' 46"	Rah	Ven	Sat
Ket (R)	Leo	16: 41' 46"	Ven	Mon	Sat
Ura	Gemini	19: 16' 49"	Rah	Mar	Rah
Nep	Virgo	24: 18' 41"	Mar	Rah	Rah
Plu	Cancer	26: 33' 52"	Mer	Jup	Sat
Fortuna	Capricorn	18: 48' 22"	Mon	Mer	Mar

Analysis of Figure 4.16

Step 1: The sub-sub lord of the ascendant is Venus that is in the sub of Mercury that is the native's Moon star. Moreover Mercury itself is in Venus star.

Step 2: The sub-sub lord of ascendant is Venus that is in its own star. Venus appears as sub lord of 5. Venus is in the sub of Mercury that appears as star lord of 11. Thus we find that the ascendant sub sub lord is not linked to the 7th cusp directly or indirectly. The sub-sub lord of the 7th cusp is Jupiter that is in Mercury star and Ven sub. Mercury is the star lord of the 11th cusp and Venus is the sub lord of 5. Thus we feel that the horoscope needs rectification.

Step 3: Promise of Divorce: The sub-sub lord of the ascendant Venus being in its own star and is linked with 6th cusp. The sub-sub lord of the 7th cusp is Jupiter that is in Mercury star and Venus sub. Jupiter has the positional status and is the star lord of the 6th cusp. These conditions do hint at problems in marital life but they do not necessarily cause for divorce. Since the chart does not promise marriage we need not analyse the chart for divorce.

Step 4: Check of compatibility:

A. The sub-sub lord of the 7th cusp is Jupiter and the Moon star of Figure 4.15 is Jupiter.

B. The planets co-ruling the 7th cusp of Figure 4.16 are Jup-Ketu only. The planets co-ruling the ascendant of Figure 4.15 are Mars-Sun-Mars-Mer. In Figure 4.16, Ketu represents Sun, and Mercury is in the sub of Jupiter. However the planet Mars has no relationship with Jupiter and Ketu.

Let us check the accuracy of the horoscope from dasa potential of the planets. The native's marriage on 6.6.1976 took place in the period of Ven-Ra-Jup-Sat. The Bhukti lord Rahu does not meet the necessary conditions to cause marriage. But since Rahu represents Saturn and can cause marriage because it is in Sun star that is the sub lord of the 11th cusp. Saturn is in the sub of Ketu that appears as the sub lord of the 7th cusp.

The above discussion reveals that this horoscope i.e. of Figure 4.16 also needs rectification.

Rectified horoscopes for both are shown in Figure 4.17 and Figure 4.18 respectively.

Fig. 4.17

Name	Fig 4.17	Place of Birth	General 1
Sex	Male	Latitude	018.55.N
Date of Birth	27/04/1947	Longitude	072.54.E
Day of Birth	Sunday	Local Birth Time	06:34:46
Time of Birth	07:13:10	Local Birth Date	27/04/1947
Sidereal Time	20:51:35	Lunar Tithi	7
Bal. of Dasha	Jup 2Y 1M 17D	K.P. (New) Ayanamsa	23:06:36
Lagan	Aries	Lagan Lord	Mars
Sign	Cancer	Sign Lord	Moon
Nakshatra	Punarvasu	Nakshatra Lord	Jupiter

Lagna Chart

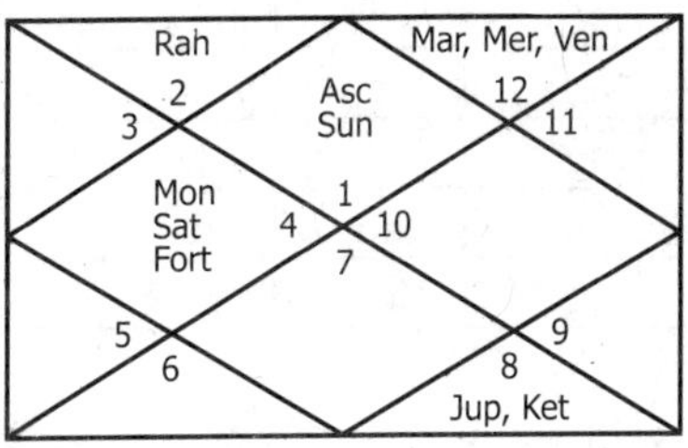

Bhava Chart

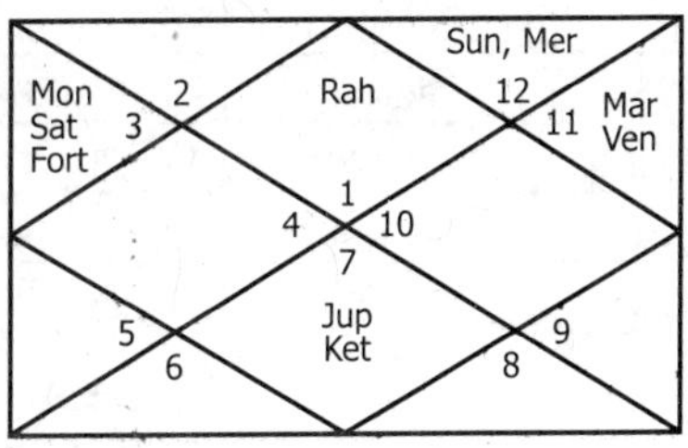

Cusp Chart

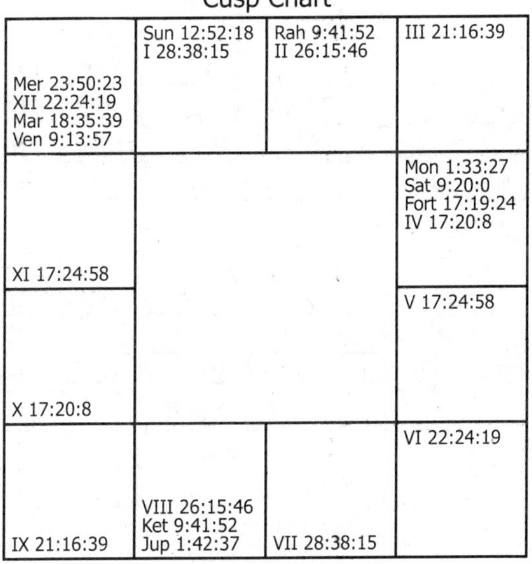

Fig. 4.17 Contd......

Nirayana Cusps

Bhav No.	Sign	Degree	Star Lord	Sub Lord	Sub-Sub Lord
1	Aries	28: 38' 15"	Sun	Mar	Jup
2	Taurus	26: 15' 46"	Mar	Jup	Jup
3	Gemini	21: 16' 39"	Jup	Jup	Mon
4	Cancer	17: 20' 08"	Mer	Mer	Ven
5	Leo	17: 24' 58"	Ven	Mar	Rah
6	Virgo	22: 24' 19"	Mon	Ven	Mer
7	Libra	28: 38' 15"	Jup	Ven	Mer
8	Scorpio	26: 15' 46"	Mer	Jup	Jup
9	Sagittarius	21: 16' 39"	Ven	Jup	Ven
10	Capricorn	17: 20' 08"	Mon	Sat	Rah
11	Aquarius	17: 24' 58"	Rah	Ven	Ket
12	Pisces	22: 24' 19"	Mer	Mon	Rah

Planetary Position

Planet	Sign	Degree	Star Lord	Sub Lord	Sub-Sub Lord
Sun	Aries	12: 52' 18"	Ket	Mer	Jup
Mon	Cancer	01: 33' 27"	Jup	Rah	Rah
Mar	Pisces	18: 35' 39"	Mer	Ket	Ket
Mer	Pisces	23: 50' 23"	Mer	Mar	Ket
Jup (R)	Scorpio	01: 42' 37"	Jup	Rah	Jup
Ven	Pisces	09: 13' 57"	Sat	Ven	Rah
Sat	Cancer	09: 20' 00"	Sat	Ven	Jup
Rah (R)	Taurus	09: 41' 52"	Sun	Ven	Mer
Ket (R)	Scorpio	09: 41' 52"	Sat	Ven	Sat
Ura	Taurus	26: 11' 20"	Mar	Jup	Jup
Nep (R)	Virgo	15: 37' 17"	Mon	Jup	Rah
Plu	Cancer	17: 52' 41"	Mer	Mer	Rah
Fortuna	Cancer	17: 19' 24"	Mer	Mer	Ven

Verification of Correctness of Figure 4.17

Step 1: The sub-sub lord of the ascendant is Jupiter that is also the Moon's star lord.

Step 2: Promise of Marriage - Jup, the sub-sub lord of the ascendant is in its own star that is the star lord of the 7th cusp. Jupiter is in the sub of Rahu that appears as the sub sub lord of the 5th cusp and star lord of 11th cusp. The sub-sub lord of the 7th cusp is Mercury that is in its own star. Mercury is in the sub of Mars that appears in 5 and 11. Thus marriage is promised.

Step 3: Promise for Divorce - The sub-sub lord of the ascendant is Jupiter that is in its own star and Rahu sub. Rahu also represents Venus. Rahu is the sub-sub lord of the 12th cusp and Venus is the sub lord of the 6th cusp. Thus ascendant also promises divorce along with the promise of marriage.

Mercury, the sub-sub lord of the 7th cusp is in its own star. Mercury appears as the sub-sub lord of the 6th cusp and star lord of the 12th cusp. All this proves that the ascendant and 7th cusp sub-sub lords promise marriage as well as divorce.

Step 4: Check of compatibility:

A. The sub-sub lord of the 7th cusp is Mercury that is the Moon's star lord of Figure 4.18.

B. The planets co-ruling the 7th cusp of Figure 4.17 are Ven, Jup and Mercury. Here we find that Venus and Mercury have direct appearance and Mars being in Mercury star in Figure 4.17 is quite appropriate for its appearance in the ascendant of Figure 4.18.

There is, thus, complete compatibility between the two horoscopes.

Let us verify the accuracy of the chart for dasa potential of the planets to causes events.

Marriage: The native's marriage on 6.6.1976 took place in the joint period of planets Mer-Mo-Mer-Ven. The Bhukti lord Moon is in Jupiter star and Rahu sub. Jupiter is the star lord of 7th cusp and Rahu is the sub-sub lord of the 5th cusp and star lord of 11th cusp.

Mercury, the Antara lord is in its own star that is the sub-sub lord of the 7th cusp. Mercury is in the sub of Mars that is the sub lord of the 5th cusp and is placed in the 11th cusp.

Venus, the Sookshma lord has the positional status and is the sub lord of the 7th and the 11th cusp. Venus is in Saturn star that appears in 11. Venus is in Venus sub that appears in 7 and 11. Thus the dasa potential of planets also justifies the event.

Separation between the couple: The native separated from his partner on 25.1.1977 when he was running the period of Mer-Mars-Rahu and Sat.

I have serious doubts about the contention of the astrologers who say that the event of divorce happens in the joint period of planets that are significators of houses 1, 6, 10 and 12. We should remember that the event of divorce means breaking away from the partner i.e. the partner has to be involved in the activity of separation. Thus, I feel while the dasa, Bhukti and Antara lords may be significators of 4, 6, 10 and 12 (I do not take the second house for matters of marriage), the Sookshma and Prana lords, which will ensure the completion of the activity of breaking away from the partner, must involve the seventh cusp in enacting the event of divorce. This

involvement can take place if the Sookshma lord is one of the planets appearing in the 7th cuspal position (preferably the sub-sub lord of the 7th cusp) or any planet that involves the 7th cusp through its star lord and commits to 6 and 12 through sub lord.

The separation takes place when the planets are linked with 1, 6 and 10. Here the dasa lord Mercury is in its own star and appears in 4, 6, 7, 8 and 12 cusps. Mars the Bhukti lord has the positional status and appears in 1, 2 and 5. Mars is in Mercury star and as such is linked to 4, 6, 7, 8 and 12. The Antara lord Rahu has the positional status. It appears in 1, 5, 10, 11 and 12. Rahu is in Sun star that appears in 12 (resident position). The Sookshma lord is Saturn that is in its own star and appears in the 10th cusp as the sub lord. Ket that represents Saturn is placed in 7th Bhava. Thus we treat that Saturn is placed in 7. Saturn is in the sub of Venus that appears in 6. Thus Saturn involves the 7th cusp and commits to 6 causing separation from the partner. Thus the planets justify the event of separation.

Divorce: The native got divorce on 22.7.1979 when he was running Mer-Ra-Ket-Sat-Jupiter period. Divorce is permanent disconnection with the partner and happens in the joint period of planets linked with cusps 1, 6, 12 when transit agrees. We have already discussed above the linkages of Mer, Ra and Saturn. Now Ketu is in Saturn star and Venus sub. Saturn is the resident of the 3rd cusp and is the sub lord of the 10th cusp. Venus is the sub lord of the 6th cusp. Moreover, Ketu has to give the results of Mars and Saturn also that are linked with the relevant cusps 1, 6, 12. Jupiter the Prana lord is in its own star and Rahu sub. Thus it is linked with 1, 6 and 12 because Rahu represents Venus. The chart's accuracy stands verified.

Fig. 4.18

Name	Fig 4.18	Place of Birth	General2
Sex	Female	Latitude	022.18.N
Date of Birth	21/08/1951	Longitude	070.56.E
Day of Birth	Tuesday	Local Birth Time	00:58:26
Time of Birth	01:44:42	Local Birth Date	21/08/1951
Sidereal Time	22:51:49	Lunar Tithi	5
Bal. of Dasha	Mer 10Y 0M 25D	K.P. (New) Ayanamsa	23:10:13
Lagan	Gemini	Lagan Lord	Mercury
Sign	Pisces	Sign Lord	Jupiter
Nakshatra	Revati	Nakshatra Lord	Mercury

Lagna Chart

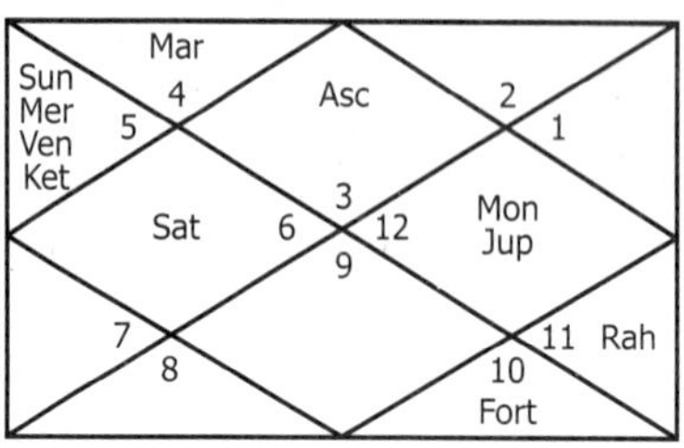

Bhava Chart

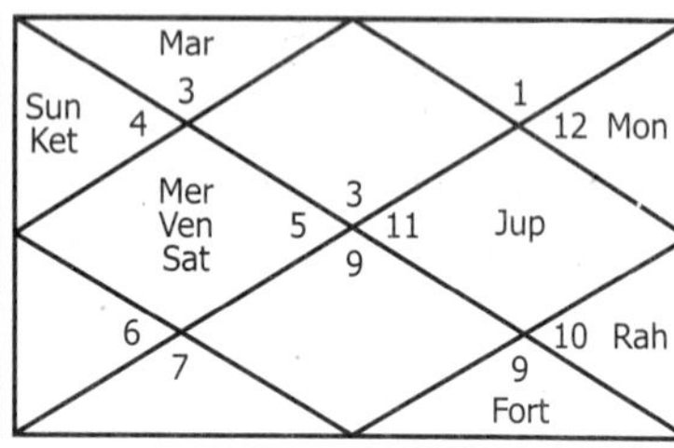

Cusp Chart

Mon 22:6:5 XI 21:46:19 Jup 20:33:23	XII 27:15:14		I 0:27:13 II 24:41:21
X 18:21:3 Rah 16:41:46			Mar 8:22:32 III 19:41:45
IX 19:41:45 Fort 18:43:59			Sun 3:49:19 Ket 16:41:46 IV 18:21:3 Mer 21:28:49 Ven 24:2:41
VIII 24:41:21 VII 0:27:13		VI 27:15:14	Sat 7:35:57 V 21:46:19

Fig. 4.18 Contd......

Nirayana Cusps

Bhav No.	Sign	Degree	Star Lord	Sub Lord	Sub-Sub Lord
1	Gemini	00: 27' 13"	Mar	Mer	Ven
2	Gemini	24: 41' 21"	Jup	Mer	Mon
3	Cancer	19: 41' 45"	Mer	Ven	Ven
4	Leo	18: 21' 03"	Ven	Rah	Rah
5	Virgo	21: 46' 19"	Mon	Ven	Jup
6	Libra	27: 15' 14"	Jup	Ven	Mar
7	Sagittarius	00: 27' 13"	Ket	Ket	Jup
8	Sagittarius	24: 41' 21"	Ven	Mer	Ven
9	Capricorn	19: 41' 45"	Mon	Ket	Ket
10	Aquarius	18: 21' 03"	Rah	Mon	Rah
11	Pisces	21: 46' 19"	Mer	Sun	Rah
12	Aries	27: 15' 14"	Sun	Sun	Ven

Planetary Position

Planet	Sign	Degree	Star Lord	Sub Lord	Sub-Sub Lord
Sun	Leo	03: 49' 19"	Ket	Mon	Mar
Mon	Pisces	22: 06' 05"	Mer	Sun	Ket
Mar	Cancer	08: 22' 32"	Sat	Ven	Ven
Mer (R)	Leo	21: 28' 49"	Ven	Jup	Mon
Jup (R)	Pisces	20: 33' 23"	Mer	Ven	Jup
Ven (R)	Leo	24: 02' 41"	Ven	Mer	Mer
Sat	Virgo	07: 35' 57"	Sun	Ket	Sat
Rah (R)	Aquarius	16: 41' 46"	Rah	Ven	Sat
Ket (R)	Leo	16: 41' 46"	Ven	Mon	Sat
Ura	Gemini	19: 16' 49"	Rah	Mar	Rah
Nep	Virgo	24: 18' 41"	Mar	Rah	Rah
Plu	Cancer	26: 33' 52"	Mer	Jup	Sat
Fortuna	Capricorn	18: 43' 59"	Mon	Mer	Mar

Verification of correctness of Figure 4.18

Step 1: Venus, the sub-sub lord of the ascendant is in Mercury sub that is the native's Moon star. Moreover Mercury Itself is in Venus star. Thus the sub-sub lord of the ascendant maintains relationship with the Moon's star lord.

Step 2: Venus, the sub-sub lord of the ascendant is in its own star; Venus appears as the sub lord of the 5th cusp. The sub-sub lord of the 7th cusp is Jupiter that has the positional status. It is in Mercury star and Venus sub. Mercury is the star lord of the 11th cusp. Thus marriage is promised.

Step 3: The sub-sub lord of the ascendant and the sub-sub lord of the 7th cusp also promise divorce. Venus is in Venus star. Venus appears as the sub lord of the 6th cusp and sub-sub lord of the 12th cusp. Jupiter, the sub-sub lord of the 7th cusp is in the sub of Venus.

Step 4: The sub-sub lord of the 7th cusp is Jupiter that is the Moon's star lord of Figure 4.17. The planets co-ruling the 7th cusp of Figure 4.18 are Jup and Ketu. The ascendant of Figure 4.17 is ruled by planets Mars, Sun and Jupiter. Now Sun is in Ketu star and Mars is in Venus sub that represents Ketu. Thus the horoscope shows compatibility with Figure 4.17.

Let us verify the accuracy of the chart from the dasa potential of planets.

Marriage: The native got married in the joint period of the planets Ven-Rahu-Jup-Sat-Jup. Rahu represents Saturn that is in Sun's star and Ketu sub. Thus Rahu gets the required qualifications to cause marriage. All other planets have the required linkages with the cusps 5, 7 and 11 to cause marriage event.

Separation: The native separated from her husband on 25.1.1977 in the joint period of the planets Ven-Rahu-Sat-Rahu-Rahu. Here also it can be seen that the planets ruling the dasa period are linked with 1, 6 and 12.

Divorce: The native got divorce on 22.7.1979 in the joint period of planets Venus-Jup-Sat-Rahu-Mercury, which are linked with 1, 6 and 12.

Both the horoscopes, thus, stand verified for accuracy. The charts can further be verified by taking transit of planets on the day of marriage etc.

Fig. 4.19

Name	Fig 4.19	Place of Birth	General3
Sex	Male	Latitude	022.00.N
Date of Birth	13/08/1918	Longitude	072.52.E
Day of Birth	Tuesday	Local Birth Time	08:16:28
Time of Birth	08:55:00	Local Birth Date	13/08/1918
Sidereal Time	5:39:27	Lunar Tithi	6
Bal. of Dasha	Rah 17Y 10M 5D	K.P. (New) Ayanamsa	22:42:34
Lagan	Virgo	Lagan Lord	Mercury
Sign	Libra	Sign Lord	Venus
Nakshatra	Swati	Nakshatra Lord	Rahu

Lagna Chart

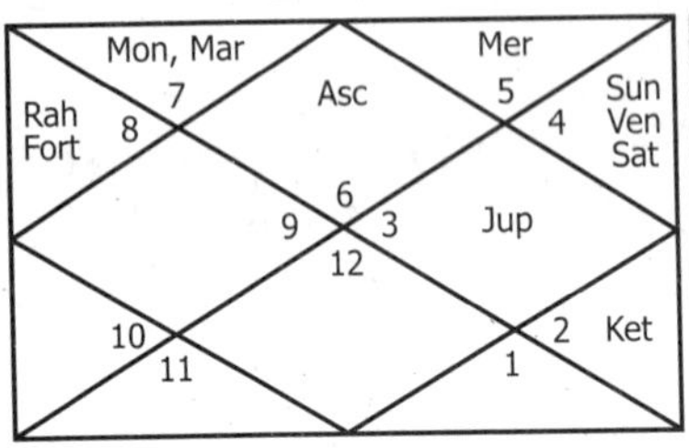

Bhava Chart

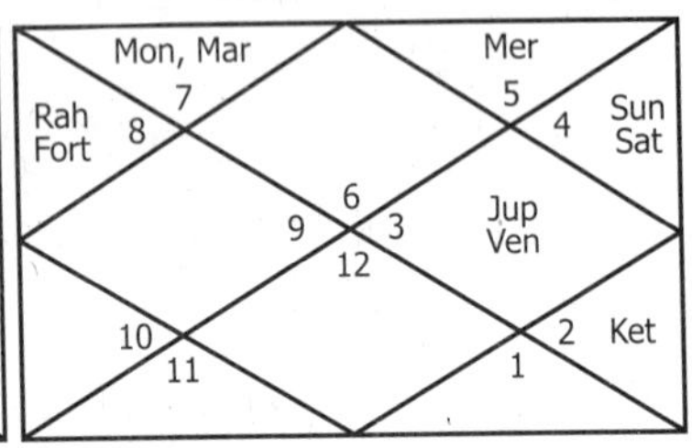

Cusp Chart

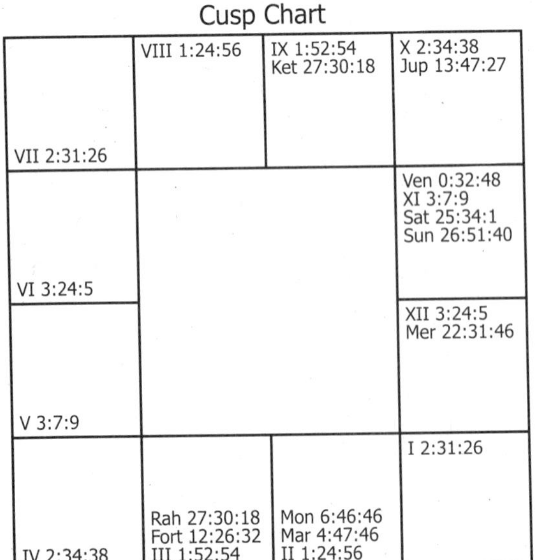

Fig. 4.19 Contd......

Nirayana Cusps

Bhav No.	Sign	Degree	Star Lord	Sub Lord	Sub-Sub Lord
1	Virgo	02: 31' 26"	Sun	Jup	Mon
2	Libra	01: 24' 56"	Mar	Mer	Jup
3	Scorpio	01: 52' 54"	Jup	Rah	Jup
4	Sagittarius	02: 34' 38"	Ket	Ven	Mer
5	Capricorn	03: 07' 09"	Sun	Sat	Sat
6	Aquarius	03: 24' 05"	Mar	Ven	Mar
7	Pisces	02: 31' 26"	Jup	Rah	Ket
8	Aries	01: 24' 56"	Ket	Ven	Mon
9	Taurus	01: 52' 54"	Sun	Jup	Mer
10	Gemini	02: 34' 38"	Mar	Ket	Mer
11	Cancer	03: 07' 09"	Jup	Rah	Mon
12	Leo	03: 24' 05"	Ket	Sun	Sat

Planetary Position

Planet	Sign	Degree	Star Lord	Sub Lord	Sub-Sub Lord
Sun	Cancer	26: 51' 40"	Mer	Jup	Mer
Mon	Libra	06: 46' 46"	Rah	Rah	Rah
Mar	Libra	04: 47' 46"	Mar	Ven	Ket
Mer	Leo	22: 31' 46"	Ven	Sat	Ket
Jup	Gemini	13: 47' 27"	Rah	Mer	Rah
Ven	Cancer	00: 32' 48"	Jup	Mon	Sun
Sat	Cancer	25: 34' 01"	Mer	Rah	Ven
Rah (R)	Scorpio	27: 30' 18"	Mer	Jup	Mon
Ket (R)	Taurus	27: 30' 18"	Mar	Jup	Mon
Ura (R)	Aquarius	03: 16' 27"	Mar	Ven	Mon
Nep	Cancer	14: 36' 49"	Sat	Rah	Mon
Plu	Gemini	13: 22' 30"	Rah	Mer	Mon
Fortuna	Scorpio	12: 26' 32"	Sat	Mar	Sat

Example 5:

Figure 4.19 is the chart of a gentleman as per his recorded birth data. The main events that happened in his life are listed below:

1. Purchased land on 4.10.1962 and constructed his house that he occupied in October 1963.
2. The right eye of the native was operated for cataract on 28.7.1979.
3. The native's father died on 6.8.1930.
4. The native's mother died on 30.1.1932
5. The native joined his first service as a teacher on 1.6.1940.
6. The native was appointed as a professor in a college on 11.11.1946
7. The native was promoted to the post of the principal of the college on 1.5.1964
8. The native retired from service on 1.9.1978
9. The native got married on 21.1.1942.
10. The native passed his B. Com on 28.5.1940 and M.Com in June 1946 and got his PhD in June 1959.
11. On 13.7.1948 he got a daughter and on 15.11.1950 he got son.

Let us analyse the chart to assess its accuracy for the promise of all events and also the daśa potential of planets that allowed the events to happen in his life.

Step 1: Since Moon is sub-sub lord of the ascendant, it maintains relationship with Moon's star lord. Planets co-ruling the positions of Sun, Moon and ascendant are linked with 1, 7 and 10.

Step 2: Promise of Marriage: The ascendant sub-sub lord Moon is in Rahu star that appears as the sub lord of the 7th as well as 11th cusp. The sub-sub lord of the 7th cusp is Ketu. It is in Mars star that does not appear in 5 or 7 or 11. However, Ketu represents Venus that is in Jupiter star that appears as the star lord of both 7th and 11th cusp. Thus we may say that marriage is promised.

Step 3: Promise of Children: The sub-sub lord of the 5th cusp is Saturn. It is in Mercury star and Rahu sub. Since Mercury is the sub lord of the 2nd cusp and Rahu is the sub lord of the 11th cusp. It promises children. However since Mercury is also the sub-sub lord of the 4th and the 10th cusp it indicates delay. Since Saturn is in the sub-sub of Venus that occupies Cancer sign, it promises female child.

Step 4: Educational Prospects: The native specialized in the subject of commerce. For this the 2nd and 11th cusp should maintain relationship with 4th and 9th cusp. The sub-sub lord of the 2nd cusp is Jupiter. It is in Rahu star and Mercury sub. Thus the 2nd cusp establishes relationship with the 4th cusp through the 11th cusp i.e. the house for fulfillment of desires. Mercury is also the sub-sub lord of the 9th cusp. Thus the 2nd cusp also maintains relationship with the 9th cusp. The sub-sub lord of the 11th cusp is Moon that is in Rahu star. Since Rahu represents Mercury as its star lord, Moon is linked with both 4th and 9th cusp. Thus the choice of commerce as the subject of education is justified.

Step 5: Professional Activities - Since the native served in an educational institution, the sub-sub lord of the 10th cusp should establish relationship with 4th or the 9th cusp either directly through its star lord or the star lord may appear in 11th cusp and sub lord in the 4th or 9th cusp or the sub-sub lord of the 10th cusp should itself appear in 4th or 9th cusp. Here Mercury is the sub-sub lord of the 10th cusp that is in Venus star that appears as the sub lord of the 4th cusp. This justifies the native's working in an educational institution. For teaching the native has to use his oratorical skill, communication skill and intellectual capability. For this the 2nd, 3rd and the 5th cusp should establish relationship with the 10th cusp. The 2nd sub-sub lord Jupiter is in Rahu star and Mercury sub. Rahu is sub lord of 11th cusp (house of fulfillment of desire) and the Mercury is the sub-sub lord of the 10th cusp. Thus the second cusp stands linked with the 10th cusp. The sub-sub lord of the 3rd cusp is also Jupiter and as explained above Jupiter is linked with the 10th cusp. The sub-sub lord of the 5th cusp is Saturn that is in Mercury star and as such 5th cusp is also linked with the 10th cusp. Thus the horoscope appears to justify his professional activities.

Step 6: Cataract In Right Eye - The native developed cataract in the right eye, which was operated. Defect in the right eye occurs if the sub-sub lord of the 2nd cusp or Sun or Venus maintains relationship with 8th and 12th cusp. The sub-sub lord of the 2nd cusp is Jupiter that is in Rahu star. Rahu represents Mars that is only the Sign lord of the 8th cusp. Jupiter is in the sub of Mercury that neither appears in 8th nor in the 12th cusp. The planet Sun maintains relationship with the 12th cusp. Venus, however, is the sub lord of the 8th cusp and its star lord Jupiter appears in 2nd cusp. It is in the sub of Moon that is the sub-sub lord of the 8th cusp. This justifies the appearance of cataract in the right eye.

Step 7: Genetical Connection - The native got his first daughter on 13.7.1948. On this date Moon's star lord was Moon up to 09hrs.10 minutes 28 seconds and then it was Mars star lord. The sub-sub lord of the 5th cusp is Saturn. It is in Rahu sub. Rahu represents Mars. So if the child is born after 09hrs.10

minutes 28 seconds this establishes the genetical connection with the 5th cusp sub-sub lord of the native. But if the child is born in Moon star then Moon does not maintain any relationship with Saturn the sub-sub lord of the 5th cusp.

The native got his 2nd child, a Son, on 15.11.1950. On this date the Moon was in Sun star up to 08hrs.11minutes 13 seconds and then it was Moon's star day. The sub-sub lord of the 7th cusp is Ketu. It is in the sub-sub of Moon. Ketu represents Venus that is in the sub of Moon and sub-sub of Sun. It appears that the Moon's star of the son should be Moon.

Thus the horoscope accurately reveals the genetical connections also. Now let us try to analyse the accuracy of the horoscope for the dasa potential of the planets for causing various events in the life of the native.

A. **Marriage:** The native got married on 21.1.1942 when he was running the period of Jup-Mer-Sun-Ketu-Sat. The dasa lord Jupiter is the star lord of 7th and 11th cusp. It is in Rahu star that is the sub lord of the 11th and 7th cusps. It is in the sub of Mercury that does not appear in the 6th cusp. Thus the dasa lord is favourable for the event of marriage. The Bhukti lord is Mercury. It does not appear in 5, 7 or 11 cusp. It is in the star of Venus that also does not appear in 5, 7 or 11 cusps. Rather it is appearing in 4, 6 and 10 cusps. This raises a serious doubt about the potential of Bhukti lord to cause the event of marriage. The horoscope thus needs to be rectified to allow Mercury to cause marriage.

B. **Birth of Daughter:** The native got daughter on 13.7.1948 when he was running the joint period of Jup-Mo-Sat-Ra-Mercury.All planets except Mercury are clearly linked with 2, 5 and 11 and justifies the event. Mercury is the sub lord of the 2nd cusp and is in the star of Venus and sub of Saturn.

Mercury does not have the positional status. Its linkage does not clearly justify the event.

C. Joining 1st Job: The native joined his first employment on 1.6.1940 when he was running the joint period of the planets Jup-Sat-Ra-Ra-Ra. The native joins service in the period of planets linked with 2, 6, and 10. The Bhukti lord Saturn is in Mercury star and Rahu sub. Mercury is the sub lord of the 2nd cusp and Rahu is the sub lord of the 11th cusp. Since Rahu represents Mars that is the star lord of 2, 6 and 10 cusps, the Bhukti lord strongly justifies the event. Rahu is in Mercury star, Jupiter sub and Moon sub-sub. Mercury is the sub sub lord of 10 and Jupiter is sub sub lord of 2. Rahu also has to give the result of Mars. Now Mars is in its own star and Venus sub. Thus Rahu completely justifies the event.

D. Cataract Operation: The right eye of the native was operated for cataract on 28.7.1979 when he was running the period of the planets Mercury-Moon-Mercury-Sat-Jupiter. The dasa and Antara lord Mercury is in Venus star that appears in 6th & 8th cusp. It is in the sub of Sat that is the sub-sub lord of the 12th. Thus Mercury has already set the stage for the deterioration of vision being the sub lord of the 2nd cusp. The Bhukti lord Moon is in Rahu star, Rahu sub and Rahu sub-sub. Rahu represents Mars and Mercury and has thus to give the same results as are given by Mercury. The planet Saturn, the Sookshma lord is the sub-sub lord of the 12th cusp, the house of hospitalization, has the positional status and thus has to offer the result of the 12th house. It is in Mercury star, Rahu sub and Venus sub-sub. This prepares the scene for hospitalization and promise recovery of vision being related to both 5th and 11th cusp. Jupiter the Prana lord however cannot account for surgery because it maintains no relationship with the 8th and the 12th houses. This also indicates that the horoscope needs rectification.

Rectification of horoscope can be attempted as follows:

To enable the planet Mercury to acquire the necessary qualifications to cause marriage, the sub-sub lord of the 7th cusp need to be changed by moving around the noted birth time in seconds.

Can we put Mercury as the sub-sub lord of the 7th cusp?

No, because Mercury does not have the positional status and as such can't itself provide results of the 7th cusp. Mercury is in Venus star that does not appear in 5, 7 or 11 but appears in 4, 6 and 8 which are not the relevant house to enact the event of marriage. The only alternative left with us is to fix the sub-sub lord of the 7th cusp as Venus that is in Jupiter star that appears as the star lord of the 7th and 11th cusp. Venus is in the sub of Moon and sub-sub of Sun that provides the necessary condition to account for the genetical connection with the 2nd child.

The True Horoscope and Its Verification: Figure 4.20 is the rectified chart.

Fig. 4.20

Name	Fig 4.20	Place of Birth	General3
Sex	Male	Latitude	022.00.N
Date of Birth	13/08/1918	Longitude	072.52.E
Day of Birth	Tuesday	Local Birth Time	08:16:52
Time of Birth	08:55:24	Local Birth Date	13/08/1918
Sidereal Time	5:39:51	Lunar Tithi	6
Bal. of Dasha	Rah 17Y 10M 4D	K.P. (New) Ayanamsa	22:42:34
Lagan	Virgo	Lagan Lord	Mercury
Sign	Libra	Sign Lord	Venus
Nakshatra	Swati	Nakshatra Lord	Rahu

Lagna Chart

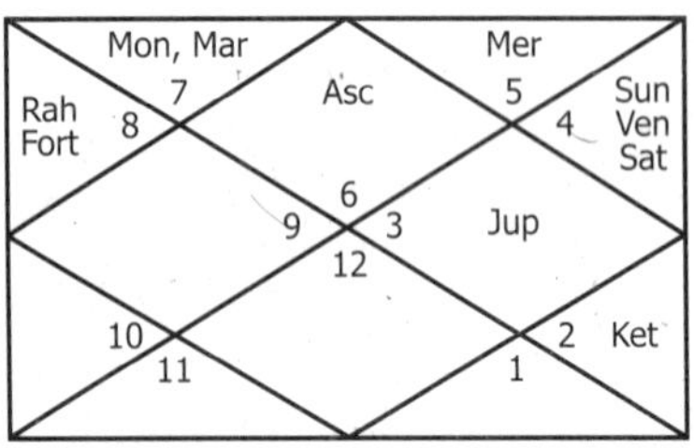

Bhava Chart

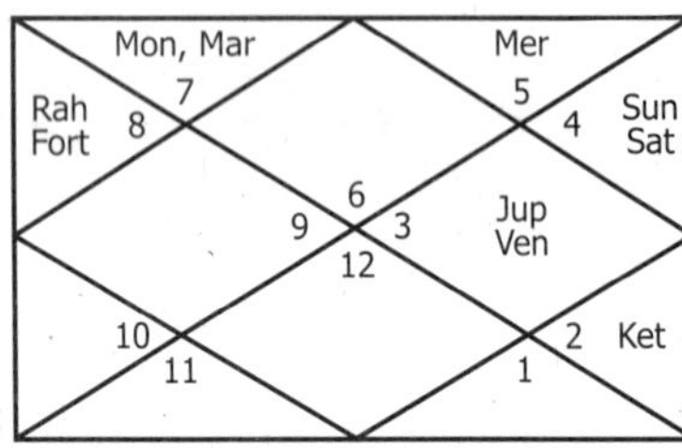

Cusp Chart

VII 2:37:1	VIII 1:30:42	IX 1:58:34 Ket 27:30:18	X 2:40:9 Jup 13:47:27
VI 3:29:46			Ven 0:32:49 XI 3:12:43 Sat 25:34:1 Sun 26:51:41
V 3:12:43			XII 3:29:46 Mer 22:31:46
IV 2:40:9	Rah 27:30:18 Fort 12:32:18 III 1:58:34	Mon 6:46:58 Mar 4:47:46 II 1:30:42	I 2:37:1

Fig. 4.20 Contd......

Nirayana Cusps

Bhav No.	Sign	Degree	Star Lord	Sub Lord	Sub-Sub Lord
1	Virgo	02: 37' 01"	Sun	Jup	Mon
2	Libra	01: 30' 42"	Mar	Mer	Jup
3	Scorpio	01: 58' 34"	Jup	Rah	Sat
4	Sagittarius	02: 40' 09"	Ket	Ven	Mer
5	Capricorn	03: 12' 43"	Sun	Sat	Sat
6	Aquarius	03: 29' 46"	Mar	Ven	Rah
7	Pisces	02: 37' 01"	Jup	Rah	Ven
8	Aries	01: 30' 42"	Ket	Ven	Mar
9	Taurus	01: 58' 34"	Sun	Jup	Mer
10	Gemini	02: 40' 09"	Mar	Ven	Ven
11	Cancer	03: 12' 43"	Jup	Rah	Mon
12	Leo	03: 29' 46"	Ket	Sun	Mer

Planetary Position

Planet	Sign	Degree	Star Lord	Sub Lord	Sub-Sub Lord
Sun	Cancer	26: 51' 41"	Mer	Jup	Mer
Mon	Libra	06: 46' 58"	Rah	Rah	Rah
Mar	Libra	04: 47' 46"	Mar	Ven	Ket
Mer	Leo	22: 31' 46"	Ven	Sat	Ket
Jup	Gemini	13: 47' 27"	Rah	Mer	Rah
Ven	Cancer	00: 32' 49"	Jup	Mon	Sun
Sat	Cancer	25: 34' 01"	Mer	Rah	Ven
Rah (R)	Scorpio	27: 30' 18"	Mer	Jup	Mon
Ket (R)	Taurus	27: 30' 18"	Mar	Jup	Mon
Ura (R)	Aquarius	03: 16' 27"	Mar	Ven	Mon
Nep	Cancer	14: 36' 49"	Sat	Rah	Mon
Plu	Gemini	13: 22' 30"	Rah	Mer	Mon
Fortuna	Scorpio	12: 32' 18"	Sat	Mar	Mer

Comparing this chart with the chart of Figure 4.19, we find that the sub-sub lords of cusps 3, 6, 7, 8, 10 and 12 have changed. The changes in the cuspal positions of 3, 6 and 10 should meet the promises in respect of professional activities of the native. Let us see if the sub-sub lords now maintain relationship with the 10th cusp or not.

Third cusp sub-sub lord is Saturn that is in Mercury star. Mercury appears as sign lord of 10. It enables the native to carry out his professional activities using 3rd house significations.

The 6th sub-sub lord has changed from Mars to Rahu. But as Rahu itself represents Mars, this change has not affected any significant difference as far as the professional activities are concerned.

The sub-sub lord of the 10th has come as Venus. Since Venus is in the star of Jupiter that is the sub lord of the 9th cusp, the native's serving in an educational institution viz. a college is justified.

Seventh sub-sub lord is now Venus. Mercury is in its star and thus gets the required qualification to cause marriage and the genetical connection with the second child.

Change of the 8th sub-sub lord and the 12th sub-sub lord allows for cataract operation. In the rectified chart, the native got operated in the joint period of the planets Mer-Moon-Ket-Ket-Mars.

Now Ketu has the positional status and is the star lord of 8th and the 12th cusp. It is in Mars star that is the star lord of 2nd cusp and sub-sub lord of the 8th cusp. Ketu is in the sub of Jupiter that is the sub lord of ascendant and sub-sub lord of the 2nd cusp. Ketu is in the sub-sub of Moon that is the sub-sub lord of the 11th cusp. This clearly sets the scene for operation on the right eye and restoration of vision. The Prana lord Mars on the day of operation is in its own star and is thus linked to 2 and 8. It is in the sub of Venus that is the sub lord of 8th cusp. This indicates surgery on the part of the body represented by the 2nd cusp i.e. right eye. Mars is in the sub-sub of Ketu that is the star lord of the 12th cusp that indicates hospitalization.

Fig. 4.21

Name	Fig 4.21	Place of Birth	General3
Sex	Male	Latitude	022.00.N
Date of Birth	28/07/1979	Longitude	072.52.E
Day of Birth	Saturday	Local Birth Time	08:21:28
Time of Birth	09:00:00	Local Birth Date	28/07/1979
Sidereal Time	4:42:17	Lunar Tithi	4
Bal. of Dasha	Ven 2Y 0M 11D	K.P. (New) Ayanamsa	23:33:36
Lagan	Leo	Lagan Lord	Sun
Sign	Leo	Sign Lord	Sun
Nakshatra	P.Phalguni	Nakshatra Lord	Venus

Fig. 4.21 Contd......

Nirayana Cusps

Bhav No.	Sign	Degree	Star Lord	Sub Lord	Sub-Sub Lord
1	Leo	18: 27' 30"	Ven	Rah	Jup
2	Virgo	16: 45' 05"	Mon	Sat	Ven
3	Libra	17: 21' 47"	Rah	Ven	Ket
4	Scorpio	18: 30' 28"	Mer	Mer	Sat
5	Sagittarius	19: 09' 08"	Ven	Rah	Mer
6	Capricorn	19: 14' 09"	Mon	Mer	Jup
7	Aquarius	18: 27' 30"	Rah	Mon	Jup
8	Pisces	16: 45' 05"	Mer	Mer	Mer
9	Aries	17: 21' 47"	Ven	Mar	Mar
10	Taurus	18: 30' 28"	Mon	Mer	Sun
11	Gemini	19: 09' 08"	Rah	Mon	Ven
12	Cancer	19: 14' 09"	Mer	Ket	Mer

Planetary Position

Planet	Sign	Degree	Star Lord	Sub Lord	Sub-Sub Lord
Sun	Cancer	10: 55' 59"	Sat	Sun	Ven
Mon	Leo	25: 18' 41"	Ven	Mer	Rah
Mar	Taurus	28: 46' 46"	Mar	Sat	Ven
Mer (R)	Cancer	16: 57' 52"	Mer	Mer	Ket
Jup	Cancer	22: 56' 07"	Mer	Mon	Mer
Ven	Cancer	03: 08' 25"	Jup	Rah	Mon
Sat	Leo	18: 22' 53"	Ven	Rah	Rah
Rah (R)	Leo	15: 11' 57"	Ven	Ven	Mer
Ket (R)	Aquarius	15: 11' 57"	Rah	Ket	Mer
Ura	Libra	23: 21' 45"	Jup	Sat	Rah
Nep (R)	Scorpio	24: 26' 52"	Mer	Rah	Jup
Plu	Virgo	23: 07' 55"	Mon	Sun	Mer
Fortuna	Libra	02: 50' 12"	Mar	Ven	Ven

Figure 4.21 shows the chart to represent the transit of planets on 28.7.1979. On the day of operation, assuming it has taken place at about 09.00 AM, Moon transits in Leo in the star of Venus, sub of Mercury and sub-sub of Rahu. Now Venus is the sub lord of the 8th cusp and Mercury is the sub-sub lord of the 12th cusp and also the sub lord of the 2nd cusp (in fig. 4.20). Rahu is the sub lord of the 11th cusp that indicates successful operation. Mars transits in its own star Mars, Saturn sub and Venus sub-sub.Thus transit fully agrees to cause the Event to happen.

Retirement from Service: The person retires on the day when the planetary period is linked with 5th and 9th cusps. On 1.9.1979 the native was running the period of the planets Mer-Moon-Mars-Rahu-Rahu. Rahu is in Mercury star that appears in 9 and 10.It is in Jupiter sub that appears in 9. Rahu represents Mercury that is in Venus star, the sub lord of the 6th and 10th cusp. Mercury is in the sub of Saturn that appears in 5th cusp. This justifies the dasa potential of the planets to cause the event. Moon on the day of retirement is in Mercury star. Thus transit also agrees.

Purchase of Land: The native purchased land on 4.10.1962 when he was running the period of planets Sat-Sun-Jup-Jup-Jup. Jupiter in the Figure 4.20 is in Rahu star and Mercury sub. Rahu is the sub lord of the 11th cusp and Mercury is the sub-sub lord of the 4th and 12th cusp. This fully justifies the linkage for the purchase of land. Moon on the day of purchase was transiting in Mercury star. The transit also agrees because Mercury is the sub-sub lord of 4th and 12th cusp.

We may verify other events also. The horoscope thus stands verified and is the true horoscope of the native.

Example 6: Figure 4.22 is the chart of a person that suffered from the fatal disease Leukemia i.e. blood cancer. The native died on 5.1.1969.

Fig. 4.22

Name	Fig 4.22	Place of Birth	N7
Sex	Male	Latitude	023.34.N
Date of Birth	05/04/1914	Longitude	072.54.E
Day of Birth	Sunday	Local Birth Time	23:02:36
Time of Birth	23:41:00	Local Birth Date	05/04/1914
Sidereal Time	11:55:21	Lunar Tithi	10
Bal. of Dasha	Sat 0Y 2M 25D	K.P. (New) Ayanamsa	22:38:55
Lagan	Scorpio	Lagan Lord	Mars
Sign	Cancer	Sign Lord	Moon
Nakshatra	Pushya	Nakshatra Lord	Saturn

Lagna Chart

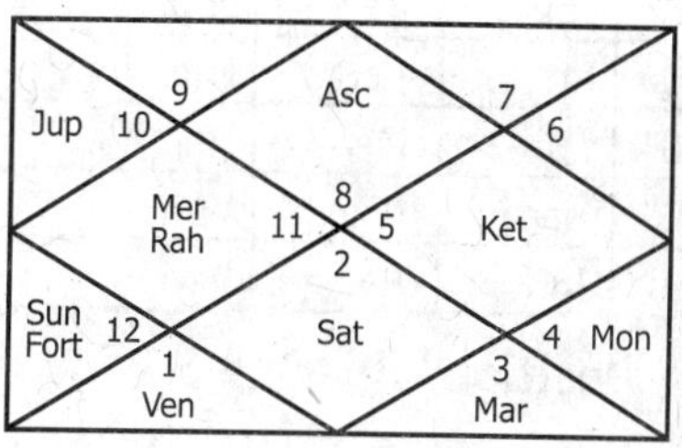

Bhava Chart

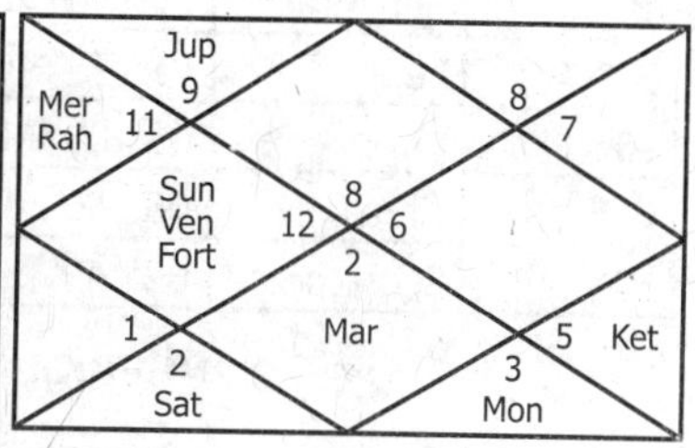

Cusp Chart

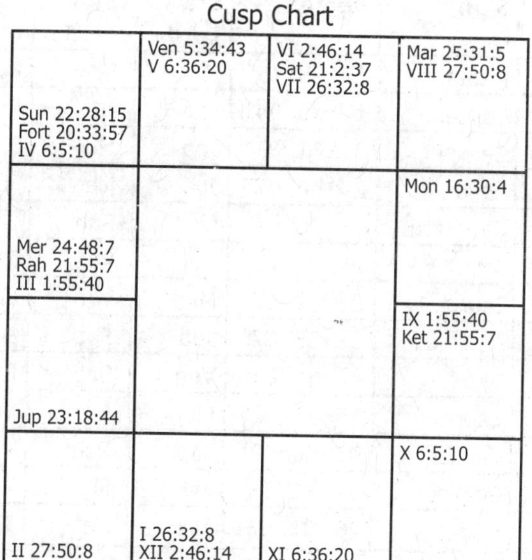

Fig. 4.22 Contd......

Nirayana Cusps

Bhav No.	Sign	Degree	Star Lord	Sub Lord	Sub-Sub Lord
1	Scorpio	26: 32' 08"	Mer	Jup	Sat
2	Sagittarius	27: 50' 08"	Sun	Mon	Sat
3	Aquarius	01: 55' 40"	Mar	Ket	Ket
4	Pisces	06: 05' 10"	Sat	Mer	Ven
5	Aries	06: 36' 20"	Ket	Rah	Mer
6	Taurus	02: 46' 14"	Sun	Jup	Rah
7	Taurus	26: 32' 08"	Mar	Jup	Sat
8	Gemini	27: 50' 08"	Jup	Ven	Jup
9	Leo	01: 55' 40"	Ket	Ven	Jup
10	Virgo	06: 05' 10"	Sun	Mer	Mar
11	Libra	06: 36' 20"	Mar	Mon	Ven
12	Scorpio	02: 46' 14"	Jup	Rah	Ven

Planetary Position

Planet	Sign	Degree	Star Lord	Sub Lord	Sub-Sub Lord
Sun	Pisces	22: 28' 15"	Mer	Mon	Rah
Mon	Cancer	16: 30' 04"	Sat	Jup	Rah
Mar	Gemini	25: 31' 05"	Jup	Mer	Sat
Mer	Aquarius	24: 48' 07"	Jup	Mer	Mon
Jup	Capricorn	23: 18' 44"	Mon	Sun	Ven
Ven	Aries	05: 34' 43"	Ket	Rah	Rah
Sat	Taurus	21: 02' 37"	Mon	Ven	Mon
Rah (R)	Aquarius	21: 55' 07"	Jup	Sat	Sat
Ket (R)	Leo	21: 55' 07"	Ven	Sat	Sat
Ura	Capricorn	18: 16' 42"	Mon	Mer	Ven
Nep	Cancer	02: 46' 49"	Jup	Rah	Ven
Plu	Gemini	06: 31' 15"	Mar	Mon	Ven
Fortuna	Pisces	20: 33' 57"	Mer	Ven	Jup

Leukemia is a malignant growth of white corpuscles in blood, which is commonly known as cancer of blood. A native usually suffers from such a disease when the ascendant sub-sub lord is simultaneously linked to 6th, 8th and 12th cusps. Also the $6^{th}/8^{th}$ cusp should be simultaneously linked with 6th, 8th and 12th cusps. Rahu and Jupiter are important planets known for causing cancer. Mars and Moon cause diseases of blood. Diseases due to blood cells are caused if the sub-sub lord of the 5th or the 11th cusp links with 6/8 cusps.

Let us analyse the chart to find out whether it promises that the native was destined to suffer that fatal disease or not.

Step 1: The sub-sub lord of the ascendant is Saturn and the native's Moon star is also Saturn.

Step 2: Analysis of Ascendant for Promise of Disease - The sub-sub lord of the ascendant is in Moon star, Venus sub and Moon sub-sub. Moon does not appear in 6th or 8th cuspal position but is resident of the 8th cusp in the Bhava chart. Venus the sub lord of the Saturn appears in 8th and 12th cusps. The ascendant sub-sub lord has thus made simultaneous relationship with 8 and 12 only. It maintains no relationship with the 6th cusp.

Step 3: Study of the 8th cusp - The sub-sub lord of the 8th cusp is Jupiter. It is in Moon star, Sun sub and Venus sub-sub. Moon is placed in the 8th Bhava. sub lord of Jupiter is Sun that appears in 6. The sub sub of Jupiter is Venus that appears in 6 as well as in 12.

Step 4: Promise for Blood Cancer: For this the 5th or the 11th cusp sub-sub lord should be linked to $6^{th}/8^{th}$ cusp. Here the sub-sub lord of the 5th cusp is Mercury that is linked with 6th, 8th and 12th cusp through its star lord Jupiter.

Step 5: Check of Longevity - The ascendant, the 3rd and the 8th sub-sub lords are at best Connected with only one Maraka house or the Badhaka house and as such the longevity of the native cannot be assumed to be medium. Moreover for the disease to be fatal the 8th cusp sub-sub lord should establish links through its star lord with Maraka and Badhaka houses or its star may appear in 6th or 8th cusp and sub in Maraka and Badhaka houses.

The horoscope has, therefore, to be rectified to ensure the following:

1. Simultaneously linkage of the ascendant sub-sub lord with the 6th, 8th and 12th house.
2. Simultaneously linkage of the 8th cusp sub-sub lord with 6th, 8th and 12th house as well as with Maraka and Badhaka houses.

To rectify the chart, the ruling planets were taken to decide the cuspal position of the 6th cusp. The RP chart is shown in Figure 4.23.

Fig. 4.23

Name	Fig 4.23	Place of Birth	Noida
Sex	Male	Latitude	028.20.N
Date of Birth	22/01/2005	Longitude	077.20.E
Day of Birth	Saturday	Local Birth Time	05:20:30
Time of Birth	05:41:10	Local Birth Date	22/01/2005
Sidereal Time	13:26:16	Lunar Tithi	12
Bal. of Dasha	Mar 3Y 0M 14D	K.P. (New) Ayanamsa	23:54:56
Lagan	Sagittarius	Lagan Lord	Jupiter
Sign	Gemini	Sign Lord	Mercury
Nakshatra	Mrigasira	Nakshatra Lord	Mars

Fig. 4.23 Contd......

Nirayana Cusps

Bhav No.	Sign	Degree	Star Lord	Sub Lord	Sub-Sub Lord
1	Sagittarius	13: 41' 44"	Ven	Ven	Ven
2	Capricorn	18: 55' 25"	Mon	Mer	Rah
3	Aquarius	26: 08' 41"	Jup	Ket	Rah
4	Pisces	29: 23' 41"	Mer	Sat	Mar
5	Aries	26: 45' 58"	Sun	Sun	Mar
6	Taurus	20: 25' 50"	Mon	Ket	Mer
7	Gemini	13: 41' 44"	Rah	Mer	Rah
8	Cancer	18: 55' 25"	Mer	Ket	Rah
9	Leo	26: 08' 41"	Ven	Ket	Mon
10	Virgo	29: 23' 41"	Mar	Sat	Mar
11	Libra	26: 45' 58"	Jup	Ven	Ven
12	Scorpio	20: 25' 50"	Mer	Ven	Rah

Planetary Position

Planet	Sign	Degree	Star Lord	Sub Lord	Sub-Sub Lord
Sun	Capricorn	08: 09' 39"	Sun	Ven	Sun
Mon	Gemini	00: 52' 32"	Mar	Mer	Mon
Mar	Scorpio	25: 01' 09"	Mer	Rah	Mer
Mer	Sagittarius	23: 15' 44"	Ven	Sat	Mon
Jup	Virgo	24: 45' 20"	Mar	Rah	Sat
Ven	Sagittarius	21: 30' 29"	Ven	Jup	Mon
Sat (R)	Gemini	29: 18' 06"	Jup	Sun	Ket
Rah (R)	Aries	03: 20' 40"	Ket	Sun	Sat
Ket (R)	Libra	03: 20' 40"	Mar	Ven	Mar
Ura	Aquarius	10: 57' 23"	Rah	Sat	Mer
Nep	Capricorn	20: 41' 02"	Mon	Ven	Ven
Plu	Scorpio	29: 31' 22"	Mer	Sat	Rah
Fortuna	Taurus	06: 24' 37"	Sun	Mer	Rah

Since Moon has come as the sub-sub lord in RP (Moon), it was decided to put it as the sub-sub lord of the 6th cusp. This also resulted in changing the sub-sub lord of the 8th cusp from Jupiter to Rahu. The rectified chart is shown in Figure 4.24.

Fig. 4.24

Name	Fig 4.24	Place of Birth	N7
Sex	Male	Latitude	023.34.N
Date of Birth	05/04/1914	Longitude	072.54.E
Day of Birth	Sunday	Local Birth Time	23:01:56
Time of Birth	23:40:20	Local Birth Date	05/04/1914
Sidereal Time	11:54:41	Lunar Tithi	10
Bal. of Dasha	Sat 0Y 2M 28D	K.P. (New) Ayanamsa	22:38:55
Lagan	Scorpio	Lagan Lord	Mars
Sign	Cancer	Sign Lord	Moon
Nakshatra	Pushya	Nakshatra Lord	Saturn

Lagna Chart

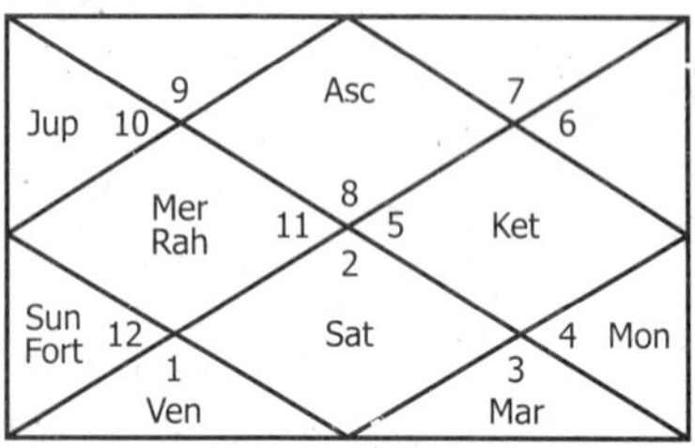

Bhava Chart

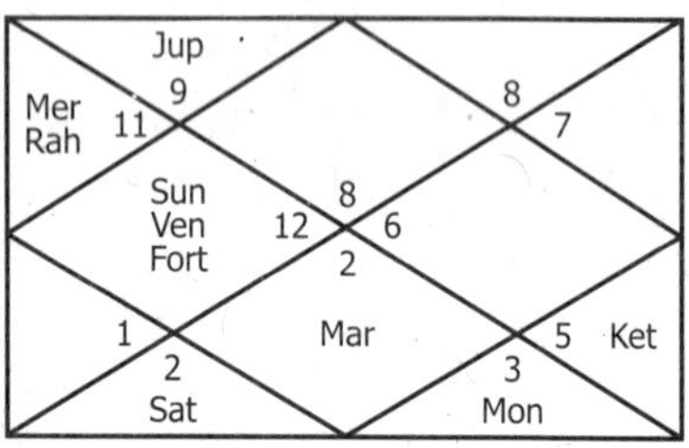

Cusp Chart

Sun 22:23:14 Fort 20:24:40 IV 5:54:15	Ven 5:34:41 V 6:26:22	VI 2:37:10 Sat 21:2:36 VII 26:23:13	Mar 25:31:4 VIII 27:40:15
Mer 24:48:6 Rah 21:55:7 III 1:44:45			Mon 16:29:41
Jup 23:18:43			IX 1:44:45 Ket 21:55:7
II 27:40:15	I 26:23:13 XII 2:37:10	XI 6:26:22	X 5:54:15

Fig. 4.24 Contd......

Nirayana Cusps

Bhav No.	Sign	Degree	Star Lord	Sub Lord	Sub-Sub Lord
1	Scorpio	26: 23' 13"	Mer	Jup	Sat
2	Sagittarius	27: 40' 15"	Sun	Mon	Jup
3	Aquarius	01: 44' 45"	Mar	Mer	Sat
4	Pisces	05: 54' 15"	Sat	Mer	Ven
5	Aries	06: 26' 22"	Ket	Rah	Mer
6	Taurus	02: 37' 10"	Sun	Jup	Mon
7	Taurus	26: 23' 13"	Mar	Jup	Sat
8	Gemini	27: 40' 15"	Jup	Ven	Rah
9	Leo	01: 44' 45"	Ket	Ven	Rah
10	Virgo	05: 54' 15"	Sun	Mer	Mon
11	Libra	06: 26' 22"	Mar	Mon	Ven
12	Scorpio	02: 37' 10"	Jup	Rah	Ven

Planetary Position

Planet	Sign	Degree	Star Lord	Sub Lord	Sub-Sub Lord
Sun	Pisces	22: 28' 14"	Mer	Mon	Rah
Mon	Cancer	16: 29' 41"	Sat	Jup	Rah
Mar	Gemini	25: 31' 04"	Jup	Mer	Sat
Mer	Aquarius	24: 48' 06"	Jup	Mer	Mon
Jup	Capricorn	23: 18' 43"	Mon	Sun	Ven
Ven	Aries	05: 34' 41"	Ket	Rah	Rah
Sat	Taurus	21: 02' 36"	Mon	Ven	Mon
Rah (R)	Aquarius	21: 55' 07"	Jup	Sat	Sat
Ket (R)	Leo	21: 55' 07"	Ven	Sat	Sat
Ura	Capricorn	18: 16' 42"	Mon	Mer	Ven
Nep	Cancer	02: 46' 49"	Jup	Rah	Ven
Plu	Gemini	06: 31' 15"	Mar	Mon	Ven
Fortuna	Pisces	20: 24' 40"	Mer	Ven	Rah

Verification of the rectified Chart

Step 1: Analysis of Ascendant: The sub-sub lord of ascendant is Saturn. It is in Moon star and Venus sub. Moon is the sub-sub lord of the 6th cusp and Venus is the sub-lord of 8th and sub-sub lord of 12th cusp. Thus the ascendant sub-sub lord is simultaneously linked to 6, 8, 9, and 12. Saturn is in the sub-sub of Moon, which also appears in 11th cusp. We can verify that the planets co-ruling ascendant, Moon and Sun satisfy the necessary conditions.

Step 2: Analysis of 6th Cusp - Moon is the sub-sub lord of the 6th cusp. It is in Saturn star and Jupiter sub and Rahu sub-sub. Moon thus involves the ascendant and commits to 6, 8, 12, where Jupiter appears. The natural significations of the planets co-ruling the degree rising on the 6th cusp do not indicate the disease the native suffered. But if we analyse their signification as per chart, it reveals everything. The nature of the disease is indicated by the sub sub lord of the 6th cusp as per its own nature as modified by the star lord in which it is placed in the horoscope. Moon is placed in Saturn star (Pushya). If we read page 121 of the revised edition of the book Basics and Traditional concepts we notice that the person is liable to suffer cancer. Since Moon is Karaka for blood it may be blood cancer. We can study other planets that are the co-ruling planets of 6th cusp.

Venus the sign lord is in Ketu star, Rahu sub and Rahu sub-sub completely controlling the 5th cuspal position and linking with 8th & 12th cusps. Sun the star lord of the 6th cusp is in Mercury star and Moon sub i.e. Sun involves the 5th house and commits to 6th house. Jupiter the sub lord of the 6th cusp is in Moon star and Sun sub.

Step 3: Study of the 8th Cusp - For serious sickness or fatal diseases we need to analyse 8th cusp. Here the sub-sub lord of the 8th cusp is Rahu that also represents Saturn and Jupiter. Rahu is in Jupiter star and as such is linked to 6, 8, 12 cusps simultaneously. The sub-sub lord of the 8th cusp is also linked with 2 and 7 cusps.

Rahu is in Aquarius the Sign that rules over the circulatory System. It is in Jupiter star (Purvabhadra). If we read the above referred book for determining the nature of the disease we get an idea that the native is likely to suffer serious disease relating to the circulatory system.

Step 4: For diseases due to blood cells, 5th or 11th house should be linked to 6th/ 8th cusp. The 5th cusp is co-ruled by Ketu as star lord, Rahu as sub lord and Mercury as sub-sub lord. All are linked with 6th or 8th cusp.

Eleventh cusp is co-ruled by Mars as star lord, Moon as sub lord and Venus as sub-sub lord. All these planets are linked with 6th and 8th cusp.

Thus the linkage of ascendant and 8th cusp with 6,8,12 indicates that the native had to suffer some serious disease. Linkages of the planets Mars and Moon from the 11th cusp reveal the nature of disease as blood cancer.

The native died on 5.1.1969 in the joint period of Moon-Sat-Mercury-Mercury-Ketu. Dasa lord Moon is placed in the 8th Bhava and as such it is considered to be a co-ruling planet in the 8th cusp. Moon is in Saturn star. The sub sub lord of 8th cusp is Rahu that represents Saturn. As such Moon is related to the sub sub lord of the 8th cusp. Now Moon is in Saturn star that is the sub sub lord of ascendant. Moon is in the sub of Jupiter that appears in 2, 7, 8 and 12. Moon is in the sub sub of Rahu that is the sub sub of 8th cusp. Moon thus satisfies all conditions to be declared as Markesh dasa Lord.

The Bhukti lord Saturn has PS. It is the sub sub lord of ascendant and as such signifies 1. It is in the sub of Venus that appears in 8. Thus Saturn is fully competent to cause death of the native.

Mercury is both Antara and Sookshama Lord. Mercury is in Jupiter star that appears in 1 and 8. It is in Mercury sub that also appears in 1 and 8. Mercury is in the sub sub of Moon that is placed in 8 with PS. Thus we find that Mercury also is fully competent in causing death of the native.

The death of the native took place in the Prana of Ketu that is placed in Badhaka with PS (exchange of Nakshatra). Ketu is in Venus star that appears in 8. Ketu is in the sub of Saturn that is the sub sub lord of 1. It is in the sub sub of Saturn that is the sub sub lord of the 7th cusp. These significations of Ketu fully justify the event of death. Ketu represents Sun and Venus. Sun appears in 6 (disease). It is in Mercury star that appears in 1. It is in the sub of Moon and sub sub of Rahu. Both Moon and Rahu appears in 8. This accounts for the cause of death.

Example 7: Figure 4.25 is the chart of a female as per her recorded birth data. The lady made an attempt to commit suicide by pouring kerosene over her body on 25.12.1971. She suffered severe burns but her life was saved.

Fig. 4.25

Name	Fig 4.25	Place of Birth	General 5
Sex	Female	Latitude	022.43.N
Date of Birth	26/02/1945	Longitude	074.39.E
Day of Birth	Monday	Local Birth Time	15:28:36
Time of Birth	17:00:00	Local Birth Date	26/02/1945
Sidereal Time	1:52:13	Lunar Tithi	15
Bal. of Dasha	Ket 2Y 9M 5D	K.P. (New) Ayanamsa	23:04:47
Lagan	Cancer	Lagan Lord	Moon
Sign	Leo	Sign Lord	Sun
Nakshatra	Magha	Nakshatra Lord	Ketu

Lagna Chart

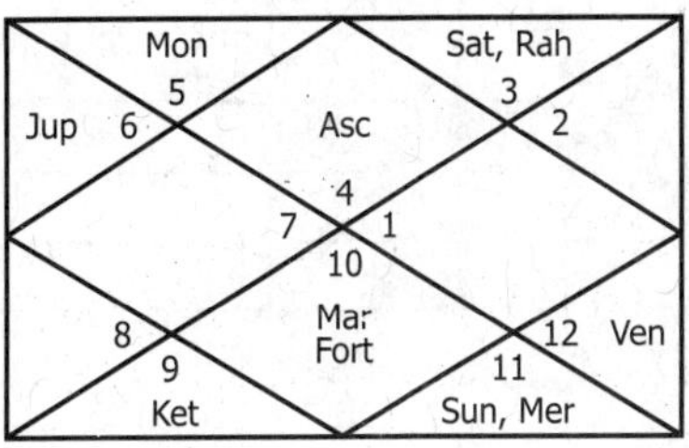

Bhava Chart

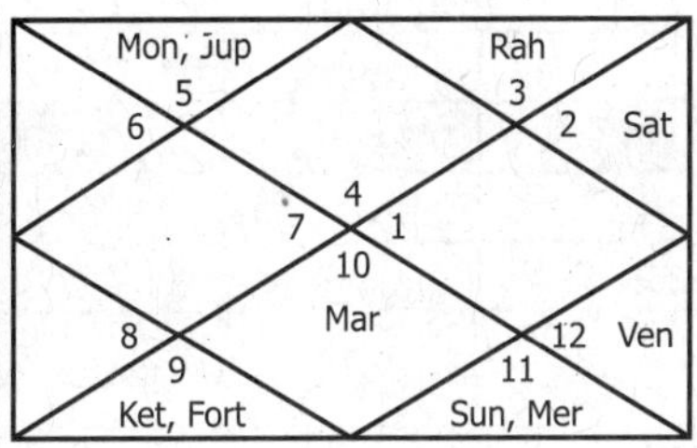

Cusp Chart

Ven 28:44:56 IX 4:55:12	X 7:4:20	XI 10:2:35	Sat 10:48:27 XII 11:28:5 Rah 24:20:43
Sun 14:24:15 Mer 12:19:24 VIII 6:9:23			I 10:59:43
Mar 16:11:57 VII 10:59:43 Fort 4:39:48			II 6:9:23 Mon 8:4:20
Ket 24:20:43 VI 11:28:5	V 10:2:35	IV 7:4:20	Jup 1:24:11 III 4:55:12

Fig. 4.25 Contd......

Nirayana Cusps

Bhav No.	Sign	Degree	Star Lord	Sub Lord	Sub-Sub Lord
1	Cancer	10: 59' 43"	Sat	Sun	Ven
2	Leo	06: 09' 23"	Ket	Rah	Sat
3	Virgo	04: 55' 12"	Sun	Sat	Jup
4	Libra	07: 04' 20"	Rah	Rah	Jup
5	Scorpio	10: 02' 35"	Sat	Ven	Mer
6	Sagittarius	11: 28' 05"	Ket	Mer	Mer
7	Capricorn	10: 59' 43"	Mon	Mon	Ven
8	Aquarius	06: 09' 23"	Mar	Mon	Sat
9	Pisces	04: 55' 12"	Sat	Sat	Rah
10	Aries	07: 04' 20"	Ket	Rah	Ven
11	Taurus	10: 02' 35"	Mon	Mon	Mon
12	Gemini	11: 28' 05"	Rah	Sat	Ven

Planetary Position

Planet	Sign	Degree	Star Lord	Sub Lord	Sub-Sub Lord
Sun	Aquarius	14: 24' 15"	Rah	Mer	Sat
Mon	Leo	08: 04' 20"	Ket	Jup	Sat
Mar	Capricorn	16: 11' 57"	Mon	Sat	Mer
Mer	Aquarius	12: 19' 24"	Rah	Sat	Jup
Jup (R)	Virgo	01: 24' 11"	Sun	Jup	Jup
Ven	Pisces	28: 44' 56"	Mer	Sat	Ven
Sat (R)	Gemini	10: 48' 27"	Rah	Sat	Mer
Rah (R)	Gemini	24: 20' 43"	Jup	Mer	Ven
Ket (R)	Sagittarius	24: 20' 43"	Ven	Mer	Ket
Ura	Taurus	16: 04' 40"	Mon	Sat	Mer
Nep (R)	Virgo	12: 42' 48"	Mon	Rah	Sat
Plu (R)	Cancer	15: 24' 29"	Sat	Jup	Mer
Fortuna	Capricorn	04: 39' 48"	Sun	Sat	Rah

Let us analyse the chart to find out whether it promises this event to happen in her life or not.

Step 1: The ascendant sub-sub lord is Venus. The Moon's star of the native is Ketu. Since Ketu is in Venus star, the ascendant sub-sub lord has established relationship with the Moon star.

Step 2: Attempt to commit suicide - Suicide is a deliberate or conscious effort of the native to kill him or herself. This happens at a time when the native is in a state of depression which may be caused by the native's own actions which ruins his or her career, position in society or other things which he or she values in life. It may be caused when the native feels incapacitated to face the struggles of life.

Since suicide is self-undoing, the ascendant sub-sub lord should link itself with the 12th cusp through its star lord and commits to the 8th cusp through its sub lord. Here the sub-sub lord of the ascendant is Venus that is in Mercury star and Saturn sub. Mercury appears in the 12th cuspal position. It is resident of 8th house. This linkage only promises mental agony and proneness to accident.

Step 3: Mode of committing suicide - The mode of committing suicide if it has to result in death has to be indicated by the sub-sub lord of the 8th cusp. Suicide is an unnatural death. For unnatural death, the following conditions should exist in the chart.

1. 8th Cusp sub- sub lord should be significator of 8th and 12th house.
2. 8th Cusp sub-sub lord and its star lord should be in cardinal and violent signs Aries, Taurus, Scorpio, Leo, Sagittarius or Capricorn.

3. Ascendant sub-sub Lord should also be connected with 8 and 12 houses to promise unnatural Death.

Here, the sub-sub lord of the 8th cusp is Saturn, that is in Rahu star and Saturn sub. Since Rahu is in Gemini sign and Jupiter star. Rahu represents Jupiter that is in Virgo. It thus does not promise death due to burning. However, Saturn has the positional status. It occupies the sub-sub arc of the 2nd cusp that rises in Leo. It is also the star lord of the 5th cusp that rises in Scorpio. This may justify the attempt of the native to burn her.

Step 4: Failure to commit suicide: The native's span of life is determined from the sub-sub lord of the ascendant. Here Venus, the sub-sub lord of the ascendant shows long life because of the absence of its links with the Maraka and Badhaka houses.

Step5: Depression and Abnormal Behaviour: A person undergoes periods of depression when the sub-sub lord of the 3rd cusp maintains simultaneous relationship with 8th and 12th cusp. Here Jupiter is the sub-sub lord of the third cusp that is in Sun star and its own sub and sub-sub. Thus Jupiter does not establish relationship with 8th and 12th cusp.

The native under the following conditions shows the abnormal behaviour:

A. The ascendant sub-sub lord should maintain relationship with 5, 8 and 12 cusps.

B. The sub-sub lord of the 5th cusp should maintain relationship with 8 and 12 cusps.

Here the sub-sub lord of the ascendant is Venus, that is in Mercury star and Saturn sub. Mercury appears in the 5th cusp as sub-sub lord and Saturn appears in the 8th cusp as sub-sub lord and as sub lord of the 12th cusp. Thus the condition as stipulated by (A) above is justified.

The 5th cusp sub-sub lord is Mercury that is in Rahu star and Saturn sub. Rahu appears as the star lord of the 12th cusp and is also the resident of the 12th house. Saturn is the sub-sub lord of the 8th cusp. The condition set by (B) above is also justified.

Step 6: The native attempted to commit suicide at 21.15 hrs on 25.12.1971 when she was running the joint period of Sun-Mer-Venus-Sat-Mercury.

As the dasa lord Sun does not maintain simultaneous relationship with 1 and 8 it ensures that the native cannot meet death during Sun dasa.

The Bhukti lord Mercury being in Rahu star, Saturn sub and Jupiter sub-sub is connected with 4, 8 and 12 cusps. This sets the scene for accident.

The Antara lord Venus being in Mercury star, Saturn sub and Venus sub-sub is linked with 3, 5, 8 and 12 and thus accounts for depression and abnormal behaviour.

The Sookshma lord Saturn is the sub-sub lord of the 8th cusp, and appears in 3, 5 and 12 cusps also. It has the positional status and is thus linked to the relevant cusps for depression and abnormal behaviour and accident.

The Prana lord Mercury, we have already discussed above is linked with the relevant cusps to allow the event to happen.

The transit of planets Sun and Moon agrees with the dasa periods. The transit position of planets at 21.15 hrs on 25.12.1971 is shown in Figure 4.26.

Fig. 4.26

Name	Fig 4.26	Place of Birth	General 5
Sex	Male	Latitude	022.43.N
Date of Birth	25/12/1971	Longitude	074.39.E
Day of Birth	Saturday	Local Birth Time	20:43:36
Time of Birth	21:15:00	Local Birth Date	25/12/1971
Sidereal Time	2:57:34	Lunar Tithi	9
Bal. of Dasha	Mer 15Y11M14D	K.P. (New) Ayanamsa	23:27:15
Lagan	Cancer	Lagan Lord	Moon
Sign	Pisces	Sign Lord	Jupiter
Nakshatra	Revati	Nakshatra Lord	Mercury

Fig. 4.26 Contd......

Nirayana Cusps

Bhav No.	Sign	Degree	Star Lord	Sub Lord	Sub-Sub Lord
1	Cancer	25: 01' 55"	Mer	Rah	Mer
2	Leo	21: 24' 00"	Ven	Jup	Mon
3	Virgo	21: 18' 02"	Mon	Ven	Rah
4	Libra	23: 24' 20"	Jup	Sat	Rah
5	Scorpio	25: 18' 16"	Mer	Rah	Ket
6	Sagittarius	25: 48' 58"	Ven	Mer	Sat
7	Capricorn	25: 01' 55"	Mar	Rah	Mer
8	Aquarius	21: 24' 00"	Jup	Jup	Mon
9	Pisces	21: 18' 02"	Mer	Ven	Mer
10	Aries	23: 24' 20"	Ven	Sat	Rah
11	Taurus	25: 18' 16"	Mar	Rah	Ket
12	Gemini	25: 48' 58"	Jup	Ket	Ket

Planetary Position

Planet	Sign	Degree	Star Lord	Sub Lord	Sub-Sub Lord
Sun	Sagittarius	09: 44' 46"	Ket	Sat	Mer
Mon	Pisces	17: 29' 09"	Mer	Mer	Mon
Mar	Pisces	05: 50' 34"	Sat	Mer	Ven
Mer	Scorpio	19: 05' 22"	Mer	Ket	Jup
Jup	Scorpio	27: 29' 04"	Mer	Jup	Mon
Ven	Capricorn	09: 30' 08"	Sun	Ven	Sat
Sat (R)	Taurus	07: 19' 49"	Sun	Ket	Rah
Rah (R)	Capricorn	12: 13' 13"	Mon	Rah	Jup
Ket (R)	Cancer	12: 13' 13"	Sat	Mar	Rah
Ura	Virgo	24: 29' 08"	Mar	Rah	Jup
Nep	Scorpio	10: 26' 17"	Sat	Sun	Mar
Plu	Virgo	08: 33' 57"	Sun	Ven	Mar
Fortuna	Scorpio	02: 46' 18"	Jup	Rah	Ven

From the above discussion, it appears that the cuspal positions of various cusps do justify the native's behaviour except for the fact that it fails to account for the native's undergoing periods of depression and suicidal tendencies. The horoscope thus needs rectification. The rectified horoscope is shown in Figure 4.27

Fig. 4.27

Name	Fig 4.27	Place of Birth	General 5
Sex	Female	Latitude	022.43.N
Date of Birth	26/02/1945	Longitude	074.39.E
Day of Birth	Monday	Local Birth Time	15:28:06
Time of Birth	16:59:30*	Local Birth Date	26/02/1945
Sidereal Time	1:51:43	Lunar Tithi	15
Bal. of Dasha	Ket 2Y 9M 6D	K.P. (New) Ayanamsa	23:54:59
Lagan	Cancer	Lagan Lord	Moon
Sign	Leo	Sign Lord	Sun
Nakshatra	Magha	Nakshatra Lord	Ketu

*** Chart is constructed after applying War Time Correction.**

Lagna Chart

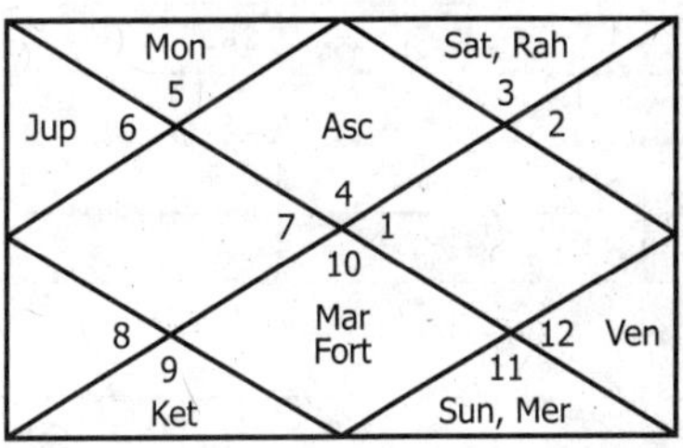

Bhava Chart

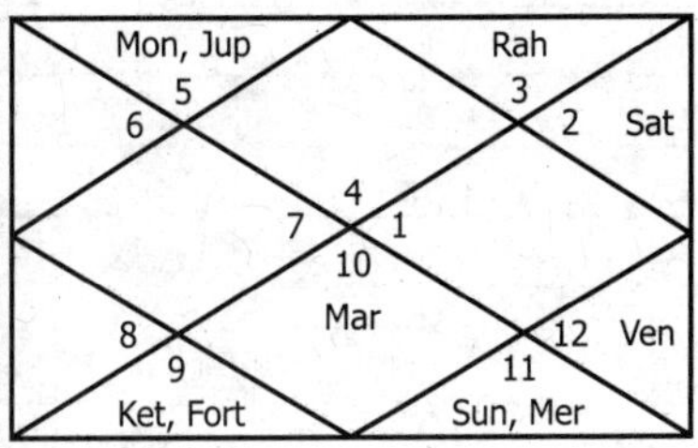

Cusp Chart

Ven 28:44:55 IX 4:47:28	X 6:56:27	XI 9:55:12	Sat 10:48:24 XII 11:21:14 Rah 24:20:43
Sun 14:24:13 Mer 12:19:21 VIII 6:2:17			I 10:53:7
Mar 46:11:56 VII 10:53:7 Fort 4:32:59			II 6:2:17 Mon 8:4:5
Ket 24:20:43 VI 11:21:14	V 9:55:12	IV 6:56:27	Jup 1:24:11 III 4:47:28

Fig. 4.27 Contd......

Nirayana Cusps

Bhav No.	Sign	Degree	Star Lord	Sub Lord	Sub-Sub Lord
1	Cancer	10: 53' 07"	Sat	Sun	Ket
2	Leo	06: 02' 17"	Ket	Rah	Jup
3	Virgo	04: 47' 28"	Sun	Sat	Rah
4	Libra	06: 56' 27"	Rah	Rah	Rah
5	Scorpio	09: 55' 12"	Sat	Ven	Mer
6	Sagittarius	11: 21' 14"	Ket	Sat	Jup
7	Capricorn	10: 53' 07"	Mon	Mon	Ven
8	Aquarius	06: 02' 17"	Mar	Mon	Sat
9	Pisces	04: 47' 28"	Sat	Sat	Mar
10	Aries	06: 56' 27"	Ket	Rah	Ven
11	Taurus	09: 55' 12"	Sun	Ven	Ket
12	Gemini	11: 21' 14"	Rah	Sat	Ven

Planetary Position

Planet	Sign	Degree	Star Lord	Sub Lord	Sub-Sub Lord
Sun	Aquarius	14: 24' 13"	Rah	Mer	Sat
Mon	Leo	08: 04' 05"	Ket	Jup	Sat
Mar	Capricorn	16: 11' 56"	Mon	Sat	Mer
Mer	Aquarius	12: 19' 21"	Rah	Sat	Jup
Jup (R)	Virgo	01: 24' 11"	Sun	Jup	Jup
Ven	Pisces	28: 44' 55"	Mer	Sat	Ven
Sat (R)	Gemini	10: 48' 27"	Rah	Sat	Mer
Rah (R)	Gemini	24: 20' 43"	Jup	Mer	Ven
Ket (R)	Sagittarius	24: 20' 43"	Ven	Mer	Ket
Ura	Taurus	16: 04' 40"	Mon	Sat	Mer
Nep (R)	Virgo	12: 42' 48"	Mon	Rah	Sat
Plu (R)	Cancer	15: 24' 29"	Sat	Jup	Mer
Fortuna	Capricorn	04: 32' 59"	Sun	Sat	Rah

Verification of the Rectified Chart

Step 1: The sub-sub lord of the ascendant is Ketu that is itself the Moon's star lord.

Step 2: Ketu is in Venus star, Mercury sub and Ketu sub-sub. It shows medium life. The native makes attempt to commit suicide if the ascendant sub-sub lord involves the 12th cusp through its star lord and commits to the 8th cusp through its sub lord. Here the star lord of Ketu appears as the sub-sub lord of the 12th cusp and its sub lord Mercury is the resident of the 8th cusp.

Step 3: Depression and Abnormal Behaviour: The sub-sub lord of the 3rd cusp is Rahu. It represents Mercury that maintains relationship with 8th and 12th cusps through its star lord and sub lord. Since Mercury is also the sub-sub lord of the 5th cusp it justifies the native's abnormal behaviour also.

Step 4: The event of attempt to commit suicide happened in the joint period of Sun-Mer-Venus-Saturn-Saturn. The Sookshma and Prana lord Saturn justifies the attempt as well as safety of life being linked with the 5th cusp by its sub-sub lord Mercury. The end result of the event is always as per the sub-sub lord of the planet.

The horoscope of Figure 4.27 is, thus the true horoscope of the native.

Example 8: Figure 4.28 is the chart of a gentleman that was doing internship in B.D.S at Banglore. He met with an accident while riding on a two-wheeler on 15.7.2004 at about 16.00 hrs and died on the spot.

Fig. 4.28

Name	Fig 4.28	Place of Birth	Meerut
Sex	Male	Latitude	029.00.N
Date of Birth	29/07/1980	Longitude	077.42.E
Day of Birth	Tuesday	Local Birth Time	12:20:48
Time of Birth	12:40:00	Local Birth Date	29/07/1980
Sidereal Time	8:49:9	Lunar Tithi	2
Bal. of Dasha	Mar 2Y 0M 10D	K.P. (New) Ayanamsa	23:54:59
Lagan	Libra	Lagan Lord	Venus
Sign	Aquarius	Sign Lord	Saturn
Nakshatra	Dhanistha	Nakshatra Lord	Mars

Lagna Chart

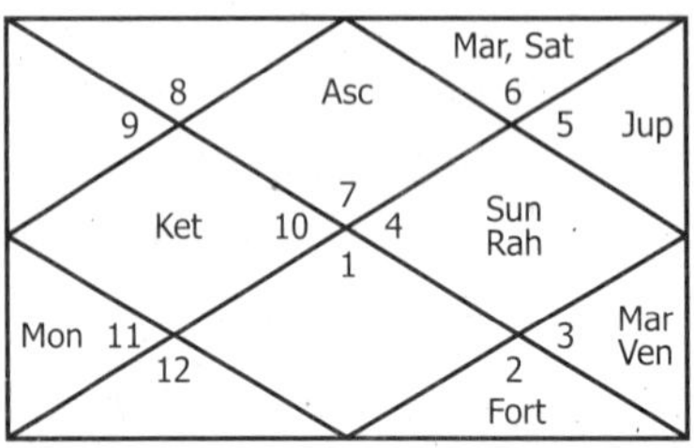

Bhava Chart

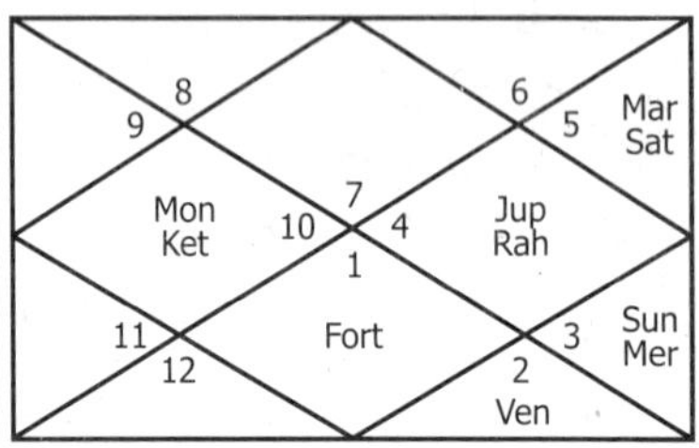

Cusp Chart

VI 17:57:50	VII 13:16:36	Fort 3:20:45 VIII 12:20:32	Ven 0:31:26 IX 13:31:16 Mer 23:46:52
V 18:36:57 Mon 2:48:33			Sun 12:44:24 X 16:16:11 Rah 26:37:18
Ket 26:37:18 IV 16:16:11			Jup 17:32:17 XI 18:36:57
III 13:31:16	II 12:20:32	I 13:16:36	Sat 0:13:18 Mar 17:8:22 XII 17:57:50

Fig. 4.28 Contd......

Nirayana Cusps

Bhav No.	Sign	Degree	Star Lord	Sub Lord	Sub-Sub Lord
1	Libra	13: 16' 36"	Rah	Mer	Sun
2	Scorpio	12: 20' 32"	Sat	Mar	Jup
3	Sagittarius	13: 31' 16"	Ven	Ven	Ven
4	Capricorn	16: 16' 11"	Mon	Sat	Mer
5	Aquarius	18: 36' 57"	Rah	Mon	Sat
6	Pisces	17: 57' 50"	Mer	Mer	Rah
7	Aries	13: 16' 36"	Ket	Mer	Sat
8	Taurus	12: 20' 32"	Mon	Rah	Jup
9	Gemini	13: 31' 16"	Rah	Mer	Mar
10	Cancer	16: 16' 11"	Sat	Jup	Mon
11	Leo	18: 36' 57"	Ven	Rah	Jup
12	Virgo	17: 57' 50"	Mon	Mer	Mer

Planetary Position

Planet	Sign	Degree	Star Lord	Sub Lord	Sub-Sub Lord
Sun	Cancer	12: 44' 24"	Sat	Mar	Ven
Mon	Aquarius	02: 48' 33"	Mar	Ven	Ven
Mar	Virgo	17: 08' 22"	Mon	Sat	Mar
Mer	Gemini	23: 46' 52"	Jup	Sat	Jup
Jup	Leo	17: 32' 17"	Ven	Mar	Jup
Ven	Gemini	00: 31' 26"	Mar	Mer	Ven
Sat	Virgo	00: 13' 18"	Sun	Rah	Mer
Rah (R)	Cancer	26: 37' 18"	Mer	Jup	Sat
Ket (R)	Capricorn	26: 37' 18"	Mar	Jup	Sat
Ura	Libra	27: 55' 43"	Jup	Ven	Jup
Nep (R)	Scorpio	26: 37' 15"	Mer	Jup	Sat
Plu	Virgo	25: 39' 19"	Mar	Rah	Ven
Fortuna	Taurus	03: 20' 45"	Sun	Sat	Mer

If the horoscope of the native is correct it should reveal the following:

1. Short Life.
2. B.D.S as the field of education.
3. Death in journey at a far off work place.
4. Dasa and Transit potential of planets to cause the event of death.

Let us check the accuracy of the horoscope of Figure 4.28

Step 1: The sub-sub lord of the ascendant is Sun. It is in Saturn star and Mars sub. Since Mars is the Moon's star lord, the sub-sub lord of the ascendant maintains relationship with Moon's star.

Step 2: Short Life: The sub-sub lord of the ascendant should be linked with Maraka and Badhaka house through its star lord and its sub lord should not negate the significations of Maraka and Badhaka houses. Here the sub-sub lord of the ascendant is Sun that is in Saturn star that appears as the star lord of the 2nd cusp and the sub-sub lord of the 7th cusp and is placed in the Badhaka house. It is in Mars sub that does not negate 2 or 7 or Badhaka. Thus we may assume that the ascendant sub-sub lord promises short life.

Step 3: B.D.S as field of Education: To have regular attendance in a college, the ascendant sub-sub lord should maintain relationship with 4th or 9th cusp. Here the sub-sub lord of ascendant is Sun whose star lord Saturn appears as the sub lord of the 4th cusp. Sun is in the sub of Mars that appears as the sub-sub lord of the 9th cusp.

The native studies medicine in the field of B.D.S when the planets Sun, Saturn, Mars and the sixth cusp maintain relationship with 4th or 9th cusp. We have already seen that Sun maintains relationship with the 4th and the 9th cusp. Saturn is in Sun star and Rahu sub. Sun is resident of 9th house and Rahu represents Moon and Mercury. Both these planets appear in the 4th cusp. Rahu and Mercury appear in the 9th cusp also. Mars is the sub-sub lord of the 9th cusp and is in Moon star and Saturn sub. Thus Mars is linked with 4th cusp. The sub-sub lord of the 6th cusp is Rahu that is in Mercury star that appears as the sub-sub lord of the 4th cusp and sub lord of the 9th cusp. All these justify his field of education.

Step 4: Mode and Place of Death: Death occurs due to accident and by getting bruised and mashed by a vehicle leading to respiratory failures, if the star lord of the sub-sub lord of the 8th cusp resides in Gemini. Here the sub-sub lord of the 8th cusp is Jupiter that is in Venus star. Venus resides in Gemini. The sub lord of the sub-sub lord of the 8th cusp will specify the place of death due to accident. Here Jupiter is in Mars sub that appears as the sub-sub lord of the 9th. This justifies death at far off work.

Step 5: The native met with an accident on 15.7.2004 at Banglore at about 16.00 hrs when he was running the joint period of Jup-Sat-Mars-Sun-Mercury/Ketu. The transit of planets at the time of accident and death is shown in Figure 4.29.

Fig. 4.29

Name	Fig 4.29	Place of Birth	Bangaluru
Sex	Male	Latitude	013.00.N
Date of Birth	15/07/2004	Longitude	077.36.E
Day of Birth	Thursday	Local Birth Time	15:40:24
Time of Birth	16:00:00	Local Birth Date	15/07/2004
Sidereal Time	11:14:50	Lunar Tithi	14
Bal. of Dasha	Rah 17Y 6M 25D	K.P. (New) Ayanamsa	23:54:30
Lagan	Scorpio	Lagan Lord	Mars
Sign	Gemini	Sign Lord	Mercury
Nakshatra	Ardra	Nakshatra Lord	Rahu

Fig. 4.29 Contd......

Nirayana Cusps

Bhav No.	Sign	Degree	Star Lord	Sub Lord	Sub-Sub Lord
1	Scorpio	20: 39' 09"	Mer	Ven	Jup
2	Sagittarius	19: 56' 15"	Ven	Rah	Mon
3	Capricorn	21: 03' 07"	Mon	Ven	Mon
4	Aquarius	23: 48' 58"	Jup	Sat	Jup
5	Pisces	25: 43' 15"	Mer	Rah	Ven
6	Aries	24: 31' 40"	Ven	Mer	Ven
7	Taurus	20: 39' 09"	Mon	Ven	Ven
8	Gemini	19: 56' 15"	Rah	Mar	Mon
9	Cancer	21: 03' 07"	Mer	Ven	Sat
10	Leo	23: 48' 58"	Ven	Sat	Jup
11	Virgo	25: 43' 15"	Mar	Rah	Ven
12	Libra	24: 31' 40"	Jup	Mer	Ven

Planetary Position

Planet	Sign	Degree	Star Lord	Sub Lord	Sub-Sub Lord
Sun	Gemini	29: 21' 47"	Jup	Sun	Ven
Mon	Gemini	06: 59' 04"	Rah	Rah	Jup
Mar	Cancer	19: 41' 19"	Mer	Ven	Ven
Mer	Cancer	23: 34' 46"	Mer	Mar	Jup
Jup	Leo	21: 42' 27"	Ven	Jup	Rah
Ven	Taurus	19: 50' 05"	Mon	Ket	Ven
Sat	Gemini	23: 48' 27"	Jup	Sat	Jup
Rah (R)	Aries	14: 27' 47"	Ven	Ven	Jup
Ket (R)	Libra	14: 27' 47"	Rah	Ket	Ket
Ura (R)	Aquarius	12: 25' 21"	Rah	Sat	Jup
Nep (R)	Capricorn	20: 39' 25"	Mon	Ven	Ven
Plu (R)	Scorpio	26: 09' 42"	Mer	Jup	Jup
Fortuna	Libra	28: 16' 26"	Jup	Ven	Sat

Death has taken place in the dasa of Jupiter, which do not show a very strong connection with the 1st and the 8th cusp.

Figure 4.30 Represents the True Horoscope. Took the RPs on 24.1.2005 at 10.20 at Noida and rectified the horoscope. Figure 4.31 shows the RP chart. Since Venus came as sub and sub-sub of RP (Moon) the sub-sub lord of the ascendant was fixed as Venus and the time was moved around a few seconds to ensure the promise of each cusp as well as the dasa potential of planets to cause the event of Death by accident.

Fig. 4.30

Name	Fig 4.30	Place of Birth	Meerut
Sex	Male	Latitude	029.00.N
Date of Birth	29/07/1980	Longitude	077.42.E
Day of Birth	Tuesday	Local Birth Time	12:20:09
Time of Birth	12:39:21	Local Birth Date	29/07/1980
Sidereal Time	8:48:29	Lunar Tithi	2
Bal. of Dasha	Mar 2Y 0M 11D	K.P. (New) Ayanamsa	23:34:27
Lagan	Libra	Lagan Lord	Venus
Sign	Aquarius	Sign Lord	Saturn
Nakshatra	Dhanistha	Nakshatra Lord	Mars

Lagna Chart

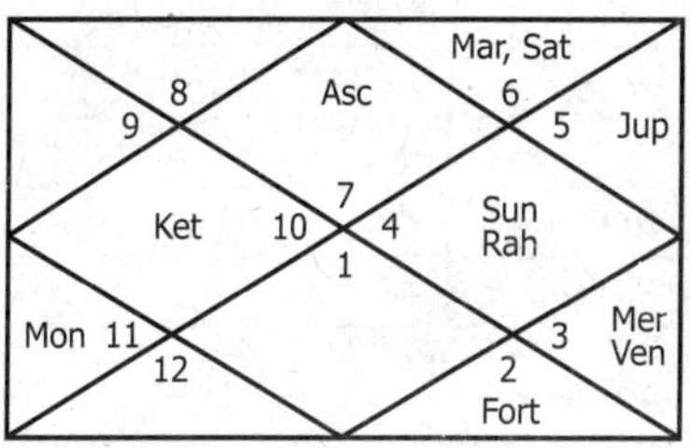

Bhava Chart

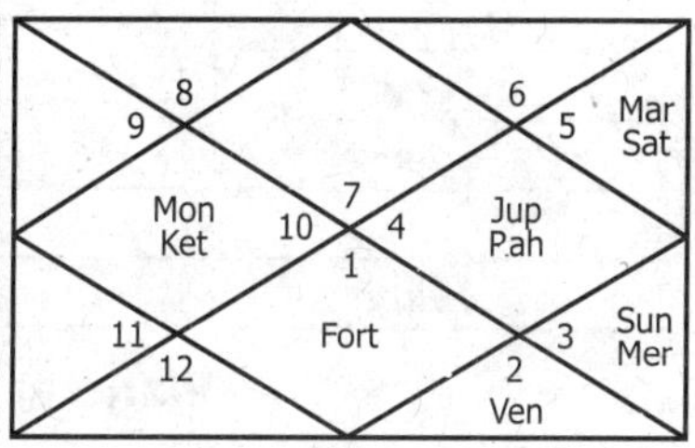

Cusp Chart

VI 17:48:41	VII 13:8:13	Fort 3:12:0 VIII 12:11:54	Ven 0:31:25 IX 13:22:10 Mer 23:46:51
V 18:27:12 Mon 2:48:10			Sun 12:44:23 X 16:6:31 Rah 26:37:18
Ket 26:37:18 IV 16:6:31			Jup 17:32:17 XI 18:27:12
III 13:22:10	II 12:11:54	I 13:8:13	Sat 0:13:18 Mar 17:8:21 XII 17:48:41

Fig. 4.30 Contd......

Nirayana Cusps

Bhav No.	Sign	Degree	Star Lord	Sub Lord	Sub-Sub Lord
1	Libra	13: 08' 13"	Rah	Mer	Ven
2	Scorpio	12: 11' 54"	Sat	Mar	Rah
3	Sagittarius	13: 22' 10"	Ven	Ven	Ven
4	Capricorn	16: 06' 31"	Mon	Sat	Mer
5	Aquarius	18: 27' 12"	Rah	Mon	Jup
6	Pisces	17: 48' 41"	Mer	Mer	Rah
7	Aries	13: 08' 13"	Ket	Mer	Sat
8	Taurus	12: 11' 54"	Mon	Rah	Jup
9	Gemini	13: 22' 10"	Rah	Mer	Mon
10	Cancer	16: 06' 31"	Sat	Jup	Sun
11	Leo	18: 27' 12"	Ven	Rah	Jup
12	Virgo	17: 48' 41"	Mon	Mer	Mer

Planetary Position

Planet	Sign	Degree	Star Lord	Sub Lord	Sub-Sub Lord
Sun	Cancer	12: 44' 23"	Sat	Mar	Ven
Mon	Aquarius	02: 48' 10"	Mar	Ven	Ven
Mar	Virgo	17: 08' 21"	Mon	Sat	Mar
Mer	Gemini	23: 46' 51"	Jup	Sat	Jup
Jup	Leo	17: 32' 17"	Ven	Mar	Jup
Ven	Gemini	00: 31' 25"	Mar	Mer	Ven
Sat	Virgo	00: 13' 18"	Sun	Rah	Mer
Rah (R)	Cancer	26: 37' 18"	Mer	Jup	Sat
Ket (R)	Capricorn	26: 37' 18"	Mar	Jup	Sat
Ura	Libra	27: 55' 43"	Jup	Ven	Jup
Nep (R)	Scorpio	26: 37' 15"	Mer	Jup	Sat
Plu	Virgo	25: 39' 19"	Mar	Rah	Ven
Fortuna	Taurus	03: 12' 00"	Sun	Sat	Sat

Fig. 4.31

Name	Fig 4.31	Place of Birth	Noida
Sex	Male	Latitude	028.20.N
Date of Birth	24/01/2005	Longitude	077.20.E
Day of Birth	Monday	Local Birth Time	09:59:20
Time of Birth	10:20:00	Local Birth Date	24/01/2005
Sidereal Time	18:13:45	Lunar Tithi	14
Bal. of Dasha	Jup 7Y 8M 19D	K.P. (New) Ayanamsa	23:54:57
Lagan	Pisces	Lagan Lord	Jupiter
Sign	Gemini	Sign Lord	Mercury
Nakshatra	Punarvasu	Nakshatra Lord	Jupiter

Fig. 4.31 Contd......

Nirayana Cusps

Bhav No.	Sign	Degree	Star Lord	Sub Lord	Sub-Sub Lord
1	Pisces	10: 57' 55"	Sat	Sun	Ven
2	Aries	17: 33' 55"	Ven	Mar	Jup
3	Taurus	15: 20' 36"	Mon	Jup	Mar
4	Gemini	09: 14' 30"	Rah	Jup	Mer
5	Cancer	03: 34' 17"	Sat	Sat	Sat
6	Leo	02: 41' 53"	Ket	Ven	Mer
7	Virgo	10: 57' 55"	Mon	Mon	Ven
8	Libra	17: 33' 55"	Rah	Sun	Mar
9	Scorpio	15: 20' 36"	Sat	Jup	Sat
10	Sagittarius	09: 14' 30"	Ket	Jup	Rah
11	Capricorn	03: 34' 17"	Sun	Sat	Mer
12	Aquarius	02: 41' 53"	Mar	Ven	Ven

Planetary Position

Planet	Sign	Degree	Star Lord	Sub Lord	Sub-Sub Lord
Sun	Capricorn	10: 23' 29"	Mon	Mon	Jup
Mon	Gemini	26: 54' 03"	Jup	Ven	Ven
Mar	Scorpio	26: 33' 10"	Mer	Jup	Sat
Mer	Sagittarius	26: 36' 56"	Ven	Ket	Mer
Jup	Virgo	24: 49' 27"	Mar	Rah	Sat
Ven	Sagittarius	24: 15' 21"	Ven	Mer	Mer
Sat (R)	Gemini	29: 07' 31"	Jup	Sun	Sat
Rah (R)	Aries	02: 52' 23"	Ket	Ven	Ket
Ket (R)	Libra	02: 52' 23"	Mar	Ven	Ven
Ura	Aquarius	11: 04' 05"	Rah	Sat	Mer
Nep	Capricorn	20: 45' 57"	Mon	Ven	Ven
Plu	Scorpio	29: 35' 25"	Mer	Sat	Rah
Fortuna	Leo	27: 28' 29"	Sun	Mon	Mar

Verification of the Chart

Step 1: The sub-sub lord of the ascendant maintains relationship with Moon's star.

Step 2: The sub-sub lord of the ascendant and 3rd cusp is Venus that shows short life.

Step 3: The sub-sub lord of the 8th cusp still remains Jupiter and accounts for the Mode and place of death.

Step 4: The linkage of the planets Sun, Saturn, Mars and the 6th cusp justify the field of education.

Step 5: The native met with the fatal accident during the joint period of Jup-Sat-Ven-Sun-Mercury. Now the dasa lord Jupiter has established the required relationship with 1 and 8. The Prana lord Mercury is in Jupiter star that is the sub-sub lord of the 8th cusp (accident) and 11th cusp (Badhaka) and is in Saturn sub. Thus Mercury is related to 1, 4,8,11 to cause accident while driving his own vehicle. Transit of planets also agrees. Moon transits in Jupiter star, Venus sub and Venus sub-sub. Jupiter is the sub-sub lord of the 8th and 11th cusp and is also the dasa lord. Venus is appearing in 1st, 3rd and 11th cusp. Moreover Venus in the Chart 4.30 is linked with 1, 4, and 12 being in the sub of Mercury. Sun transits in Moon star, Moon sub and Jupiter sub-sub. Moon in the chart 4.30 is the star lord of 4th and 12th cusp and Jupiter is the sub-sub lord of 8th and 11th cusp. Thus transit of planets Sun and Moon is in consonance with the nature of the event. Transit of dasa planets also justifies the event.

Example 9: Figure 4.32 is the horoscope of a child as per his noted birth time. The child was born with the following defects:

1. Deformed shape of head.
2. Cannot speak.
3. Legs too weak to allow him to walk.

Fig. 4.32

Name	Fig 4.32	Place of Birth	Delhi
Sex	Male	Latitude	028.39.N
Date of Birth	03/04/1997	Longitude	077.13.E
Day of Birth	Thursday	Local Birth Time	20:50:52
Time of Birth	21:12:00	Local Birth Date	03/04/1997
Sidereal Time	9:38:52	Lunar Tithi	11
Bal. of Dasha	Mar 4Y 8M 28D	K.P. (New) Ayanamsa	23:48:24
Lagan	Libra	Lagan Lord	Venus
Sign	Capricorn	Sign Lord	Saturn
Nakshatra	Dhanistha	Nakshatra Lord	Mars

Lagna Chart

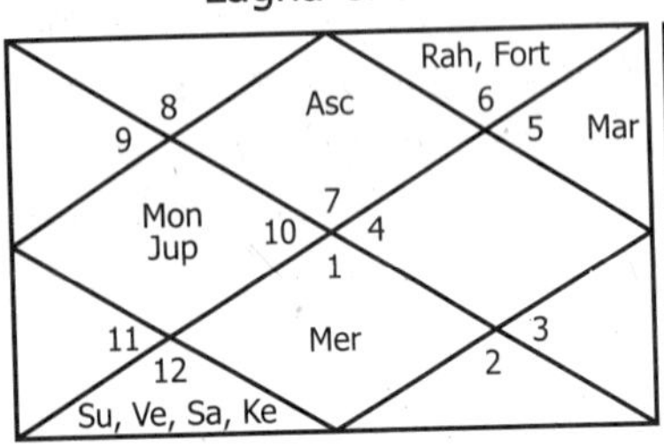

Bhava Chart

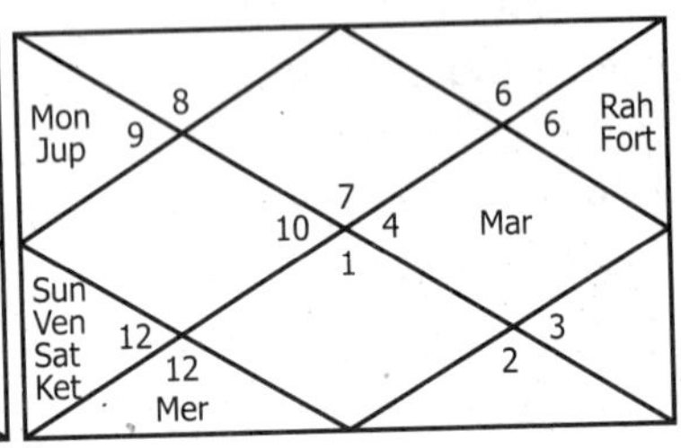

Cusp Chart

VI 29:21:19 Ven 20:24:12 Sun 20:7:15 Sat 16:55:0 Ket 4:53:15 V 0:51:26	Mer 8:54:48 VII 23:46:40	VIII 23:14:14	IX 25:6:8
			X 28:33:14
IV 28:33:14 Mon 27:37:55 Jup 21:40:41			Mar 26:40:9
III 25:6:8	II 23:14:14	I 23:46:40	XI 0:51:26 Fort 1:17:20 Rah 4:53:15 XII 29:21:19

Fig. 4.32 Contd......

Nirayana Cusps

Bhav No.	Sign	Degree	Star Lord	Sub Lord	Sub-Sub Lord
1	Libra	23: 46' 40"	Jup	Sat	Jup
2	Scorpio	23: 14' 14"	Mer	Mon	Ven
3	Sagittarius	25: 06' 08"	Ven	Mer	Rah
4	Capricorn	28: 33' 14"	Mar	Sat	Ket
5	Pisces	00: 51' 26"	Jup	Mar	Sat
6	Pisces	29: 21' 19"	Mer	Sat	Mar
7	Aries	23: 46' 40"	Ven	Sat	Jup
8	Taurus	23: 14' 14"	Mon	Sun	Ven
9	Gemini	25: 06' 08"	Jup	Mer	Rah
10	Cancer	28: 33' 14"	Mer	Sat	Ket
11	Virgo	00: 51' 26"	Sun	Rah	Sun
12	Virgo	29: 21' 19"	Mar	Sat	Mar

Planetary Position

Planet	Sign	Degree	Star Lord	Sub Lord	Sub-Sub Lord
Sun	Pisces	20: 07' 15"	Mer	Ven	Mar
Mon	Capricorn	27: 37' 55"	Mar	Jup	Rah
Mar (R)	Leo	26: 40' 09"	Sun	Sun	Sun
Mer	Aries	08: 54' 48"	Ket	Jup	Mon
Jup	Capricorn	21: 40' 41"	Mon	Ven	Jup
Ven	Pisces	20: 24' 12"	Mer	Ven	Rah
Sat	Pisces	16: 55' 00"	Mer	Mer	Mer
Rah (R)	Virgo	04: 53' 15"	Sun	Sat	Jup
Ket (R)	Pisces	04: 53' 15"	Sat	Sat	Rah
Ura	Capricorn	14: 13' 55"	Mon	Jup	Sat
Nep	Capricorn	05: 56' 04"	Sun	Mer	Mon
Plu (R)	Scorpio	11: 36' 20"	Sat	Mon	Sat
Fortuna	Virgo	01: 17' 20"	Sun	Jup	Jup

A child is born with a defect in his body parts when the following conditions exist in the horoscope.

A. The sub-sub lord of the ascendant should establish a link with 12th cusp through its star lord.The sub lord of the sub-sub lord of the ascendant will indicate the defective part as per its position in the cusp. If the sub-sub lord of the ascendant sub-sub lord is linked to cusps 5 or 11, the defect is curable. Linkage of the sub-sub lord of the ascendant sub-sub lord with 6th, 8th, or 12th cusp indicates no hope for cure.

B. The sub-sub lord of the cusp that represents the defective part should be linked with 8 or 12 through its star lord. If the star lord appears in 8th cusp and the sub lord in the 12th or the star lord appears in 12th and sub lord in the 8th cusp, this indicate permanent danger or defect in that part.

Check of Accuracy of Figure 4.32

Step 1: The sub-sub lord of the ascendant is Jupiter. The Moon's star lord at the time of birth is Mars. There is no relationship between the two.

Step 2: The Moon's star lord Mars maintains no relationship with the cusps 1, 7 and 10. (Refer Example 1 for reasons).

Step 3: The sub-sub lord of the ascendant is Jupiter. It is in Moon star. Moon does not appear in the 12th house, which is the house of defect.

Step 4: The child is born when he was running the period of planets Mars-Jup-Ra-Ra-Jup. The dasa potential of planets also does not promise birth with defective parts.

All the above factors indicate that the horoscope needs rectification. For this the ruling planets were taken on 28.1.2005 at 12.25 hrs at Noida. The RP planetary and cuspal positions are shown in Figure 4.33.

Fig. 4.33

Name	Fig 4.33	Place of Birth	Noida
Sex	Male	Latitude	028.20.N
Date of Birth	28/01/2005	Longitude	077.20.E
Day of Birth	Friday	Local Birth Time	12:04:20
Time of Birth	12:25:00	Local Birth Date	28/01/2005
Sidereal Time	20:34:52	Lunar Tithi	3
Bal. of Dasha	Ven 16Y 1M 1D	K.P. (New) Ayanamsa	23:54:57
Lagan	Aries	Lagan Lord	Mars
Sign	Leo	Sign Lord	Sun
Nakshatra	P.Phalguni	Nakshatra Lord	Venus

Fig. 4.33 Contd......

Nirayana Cusps

Bhav No.	Sign	Degree	Star Lord	Sub Lord	Sub-Sub Lord
1	Aries	27: 17' 24"	Sun	Sun	Ven
2	Taurus	24: 32' 34"	Mar	Rah	Jup
3	Gemini	18: 06' 51"	Rah	Mon	Mon
4	Cancer	12: 25' 13"	Sat	Mar	Sat
5	Leo	11: 14' 17"	Ket	Sat	Jup
6	Virgo	17: 17' 40"	Mon	Sat	Rah
7	Libra	27: 17' 24"	Jup	Ven	Mar
8	Scorpio	24: 32' 34"	Mer	Rah	Jup
9	Sagittarius	18: 06' 51"	Ven	Rah	Rah
10	Capricorn	12: 25' 13"	Mon	Rah	Jup
11	Aquarius	11: 14' 17"	Rah	Sat	Ven
12	Pisces	17: 17' 40"	Mer	Mer	Ven

Planetary Position

Planet	Sign	Degree	Star Lord	Sub Lord	Sub-Sub Lord
Sun	Capricorn	14: 32' 38"	Mon	Jup	Mer
Mon	Leo	15: 56' 30"	Ven	Sun	Sat
Mar	Scorpio	29: 24' 58"	Mer	Sat	Rah
Mer	Capricorn	02: 59' 47"	Sun	Jup	Rah
Jup	Virgo	24: 54' 44"	Mar	Rah	Sat
Ven	Sagittarius	29: 22' 30"	Sun	Rah	Rah
Sat (R)	Gemini	28: 48' 12"	Jup	Sun	Sun
Rah (R)	Aries	01: 58' 33"	Ket	Ven	Jup
Ket (R)	Libra	01: 58' 33"	Mar	Ket	Ven
Ura	Aquarius	11: 16' 51"	Rah	Sat	Ven
Nep	Capricorn	20: 55' 11"	Mon	Ven	Sun
Plu	Scorpio	29: 42' 41"	Mer	Sat	Rah
Fortuna	Scorpio	28: 41' 16"	Mer	Sat	Ven

The sub-sub lord of RP Moon was Saturn. Since Saturn does not establish any relationship with the Moon's star at birth it was rejected. The sub of RP Moon was Sun. As the Moon's star at birth is Mars, it bears relationship with it because Mars is in Sun star. It was decided to put Sun as the sub-sub lord of the ascendant. The rectified horoscope was obtained by moving around in seconds to ensure that other cuspal positions are fixed to match the promise of the horoscope. The rectified horoscope is shown in Figure 4.34.

Fig. 4.34

Name	Fig 4.34	Place of Birth	Delhi
Sex	Male	Latitude	028.39.N
Date of Birth	03/04/1997	Longitude	077.13.E
Day of Birth	Thursday	Local Birth Time	20:47:07
Time of Birth	21:08:15	Local Birth Date	03/04/1997
Sidereal Time	9:35:6	Lunar Tithi	11
Bal. of Dasha	Mar 4Y 9M 4D	K.P. (New) Ayanamsa	23:48:24
Lagan	Libra	Lagan Lord	Venus
Sign	Capricorn	Sign Lord	Saturn
Nakshatra	Dhanistha	Nakshatra Lord	Mars

Lagna Chart

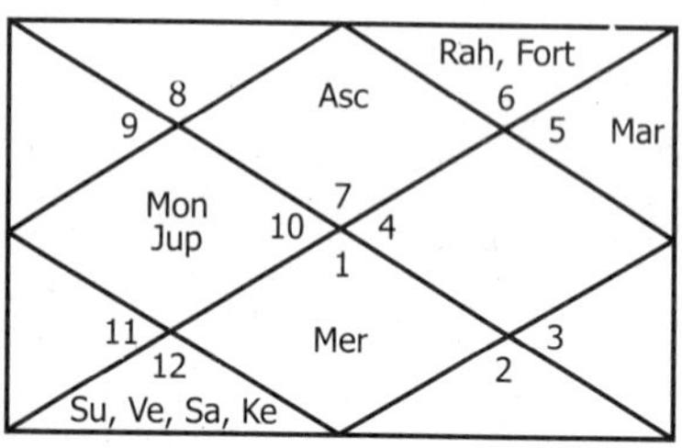

Bhava Chart

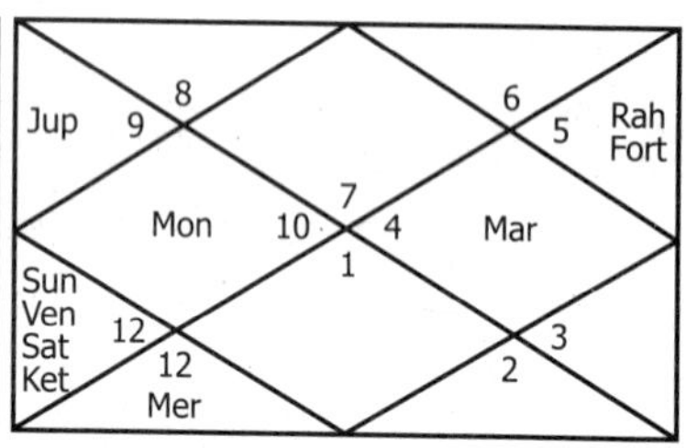

Cusp Chart

VI 28:28:59 Ven 20:24:1 Sun 20:7:6 Sat 16:54:59 Ket 4:53:15	Mer 8:54:37 VII 22:58:35	VIII 22:24:0	IX 24:11:55
V 29:54:30			X 27:35:28
Mon 27:35:38 IV 27:35:28 Jup 21:40:39			Mar 26:40:12 IX 29:54:30
III 24:11:55	II 22:24:0	I 22:58:35	Fort 0:27:7 Rah 4:53:15 XII 28:28:59

Fig. 4.34 Contd......

Nirayana Cusps

Bhav No.	Sign	Degree	Star Lord	Sub Lord	Sub-Sub Lord
1	Libra	22: 58' 35"	Jup	Sat	Sun
2	Scorpio	22: 24' 00"	Mer	Mon	Rah
3	Sagittarius	24: 11' 55"	Ven	Mer	Mer
4	Capricorn	27: 35' 28"	Mar	Jup	Mar
5	Aquarius	29: 54' 30"	Jup	Mon	Jup
6	Pisces	28: 28' 59"	Mer	Sat	Mer
7	Aries	22: 58' 35"	Ven	Sat	Ven
8	Taurus	22: 24' 00"	Mon	Ven	Mer
9	Gemini	24: 11' 55"	Jup	Mer	Ket
10	Cancer	27: 35' 28"	Mer	Jup	Mar
11	Leo	29: 54' 30"	Sun	Rah	Sat
12	Virgo	28: 28' 59"	Mar	Sat	Mer

Planetary Position

Planet	Sign	Degree	Star Lord	Sub Lord	Sub-Sub Lord
Sun	Pisces	20: 07' 06"	Mer	Ven	Mar
Mon	Capricorn	27: 35' 38"	Mar	Jup	Mar
Mar (R)	Leo	26: 40' 12"	Sun	Sun	Sun
Mer	Aries	08: 54' 37"	Ket	Jup	Mon
Jup	Capricorn	21: 40' 39"	Mon	Ven	Jup
Ven	Pisces	20: 24' 01"	Mer	Ven	Rah
Sat	Pisces	16: 54' 59"	Mer	Mer	Mer
Rah (R)	Virgo	04: 53' 15"	Sun	Sat	Jup
Ket (R)	Pisces	04: 53' 15"	Sat	Sat	Rah
Ura	Capricorn	14: 13' 55"	Mon	Jup	Sat
Nep	Capricorn	05: 56' 04"	Sun	Mer	Mon
Plu (R)	Scorpio	11: 36' 20"	Sat	Mon	Sat
Fortuna	Virgo	00: 27' 07"	Sun	Rah	Ket

Step 1: As stated above the sub-sub lord of the ascendant maintains relationship with the Moon's star lord at the Time of Birth.

Step 2: The Moon's star lord Mars itself appears as the sub-sub lord of the 10th cusp. It is in the star of Sun that is the sub-sub lord of the ascendant.

Step 3: The sub-sub lord of the ascendant is Sun. It is in Mercury star that appears as the sub-sub lord of the 12th cusp. It is in Venus sub that appears in the 3rd as well as in the 8th cusp. Third cusp indicates the child is not able to communicate. Sun is in the sub-sub of Mars that appears as the star lord of the 12th cusp and sub-sub lord of the 4th and the 10th cusp. The cure looks to be difficult.

Step 4: 3rd cusp SSL is Mercury, that is in Ketu star. Since Ketu represents Saturn being in its star, Mercury is as good as in Saturn star that is the sub lord of the 12th as well as the 6th cusp. Mercury is in the sub of Jupiter that is resident of 3rd cusp. Mercury is in the sub-sub of Moon that is the star lord of the 8th cusp but also the sub lord of the 5th cusp. Since Mercury is also the sub-sub lord of 12th cusp and it is in the star of Saturn (12th cusp) and sub of Jupiter that appears in 9th and 10th cusp, it justifies defect in legs also.

Step 5: The child was born when he was running the period of Mars-Jup-Mars-Venus-Venus. The Sookshma and Prana Lord Venus is in Mercury star and Venus sub. Mercury is the sub-sub lord of the 12th cusp and Venus is the sub lord of 3 and 8. The dasa periods also justifies the native's agony and defects at the time of birth.

The horoscope thus is rectified to be the correct horoscope.

Example10: Figure 4.35 is the chart of a gentleman as per his recorded birth time. The gentleman gave the following details of his life and wanted a correct horoscope.

1. Date of Marriage: 7.5.1981. The wife's Moon star is Ketu.
2. Date of birth of the first female child: 10.4.1982 at 04.42 A.M.
3. Transplantation of Kidney: 4.12.1997.

Fig 4.35

Name	Fig 4.35	Place of Birth	Amritsar
Sex	Male	Latitude	031.36.N
Date of Birth	09/06/1951	Longitude	074.54.E
Day of Birth	Saturday	Local Birth Time	09:47:36
Time of Birth	10:18:00	Local Birth Date	09/06/1951
Sidereal Time	2:54:34	Lunar Tithi	5
Bal. of Dasha	Sat 4Y 4M 12D	K.P. (New) Ayanamsa	23:10:03
Lagan	Cancer	Lagan Lord	Moon
Sign	Cancer	Sign Lord	Moon
Nakshatra	Pushya	Nakshatra Lord	Saturn

Lagna Chart

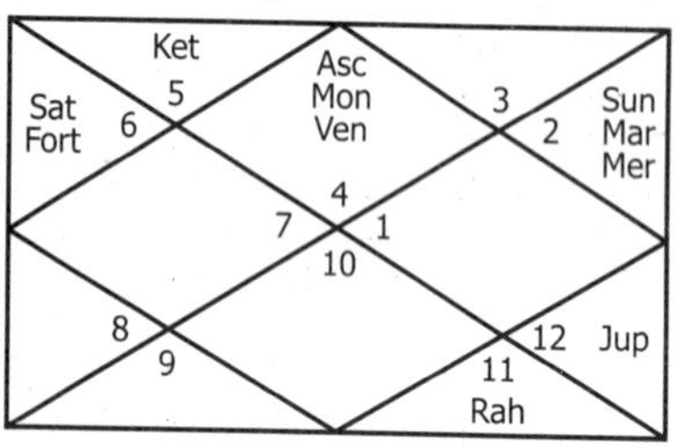

Bhava Chart

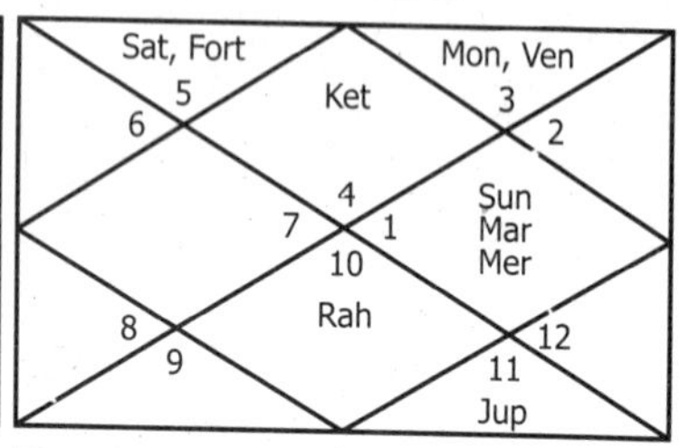

Cusp Chart

IX 20:27:59 Jup 16:18:5	X 22:56:45	Mer 6:33:11 Mar 19:52:2 Sun 24:23:55 XI 26:24:46	XII 28:9:41
VIII 21:43:1 Rah 20:34:48			Ven 8:55:50 Mon 13:36:2 I 27:17:6
VII 27:17:6			Ket 20:34:48 II 21:43:1
VI 28:9:41	V 26:24:46	IV 22:56:45	Sat 2:28:37 Fort 16:29:13 III 20:27:59

Fig. 4.35 Contd......

Nirayana Cusps

Bhav No.	Sign	Degree	Star Lord	Sub Lord	Sub-Sub Lord
1	Cancer	27: 17' 06"	Mer	Jup	Sun
2	Leo	21: 43' 01"	Ven	Jup	Rah
3	Virgo	20: 27' 59"	Mon	Ven	Ven
4	Libra	22: 56' 45"	Jup	Sat	Sun
5	Scorpio	26: 24' 46"	Mer	Jup	Sat
6	Sagittarius	28: 09' 41"	Sun	Mon	Ket
7	Capricorn	27: 17' 06"	Mar	Jup	Sun
8	Aquarius	21: 43' 01"	Jup	Jup	Rah
9	Pisces	20: 27' 59"	Mer	Ven	Jup
10	Aries	22: 56' 45"	Ven	Sat	Ven
11	Taurus	26: 24' 46"	Mar	Jup	Sat
12	Gemini	28: 09' 41"	Jup	Ven	Sat

Planetary Position

Planet	Sign	Degree	Star Lord	Sub Lord	Sub-Sub Lord
Sun	Taurus	24: 23' 55"	Mar	Rah	Rah
Mon	Cancer	13: 36' 02"	Sat	Rah	Sat
Mar	Taurus	19: 52' 02"	Mon	Ket	Sun
Mer	Taurus	06: 33' 11"	Sun	Mer	Jup
Jup	Pisces	16: 18' 05"	Sat	Jup	Mar
Ven	Cancer	08: 55' 50"	Sat	Ven	Rah
Sat	Virgo	02: 28' 37"	Sun	Jup	Sun
Rah (R)	Aquarius	20: 34' 48"	Jup	Jup	Mer
Ket (R)	Leo	20: 34' 48"	Ven	Jup	Sat
Ura	Gemini	15: 08' 47"	Rah	Ket	Mer
Nep (R)	Virgo	23: 41' 08"	Mar	Mar	Sat
Plu	Cancer	24: 36' 41"	Mer	Rah	Jup
Fortuna	Virgo	16: 29' 13"	Mon	Sat	Ven

Check of Accuracy of the horoscope of Figure 4.35

Step 1: The sub-sub lord of the ascendant is Sun. The Moon's star lord at the time of birth is Saturn that is in Sun star. Thus the sub-sub lord of the ascendant maintains relationship with the Moon's star lord.

Step 2: The native married on 7.5.1981 when he was running the joint period of Ven-Ven-Rahu-Venus-Mars/Rahu. The planet Venus has shown prominence in enacting the event. Now Venus is in Saturn star that appears in 4, 5, 7, 10, 11 and 12 cuspal positions. However Venus is in the sub of Venus that appears in 2, 3,9,10, 11 and 12 cuspal positions. The sub lord's linkages of dasa and Bhukti lord have the potential to cause the event of Marriage but with problems.

Step 3: The native got a female child on 10.4.1982 in the dasa period of planets Ven-Ven-Saturn-Moon-Mercury. The dasa potential of the planets justifies the event. The sub-sub lord of the 5th cusp is Saturn. It is in the sub-sub of Sun that occupies female sign Taurus. We may say that the native got the female child as promised by the sub-sub lord of the 5th cusp. The female child was born in the Moon's star of Rahu. Since Rahu represents Saturn, the 5th cusp sub-sub lord justifies the genetical connection also.

Step 4: Transplantation of Kidney: The native faces a serious disease of such a nature when the following conditions exist in the chart.

A. The sub-sub lord of the ascendant should be linked to 6th, 8th or 12th cusp through its star lord. The sub-lord of the ascendant sub-sub lord indicates the part of the body likely to be affected due to disease.

B. The 6th and the 8th sub-sub lords should be linked through star lords to 6 or 8 or 12 cusps. Their sub-lords will indicate the part of the body affected.

C. For Transplantation of an organ, the sub-sub lord of the 9th cusp should be linked to 6 or 8 or 12 through its star lord. The sub lord of the sub-sub lord of the 9th cusp will show the part due to which the change in the structure of the body occurs. The sub-sub lord of the sub-sub lord of the 9th cusp if connected with 1, 5 or 11 it shows recovery after transplantation. If the sub-sub lord of the sub-sub lord of the 9th cusp is linked to Maraka and Badhaka houses, it promises death after surgery.

D. The dasa potential of the planets at the time of transplantation and their transit along with the transit of Sun and Moon should justify the event.

In this chart, the sub-sub lord of the ascendant is Sun that is in Mars star. Mars does not appear in 6 or 8 or 12.

The sub-sub lord of the 6th cusp is Ketu that is in Venus star. Venus appears in the 12th cusp. Ketu is in the sub of Jupiter that appears in 7th and 8th cusp. Ketu also represents Venus that is in Saturn star and its own sub. This linkage justifies kidney problem.

The sub-sub lord of the 8th is Rahu that is in Jupiter star and Jupiter sub. This also establishes link with 7, 8 and 12 cusps. Rahu is in the sub-sub of Mercury that appears as the star lord of the 1st and the 5th cusp. The linkages of 8th and 9th sub-sub lord justify the native's undergoing successful kidney transplantation. The sub-sub lord of the 9th cusp is Jupiter that is in Saturn's star and Jupiter sub. The linkages of the 9th sub-sub lord also justify Kidney transplantation.

The Kidney transplantation was carried on 4.12.1997 when the native was running the period of Ven-Mer-Mars-Jup-Jup. It can be seen that the dasa potential justifies the event.

Above discussion indicates that the horoscope needs correction especially to justify the native's suffering from serious kidney problem by the sub sub lord of the ascendant.

To rectify the horoscope, the RP chart was prepared as per the date and time of judgement. Figure 4.36 shows the planetary and cuspal positions of RP chart.

Fig. 4.36

Name	Fig 4.36	Place of Birth	Noida
Sex	Male	Latitude	028.20.N
Date of Birth	29/01/2005	Longitude	077.20.E
Day of Birth	Saturday	Local Birth Time	05:25:14
Time of Birth	05:45:54	Local Birth Date	29/01/2005
Sidereal Time	13:58:37	Lunar Tithi	4
Bal. of Dasha	Ven 2Y 10M 0D	K.P. (New) Ayanamsa	23:54:57
Lagan	Sagittarius	Lagan Lord	Jupiter
Sign	Leo	Sign Lord	Sun
Nakshatra	P.Phalguni	Nakshatra Lord	Venus

Fig. 4.36 Contd......

Nirayana Cusps

Bhav No.	Sign	Degree	Star Lord	Sub Lord	Sub-Sub Lord
1	Sagittarius	21: 34' 48"	Ven	Jup	Mar
2	Capricorn	28: 12' 35"	Mar	Sat	Sat
3	Pisces	05: 40' 41"	Sat	Mer	Mer
4	Aries	07: 54' 26"	Ket	Jup	Sat
5	Taurus	04: 17' 34"	Sun	Sat	Mon
6	Taurus	27: 39' 07"	Mar	Jup	Rah
7	Gemini	21: 34' 48"	Jup	Jup	Rah
8	Cancer	28: 12' 35"	Mer	Sat	Sat
9	Virgo	05: 40' 41"	Sun	Mer	Ven
10	Libra	07: 54' 26"	Rah	Rah	Ket
11	Scorpio	04: 17' 34"	Sat	Sat	Ven
12	Scorpio	27: 39' 07"	Mer	Jup	Rah

Planetary Position

Planet	Sign	Degree	Star Lord	Sub Lord	Sub-Sub Lord
Sun	Capricorn	15: 16' 41"	Mon	Jup	Mon
Mon	Leo	24: 46' 46"	Ven	Mer	Sun
Mar	Scorpio	29: 55' 24"	Mer	Sat	Jup
Mer	Capricorn	04: 08' 37"	Sun	Sat	Sun
Jup	Virgo	24: 55' 20"	Mar	Rah	Sat
Ven	Capricorn	00: 16' 49"	Sun	Rah	Mer
Sat (R)	Gemini	28: 44' 50"	Jup	Ven	Ket
Rah (R)	Aries	01: 52' 35"	Ket	Ven	Rah
Ket (R)	Libra	01: 52' 35"	Mar	Mer	Sat
Ura	Aquarius	11: 19' 09"	Rah	Sat	Ven
Nep	Capricorn	20: 56' 49"	Mon	Ven	Mon
Plu	Scorpio	29: 43' 56"	Mer	Sat	Jup
Fortuna	Leo	01: 04' 53"	Ket	Ven	Ven

We notice that Sun has appeared as the sub-sub lord of the RP (Moon). Since Sun placed as the sub-sub lord of the ascendant of the native's chart does not justify the nature of serious disease, we have to reject it. The sub lord of RP (Moon) is Mercury that does not maintain any relation with the Moon's star lord Saturn at the time of birth. This was also rejected. The next planet in the RP (Moon) series is Venus. Since Venus maintains relationship with the Moon's star lord Saturn, it was decided to put Venus as the sub-sub lord of the ascendant of the Native. The corrected chart of the native is shown in Fig. 4.37.

Fig. 4.37

Name	Fig 4.37	Place of Birth	Amritsar
Sex	Male	Latitude	031.36.N
Date of Birth	09/06/1951	Longitude	074.54.E
Day of Birth	Saturday	Local Birth Time	09:47:34
Time of Birth	10:17:58	Local Birth Date	09/06/1951
Sidereal Time	2:54:32	Lunar Tithi	5
Bal. of Dasha	Sat 4Y 4M 12D	K.P. (New) Ayanamsa	23:10:03
Lagan	Cancer	Lagan Lord	Moon
Sign	Cancer	Sign Lord	Moon
Nakshatra	Pushya	Nakshatra Lord	Saturn

Lagna Chart

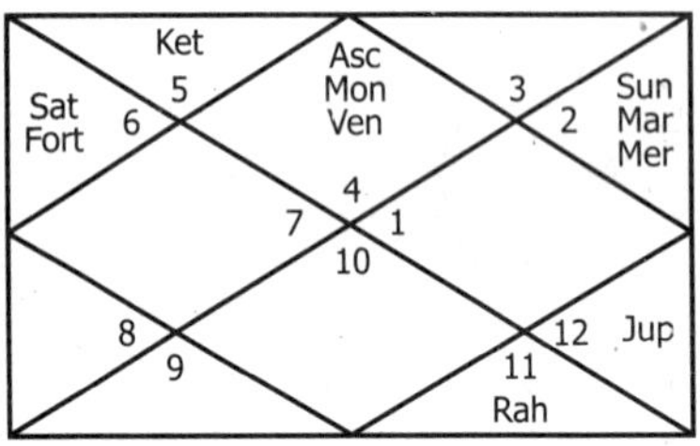

Bhava Chart

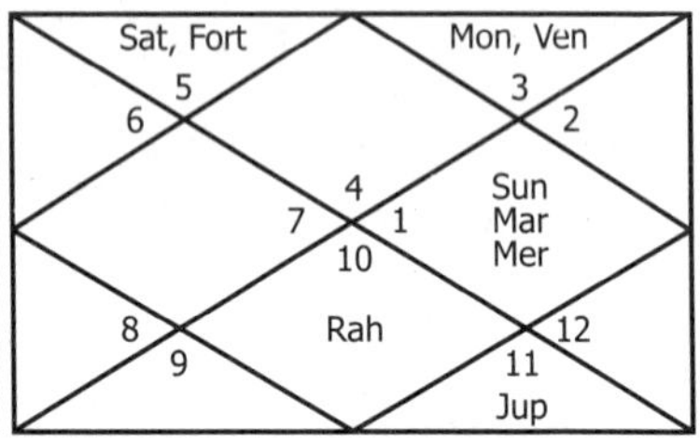

Cusp Chart

IX 20:27:29 Jup 16:18:5	X 22:56:14	Mer 6:33:11 Mar 19:52:2 Sun 24:23:54 XI 26:24:17	XII 28:9:14
VIII 21:42:33 Rah 20:34:48			Ven 8:55:50 Mon 13:36:1 I 27:16:41
VII 27:16:41			Ket 20:34:48 II 21:42:33
VI 28:9:14	V 26:24:17	IV 22:56:14	Sat 2:28:37 Fort 16:28:48 III 20:27:29

Fig. 4.37 Contd......

Nirayana Cusps

Bhav No.	Sign	Degree	Star Lord	Sub Lord	Sub-Sub Lord
1	Cancer	27: 16' 41"	Mer	Jup	Ven
2	Leo	21: 42' 33"	Ven	Jup	Rah
3	Virgo	20: 27' 29"	Mon	Ven	Ven
4	Libra	22: 56' 14"	Jup	Sat	Sun
5	Scorpio	26: 24' 17"	Mer	Jup	Sat
6	Sagittarius	28: 09' 14"	Sun	Mon	Ket
7	Capricorn	27: 16' 41"	Mar	Jup	Ven
8	Aquarius	21: 42' 33"	Jup	Jup	Rah
9	Pisces	20: 27' 29"	Mer	Ven	Rah
10	Aries	22: 56' 14"	Ven	Sat	Ven
11	Taurus	26: 24' 17"	Mar	Jup	Sat
12	Gemini	28: 09' 14"	Jup	Ven	Sat

Planetary Position

Planet	Sign	Degree	Star Lord	Sub Lord	Sub-Sub Lord
Sun	Taurus	24: 23' 54"	Mar	Rah	Rah
Mon	Cancer	13: 36' 01"	Sat	Rah	Sat
Mar	Taurus	19: 52' 02"	Mon	Ket	Sun
Mer	Taurus	06: 33' 11"	Sun	Mer	Jup
Jup	Pisces	16: 18' 05"	Sat	Jup	Mar
Ven	Cancer	08: 55' 50"	Sat	Ven	Rah
Sat	Virgo	02: 28' 37"	Sun	Jup	Sun
Rah (R)	Aquarius	20: 34' 48"	Jup	Jup	Mer
Ket (R)	Leo	20: 34' 48"	Ven	Jup	Sat
Ura	Gemini	15: 08' 47"	Rah	Ket	Mer
Nep (R)	Virgo	23: 41' 08"	Mar	Mar	Sat
Plu	Cancer	24: 36' 41"	Mer	Rah	Jup
Fortuna	Virgo	16: 28' 48"	Mon	Sat	Ven

Verification of the Accuracy of Figure 4.37

Step 1: The sub-sub lord of the ascendant Venus is in the star of Saturn that is the Moon's star lord.

Step 2: The native married on 7.5.1981 in the joint period of Ven-Ven-Rahu-Ven-Rahu. Now Venus being in its own sub that has come as the sub-sub lord of the 7th cusp and sign lord of 11 allows marriage to take place in its Bhukti. Venus is the sub-sub lord of the 7th cusp and being in the sub-sub of Rahu also justifies marriage with a lady born under Rahu star.

Step 3: The native got the female child on 10.4.1982 in the dasa period of planets Ven-Ven-Saturn-Moon-Mercury. The 5th cusp sub-sub lord remains Saturn in the corrected chart and also the birth of the child has appeared in the same dasa periods, which was running as per the recorded time chart (Figure 4.35). We have already seen above that this completely justifies the event.

Step 4: Kidney Transplantation: In the rectified chart the sub-sub lord of the ascendant is Venus that is in Saturn star, Venus sub and Rahu sub-sub. Saturn appears in the 12th cusp as sub-sub lord and is the Sign lord of the 8th cusp. The sub lord of Venus is Venus that appears in the 7th cusp. The sub-sub lord of Venus is Rahu that represents both Saturn and Jupiter. These planets are linked with 8th and 12th cusps but also with the 5th and 11th cusp. Serious disease and possibility of recovery through surgery is indicated.

The sub-sub lord of the 6th cusp is Ketu that is in Venus star, Jupiter sub and Saturn sub-sub. This also justifies that the native has to undergo serious health problems. Since Ketu is in Venus star that appears as the sub-sub lord of the 7th cusp, Kidney disease looks prominent.

The sub-sub lord of the 8th cusp and the 9th cusp are Rahu. We have seen above this justifies the Kidney transplantation.

The native had the kidney transplant on 4.12.1997 when he was running the joint period of Ven-Mer-Mar-Jup-Jup, which justifies the event.

The horoscope of Figure 4.37 therefore stands corrected.

Chapter 5

Advanced Technique of Birth Time Rectification

Research findings of the astrologer have lead to carry out certain amendments in the basic technique of rectification. The amendments are listed below:

1. **Use of RPs:** RPs should be taken up to the Prana level that is SSSS level. This is needed because invariably we find that the position of Sun may not change during the Antara or sub- sub level and we may take it as the final position of Sun. But even during a small change in time sometimes the position of Sun changes at Sookshama (SSS Level) or Prana (SSSS Level) level which may be the actual position of Sun for the correct chart. Ruling planets are used to correct the position of planets which are liable to change during the interval of time period in which we are seeking to fix the correct chart.

   Cast the chart as per given data. Set the position of Sun. Look for the time at which Sun's position show a change at SSS or SSSS level. Here we have to take a decision whether to retain the changed position or the previous one. This is done by comparing the changed position planet and the previous planet with the RPs ascendant planets. Select the planet which is a ruling planet and reject the other. If both happen to be RPs then select the stronger one. Remember strength of the RPs is from the SSSS position to the Sign lord.

Having set the Sun's position we fix the Moon position in similar fashion.

This will give almost a correct position of ascendant. We may however have to do micro adjustment to satisfy necessary conditions for the SS lord of the ascendant. This is done by using planets from RP (Moon) series.

2. **Promise of Various Aspects of Life:** We need to amend the technique of deciding the promise of significant aspects of life. It is observed that an aspect is said to be promised if the SS lord of ascendant and SS lord of the Primary cusp of the aspect gets related to the Primary cusp directly or indirectly. Direct linkage means the star Lord of SS lord is in the primary cusp and the sub lord appears in one of the supporting cusp. Indirectly related means that the star lord of the SS lord is in one of the supporting cusp and the sub lord appears in the Primary cusp.

3. **Promise of Execution of Events:** An event is promised to happen only at a specific time what we call as when destined to happen. Destiny wheel is related to the concept of Progression. Each cusp and each planet progresses from its position at the time of ascendant at the rate fixed by the philosophy of Vimsottary Dasa. In other words we may say that the natal chart SS lords of ascendant and the relevant cusp declares the promise of various aspects of life but it is the progressed position of the ascendant that declares the destined time of the execution of the promised event.

Planets co-ruling the progressed ascendant at any time reveal the promise of the events likely to happen at that time as per their significations in the natal chart.

Progressed chart at any day an event happens confirms the execution of the promised event as per the significations of Dasa period lords in the progressed chart.

4. **Timing Significant Events:** The statement that a promised event happens in the joint period of planets those are fruitful significators of the houses that take part in enacting the event when transit agrees appears to be incomplete. Many a times we find that the native was running the period of fruitful significators and transit also agreed but the event did not take place. **This has necessitated extending the above statement. We need to say that a promised event happens in the joint period of planets those are fruitful significators of the houses that take part in enacting the event provided transit and progressed position of ascendant, Primary cusp, Sun and Moon agree. Progressed chart should also justify the event.**

We also need to remember that there are some specific conditions for Dasa period lords that need be satisfied. For example events of death take place only in specific Dasas. Criterion for Markesh Dasa may be stated as below:

1. Dasa Lord should be a co-ruling planet in 1st cusp or 8th cusp or Badhaka. Planets placed in 1st or 8th cusp are to be treated as co-ruling planets with PS or no PS. Dasa lord should be related to the SS lord of the 8th cusp or planets placed in 8th Bhava. A planet is said to be related to another planet when both the planets are in the same star. This concept is in addition to other methods which we have stated in earlier chapters.

2. In case of Rahu/Ketu either they themselves should be co-ruling planets in 1st or 8th or Badhaka or the planets they represent should be co-ruling planets.

3. Dasa lord should justify necessary and essential conditions for death both as per PS and Stellar status.
4. In case of Rahu or Ketu Dasa, Rahu as Rahu or Ketu as Ketu as well as the planets Rahu/Ketu represent all should fulfill necessary & essential conditions for death.

Role of Dasa Period Lords for Significant Events:

Dasa should permit the event.

Bhukti should be linked to primary cusp directly or indirectly.

If, however, Bhukti lord appears as a co-ruling planet of primary cusp and signifies supporting cusps, then it can allow the event to happen.

Antara: Same as for Bhukti Lord.

Sookshma & Prana lords should satisfy above conditions as well as some specific conditions.

Example: If a person commits suicide the Prana lord has to be one of the co-ruling planets in the ascendant. In other words Prana Lord's cuspal position indicates how the event happens.

Role of Transit

1. Dasa Period lords should also signify event in transit.
   a) They should excite the cuspal positions of relevant cusps fruitfully.
   b) They should transit in sign/star/sub and sub sub that should be independently significator of relevant cusps.
2. Transit of Jupiter, Sun & Moon should in addition to the above conditions 'a' & 'b' meet some specific conditions. For example Moon's star Lord on the day of happening of the

event should be related to the SS lord of the Primary cusp and should be significator of the event. Similarly the Sub Lord of Sun at the time of happening should be strong significator of the event and invariably be related to the SS lord of the Primary cusp.

Fixing Dasa period lords and Transit for specific events

1. Planets placed in a Bhava with PS or without PS may be treated as virtual SS lord of the Bhava.
2. Dasa period lords should be related to the primary cusp directly or indirectly.
3. Transit of Jup, Sun & Moon etc. has to be decided by the SSL of the Primary cusp or its star lord (if they signify relevant event).
4. Relation with SSL of the primary cusp can be established as follows:-
   a) Planet may be in the star of the planet that is either itself be the SSL of the primary cusp or its star lord if they signify the event.
   b) A planet may involve the supporting cusp and is in the sub of the planet that is the SSL of the primary cusp.
   c) Or both planets are in same star.

Conditions for Immediate Death

1. Dasa period lords should be co-ruling planets of ascendant or 8th cusp.
2. Dasa lord should justify the criterion for Markesh Dasa.

3. Planets co-ruling ascendant especially the SSL of ascendant should involve and commit to 1st & 8th or Badhaka.

4. Transit of Saturn should meet the necessary criteria. **The lord of the Sign in which Saturn transits should be a co ruling planet in 8th cusp or Badhaka. It should be related to the SS lord of the 8th cusp and be a strong significator of death. This criterion applies to all events of death.**

5. Transit of Jupiter, Sun, Moon & Dasa period lords should agree.

Moment of Event-Formation of ascendant

1. Planets co-ruling ascendant need to be significator of the event in the natal chart.

2. Planets co-ruling the ascendant need also signify the relevant cusps as per their transit positions.

We will explain the use of the advanced technique through examples.

It may be noted that charts in this chapter are cast using True Astrology Software version 4.0.3 and using Khullar (hourly) Ayanamsa, Geocentric Latitude, Nutation Apply, and True Nodes.

Example 1: A Mumbai KCIL follower was asked to rectify the chart of a person. The following data was provided to the Astrologer:

Date of birth: 23rd July 1973 at Berhampur, Orissa. 84 E 47; 19 N 19

Birth time: It is reported to be between 12-15 Hrs and 12-25 Hrs.

Moon star of: Father-Venus; Mother-Mars; Elder sister-Mars.

Profession: The native is in service.

The Astrologer decided to do the rectification of the chart on 10th Jan, 2011 at 0700 hrs. at his place of residence (Long 073.11.16 E); Latitude 019.11.37). The ruling planets of ascendant and Moon were as follows.

RP (Ascendant): Jupiter-Venus-Jupiter-Sun-Venus-Mars

RP (Moon): Saturn-Jupiter-Sun-Saturn-Ketu-Mercury

The Astrologer followed step by step the procedure as laid down above. He casted the Horoscope using the given data and time of birth as 12.15hrs. He noticed that the position of Sun does not change from 12.15 to 12.25 which was the given range of time of birth. Next he found that Moon's position remains in SS of Mercury up to 12.20.26 hrs. Since Mercury is not coming in RP (ascendant) series it was decided that birth of the native could not have taken place before 12.20.26 hrs. After this time Moon enters in Ketu SS. Since Jupiter appears two times in RP (ascendant) and Ketu represents Jupiter on that day he decided to keep Ketu as Moon's SS. Next since Venus appeared two times in RP (ascendant) he decided to place Venus as SSS of Moon. This position corresponds to 12.22 hrs and gave the ascendant as Libra in Rahu star Mercury Sub and SS.

The Astrologer then started to do micro rectification to fine tune the position of ascendant and other cuspal positions by using the planets from the RP (Moon) series. To do this he followed the following steps:

Fix the sub sub lord of ascendant to establish link with the Moon's star lord at the time of birth.

1. Check that the planets co-ruling the positions of Sun, Moon and ascendant are related to 1,7,10. Since the native's chart is an event chart with respect to 9th cusp the relationship of planets has to be verified using the concepts of transit theory as explained in KCIL.

2. Having done this he had to ensure that sub sub lords of relevant cusps establish relationship with the Moon stars of Mother, Father and elder sister.

3. Since heredity plays a significant role in the formation of the horoscope the astrologer has to adjust the sub sub lord of the 9th cusp so that it establishes relationship with father's Moon star as well as is related to cusps 3, 6 and 9. Father of the native is child of his father who is represented by 5th cusp.

This exercise ultimately resulted in fixing the chart at time 12.22.34 hrs. This gave an ascendant of Libra 12.49.48 degree with Ketu as the sub sub lord of the ascendant. Fig 5.1 is the rectified horoscope. Correct longitude and latitude at place of birth has been used.

Fig. 5.1

Name	Fig 5.1	Place	Berhampur
Longitude	84-48-31-E	Latitude	19-18-31-N
Sidereal Time	08-35-17	Date	23/7/1973
Day	Monday	Geocentric Latitude	19-11-20-N
Nakshatra	Ashwini-3 Qtr.	Time	12:22:34
Lunar Nodes	True	Tithi	Krishna Paksha - Asthami
Time Zone	+5:30:0	DST	00:00
Ayanamsa	23-28-35	House System	Placidus

Rashi Chart

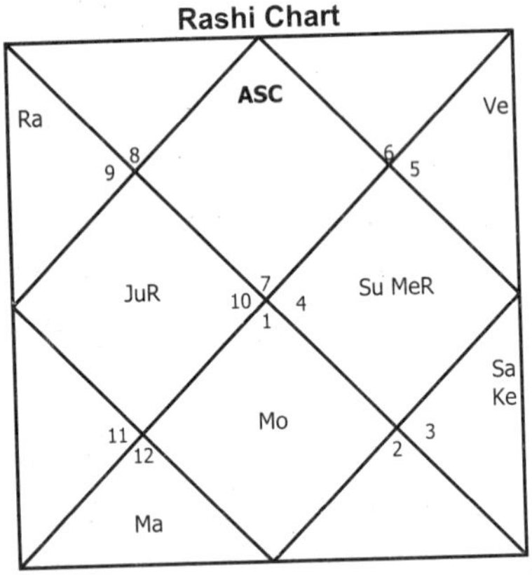

Bhava Chart

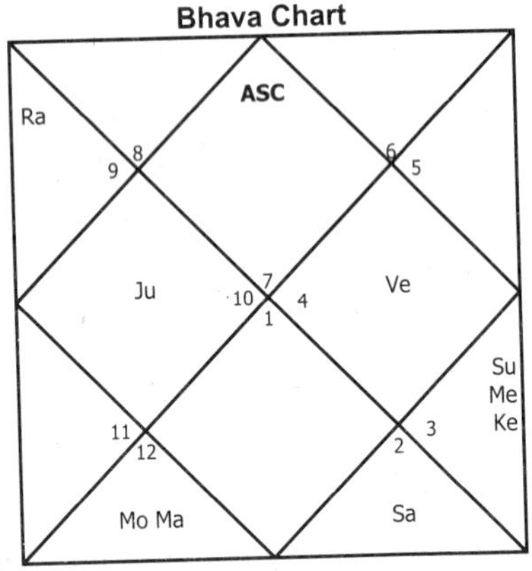

Cusp Chart

Ma 26-22-21 VI 15-15-10	Mo 08-20-47 VII 12-49-48	VIII 12-04-38	Sa 05-24-55 IX 11-58-52 Ke 13-58-32
V 14-41-24			MeR 01-55-56 Su 06-47-42 X 12-57-37
JuR 14-39-29 IV 12-57-37			Ve 04-20-07 XI 14-41-24
Ra 13-58-32 III 11-58-52	II 12-04-38	I 12-49-48	XII 15-15-10

Fig. 5.1 Contd......

Planetary Position

Planet	Sign	D-M-S	R L	STL	SL	SSL	Hse	D	S
Sun	Can	06-47-42	Mo	Sa	Me	Ju	9	P	
Moon	Ari	08-20-47	Ma	Ke	Ju	Ke	6		
Mars	Pis	26-22-21	Ju	Me	Ju	Sa	6		
Mercury	Can	01-55-56	Mo	Ju	Ra	Sa	9	R	
Jupiter	Cap	14-39-29	Sa	Mo	Ju	Me	4	R	
Venus	Leo	04-20-07	Su	Ke	Mo	Me	10	P	
Saturn	Gem	05-24-55	Me	Ma	Su	Ke	8		
T.Rahu	Sag	13-58-32	Ju	Ve	Ve	Mo	3		
T.Ketu	Gem	13-58-32	Me	Ra	Me	Ju	9	P	

Cuspal Position

Cusp	Sign	D-M-S	R L	STL	SL	SSL	% Arc
Cusp I	Lib	12-49-48	Ve	Ra	Me	Ke	06.28
Cusp II	Sco	12-04-38	Ma	Sa	Mo	Su	38.95
Cusp III	Sag	11-58-52	Ju	Ke	Me	Ve	50.46
Cusp IV	Cap	12-57-37	Sa	Mo	Ra	Me	66.37
Cusp V	Aqu	14-41-24	Sa	Ra	Ke	Mo	48.81
Cusp VI	Pis	15-15-10	Ju	Sa	Ju	Sa	45.11
Cusp VII	Ari	12-49-48	Ma	Ke	Me	Ju	18.93
Cusp VIII	Tau	12-04-38	Ve	Mo	Ra	Ra	62.77
Cusp IX	Gem	11-58-52	Me	Ra	Sa	Ra	07.47
Cusp X	Can	12-57-37	Mo	Sa	Ra	Ra	23.79
Cusp XI	Leo	14-41-24	Su	Ve	Ve	Ju	76.61
Cusp XII	Vir	15-15-10	Me	Mo	Ju	Mo	70.70

Verification of the Accuracy of the Chart:

Accuracy of Sun, Moon and Ascendant: It can be verified that the planets co-ruling the positions of Sun, Moon and ascendant are related to 1st, 7th, and 10th cusps.

It may be remembered that it is not a must that planets should be related to 1st, 7th and 10th all simultaneously. Planets may be related to 1st and 7th, 7th and 10th like that.

Sub-sub lord of ascendant is Ketu that is the Moon star of the native. Sub-sub arc of Ketu is in first half. Since male Sign rises on the ascendant it justifies the sex of the native.

Genetical Connections: Sub sub lord of 4th cusp is Mercury. Moon star of mother is Mars that is in Mercury star. Sub sub lord of 11th cusp is Jupiter. Moon star of elder sister is Mars that is in the sub of Jupiter. Moon star of father is Venus that is in Ketu star. Since Ketu is placed in the 9th Bhava it satisfies the linkage of Moon star of father with 9th cusp. Planet placed in a Bhava acts as virtual sub sub lord of the cusp.

Service as Profession: Sub sub lord of the 6th cusp is Saturn. It is also available in 10th cusp. Saturn is in Mars star that is placed in 6 and also appears as Sign lord of 2. Saturn is in the sub of Sun that is the sub sub lord of 2. This justifies earning of the native through service.

Since no significant event details were provided the native took it to be the right horoscope.

Example 2: Ms Jacqueline Kennedy Onassis is no more with us but the study of her horoscope provides a lot to learn for astrologers. Her birth details as notified are as follows:

D.O.B: 28 Jul 1929

T.O.B: 14.30 hrs. EDT +4.00

P.O.B: Southampton, New York (Long 072.23.24; Latitude 40.53.03 N).

Genitical Connections: Moon stars of relative's are shown below:

First Husband –Venus; first child (female)- Moon; second child (male)-Rahu; third child (male)- Rahu

She had a younger sister born in the year 1933.

She published books.

Significant Events:

First Marriage: 12th September 1953

She had a miscarriage in 1955. She delivered a still born child on 23.08.1956.

First child (female): 27.11.1957

Second child (male): 25.11.1960

Third child (male): 07.08.1963

Death of third child: 09.08.1963

Death of first husband: 22.11.1963

Second marriage: 20.10.1968

Death of second husband: 28.07.1974

Figure 5.2 indicates the chart of the native cast as per the given data.

Fig. 5.2

Name	Fig 5.2	Place	Southampton
Longitude	72-23-24-W	Latitude	40-53-3-N
Sidereal Time	10-04-10	Date	28/7/1929
Day	Sunday	Geocentric Latitude	40-41-38-N
Nakshatra	Ashwini- 1 Qtr.	Time	14:30:00
Lunar Nodes	True	Tithi	Krishna Paksha - Saptami
Time Zone	-4:0:0	DST	00:00
Ayanamsa	22-51-46	House System	Placidus

Rashi Chart

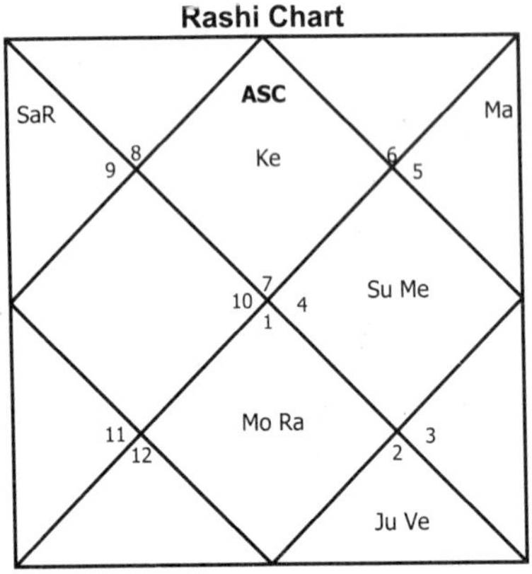

Bhava Chart

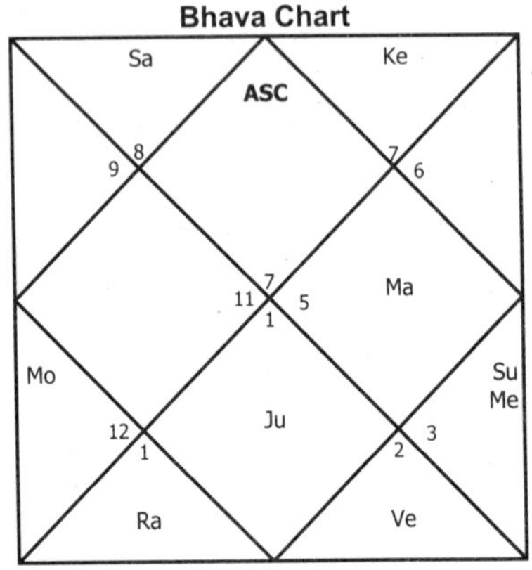

Cusp Chart

V 08-08-51	Mo 02-44-39 VI 04-04-37 Ra 24-54-49 VII 25-11-21	Ju 16-42-41 VIII 25-02-00 Ve 28-54-38	IX 29-45-16
IV 06-02-25			Me 09-32-32 Su 12-17-58
			X 06-02-25 Ma 21-57-58
III 29-45-16 SaR 01-47-37	II 25-02-00	I 25-11-21 Ke 24-54-49 XII 04-04-37	XI 08-08-51

Fig. 5.2 Contd......

Planetary Position

Planet	Sign	D-M-S	R L	STL	SL	SSL	Hse	D	S
Sun	Can	12-17-58	Mo	Sa	Ma	Ju	9	P	
Moon	Ari	02-44-39	Ma	Ke	Ve	Me	5	P	
Mars	Leo	21-57-58	Su	Ve	Sa	Sa	10	P	
Mercury	Can	09-32-32	Mo	Sa	Ve	Sa	9	P	
Jupiter	Tau	16-42-41	Ve	Mo	Sa	Ve	7		
Venus	Tau	28-54-38	Ve	Ma	Sa	Ve	8	P	
Saturn	Sag	01-47-37	Ju	Ke	Ve	Ra	2	R	
T.Rahu	Ari	24-54-49	Ma	Ve	Me	Mo	6	P	
T.Ketu	Lib	24-54-49	Ve	Ju	Me	Ma	12		

Cuspal Position

Cusp	Sign	D-M-S	R L	STL	SL	SSL	% Arc
Cusp I	Lib	25-11-21	Ve	Ju	Me	Ra	86.73
Cusp II	Sco	25-02-00	Ma	Me	Ra	Me	13.73
Cusp III	Sag	29-45-16	Ju	Su	Ra	Ju	87.07
Cusp IV	Aqu	06-02-25	Sa	Ma	Mo	Sa	07.11
Cusp V	Pis	08-08-51	Ju	Sa	Ve	Ve	09.84
Cusp VI	Ari	04-04-37	Ma	Ke	Mo	Ju	58.12
Cusp VII	Ari	25-11-21	Ma	Ve	Me	Ra	47.52
Cusp VIII	Tau	25-02-00	Ve	Ma	Ra	Me	13.73
Cusp IX	Gem	29-45-16	Me	Ju	Mo	Ra	91.53
Cusp X	Leo	06-02-25	Su	Ke	Ra	Ju	69.27
Cusp XI	Vir	08-08-51	Me	Su	Ve	Ve	99.84
Cusp XII	Lib	04-04-37	Ve	Ma	Ve	Ju	94.68

On a casual look the chart appears to satisfy conditions for Genitical connections and also the planets co-ruling Sun, Moon and ascendant appears to satisfy the necessary linkages with 1st, 7th, and 10th cusps. However detailed analysis of the chart for various events, promises of various aspects of life reveals that the chart needs micro rectification. As such the ruling planets were taken on 13.07.2011 at 07.50.53 hrs at Noida (Long 77.21.6 E; Latitude 28.33.50 N).

These were as follows:

RP (Ascendant): Moon-Mercury-Rahu-Mercury-Mars-Venus

RP (Moon): Mars-Mercury-Saturn-Moon-Sun-Rahu

On this day Rahu represented Mars and Mercury. Ketu represented Venus and Mars.

The chart was rectified by first fixing the position of Sun and then of Moon. It was observed that at 14.28.02 hrs Sun is in the SSSS of Mars and Moon is in the SSS of Mars and SSSS of Venus. Both Mars and Venus are planets that appear in position of strength in RP (ascendant) series. Corresponding to this position of Sun and Moon we get the ascendant with Mercury as sub lord and Moon as the SS lord. Both Mercury and Moon appear in RP (Moon) series.

Figure 5.3 represents the rectified chart of the native.

Fig. 5.3

Name	Fig 5.3	Place	Southampton
Longitude	72-23-24-W	Latitude	40-53-3-N
Sidereal Time	10-02-12	Date	28/7/1929
Day	Sunday	Geocentric Latitude	40-41-38-N
Nakshatra	Ashwini- 1 Qtr.	Time	14:28:02
Lunar Nodes	True	Tithi	Krishna Paksha - Saptami
Time Zone	-4:0:0	DST	00:00
Ayanamsa	22-51-46	House System	Placidus

Rashi Chart

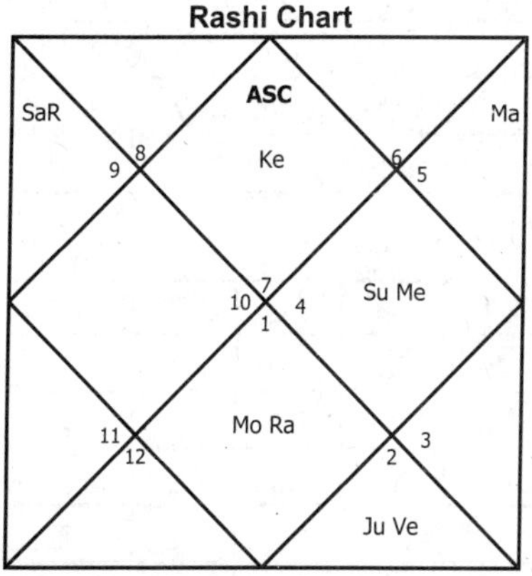

Bhava Chart

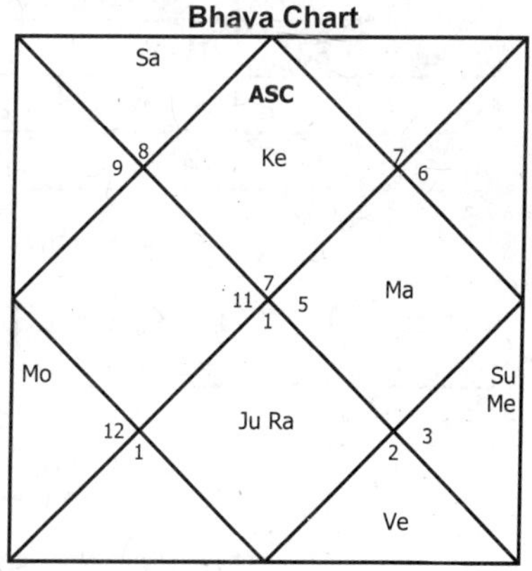

Cusp Chart

V 07-40-10	Mo 02-43-34 VI 03-39-12 VII 24-48-13 Ra 24-54-49	Ju 16-42-40 VIII 24-36-13 Ve 28-54-33	IX 29-15-48
IV 05-31-33			Me 09-32-21 Su 12-17-54
			X 05-31-33 Ma 21-57-55
III 29-15-48 SaR 01-47-37	II 24-36-13	Ke 24-54-49 I 24-48-13 XII 03-39-12	XI 07-40-10

Fig. 5.3 Contd......

Planetary Position

Planet	Sign	D-M-S	R L	STL	SL	SSL	Hse	D	S
Sun	Can	12-17-54	Mo	Sa	Ma	Ju	9	P	
Moon	Ari	02-43-34	Ma	Ke	Ve	Me	5	P	
Mars	Leo	21-57-55	Su	Ve	Sa	Sa	10	P	
Mercury	Can	09-32-21	Mo	Sa	Ve	Sa	9	P	
Jupiter	Tau	16-42-40	Ve	Mo	Sa	Ve	7		
Venus	Tau	28-54-33	Ve	Ma	Sa	Ve	8	P	
Saturn	Sag	01-47-37	Ju	Ke	Ve	Ra	2	R	
T.Rahu	Ari	24-54-49	Ma	Ve	Me	Mo	7	P	
T.Ketu	Lib	24-54-49	Ve	Ju	Me	Ma	1		

Cuspal Position

Cusp	Sign	D-M-S	R L	STL	SL	SSL	%Arc
Cusp I	Lib	24-48-13	Ve	Ju	Me	Mo	81.03
Cusp II	Sco	24-36-13	Ma	Me	Ra	Ju	72.23
Cusp III	Sag	29-15-48	Ju	Su	Ra	Ra	13.66
Cusp IV	Aqu	05-31-33	Sa	Ma	Su	Ve	73.33
Cusp V	Pis	07-40-10	Ju	Sa	Ke	Ra	10.43
Cusp VI	Ari	03-39-12	Ma	Ke	Su	Ve	88.09
Cusp VII	Ari	24-48-13	Ma	Ve	Me	Mo	10.44
Cusp VIII	Tau	24-36-13	Ve	Ma	Ra	Ju	72.23
Cusp IX	Gem	29-15-48	Me	Ju	Su	Me	66.92
Cusp X	Leo	05-31-33	Su	Ke	Ma	Mo	54.28
Cusp XI	Vir	07-40-10	Me	Su	Ke	Me	01.81
Cusp XII	Lib	03-39-12	Ve	Ma	Ve	Ra	57.14

Verification of the rectified Chart:

Accuracy of Sun, Moon and Ascendant positions: It can be verified that the planets co-ruling Sun, Moon and ascendant are showing required relationships with the houses 1, 7 and 10. **It may be remembered that it is not a must that planets should be related to 1st, 7th and 10th cusps all simultaneously. Planets may be related to 1st and 7th, 7th and 10th like that.**

Sub sub lord of the ascendant is Moon which establishes relationship with the Moon star of the native. Moon is in the SS of Mercury that is placed in female sign Cancer. More over the ascendant rises in male Sign Libra and SS arc of Moon is in second half. This justifies the sex of the native.

Genitical Connections:

The sub sub lord of 7th cusp is Moon that is in Ketu star and Venus sub. Husband's Moon star is Venus.

Sub sub lord of the 5th cusp is Rahu and Moon is placed in the 5th bhava (since Moon is placed in 5th bhava, it acts as virtual sub sub lord of 5th bhava). Moon is the Moon's star lord of the first child.

Rahu is the Moon star of second child. Rahu itself is placed in 7th bhava and becomes virtual sub sub lord of 7th bhava.

The Moon star of third child is Rahu. Mercury is the sub sub lord of the 9th cusp. Rahu is in Mercury sub which justifies the Moon star of the third child.

Verification of Various Aspects:

Promise of younger co-born: A person gets a younger co-born when the sub sub lord of the ascendant is linked through its star lord with the 3rd cusp. Sub sub lord of ascendant is Moon that is in Ketu star. Since Ketu represents Jupiter we say Moon is as good as in Jupiter star. Jupiter appears in the 3rd cusp. Thus it justifies the promise of younger co-born.

Promise of Marriage: Moon is the sub sub lord of the ascendant as well as of the 7th cusp. It is in Ketu star and Venus sub. Ketu appears in 5 and 11 and Venus appears in 7. Thus marriage is promised.

Promise of Second Marriage: Moon the sub sub lord of ascendant and 7th cusp is in Ketu star. Ketu represents Jupiter which appears in 9. Sub sub lord of 9th cusp is Mercury that has PS and it appears as sub lord of the 7th cusp. Thus by PS Mercury establishes link between 9 and 7. Mercury is in Venus sub that appears in 7. Thus the chart promises second marriage.

Promise of Children: Sub sub lord of the 5th cusp is Rahu that has PS. It is the sub lord of second cusp. Rahu is in the sub of Mercury that appears as the sub sub lord of 11. Thus the native is procreative.

The native can produce more than one child if the sub sub lord of 5th cusp is linked with 7th cusp which is 3rd from 5th. In Astrology we say that the third house to any house is the house of multiplications of the significations of that house. Here sub sub lord of 5th cusp Rahu itself is placed in 7th house with PS. Thus the native can produce more than one child.

Sex of the child is not controlled by the mother. As such no verification of this aspect is done. However 11th cusp that is 5th from 7 (spouse) rises in Virgo and the SS arc is in the first half. This may account for the first child as daughter.

Promise of Loss of Pregnancies: Sub sub lord of 5th is Rahu that is in Venus star. Venus is the sub sub lord of 4 (12th to 5th) and sub lord of 12th (8th to 5th). This promises loss of pregnancies,

Publishing Books: A native can be an author and get his/ her books published if 3rd cusp sub sub lord is linked with 3, 9 and

11. Sub sub lord of 3rd cusp is Rahu that has PS. As such it signifies 3 (writing capability). It is in the sub of Mercury that is the sub sub lord of 9 (publication) and 11. We have already indicated above that sub sub lord of ascendant (Moon) is linked with 3. Moon is also establishing relationship with 9 because its star lord Ketu represents Jupiter that appears in 9. Moon is in Ketu star that is the sub Lord of 11. Thus the sub sub lord of ascendant also promises that the native has the writing capability and ensure publication of his works.

Verification of Significant Events:

Marriage: The native got married on 12.09.1953 when she was running the period of Venus- Mercury-Saturn-Venus-Venus.

We notice Venus appears as Dasa, Sookshma and Prana lord. A planet repeats in Dasa periods only when it is strongly related to the primary and supporting cusps. In the chart Venus is in Mars star that is the star lord of 7. Rahu that represents Mars is placed in 7. Thus Venus is as good as in the star of the planet that occupies the primary house. Venus is in the sub of Saturn that appears as the star lord of 5th cusp. Saturn does not appear in 6 or 12. Venus is in the SS of Venus that appears in 7, 6 and 12. Thus this hints for short married life.

Bhukti lord Mercury is the sub lord of 7 and sub sub lord of 11. Mercury has PS and thus by its PS it signifies 7 and 11. Mercury is in the sub of Venus that appears in 7. At Stellar status also Mercury is a strong significator of Marriage. It is in Saturn star that is the star lord of 5. It is in Venus sub that appears as star lord of 7. It should be noticed that Rahu represents Venus. As such Venus is considered to be the occupant of 7th Bhava. It has PS through exchange of Nakshatra with Mars. Mercury is in the SS of Saturn that is in 5th cusp.

Antara Lord Saturn is in Ketu star that is the sub Lord of 5 and 11. Saturn is in the sub of Venus that appears in 7.

Thus we find that the Dasa period lords justify the event of marriage. Figure 5.4 represents the transit position of planets on the day of Marriage.

Fig. 5.4 Transit on 12.09.1953

Planetary Position

Planet	Sign	D-M-S	R L	STL	SL	SSL	Hse	D	S
Sun	Leo	26-22-50	Su	Ve	Ke	Ju	10		
Moon	Lib	13-44-20	Ve	Ra	Me	Ra	12	P	
Mars	Leo	05-28-44	Su	Ke	Ma	Su	9	P	
Mercury	Vir	01-01-57	Me	Su	Ra	Mo	10		
Jupiter	Gem	01-35-24	Me	Ma	Me	Sa	7	P	
Venus	Can	22-57-03	Mo	Me	Mo	Me	9		
Saturn	Lib	02-09-53	Ve	Ma	Ke	Mo	11		
T.Rahu	Cap	08-51-49	Sa	Su	Ve	Ra	3		
T.Ketu	Can	08-51-49	Mo	Sa	Ve	Ma	9		

Jupiter transits in Mercury-Mars-Mercury-Saturn. Mercury is the Bhukti lord and Saturn is the Antara Lord. Mars is in Venus star (7) and Saturn sub and SS that is the star lord of 5. Similarly we can verify the transit position of other planets.

Marriage was celebrated on Rahu star day. Rahu is placed in 7 with PS. It is in the sub of Mercury that is the sub lord of 7 and sub sub lord of 11.Rahu is in the SS of Moon that is the sub sub lord of 7.

This discussion indicates that the promised event of marriage happened in the joint period of fruitful significators of marriage when transit agreed. Let us study the progressed chart to confirm that the event has happened as destined. Figure 5.5 represents the Progressed chart on 12.09.1953.

Fig. 5.5 Prog 12.09.1953

Name	Fig 5.5	Place	Southampton
Longitude	72-23-24-W	Latitude	40-53-3-N
Sidereal Time	10-02-12	Date	28/7/1929
Day	Sunday	Geocentric Latitude	40-41-38-N
Nakshatra	Ashwini- 1 Qtr.	Time	14:28:02
Lunar Nodes	True	Tithi	Krishna Paksha - Saptami
Time Zone	-4:0:0	DST	00:00
Ayanamsa	22-51-46	House System	Placidus

Rashi Chart

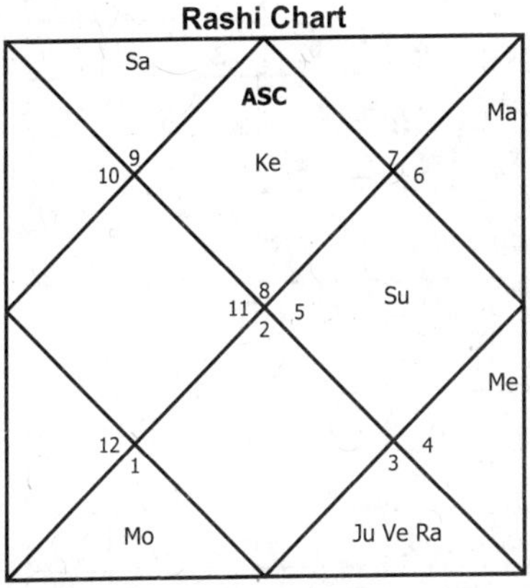

Bhava Chart

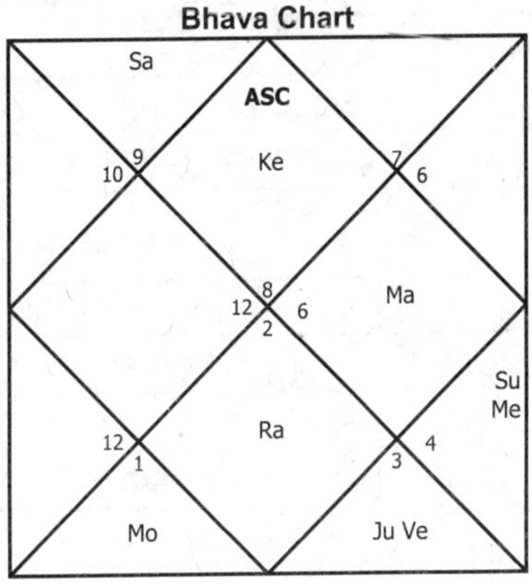

Cusp Chart

V 29-55-42 IV 00-13-17	VI 23-18-04 Mo 25-42-16	VII 13-04-50	Ra 03-48-08 VIII 15-38-00 Ju 15-40-24 Ve 21-42-39
			IX 23-36-01 Me 27-37-22
III 23-36-01			Su 01-42-56
Sa 25-22-42 II 15-38-00	Ke 13-10-24 I 13-04-50	XII 23-18-04	X 00-13-17 Ma 25-22-41 XI 29-55-42

Fig. 5.5 Contd......

Planetary Position

Planet	Sign	D-M-S	R L	STL	SL	SSL	Hse	D	S
Sun	Leo	01-42-56	Su	Ke	Ve	Ra	9	P	
Moon	Ari	25-42-16	Ma	Ve	Me	Sa	6	P	
Mars	Vir	25-22-41	Me	Ma	Ra	Ke	10	P	
Mercury	Can	27-37-22	Mo	Me	Ju	Ra	9	P	
Jupiter	Gem	15-40-24	Me	Ra	Ve	Su	8		
Venus	Gem	21-42 39	Me	Ju	Ju	Ra	8		
Saturn	Sag	25-22-42	Ju	Ve	Me	Ju	2		
Rahu	Gem	03-48-08	Me	Ma	Ve	Ju	7		
Ketu	Sco	13-10-24	Ma	Sa	Ra	Ra	1		

Cuspal Position

Cusp	Sign	D-M-S	R L	STL	SL	SSL	% Arc
Cusp I	Sco	13-04-50	Ma	Sa	Ra	Ra	63.91
Cusp II	Sag	15-38-00	Ju	Ve	Su	Mo	80.07
Cusp III	Cap	23-36-01	Sa	Ma	Ma	Sa	00.99
Cusp IV	Pis	00-13-17	Ju	Ju	Mo	Me	81.85
Cusp V	Pis	29-55-42	Ju	Me	Sa	Ju	74.53
Cusp VI	Ari	23-18-04	Ma	Ve	Sa	Ma	18.16
Cusp VII	Tau	13-04-50	Ve	Mo	Ra	Ke	21.48
Cusp VIII	Gem	15-38-00	Me	Ra	Ve	Su	36.70
Cusp IX	Can	23-36-01	Mo	Me	Ma	Sa	00.99
Cusp X	Vir	00-13-17	Me	Su	Ra	Me	40.90
Cusp XI	Vir	29-55-42	Me	Ma	Sa	Ju	74.53
Cusp XII	Lib	23-18-04	Ve	Ju	Sa	Ra	03.26

Progressed ascendant on 12.09.1953 was co ruled by Mars-Saturn-Rahu-Rahu. We have seen above that all these planets are strong significators of the event of marriage in the natal chart.

Let us study the progressed chart independently. The event of marriage happened when Moon was progressing in Mars-Venus-Mercury-Saturn-Venus-Venus.

Dasa, Sookshma and Prana lord Venus in the progressed chart is in Jupiter star Jupiter sub and Rahu SS. Jupiter appears in 5 and 11 as sub sub lord of these cusps. Rahu is the sub lord of 7.

Bhukti Lord Mercury in the progressed chart is in Mercury star that appears as star lord of 5, as Sign lord of 11 and placed in 7 (through Rahu that represents Mercury). Mercury is in the sub of Jupiter that is the sub sub lord of 5 and 11.

Antara Lord Saturn in the progressed chart is in Venus star (7) and sub of Mercury (5, 7 and 11). Saturn is in the SS of Jupiter (5 and 11).

Thus we find that the event of marriage is confirmed by the analysis of the progressed chart.

The marriage was celebrated on Rahu star day. Rahu in the progressed chart is in Mars star that is the star lord of 11. Rahu is placed in 7 and represents Mars. Thus Mars is assumed to be placed in 7. Thus Rahu signifies 7 and 11. Rahu is in the sub of Venus (7). Rahu is in the SS of Jupiter (5 and 11). Thus we find the chart justifies transit also.

Birth of First Daughter: The native was blessed with the birth of first daughter on 27.11.1957 when she was running the period of Sun-Jupiter-Rahu-Saturn-Saturn.

Sun in the chart has PS and being the star Lord of 11 signifies 11. Sun is in Saturn star (2 and 5) and in the sub of Mars that appears in 2. Sun is in the SS of Jupiter that appears in 5.

Bhukti lord Jupiter acquires the PS because Jupiter is in Moon star and Moon is in Ketu star that represents Jupiter. Thus Jupiter signifies 2 and 5. Jupiter is in the sub of Saturn that appears as the star lord of 5.

Antara Lord Rahu has PS and appears as sub Lord of 2 and sub sub lord of 5. It is in the sub of Mercury that is the sub sub lord of 11.

Sookshma and Prana lord is Saturn that is in the star of Ketu that is the sub lord of 5 and 11. Since Ketu represents Jupiter we may say that Saturn is in Jupiter star that appears as the sub sub lord of 2 and Sign lord of 5. Thus Saturn signifies 2, 5 and 11. It is in the sub of Venus that appears in favourable as well as unfavourable cusps. This accounts for related problems at the time of delivery.

Thus we see that the Dasa Period justifies the enactment of the event of birth of first daughter.

Figure 5.6 indicates the transit position of planets on 27.11.1957.

Fig. 5.6 Transit on 27.11.1957

Planetary Position

Planet	Sign	D-M-S	R L	STL	SL	SSL	Hse	D	S
Sun	Sco	11-53-53	Ma	Sa	Mo	Ve	10		
Moon	Cap	24-03-40	Sa	Ma	Ma	Mo	1	P	
Mars	Lib	19-22-16	Ve	Ra	Ma	Ra	9		
Mercury	Sag	00-14-29	Ju	Ke	Ke	Mo	11		
Jupiter	Vir	29-50-40	Me	Ma	Sa	Ju	8	P	
Venus	Sag	28-43-28	Ju	Su	Ma	Sa	12		
Saturn	Sco	22-09-37	Ma	Me	Su	Ve	10		
T.Rahu	Lib	16-59-24	Ve	Ra	Ve	Sa	9	P	
T.Ketu	Ari	16-59-24	Ma	Ve	Mo	Me	3		

It can be verified that transit supports the event. Jupiter transits in Mercury-Mars-Saturn-Jupiter. All these planets signify 2, 5 and 11. Similarly we can check the transit position of other planets.

Figure 5.7 is the progressed chart for the event of birth of first daughter.

Fig. 5.7 Progress on 27.11.1957.

Name	Fig 5.7	Place	Southampton
Longitude	72-23-24-W	Latitude	40-53-3-N
Sidereal Time	10-02-12	Date	28/7/1929
Day	Sunday	Geocentric Latitude	40-41-38-N
Nakshatra	Ashwini- 1 Qtr.	Time	14:28:02
Lunar Nodes	True	Tithi	Krishna Paksha - Saptami
Time Zone	-4:0:0	DST	00:00
Ayanamsa	22-51-46	House System	Placidus

Rashi Chart

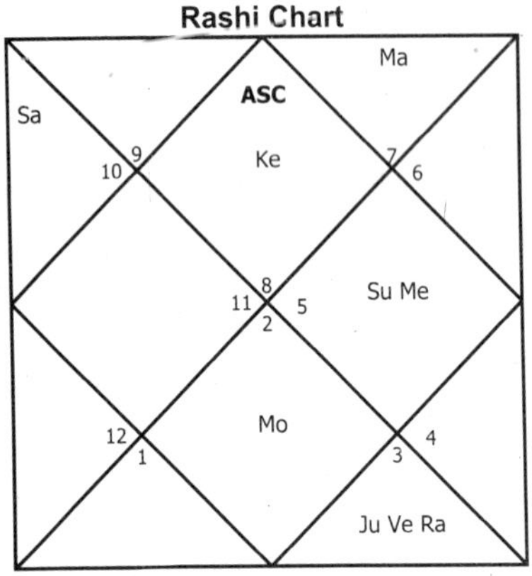

Bhava Chart

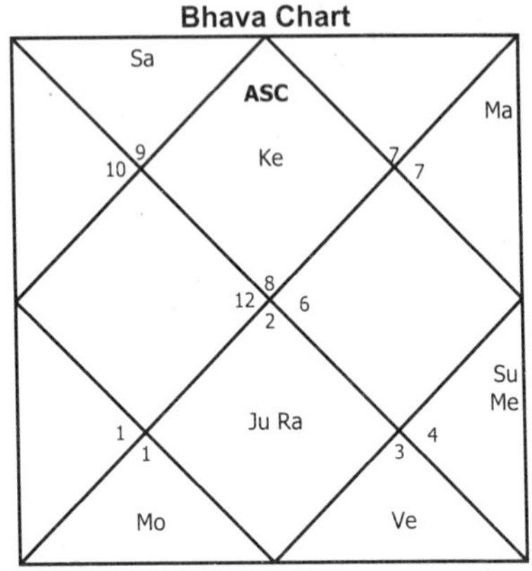

Cusp Chart

IV 04-11-21	V 03-23-28 VI 26-22-19	Mo 02-48-39 VII 16-02-01	Ra 08-40-11 Ju 18-47-26 VIII 19-10-51 Ve 25-13-03
			IX 27-42-16
III 27-42-16 Sa 01-43-23			Me 02-14-32 Su 09-43-51
II 19-10-51	Ke 16-07-35 I 16-02-01	XII 26-22-19 Ma 03-23-36 XI 03-23-28	X 04-11-21

Fig. 5.7 Contd......

Planetary Position

Planet	Sign	D-M-S	R L	STL	SL	SSL	Hse	D	S
Sun	Leo	09-43-51	Su	Ke	Sa	Me	9	P	
Moon	Tau	02-48-39	Ve	Su	Ju	Ra	6	P	
Mars	Lib	03-23-36	Ve	Ma	Ve	Ma	11	P	
Mercury	Leo	02-14-32	Su	Ke	Ve	Sa	9	P	
Jupiter	Gem	18-47-26	Me	Ra	Mo	Me	7		
Venus	Gem	25-13-03	Me	Ju	Me	Ra	8	P	
Saturn	Cap	01-43-23	Sa	Su	Ju	Sa	2		
Rahu	Gem	08-40-11	Me	Ra	Ju	Ju	7	P	
Ketu	Sco	16-07-35	Ma	Sa	Ju	Su	1		

Cuspal Position

Cusp	Sign	D-M-S	R L	STL	SL	SSL	% Arc
Cusp I	Sco	16-02-01	Ma	Sa	Ju	Ve	91.35
Cusp II	Sag	19-10-51	Ju	Ve	Ra	Me	65.75
Cusp III	Cap	27-42-16	Sa	Ma	Ju	Ra	30.85
Cusp IV	Pis	04-11-21	Ju	Sa	Sa	Ve	28.27
Cusp V	Ari	03-23-28	Ma	Ke	Su	Sa	70.60
Cusp VI	Ari	26-22-19	Ma	Ve	Ke	Ju	40.87
Cusp VII	Tau	16-02-01	Ve	Mo	Sa	Me	10.94
Cusp VIII	Gem	19-10-51	Me	Ra	Mo	Su	25.32
Cusp IX	Can	27-42-16	Mo	Me	Ju	Ra	30.85
Cusp X	Vir	04-11-21	Me	Su	Sa	Su	76.68
Cusp XI	Lib	03-23-28	Ve	Ma	Ve	Ma	44.63
Cusp XII	Lib	26-22-19	Ve	Ju	Ke	Sa	40.43

Progressed ascendant was co-ruled by planets Mars-Saturn-Jupiter-Venus. We have seen above that these planets signify 2, 5 and 11 in the natal chart. Let us study the progressed chart independently.

Birth of first child took place when Moon was progressing in Sun-Jupiter-Rahu-Sat-Sat.

Sun in the progressed chart is in Ketu star (star lord of 5). Ketu represents Mars and Saturn. Thus Sun can be assumed to be in Mars star (11) and also in Saturn star (2). Sun is in Saturn sub that is the sub sub lord of 5.

Jupiter is in Rahu star (sub lord of 2, and as Mercury sub sub lord of 2). Jupiter is in Moon sub that appears in favourable as well as unfavourable positions. But Jupiter is in the SS of Mercury that is sub sub lord of 2.

Rahu represents Mercury that is in Ketu star (star lord of 5) and in the sub of Venus (2 and 11). It is in the SS of Saturn that is the sub sub lord of 5.

Saturn is in Sun star (sub lord of 5) and in Jupiter sub that appears in 2. Saturn is in the SS of Saturn that appears as sub sub lord of 5.

Thus the analysis of progressed chart confirms the enactment of the event of birth of first daughter.

Death of First Husband: Native lost her first husband on 22.11.1963 when she was running the period of Moon-Rahu-Moon-Jupiter-Venus.

Dasa and Antara Lord Moon: Moon is the sub sub lord of 7th cusp that represents the first husband. Moon is in Ketu star. Since Ket represents Jupiter we say Moon is in Jupiter star that is the sub sub lord of 2 which is 8th from 7. Moon is in the sub of Venus that is the star lord of 7. Moon is in the SS of Mercury that appears in 2. Thus we see that the Dasa lord justifies all conditions for Markesh Dasa.

Bhukti Lord Rahu: Rahu has PS. It is the sub lord of 2 and is placed in 7. Thus by PS it signifies houses 1 and 8 with respect to 7. It is in the sub of Mercury that appears in 2 and 7 (8 and 1 from 7). Rahu is in the SS of Moon that appears in 1 (7th from 7). Even as per its stellar status Rahu is in Venus star (7) and Mercury sub (2). Thus Rahu justifies the role of Bhukti lord in causing the death of the first husband.

Sookshma Lord Jupiter: Jupiter is in Moon star and Saturn sub. Moon is the sub sub lord of 7 (ascendant of spouse) and Saturn is the star lord of 5 that is Badhaka house for 7. Jupiter is in the SS of Venus that appears in 1, 6 and 8 (Maraka houses for 7).

Prana Lord Venus: Venus is in Mars star that appears in house 1, 2, 8, and 12 from 7(only relevant positions shown). Venus is in the sub of Saturn that is the star lord of Badhaka house. These linkages of the Prana lord not only justify death but also clearly indicate un-natural death.

Figure 5.8 indicate the Progressed chart for the event of death of the first husband.

Fig. 5.8 Progressed chart 22.11.1963.

Name	Fig 5.8	Place	Southampton
Longitude	72-23-24-W	Latitude	40-53-3-N
Sidereal Time	10-02-12	Date	28/7/1929
Day	Sunday	Geocentric Latitude	40-41-38-N
Nakshatra	Ashwini- 1 Qtr.	Time	14:28:02
Lunar Nodes	True	Tithi	Krishna Paksha - Saptami
Time Zone	-4:0:0	DST	00:00
Ayanamsa	22-51-46	House System	Placidus

Rashi Chart

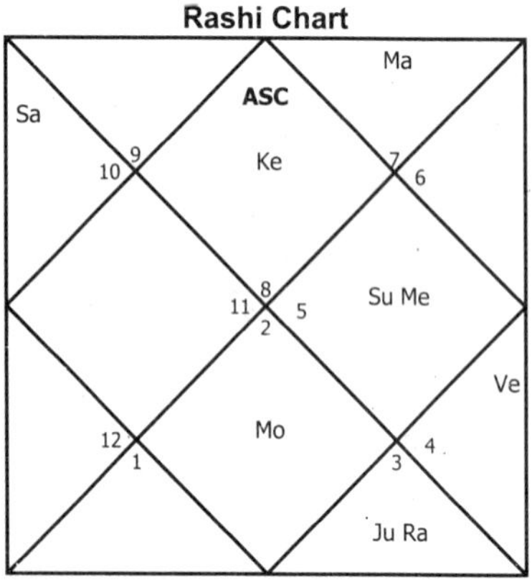

Bhava Chart

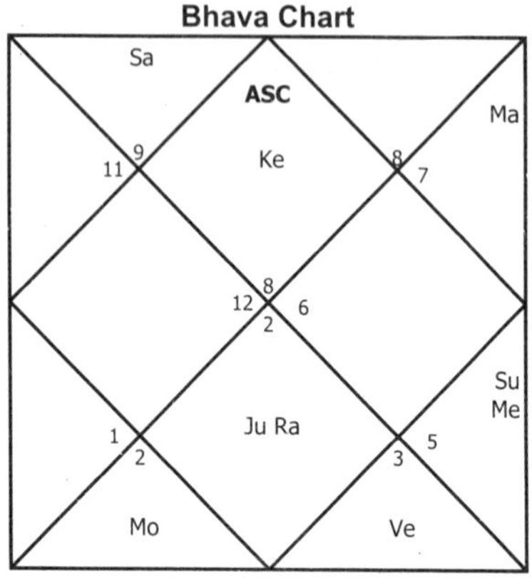

Cusp Chart

IV 10-19-00	V 08-41-44	VI 01-06-11 Mo 13-39-59 VII 20-39-12	Ra 13-06-11 Ju 23-37-36 VIII 24-49-12
III 04-10-35			Ve 00-12-18
Sa 13-00-50			IX 04-10-35 Me 13-26-29 Su 16-03-45
II 24-49-12	Ke 20-45-25 I 20-39-12 XII 01-06-11	Ma 09-49-37 XI 08-41-44	X 10-19-00

Fig. 5.8 Contd......

Planetary Position

Planet	Sign	D-M-S	R L	STL	SL	SSL	Hse	D	S
Sun	Leo	16-03-45	Su	Ve	Su	Me	9	P	
Moon	Tau	13-39-59	Ve	Mo	Ra	Mo	6	P	
Mars	Lib	09-49-37	Ve	Ra	Ju	Ve	11	P	
Mercury	Leo	13-26-29	Su	Ve	Ve	Ve	9		
Jupiter	Gem	23-37-36	Me	Ju	Sa	Ju	7	P	
Venus	Can	00-12-18	Mo	Ju	Mo	Me	8		
Saturn	Cap	13-00-50	Sa	Mo	Ra	Me	2	P	
Rahu	Gem	13-06-11	Me	Ra	Me	Ve	7	P	
Ketu	Sco	20-45-25	Ma	Me	Ve	Ju	1	P	

Cuspal Position

Cusp	Sign	D-M-S	R L	STL	SL	SSL	% Arc
Cusp I	Sco	20-39-12	Ma	Me	Ve	Ju	64.22
Cusp II	Sag	24-49-12	Ju	Ve	Me	Mo	20.94
Cusp III	Aqu	04-10-35	Sa	Ma	Ve	Sa	23.83
Cusp IV	Pis	10-19-00	Ju	Sa	Ve	Ke	87.12
Cusp V	Ari	08-41-44	Ma	Ke	Ju	Ve	89.76
Cusp VI	Tau	01-06-11	Ve	Su	Ra	Mo	98.43
Cusp VII	Tau	20-39-12	Ve	Mo	Ve	Ve	56.38
Cusp VIII	Gem	24-49-12	Me	Ju	Me	Mo	91.53
Cusp IX	Leo	04-10-35	Su	Ke	Mo	Sa	21.35
Cusp X	Vir	10-19-00	Me	Mo	Mo	Ra	95.54
Cusp XI	Lib	08-41-44	Ve	Ra	Ju	Ju	12.20
Cusp XII	Sco	01-06-11	Ma	Ju	Ma	Ve	02.26

Planets co-ruling the Ascendant of progressed chart for the event of death of first husband are Mars-Mercury-Venus-Jupiter. All these planets in the natal chart are strong significators of the event of death of the first husband.

Let us study the progressed chart independently. The event happened when Moon was progressing in Moon-Rahu-Moon-Jupiter-Venus.

Dasa and Antara Lord are Moon that is in Moon star (sub sub lord of 2 that is 8th from 7) and sub of Rahu that has PS and is placed in 7 (the ascendant for husband). Moon is in the SS of Moon that is sub sub lord of 8 with respect to 7.

Bhukti lord Rahu is in Rahu star. Rahu is placed in 7(ascendant of husband) and Mercury sub that is the sub lord of 2 (8 for husband).

Sookshma Lord Jupiter is in Jupiter star that is placed in the 7th house and is also the sign lord of 2. It is in the sub of Saturn that is the sub sub lord of 3 which is Badhaka house for 7 in the progressed chart.

Prana lord Venus is in Jupiter star that is placed in 7 and sub of Moon that is the sub sub lord of 2.

Thus we see that the analysis of the progressed chart confirms that the event of death of first husband happened as destined.

On the date of death Saturn was transiting in Sat-Mars-Mars-Venus. Saturn in the progressed chart is in Moon star that is the sub sub lord of 8th cusp with respect to the ascendant of first husband. It is in Rahu sub that has PS and is placed in the ascendant of husband. Thus transit of Saturn in Saturn Sign meets all the necessary conditions. Mars and Venus are strong significators of death both in the natal and progressed chart.

Death took place on the day when Moon was in Moon star that is the sub sub lord of 8 with respect to ascendant of husband. We have seen above that Moon is both the Dasa as well as the Antara lord on the day of death.

Second Marriage: It is said that the native celebrated her second marriage on 20.10.1968 when she was running the period of Moon-Ketu-Sat-Sat-Mercury. The second marriage takes place in the joint period of planets those are fruitful significators of 5, 9 and 11. Remember the Primary cusp for second marriage is 9th house. All the planets that are the Dasa period lords have to be linked with 9th cusp directly or indirectly. Readers can verify that in the natal chart Moon-Ketu-Sat-Sat-Mercury satisfy the necessary conditions to enact the promised event of second marriage. The analysis of the progressed chart, however, does not confirm this. It could not have been her second marriage. I would not venture to discuss this further.

We feel that the step by step analysis of the chart certifies the correctness of the chart.

Example 3: A person approached the author with a request to fix his chart. He gave the following details:

D.O.B: 26.02.1949. P.O.B: Karolbagh, Delhi, India T.O.B: Between 11 hrs and 16 hrs

Genetical Connections:

Moon stars of:

Wife —Mars, Father—Saturn/Mercury, First daughter—Venus, Second daughter—Rahu, Third child son—Rahu, Immediate elder sister—Jupiter/Saturn, Immediate younger sister—Ketu/Venus

Significant Events:

Death of Mother—23.01.1954 about 04 to 05 hrs

Death of Father—27.12.1998 at 22 hrs

Date of Marriage—23.05.1971

First child (female) –07.06.1974 at 18.39.16 hrs in Holy Family Hospital, Delhi.India

Second child (female)—11.08.1978 at 14.55.57 hrs in Holy Family Hospital, Delhi.India

Third child (male)—17.05.1981 at 18.03.14 hrs in Holy Family Hospital, Delhi.India

Recent Foreign Journey: –From 01.04.2011 to 18.04.2011 departure time 01 hrs. Native in fact had many foreign journeys.

The author took up the job of rectification on 09.07.2011 at 04.00.13 at Noida.

The ruling planets at that time were as follows:

RP (ascendant): Mercury-Mars-Mercury-Jupiter-Jupiter-Mercury

RP (Moon): Venus-Mars-Mercury-Rahu-Venus-Rahu

Rahu on this day represented Mars and Mercury. Ketu represented Venus and Mars.

The correct chart was fixed by following step by step procedure as illustrated below:

The chart was cast as per the given data using time of birth as 11.0hrs. This chart shows that the Sun was in the SS of Saturn. The time of birth was then changed to 16.0 hrs. We noticed that Sun still remained in Saturn SS. Thus we had to believe that the Sun's position in SS has to be accepted though it is not a RP. We shifted the time of birth back to 11.0hrs and tried to put the SSS position of Sun using planets from RP (ascendant) series. Since

Mercury is the strongest planet in RP we decided to put Mercury as the sub sub lord of Sun's position. This occurred at 11.37 hrs. Corresponding to this we noticed that Moon is in Jupiter sub and Saturn SS. Saturn is not a co-ruling planet in RP (ascendant) series. Since Mercury appeared three times in RP we decided to keep Mercury as SS of Moon. This comes at time 11.56.09.

Corresponding to this time we notice that Sun is in the SSSS of Venus that is not a ruling planet in RP (ascendant) series. The earliest planet that can come as SSSS of Sun is Mars. This occurs at time 12.06.43 hrs and next position is Rahu. Both these planets are strong RPs. Thus we decided that keeping Mars or Rahu as the SSSS of Sun we should adjust the position of Moon.

At 12.15.33 we found that Sun is in Rahu SSSS and Moon is in Rahu SSS and Mercury SSSS.

Having set the position of Sun and Moon we need now to set the position of sub and SS of ascendant using planets from RP (Moon) series. At 12.15.34 we noticed that Rahu is the sub lord and Venus is the sub sub lord of ascendant. Both these planets are strong in RP (Moon) series. At 12.15.34 we get SSS and SSSS of ascendant as Rahu. This appeared to be the most accurate position of ascendant.

However this indicated that the SS arc of the sub sub lord of ascendant is in the first half when female Sign rises in the ascendant. But as Venus the sub sub lord of ascendant is in the SS of Saturn that is placed in male sign Leo it was accepted that this justifies the sex of the native.

Figure 5.9 represents the rectified chart.

Fig. 5.9 Natal Chart

Name	Fig 5.9	Place	Karolbagh, Delhi
Longitude	77-11-0-E	Latitude	28-40-0-N
Sidereal Time	22-17-27	Date	26/2/1949
Day	Saturday	Geocentric Latitude	28-30-18-N
Nakshatra	Dhanishtha-2 Qtr.	Time	12:15:34
Lunar Nodes	True	Tithi	Krishna Paksha - Chaturdasi
Time Zone	+5:30:0	DST	00:00
Ayanamsa	23-08-09	House System	Placidus

Rashi Chart

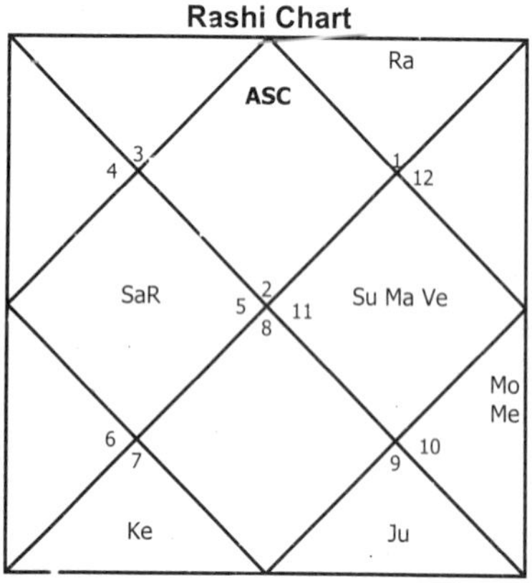

Bhava Chart

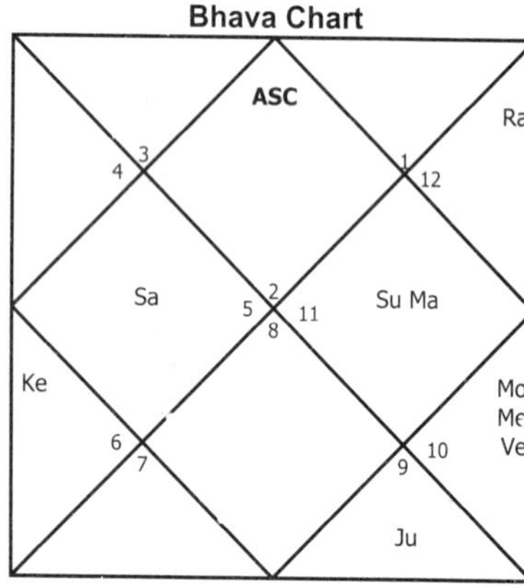

Cusp Chart

XI 12-01-14	Ra 03-38-49 XII 19-30-13	I 25-31-13	II 19-00-27
Ma 18-20-22 Su 14-13-12 X 09-14-53 Ve 01-43-30			III 12-25-41
Mo 26-47-32 Me 17-18-43 IX 12-25-41			IV 09-14-53 SaR 09-17-44
Ju 29-39-14 VIII 19-00-27	VII 25-31-13	VI 19-30-13 Ke 03-38-49	V 12-01-14

Fig. 5.9 Contd......

Planetary Position

Planet	Sign	D-M-S	R L	STL	SL	SSL	Hse	D	S
Sun	Aqu	14-13-12	Sa	Ra	Me	Sa	10		
Moon	Cap	26-47-32	Sa	Ma	Ju	Me	9		
Mars	Aqu	18-20-22	Sa	Ra	Mo	Ra	10	P	
Mercury	Cap	17-18-43	Sa	Mo	Sa	Ra	9	P	
Jupiter	Sag	29-39-14	Ju	Su	Ra	Ju	8	P	
Venus	Aqu	01-43-30	Sa	Ma	Me	Sa	9	P	
Saturn	Leo	09-17-44	Su	Ke	Ju	Ra	4	R	P
T.Rahu	Ari	03-38-49	Ma	Ke	Su	Ve	11	P	
T.Ketu	Lib	03-38-49	Ve	Ma	Ve	Ra	5		

Cuspal Position

Cusp	Sign	D-M-S	R L	STL	SL	SSL	% Arc
Cusp I	Tau	25-31-13	Ve	Ma	Ra	Ve	37.78
Cusp II	Gem	19-00-27	Me	Ra	Mo	Ve	14.10
Cusp III	Can	12-25-41	Mo	Sa	Ma	Sa	41.61
Cusp IV	Leo	09-14-53	Su	Ke	Ju	Ra	67.97
Cusp V	Vir	12-01-14	Me	Mo	Ra	Ra	43.92
Cusp VI	Lib	19-30-13	Ve	Ra	Ma	Sa	12.67
Cusp VII	Sco	25-31-13	Ma	Me	Ra	Ve	37.78
Cusp VIII	Sag	19-00-27	Ju	Ve	Ra	Me	04.64
Cusp IX	Cap	12-25-41	Sa	Mo	Ra	Ju	89.70
Cusp X	Aqu	09-14-53	Sa	Ra	Ju	Me	24.91
Cusp XI	Pis	12-01-14	Ju	Sa	Mo	Ve	81.15
Cusp XII	Ari	19-30-13	Ma	Ve	Ra	Ve	32.74

Verification of the Accuracy of the Rectified Chart:

Accuracy of Sun, Moon and Ascendant Positions: It can be verified that the planets co-ruling the positions of Sun, Moon and ascendant are related to 1, 7 and 10. **It may be remembered that it is not a must that planets should be related to 1, 7 and 10 all simultaneously. Planets may be related to 1 and 7, 7 and 10 like that.**

Sub sub lord of the ascendant is Venus that is in Mars star that is the star lord of the native.

Genetical Connections:

Seventh cusp sub sub lord is Venus that is in Mars star which is the star lord of the wife. More over Mars is in Rahu star that represents Venus through Ketu. Note Rahu is the Moon star of the Second child. Thus the sub sub lord justifies the Moon star of wife as well as the second child.

Fifth cusp sub sub lord is Rahu that is in Ketu star that represents Venus that is the Moon star of the first child.

Ninth cusp sub sub lord is Jupiter that is in Rahu sub which is the Moon star of the third child. More over Rahu is in Ketu star that represents Venus that is placed in the 9th Bhava. Thus this justifies the Moon star of the third child. It is stated by the native that the Moon star of his father could be Saturn or Mercury. Now Saturn is in Ketu star that represents Venus that is placed in the 9th Bhava. Mercury itself is placed in 9th Bhava. Thus the chart justifies the linkage with the Moon star of the father.

Eleventh sub sub lord is Venus and Rahu is placed in the 11th Bhava. It is stated that the Moon star of the immediate elder sister could be Jupiter or Saturn. Now Jupiter is in the sub of

Rahu and Saturn is in Ketu star that represents Venus. Thus the relationship of 11th cusp with the Moon star of the immediate elder sister is established.

Third sub sub lord is Saturn that is in Ketu star that represents Venus. It is stated that the Moon star of the immediate younger could be Ketu or Venus. Thus the sub sub lord of the 3rd cusp establishes relationship with the Moon star of the immediate younger sister.

Promise of Aspects of Life:

Marriage: Venus is the sub sub lord of 1 and 7. It has PS and appears as sub sub lord of 7 and 11. It is in the sub of Mercury that appears in 5 & 7. More over Venus is in the star of Mars that appears in 7. Thus marriage is promised.

Birth of Children: Sub sub lord of 5th cusp is Rahu that is in Ketu star that represents Venus. Notice Venus appears as the sub sub lord of 2 and 11. Rahu is in the sub of Sun that does not negate 2. Rahu is in the SS of Venus that appears in relevant cusps 2 and 11. This shows that the native has the necessary procreative power to produce children.

A native can produce more than one child if the sub sub lord of 5th cusp is related through its star lord with 7 that is third from 5. **In Astrology, we say that third house to any house is the house of multiplications of the significations of that house**. Rahu the sub sub lord of 5th cusp is in Ketu star that represents Venus that is the sub sub lord of 7th cusp. This shows that native could produce more than one child.

Since Rahu is linked with 4 and 12 which are negative houses with respect to 5th cusp this indicates delay or the possibilities of loss of some pregnancies.

Promise of Foreign Travels: Ascendant sub sub lord is in Mars star that appears in 3 and 12. It is in Mercury sub that appears in 9. Thus the chart promises that native could make foreign travels.

Promise of Execution of Events and Progression: The natal chart sub sub lords of ascendant and the relevant cusp declares the promise of various aspects of life but it is the progressed position of the ascendant that declares the destined time of the execution of the promised event.

Native is born in Taurus ascendant and then it enters in Gemini around 6.7.1951. It means the native lost his mother when the ascendant was progressing in Mercury sign Gemini. The necessary conditions for the Progressed sign lord to declare the execution of death events that the native may have to experience are:

a. Mercury in the natal chart should signify 12 (Loss), and 8 (Death). Here in this chart we find that Mercury with PS appears as the sub sub lord of 8. It is in the sub of Saturn that appears as SSSS of 12. Thus it shows that the native will experience some death events during the time ascendant progresses in Mercury Sign.

b. To decide whose death will occur we have to notice in which cusp Mercury appears. Death will take place of a person for whom it appears in the 8th cusp or the ascendant. Mercury also has to have the power to inflict death of the concerned relative. Here Mercury is the SSS lord of the 11th cusp which is 8th from 4 (Mother). Mercury is a co-ruling planet in 8th house from 4. Mercury is in Moon star that is the sub lord of 11 (8th from 4) and sub of Saturn that is placed in 4 (ascendant for mother).Mercury is in the SS of Rahu that appears in Maraka houses with respect to 4. Thus the chart clearly indicates the possibility of death of mother.

c. Ascendant progresses to Gemini sign and remain there up to 5.1.1985. During this period the native experienced the events of marriage, and birth of three children. This means Mercury in the natal chart should be related to the relevant cusps which take part in enacting these events.

Mercury has PS and appears in 2, 5, 7, 8, 9, and 10. Mercury is in the sub of Saturn that also has PS and appears in 3, 4, 6, 9, 10, and 11. Thus by PS alone it promises the execution of Marriage (5, 7 and 11), birth of first child (2, 5, and 11), birth of second child (2, 7, and 11), birth of 3rd child (2, 9 and 11). Thus we find the progressed ascendant Sign lord justifies the execution of these events.

Verification of Events:

Marriage: Native got married on 23.05.1971 when he was running the Dasa period of Rahu-Mars-Rahu-Jupiter-Moon.

Rahu is Dasa as well as Antara lord. Rahu is in Ketu star that represents Venus that is the sub sub lord of 7 and 11. Ketu itself is in 5. Rahu is in Sun sub that does not negate 7. Thus we say that the Dasa lord allows the event of marriage. Bhukti lord Mars is in Rahu star (5 and 7) and sub of Moon that is the sub lord of 11. Mars is in the SS of Rahu that is in 5 and 7.

Sookshama Lord Jupiter has PS and is the Sign lord of 11. It is in the sub of Rahu that is the sub and sub sub lord of 5 and sub lord of 7. Rahu is in the SS of Jupiter that is in 11.

Prana lord could be Moon or Mars. Both these planets promise the execution of the event of marriage.

Figure 5.10 shows the transit position of planets at 23 hours on 23.05.1971. Study of transit clearly indicates that it supports the event.

Fig 5.10 transit on 23.05.1971

Planetary Position

Planet	Sign	D-M-S	R L	STL	SL	SSL	Hse	D	S
Sun	Tau	08-29-05	Ve	Su	Ve	Ma	4	P	
Moon	Ari	27-49-29	Ma	Su	Mo	Sa	4		
Mars	Cap	16-08-55	Sa	Mo	Sa	Me	1		
Mercury	Ari	13-47-10	Ma	Ve	Ve	Su	3		
Jupiter	Sco	08-05-53	Ma	Sa	Ke	Me	10	R	P
Venus	Ari	12-50-14	Ma	Ke	Me	Ju	3	P	
Saturn	Tau	03-17-25	Ve	Su	Sa	Sa	4		
T.Rahu	Cap	24-14-31	Sa	Ma	Ra	Ra	1	P	
T.Ketu	Can	24-14-31	Mo	Me	Ra	Ra	7		

Figure 5.11 represents the Progressed chart for the event of Marriage. We notice that the progressed ascendant is co-ruled by Mercury-Rahu-Moon-Mercury. All these planets are strong significators of the event of marriage in the natal chart.

In the progressed chart Moon was progressing in Sat-Rahu-Mars-Rahu-Jup-Moon/Mars. All these planets are strongly related to 5, 7 and 11 in the Natal chart.

Fig. 5.11 Progress

Name	Fig 5.11	Place	Karolbagh Delhi
Longitude	77-11-0-E	Latitude	28-40-0-N
Sidereal Time	22-17-27	Date	26/2/1949
Day	Saturday	Geocentric Latitude	28-30-18-N
Nakshatra	Dhanishtha-2 Qtr.	Time	12:15:34
Lunar Nodes	True	Tithi	Krishna Paksha - Chaturdasi
Time Zone	+5:30:0	DST	00:00
Ayanamsa	23-08-09	House System	Placidus

Rashi Chart

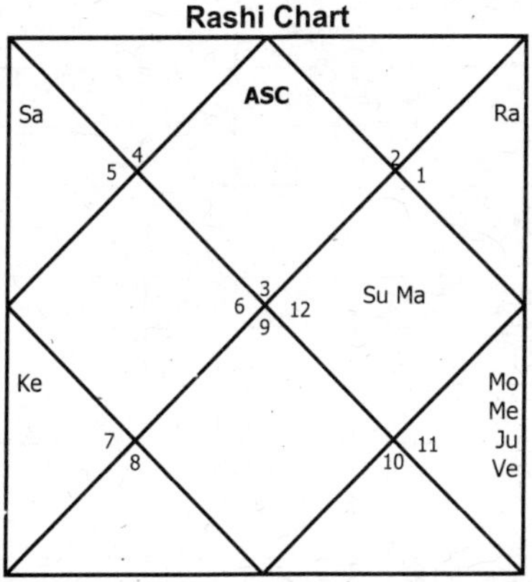

Bhava Chart

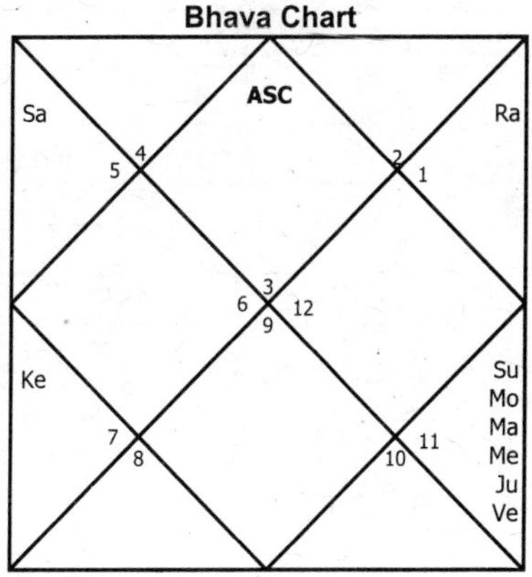

Cusp Chart

X 06-32-47 Ma 06-08-09 Su 02-01-37	XI 11-13-59 Ra 24-46-00	XII 16-38-41	I 18-48-09
Ve 21-22-03 Mo 19-17-50 Me 14-36-25 Ju 07-05-45 IX 06-35-51			II 11-27-56
VIII 11-27-56			III 06-35-51 Sa 26-55-23
VII 18-48-09	VI 16-38-41	Ke 22-12-30 V 11-13-59	IV 06-32-47

Fig. 5.11 Contd......

Planetary Position

Planet	Sign	D-M-S	R L	STL	SL	SSL	Hse	D	S
Sun	Pis	02-01-37	Ju	Ju	Ra	Sa	9		
Moon	Aqu	19-17-50	Sa	Ra	Ma	Ra	9	P	
Mars	Pis	06-08-09	Ju	Sa	Me	Ve	9	P	
Mercury	Aqu	14-36-25	Sa	Ra	Ke	Ve	9	P	
Jupiter	Aqu	07-05-45	Sa	Ra	Ra	Ju	9	P	
Venus	Aqu	21-22-03	Sa	Ju	Ju	Mo	9		
Saturn	Leo	26-55-23	Su	Su	Su	Ju	3		
Rahu	Ari	24-46-00	Ma	Ve	Me	Su	11		
Ketu	Lib	22-12-30	Ve	Ju	Sa	Me	5	P	

Cuspal Position

Cusp	Sign	D-M-S	R L	STL	SL	SSL	% Arc
Cusp I	Gem	18-48-09	Me	Ra	Mo	Me	27.53
Cusp II	Can	11-27-56	Mo	Sa	Mo	Ju	95.47
Cusp III	Leo	06-35-51	Su	Ke	Ra	Me	56.00
Cusp IV	Vir	06-32-47	Me	Su	Me	Ju	38.68
Cusp V	Lib	11-13-59	Ve	Ra	Sa	Ve	09.15
Cusp VI	Sco	16-38-41	Ma	Sa	Ju	Ra	91.74
Cusp VII	Sag	18-48-09	Ju	Ve	Ra	Sa	39.42
Cusp VIII	Cap	11-27-56	Sa	Mo	Ma	Sa	71.99
Cusp IX	Aqu	06-35-51	Sa	Ma	Mo	Ve	92.67
Cusp X	Pis	06-32-47	Ju	Sa	Me	Ra	16.74
Cusp XI	Ari	11-13-59	Ma	Ke	Sa	Ju	24.92
Cusp XII	Tau	16-38-41	Ve	Mo	Sa	Ve	62.95

Let us study the Progressed chart independently.

Dasa and Antara Lord Rahu is in Venus star and Mercury sub. Venus is the sub sub lord of 5 and star lord of 7. Rahu represents Venus and it is placed in 11. Thus we take that Venus is placed in 11. Thus Rahu involves all the relevant houses and its sub lord supports the event.

Bhukti Lord Mars is in Saturn star that is the sub sub lord of 7 and sub lord of 5 and 11. Mars is in the sub of Mercury that is placed in 9 and has PS. 9th house is a favourable house with respect to 5, 7 and 11.

Sookshama Lord Jupiter is in Rahu star Rahu sub and Jupiter SS. **When a planet is in the star and sub of the same planet we treat it as a case of bunching and treat the planet as if it is in the star of that planet and the sub sub lord of the planet takes upon the role of sub as well as SS.**

Thus Jupiter is taken in Rahu star and Jupiter sub. Rahu appears in 5 and 7 and Jupiter is the sub sub lord of 11.

Prana lord Moon is in Rahu star (5 and 7) and in Mars sub that appears in 11.

Thus we find that a promised event of marriage has happened in the joint period of fruitful significators of 5, 7 and 11 when transit agreed. It also clearly illustrates that the event happened only as destined which is shown by the progressed chart.

We may also note the progressed position of the primary cusp 7 for the event of marriage. We notice that the 7th cusp has progressed to Jupiter-Venus-Rahu-Venus. All these planets are strong significators of 5, 7 and 11. We need to look for the progressed position of 7th cusp independently and not from the progressed chart.

Death of Father: The native lost his father on 27.12.1998 at 22.0 hrs approximately. At that time he was running Dasa period of Saturn-Sun-Mercury-Mars-Mercury.

Dasa Lord Saturn has PS and is placed in 4 (8th from 9). Saturn is in Ketu star (star lord of 4) and sub of Jupiter that is the sub sub lord of 9. Thus we find Saturn satisfies all the conditions for a Markesh Dasa.

Bhukti Lord Sun is in Rahu star that is the sub sub lord of 4 and sub lord of 7 (Badhaka for 9) and 9. Sun is in the sub of Mercury that is placed in 9 with PS. Sun is in Saturn SS that is in Maraka houses.

Mercury the Antara and Prana Lord is placed in 9 with PS. It is in the sub of Saturn that is placed in 4 with PS. Thus as per its PS it is a very strong significator of death of father. Mercury is in Moon star and Sat sub. Moon appears as star lord of 9 and Sat is the resident of 4 with PS. Thus at stellar level also Mercury is a strong significator of death of father.

Sookshama lord Mars is in Rahu star that is the sub sub lord of 4 and sub lord of 9 and 7. Mars is in the sub of Moon that is in 9. Mars is in the SS of Rahu. Thus Mars has the power to inflict death of father.

Figure 5.12 represents the transit position of planets on the day of Death of the Father.

Fig. 5.12 Transit chart on 27.12.1998 at 22 hrs.

Planetary Position

Planet	Sign	D-M-S	R L	STL	SL	SSL	Hse	D	S
Sun	Sag	11-53-01	Ju	Ke	Me	Ve	5	P	
Moon	Pis	28-03-48	Ju	Me	Sa	Sa	8		
Mars	Vir	22-23-44	Me	Mo	Ve	Me	2		
Mercury	Sco	21-35-26	Ma	Me	Su	Mo	4	P	
Jupiter	Aqu	27-30-09	Sa	Ju	Ve	Ra	7	P	
Venus	Sag	26-08-48	Ju	Ve	Ke	Mo	5	P	
Saturn	Ari	02-56-34	Ma	Ke	Ve	Ke	8	R	P
T.Rahu	Can	29-26-29	Mo	Me	Sa	Ra	12	P	
T.Ketu	Cap	29-26-29	Sa	Ma	Sa	Ra	6		

We notice that Saturn was transiting in Mars sign Aries and in Ketu star, Venus sub and Ketu SS. The Sign Lord Mars is related to the sub sub lord of 4 that is sub sub lord of 8 with respect to 9 because Rahu the sub sub lord of 4 represents Mars. We have already seen that Mars has the potential to cause the death of the father of the native. Ketu represents both Venus and Mars. As such we find that transit of Saturn fully justifies the event of death. Similarly we can verify that transit position of other planets support the event.

Let us discuss the Progressed chart for the event of death of the native's father. Figure 5.13 represents the progressed chart.

Fig. 5.13 Progress on 27.12.1998 at 22 hrs.

Name	TH Fig 5.9	Place	Karolbagh Delhi
Longitude	77-11-0-E	Latitude	28-40-0-N
Sidereal Time	22-17-27	Date	26/2/1949
Day	Saturday	Geocentric Latitude	28-30-18-N
Nakshatra	Dhanishtha-2 Qtr.	Time	12:15:34
Lunar Nodes	True	Tithi	Krishna Paksha - Chaturdasi
Time Zone	+5:30:0	DST	00:00
Ayanamsa	23-08-09	House System	Placidus

Rashi Chart

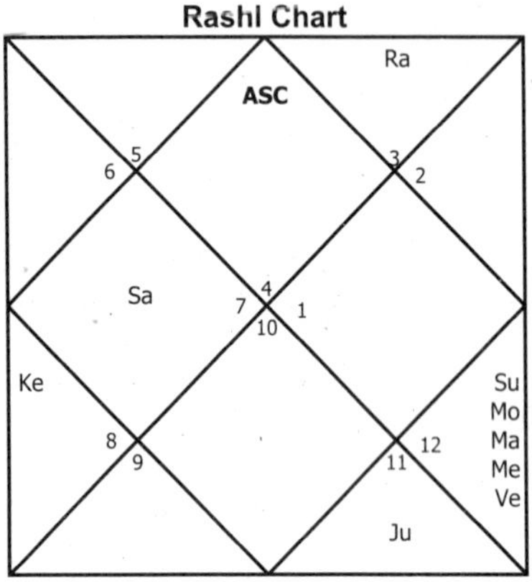

Bhava Chart

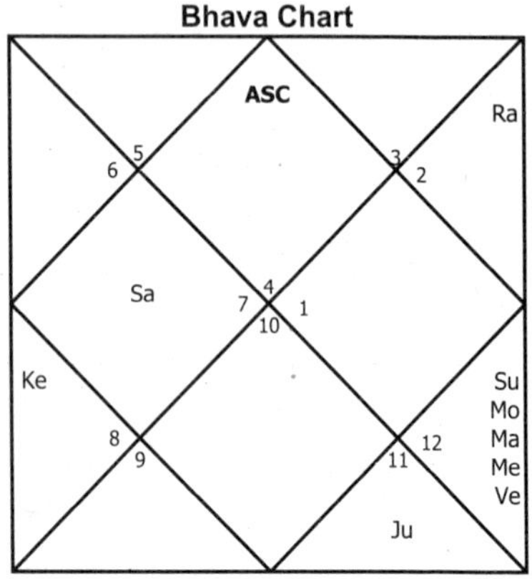

Cusp Chart

Ma 26-32-31 Su 22-10-49 Ve 12-37-24 Mo 10-48-22 Me 06-21-45 IX 01-34-32	X 03-33-36	XI 07-38-49	Ra 07-57-40 XII 10-22-34
Ju 28-28-51 VIII 04-01-01			I 10-20-15
VII 10-20-15			II 04-01-01
VI 10-22-34	Ke 13-19-53 V 07-38-49	Sa 10-09-28 IV 03-33-36	III 01-34-32

Fig. 5.13 Contd......

Planetary Position

Planet	Sign	D-M-S	R L	STL	SL	SSL	Hse	D	S
Sun	Pis	22-10-49	Ju	Me	Su	Ve	9	P	
Moon	Pis	10-48-22	Ju	Sa	Su	Me	9	P	
Mars	Pis	26-32-31	Ju	Me	Ju	Sa	9	P	
Mercury	Pis	06-21-45	Ju	Sa	Me	Mo	9		
Jupiter	Aqu	28-28-51	Sa	Ju	Ve	Me	8	P	
Venus	Pis	12-37-24	Ju	Sa	Ma	Ke	9	P	
Saturn	Lib	10-09-28	Ve	Ra	Ju	Ma	4	P	
Rahu	Gem	07-57-40	Me	Ra	Ra	Ve	11	P	
Ketu	Sco	13-19-53	Ma	Sa	Ra	Ju	5	P	

Cuspal Position

Cusp	Sign	D-M-S	R L	STL	SL	SSL	% Arc
Cusp I	Can	10-20-15	Mo	Sa	Su	Su	12.49
Cusp II	Leo	04-01-01	Su	Ke	Mo	Ju	17.75
Cusp III	Vir	01-34-32	Me	Su	Ju	Sa	41.31
Cusp IV	Lib	03-33-36	Ve	Ma	Ve	Ra	29.08
Cusp V	Sco	07-38-49	Ma	Sa	Ke	Ma	76.98
Cusp VI	Sag	10-22-34	Ju	Ke	Sa	Ve	81.39
Cusp VII	Cap	10-20-15	Sa	Mo	Mo	Ju	09.06
Cusp VIII	Aqu	04-01-01	Sa	Ma	Ve	Ju	74.50
Cusp IX	Pis	01-34-32	Ju	Ju	Ra	Ra	80.73
Cusp X	Ari	03-33-36	Ma	Ke	Su	Ve	03.91
Cusp XI	Tau	07-38-49	Ve	Su	Ke	Sa	83.25
Cusp XII	Gem	10-22-34	Me	Ra	Ju	Ra	74.40

We notice that the progressed position of ascendant is co-ruled by planets Moon -Sat- Sun-Sun. Death of father has taken place in Saturn Dasa and Sun Bhukti. Moon is also a strong significator of father's death. Moon is placed in 9, ascendant of Father. It is in Mars star that is in 7 (Badhaka for 9) and in Jupiter sub that is the sub sub lord of 9 and sub lord of 4th.

We can also check that during the progressed position of ascendant in Moon sign the native will experience some death event or not. Moon is in Mars star (12) and Jupiter sub (8). This shows that the native is destined to experience some death event.

We may analyse the progressed chart independently. Dasa lord Saturn is placed in 4 in the progressed chart. Saturn acquires the positional status because of exchange of Nakshatra with Mercury through Rahu. Saturn is in Rahu star that is the sub sub lord of 4 and 9. Saturn is in the sub of Jupiter that is in 9 as well as in 3 (both Maraka and Badhaka for 9). Saturn thus satisfies necessary conditions to be the Markesh Dasa. Similarly we can verify that all planets in the Progressed position of Moon justify death in the Progressed chart also.

We can study the progressed chart along with transit chart. For example Saturn in transit was in Aries ruled by Mars. In the progressed chart Mars is in Mercury star that is placed in 9. Mars is in the sub of Jupiter that is in Badhaka.

Birth of First Daughter: The native was blessed with the birth of his first female child on 07.06.1974 at 18.39.16 hrs when he was running the period of Jupiter-Jupiter-Rahu-Moon-Rahu.

Dasa and Bhukti lord Jupiter has PS and appears in 11.It is in the sub of Rahu that appears in 2 and 5.

Antara and Prana lord Rahu is in Ketu star that is placed in 5. Since Ketu represents Venus we may say that Rahu is in Venus star that is the sub sub lord of 2 and 11. Thus we notice that Rahu involves all three relevant houses. Rahu is in the sub of Sun that does not negate 2. Rahu represents Mars and thus has also to cause results of Mars. Mars is in Rahu star (2, 5 and 11) and Moon sub that is the sub lord of 2 and 11 and star lord of 5. Mars is in the SS of Rahu that appears in all the relevant cusps. Thus we find that Rahu is a very strong significator of the event of birth of the first child.

Sookshama lord Moon is in Mars star and Jupiter sub. We notice that in this chart both Rahu and Ketu represent Mars. Ketu is placed in 5 and Rahu is placed in 11. Thus we find Moon involves 5 and 11. Moon is in the sub of Jupiter that appears in 11. Moon is in the SS of Mercury that appears in 2.

Figure 5.14 shows the transit position of planets at the time of birth of the child.

Fig. 5.14 07.06.1974 18.39.16 Holy family

Planetary Position

Planet	Sign	D-M-S	R L	STL	SL	SSL	Hse	D	S
Sun	Tau	22-54-48	Ve	Mo	Su	Ju	7	P	
Moon	Sag	22-12-09	Ju	Ve	Sa	Sa	2		
Mars	Can	05-35-50	Mo	Sa	Me	Me	8		
Mercury	Gem	16-07-42	Me	Ra	Ve	Ra	7	P	
Jupiter	Aqu	22-56-58	Sa	Ju	Sa	Su	3	P	
Venus	Ari	14-53-48	Ma	Ve	Ve	Sa	5	P	
Saturn	Gem	11-52-49	Me	Ra	Sa	Ma	7	P	
T.Rahu	Sco	25-54-08	Ma	Me	Ra	Mo	1	P	
T.Ketu	Tau	25-54-08	Ve	Ma	Ra	Mo	7	P	

The native got the child in Venus Moon star. **An event happens when the Moon star is related to the sub sub lord of the primary cusp and it signifies the relevant houses.** In this case Rahu is the sub sub lord of the 5th cusp that represents Venus through Ketu. Venus is in Mars star. Both Ketu and Rahu represent Mars and Venus. Thus Venus involves 2, 5 and 11. Venus is in the sub of Mercury that appears in 2.

We can check transit of all planets and confirm that transit supports the event.

Figure 5.15 represents the Progressed chart at the time of birth of the first daughter.

Fig. 5.15 Progress chart of 07.06.1974

Name	Fig 5.9	Place	Karolbagh Delhi
Longitude	77-11-0-E	Latitude	28-40-0-N
Sidereal Time	22-17-27	Date	26/2/1949
Day	Saturday	Geocentric Latitude	28-30-18-N
Nakshatra	Dhanishtha-2 Qtr.	Time	12:15:34
Lunar Nodes	True	Tithi	Krishna Paksha - Chaturdasi
Time Zone	+5:30:0	DST	00:00
Ayanamsa	23-08-09	House System	Placidus

Rashi Chart

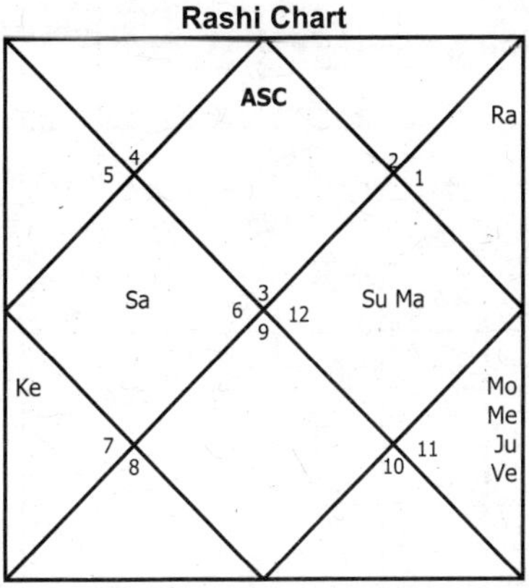

Bhava Chart

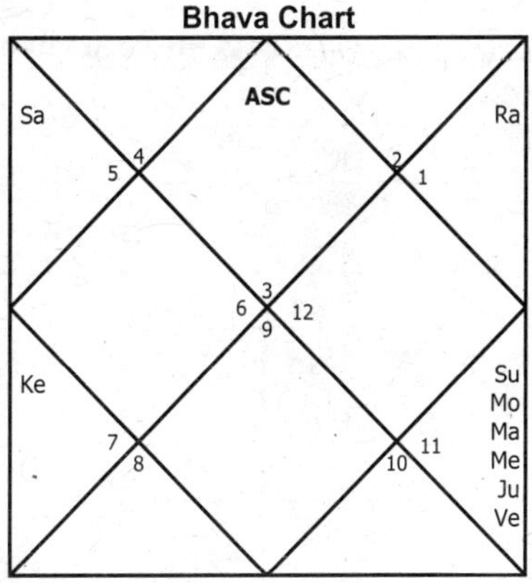

Cusp Chart

X 09-31-10 Ma 08-16-12 Su 04-22-03	XI 14-14-36 Ra 27-05-29	XII 19-20-54	I 21-11-14
Ve 23-54-07 Mo 21-44-38 Me 16-51-35 Ju 09-20-55 IX 09-16-20			II 13-53-23
VIII 13-53-23			III 09-16-20
VII 21-11-14	VI 19-20-54	Ke 24-44-34 V 14-14-36	Sa 03-40-53 IV 09-31-10

Fig. 5.15 Contd......

Planetary Position

Planet	Sign	D-M-S	R L	STL	SL	SSL	Hse	D	S
Sun	Pis	04-22-03	Ju	Sa	Sa	Ve	9	P	
Moon	Aqu	21-44-38	Sa	Ju	Ju	Ra	9	P	
Mars	Pis	08-16-12	Ju	Sa	Ve	Ve	9	P	
Mercury	Aqu	16-51-35	Sa	Ra	Ve	Sa	9	P	
Jupiter	Aqu	09-20-55	Sa	Ra	Ju	Me	9		
Venus	Aqu	23-54-07	Sa	Ju	Me	Me	9	P	
Saturn	Vir	03-40-53	Me	Su	Sa	Ke	3	P	
Rahu	Ari	27-05-29	Ma	Su	Su	Me	11		
Ketu	Lib	24-44-34	Ve	Ju	Me	Mo	5	P	

Cuspal Position

Cusp	Sign	D-M-S	R L	STL	SL	SSL	% Arc
Cusp I	Gem	21-11-14	Me	Ju	Ju	Su	19.05
Cusp II	Can	13-53-23	Mo	Sa	Ra	Me	41.48
Cusp III	Leo	09-16-20	Su	Ke	Ju	Ra	77.10
Cusp IV	Vir	09-31-10	Me	Su	Ve	Sa	89.75
Cusp V	Lib	14-14-36	Ve	Ra	Me	Sa	32.74
Cusp VI	Sco	19-20-54	Ma	Me	Ve	Ve	04.06
Cusp VII	Sag	21-11-14	Ju	Ve	Ju	Ve	68.21
Cusp VIII	Cap	13-53-23	Sa	Mo	Ju	Ju	00.37
Cusp IX	Aqu	09-16-20	Sa	Ra	Ju	Me	34.58
Cusp X	Pis	09-31-10	Ju	Sa	Ve	Ju	94.08
Cusp XI	Ari	14-14-36	Ma	Ve	Ve	Ra	34.10
Cusp XII	Tau	19-20-54	Ve	Mo	Me	Ju	92.37

The progressed ascendant is co-ruled by planets Mercury-Jupiter-Jupiter-Sun. We have discussed earlier that Mercury promises the execution of the first child birth. Jupiter is Dasa and Bhukti lord at the time of birth of the child. Sun in the natal chart is in Rahu star (2, 5 and 11) and sub of Mercury that is in 2. Thus we find that the co-ruling planets of progressed ascendant are strong significators of the event.

We can study the progressed chart independently.

Refer page 303, Dasa and Bhukti lord Jupiter is in Rahu star that is the sub sub lord of 11, sub lord of 2 and star lord of 5. Jupiter is in the sub of Jupiter that appears in 9 and 1 and thus supports the houses 5 and 11 but negates 2. This accounts for the reason that Jupiter could not enact the event in its Antara.

Antara and Prana lord Rahu represents Mars and Sun. Both these planets are strong significators of 2, 5 and 11. Rahu is in Sun star Sun sub and Mercury SS. It will be considered that Rahu is in Sun star and Mercur sub. Sun as Rahu is placed in 11 and Mercury appears in 2.

Sookshama lord Moon is in Jupiter star and Rahu sub. Ketu which represents Jup is placed in 5. Thus Moon involves 5 and its sub lord Rahu appears in 2 and 11.

Thus the Progressed chart justifies the event.

We can see that the event happened when the 5th cusp progressed to the planets co ruled by Ven-Rahu-Mercury and Jupiter that are all strong significators of the event. **Note we have to see the progression of 5th cusp independently and not the 5th cusp as it appears in the progressed chart.**

Foreign Travel: The native went overseas on 01.04.2011 when he was running the period of Mercury-Venus-Sun-Rahu-Saturn and Moon star at the time of departure was Rahu. All the Dasa period lords are significators of 3, 9 and 12.

Moon star Rahu is Sookshama lord. Rahu is in Ketu star that represents Venus which is placed in 9 and is the sub sub lord of 12. Ketu also represents Mars that is the sub lord of 3.

Thus we find that the chart justifies the event as per Dasa and transit potential.

Figure 5.16 represents the Progressed chart at the time of start of the Journey.

Fig. 5.16 Progress on 01.04.2011 at 01 hrs.

Name	Fig 5.16	Place	Karolbagh Delhi
Longitude	77-11-0-E	Latitude	28-40-0-N
Sidereal Time	22-17-27	Date	26/2/1949
Day	Saturday	Geocentric Latitude	28-30-18-N
Nakshatra	Dhanishtha-2 Qtr.	Time	12:15:34
Lunar Nodes	True	Tithi	Krishna Paksha - Chaturdasi
Time Zone	+5:30:0 DST	00:00	
Ayanamsa	23-08-09	House System	Placidus

Rashi Chart

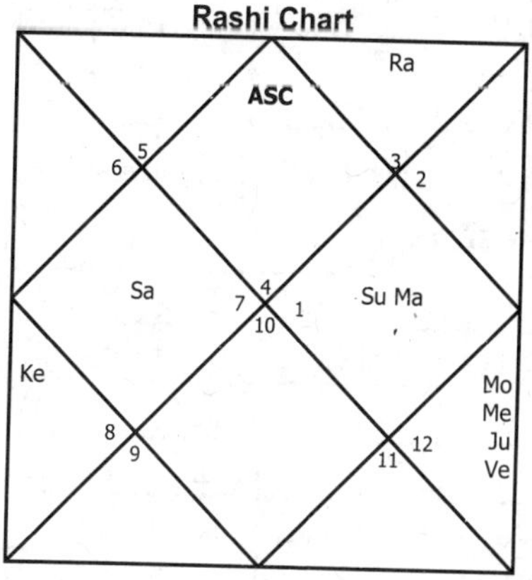

Bhava Chart

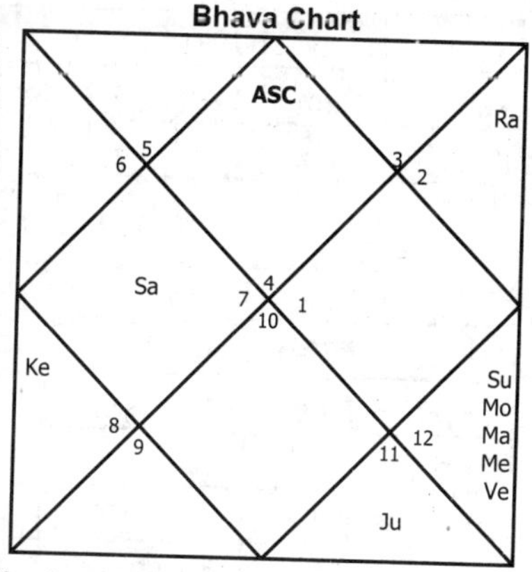

Cusp Chart

Ve 21-45-42 Mo 19-43-50 Me 14-57-52 IX 12-06-19 Ju 07-50-56	Su 04-21-26 Ma 13-53-57 X 14-24-33	XI 17-52-14	Ra 17-02-27 XII 19-44-40
VIII 13-37-02			I 19-12-24
VII 19-12-24			II 13-37-02
VI 19-44-40	Ke 22-33-11 V 17-52-14	Sa 19-14-15 IV 14-24-33	III 12-06-19

Fig. 5.16 Contd......

Planetary Position

Planet	Sign	D-M-S	R L	STL	SL	SSL	Hse	D	S
Sun	Ari	04-21-26	Ma	Ke	Mo	Me	9	P	
Moon	Pis	19-43-50	Ju	Me	Ve	Su	9	P	
Mars	Ari	13-53-57	Ma	Ve	Ve	Mo	9	P	
Mercury	Pis	14-57-52	Ju	Sa	Ju	Ju	9		
Jupiter	Pis	07-50-56	Ju	Sa	Ke	Ju	8	P	
Venus	Pis	21-45-42	Ju	Me	Su	Ra	9		
Saturn	Lib	19-14-15	Ve	Ra	Ma	Ma	4	P	
Rahu	Gem	17-02-27	Me	Ra	Ve	Me	11	P	
Ketu	Sco	22-33-11	Ma	Me	Mo	Ju	5		

Cuspal Position

Cusp	Sign	D-M-S	R L	STL	SL	SSL	% Arc
Cusp I	Can	19-12-24	Mo	Me	Ke	Sa	86.70
Cusp II	Leo	13-37-02	Su	Ve	Ve	Ve	76.65
Cusp III	Vir	12-06-19	Me	Mo	Ra	Ra	72.16
Cusp IV	Lib	14-24-33	Ve	Ra	Me	Sa	88.16
Cusp V	Sco	17-52-14	Ma	Me	Me	Ra	52.70
Cusp VI	Sag	19-44-40	Ju	Ve	Ra	Su	16.65
Cusp VII	Cap	19-12-24	Sa	Mo	Me	Ju	36.14
Cusp VIII	Aqu	13-37-02	Sa	Ra	Me	Ra	02.49
Cusp IX	Pis	12-06-19	Ju	Sa	Mo	Su	89.66
Cusp X	Ari	14-24-33	Ma	Ve	Ve	Ra	83.82
Cusp XI	Tau	17-52-14	Ve	Mo	Me	Me	34.69
Cusp XII	Gem	19-44-40	Me	Ra	Ma	Ke	50.98

The Progressed ascendant is co-ruled by Moon-Mercury-Ketu-Saturn. All these planets are strong significators of 3, 9 and 11. See Saturn that is ruling the sub sub lord position of the progressed ascendant. It is in Ketu star (Mars and Venus-3, 9 and 12) and Jupiter sub (sub sub lord of 9) and Rahu SS (3, 9 and 12). (Refer natal chart fig. 5.9)

We can verify the event by studying the progressed chart independently. Let us take the Sookshama lord Rahu. It is in Rahu star (3 and 12). Prana lord Saturn is in Rahu star (3 and 12) and Mars sub (sub sub lord of 9).

Thus we say that the execution of the event is justified by the progressed chart.

From the above discussion we can say that the rectified chart is the true horoscope of the native.

Example 4: A female provided the following details with a request to fix the correct chart.

My DOB: 25 dec1973

Time of Birth: 08.50 Hrs.

Place: Amarjain Hospital, Rajasthan, India

Longitude: 75 deg 49 min 15 sec-East

Latitude: 26 deg 55 min 17 sec-North

Qualification: B.A (1995); M.B.A.(1997)

Death of father: 19th Dec. 1991 approx time: 1.30 hrs. in Jaipur

Death of mother: 10th Sep. 2008 approx time: 15.50 hrs Delhi

Younger sister: DOB-1st Oct 1975 at 19.30 hrs.

Younger brother: DOB-28th May 1977 at 02.15 hrs.

Elder daughter: DOB-10th Oct 2002; TOB- 1.41.26 p.m. at Noida

Younger son: DOB-1st Mar 2006; TOB-10.15 a.m. at Noida

My wedding ceremony date: 19th Nov 1999

My husband's DOB- 23rd June 1973; in Delhi

Date of joining of first job: 1st June 1997

First Foreign Travel: 15th May 2010 Time of departure 5 a.m.

The job of rectification of this chart was taken on 18.07.2011 at 18.55.57 at Noida. The ruling planets at that time were as follows:

RP (Ascendant): Jupiter-Venus-Ketu-Mercury-Jupiter-Mercury

RP (Moon): Saturn-Rahu-Jupiter-Rahu-Jupiter-Saturn

On this date Rahu represented Mars and Mercury. Ketu represented Venus and Mars.

The process of rectification was done by following the step by step procedure as discussed above. It was found that at 08.48.02 hrs the positions of Sun, Moon and ascendant match the ruling planets. The rectified horoscope is represented by Figure 5.17.

Fig. 5.17 Natal

Name	Fig 5.17	Place	Amarjain Hospital
Longitude	75-49-15-E	Latitude	26-55-17-N
Sidereal Time	14-35-19	Date	25/12/1973
Day	Tuesday	Geocentric Latitude	26-45-59-N
Nakshatra	P.Ashadha-1 Qtr.	Time	08:48:02
Lunar Nodes	True	Tithi	Shukla Paksha - Pratipada
Time Zone	+5:30:0	DST	00:00
Ayanamsa	23-28-56	House System	Placidus

Rashi Chart

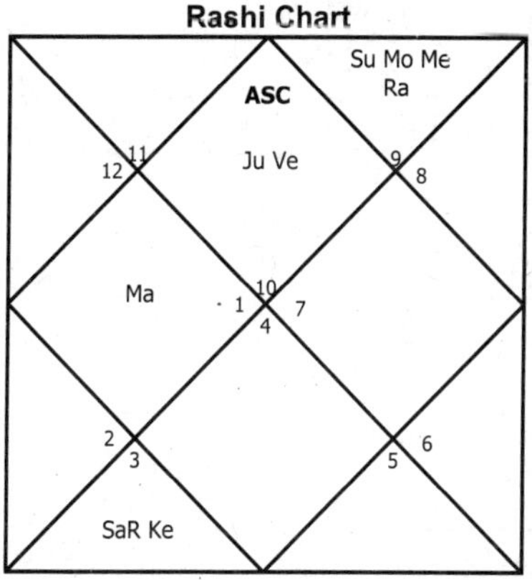

Bhava Chart

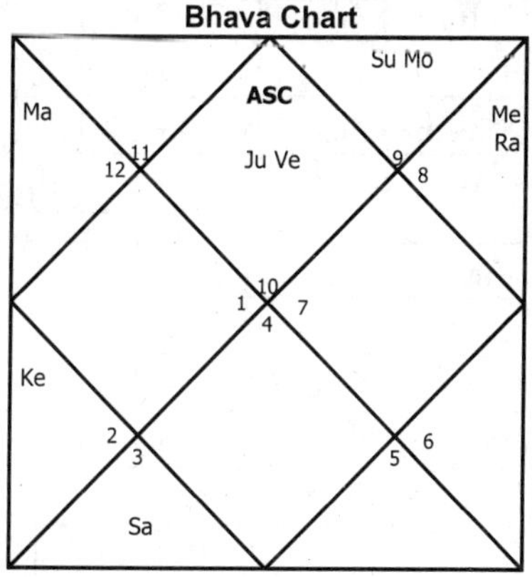

Cusp Chart

III 16-52-40	Ma 06-45-27 IV 17-46-41	V 13-22-23	Ke 05-07-32 VI 06-53-31 SaR 07-37-04
II 09-56-00			VII 02-11-56
Ju 19-27-16 Ve 16-16-38 I 02-11-56			VIII 09-56-00
Mo 15-10-51 Su 09-42-17 XII 06-53-31 Ra 05-07-32 Me 01-04-03	XI 13-22-23	X 17-46-41	IX 16-52-40

Fig. 5.17 Contd......

Planetary Position

Planet	Sign	D-M-S	R L	STL	SL	SSL	Hse	D	S
Sun	Sag	09-42-17	Ju	Ke	Sa	Me	12	P	
Moon	Sag	15-10-51	Ju	Ve	Ve	Me	12	P	
Mars	Ari	06-45-27	Ma	Ke	Ra	Ke	3	P	
Mercury	Sag	01-04-03	Ju	Ke	Ve	Ve	11	P	
Jupiter	Cap	19-27-16	Sa	Mo	Me	Sa	1	P	
Venus	Cap	16-16-38	Sa	Mo	Sa	Me	1	P	
Saturn	Gem	07-37-04	Me	Ra	Ra	Me	6	R	P
T.Rahu	Sag	05-07-32	Ju	Ke	Ma	Sa	11		
T.Ketu	Gem	05-07-32	Me	Ma	Su	Ju	5	P	

Cuspal Position

Cusp	Sign	D-M-S	R L	STL	SL	SSL	% Arc
Cusp I	Cap	02-11-56	Sa	Su	Ju	Ve	34.60
Cusp II	Aqu	09-56-00	Sa	Ra	Ju	Mo	05.05
Cusp III	Pis	16-52-40	Ju	Me	Me	Me	78.84
Cusp IV	Ari	17-46-41	Ma	Ve	Ma	Me	50.69
Cusp V	Tau	13-22-23	Ve	Mo	Ra	Ve	60.22
Cusp VI	Gem	06-53-31	Me	Ra	Ra	Ra	75.07
Cusp VII	Can	02-11-56	Mo	Ju	Ra	Sa	94.36
Cusp VIII	Leo	09-56-00	Su	Ke	Sa	Me	88.88
Cusp IX	Vir	16-52-40	Me	Mo	Sa	Su	97.24
Cusp X	Lib	17-46-41	Ve	Ra	Su	Sa	16.07
Cusp XI	Sco	13-22-23	Ma	Sa	Ra	Ju	69.02
Cusp XII	Sag	06-53-31	Ju	Ke	Ra	Ve	15.90

Verification of Accuracy of the Chart:

Planets co-ruling the positions of Sun, Moon and ascendant establish links with 1, 7 and 10. **It may be remembered that it is not a must that planets should be related to 1, 7 and 10 all simultaneously. Planets may be related to 1 and 7, 7 and 10 like that.**

Moon star of the native is Venus that is placed in ascendant with PS. More over Venus is the sub sub lord of the ascendant. Thus the Moon star lord establishes relationship with the sub sub lord of the ascendant.

Verification of Promises:

Marriage: Sub sub lord of ascendant is Venus that is in Moon star (5 and 7) and Saturn sub (7 and 11). Sub sub lord of 7th cusp is Saturn that is in Rahu star (5, 7 and 11) and sub of Mercury (11). Thus the chart promises marriage.

Birth of Children: Sub sub lord of 5 is Venus that is in Moon star (5 and 2) and Saturn sub (2 and 11). This promises that the native is procreative and could produce children.

A native can produce more than one child if the sub sub lord of 5 is linked with 7. Here Venus is in Moon star that appears in 7. Thus the native could produce more than one child.

Since sub sub lord of 5th cusp Venus has PS and thus gets connected to 4 and 12. This promises possible loss of pregnancies.

Promise of Higher Education: Sub sub lord of 4th cusp is Mercury that has PS and appears in 9th cusp. This promises that the native could have higher education. Since 7th cusp sub sub lord is Saturn that has PS and it appears as sub lord of 9th cusp; it justifies that native could do MBA.

Genitical Connections: It can be verified that the sub sub lords of 3, 5, and 7 relates to the Moon stars of the younger sister, first daughter, second child and husband.

Promise of Execution of Events and Progression: The natal chart sub sub lords of ascendant and the relevant cusp declares the promise of various aspects of life but it is the progressed position of the ascendant that declares the destined time of the execution of the promised event.

The native took birth in Capricorn ascendant ruled by Saturn. The ascendant will then progress to Aquarius which is also ruled by Saturn. This indicates that up to approximately May 2024 the native will experience all those events which are indicated by Saturn.

The native has already experienced the events of deaths of Parents, birth of children, marriage and service as profession, and could travel abroad. Let us see does Saturn promise all this? Saturn has PS and appears in 1, 2, 6, 7, 8, 9, 10 and 11. It is in the sub of Rahu that appears in 2, 5, 6, 7, 10, 11, and 12. Rahu represents Mars through Ketu that is placed in 3 with PS. Thus we find Saturn is linked with all the 12 houses directly or indirectly and justifies the execution of all events.

Verification of Events:

Marriage: The native got married on 19.11.1999 when she was running the period of Moon-Rahu-Sun-Saturn-Mars. All these planets are linked with 5, 7 and 11.

Dasa Lord Moon has PS and appears in 5 and 7. It is in the sub of Venus that is the sub sub lord of 5. Moon is in Venus star Venus sub and Mercury SS. We may say that Moon is in Venus star (5) and Mercury sub that is placed in 11with PS. Similarly we can check that Bhukti, Antara and Sookshma lord justify the enactment of the event.

It can be verified that transit of planets on that date support the event. Let us take the case of Moon. Moon was transiting on that date in Jupiter-Saturn-Rahu-Mercury.

Jupiter in the natal chart is in Moon star (5 and 7) and in Mercury sub (11). Saturn in the Natal chart is in Rahu star Rahu sub (5, 7 and 11) and Mercury SS (11). Rahu is the sub lord of 7. It is in Ketu star (5) and Mars sub 11. Mercury is placed in 11 with PS. It is in Venus sub that is the sub sub lord of 5.

Similarly we can verify the transit of other planets.

Verification of the event of Marriage from Progressed Chart: Figure 5.18 represents the Progressed chart on the day of Marriage.

Fig. 5.18 Progression on 19.11.1999 at 23 hrs

Name	Fig 5.18	Place	Amarjain Hospital
Longitude	75-49-15-E	Latitude	26-55-17-N
Sidereal Time	14-35-19	Date	25/12/1973
Day	Tuesday	Geocentric Latitude	26-45-59-N
Nakshatra	P.Ashadha-1 Qtr.	Time	08:48:02
Lunar Nodes	True	Tithi	Shukla Paksha - Pratipada
Time Zone	+5:30:0 DST	00:00	
Ayanamsa	23-28-56	House System	Placidus

Rashi Chart

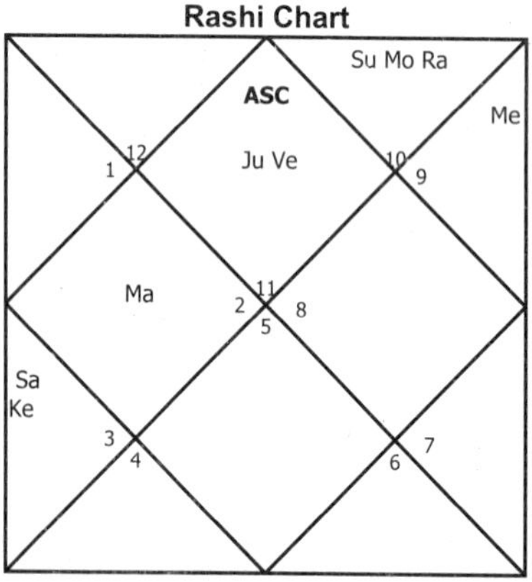

Bhava Chart

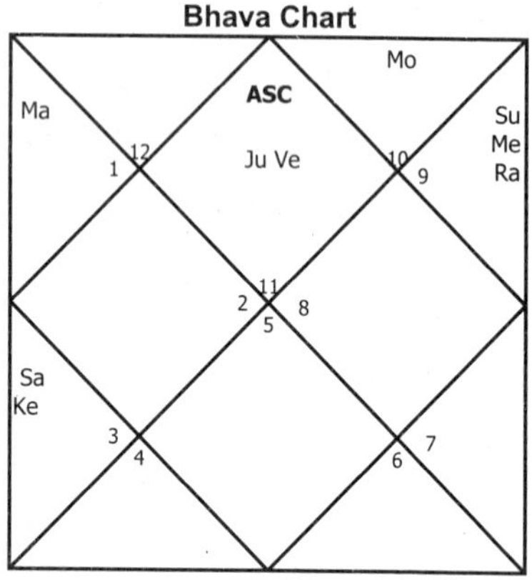

Cusp Chart

II 20-38-58	III 23-01-32	Ma 02-06-35 IV 19-06-12	V 12-53-43 Ke 25-54-38 Sa 27-39-17
Ju 18-30-47 Ve 16-44-52 I 10-39-36			VI 08-26-17
Mo 13-33-50 XII 08-26-17 Su 05-32-54 Ra 00-12-21			VII 10-39-36
Me 26-18-29 XI 12-53-43	X 19-06-12	IX 23-01-32	VIII 20-38-58

Fig. 5.18 Contd......

Planetary Position

Planet	Sign	D-M-S	R L	STL	SL	SSL	Hse	D	S
Sun	Cap	05-32-54	Sa	Su	Me	Ve	11	P	
Moon	Cap	13-33-50	Sa	Mo	Ra	Su	12	P	
Mars	Tau	02-06-35	Ve	Su	Ju	Ve	3	P	
Mercury	Sag	26-18-29	Ju	Ve	Ke	Ra	11	P	
Jupiter	Aqu	18-30-47	Sa	Ra	Mo	Ju	1	P	
Venus	Aqu	16-44-52	Sa	Ra	Ve	Sa	1		
Saturn	Gem	27-39-17	Me	Ju	Ve	Ra	5	P	
Rahu	Cap	00-12-21	Sa	Su	Ra	Me	11		
Ketu	Gem	25-54-38	Me	Ju	Ke	Ve	5	P	

Cuspal Position

Cusp	Sign	D-M-S	R L	STL	SL	SSL	% Arc
Cusp I	Aqu	10-39-36	Sa	Ra	Sa	Sa	64.52
Cusp II	Pis	20-38-58	Ju	Me	Ve	Ju	62.96
Cusp III	Ari	23-01-32	Ma	Ve	Sa	Su	26.85
Cusp IV	Tau	19-06-12	Ve	Mo	Me	Ra	95.60
Cusp V	Gem	12-53-43	Me	Ra	Me	Ke	65.38
Cusp VI	Can	08-26-17	Mo	Sa	Ve	Ve	88.25
Cusp VII	Leo	10-39-36	Su	Ke	Sa	Mo	64.17
Cusp VIII	Vir	20-38-58	Me	Mo	Ve	Ve	55.37
Cusp IX	Lib	23-01-32	Ve	Ju	Sa	Mo	19.27
Cusp X	Sco	19-06-12	Ma	Me	Ke	Sa	02.66
Cusp XI	Sag	12-53-43	Ju	Ke	Me	Ju	44.78
Cusp XII	Cap	08-26-17	Sa	Su	Ve	Mo	96.50

We notice that the Progressed ascendant is co-ruled by the planets Saturn-Rahu-Saturn-Saturn. We have already discussed above that Saturn and Rahu allows the enactment of the event of marriage in the natal chart.

Let us study the progressed chart independently. The event of Marriage happened when Moon was progressing in Moon – Rahu-Sun-Saturn-Mars. In the Progressed chart Moon is the sub sub lord of 7th cusp. It is in Rahu sub that appears in 5. Rahu the Bhukti lord is in Sun star (7 and 11) and in Rahu sub (5). Sun the Antara lord is in Sun star (7 and 11) and Mercury sub (5 and 11). Sookshama lord Saturn has PS and is the sub lord of 7 and is placed in 5. Saturn is in the star of Jupiter that is the sub sub lord of 11. It is in Venus sub that does not negate 5 and 11. Prana lord Mars is in Sun star (7 and 11) and in Jupiter sub that is the sub sub lord of 11.

Thus we find Progressed chart justifies the event of marriage.

Death of Father: The native lost her father on 19.12.1991 at about 01.30 hrs. She was at that time running the period of Sun-Moon-Venus-Saturn-Sun.

Dasa Lord Sun is a co-ruling planet in the ascendant. It is in Ketu star that represents Mercury the sub sub lord of the 4th cusp (8th from 9). Sun is in the sub of Saturn that is the sub lord of 9. Sun is in the SS of Mercury that appears in 4. Thus the Dasa lord meets all the conditions of a Markesh Dasa.

Bhukti lord Moon has PS and appears in 9. Moon is in Venus star and Venus sub and Mercury SS. We may Say that Mercury takes the role of sub lord. Thus Moon in 9 and Mercury is the sub sub lord of 3 & 4 that is the Badhaka & 8th for father.

Antara lord Venus, Sookshma lord Saturn and Prana lord Sun are all significators of father's death.

On the date of father's death Saturn was transiting in Saturn-Moon-Moon-Mercury. Saturn is in Rahu star Rahu sub. Rahu represents Mercury through Ketu. Mercury is the sub sub lord of 4 (8th from 9). Saturn signifies death of father. Moon is the Bhukti lord. Mercury has PS. It is in the sub of Venus that appears in 10 (2nd from 9th). Thus we find that Mercury is linked with Maraka and Badhaka house and justifies the death of father.

We can notice that death of father took place when Moon was transiting in Sun star that meets all the conditions for father's death as stated above.

We can anlyse the progressed chart of the event. Figure 5.19 represents the progressed chart.

Fig 5.19 Prog 19.12.1991

Name	Fig 5.19	Place	Amarjain Hospital
Longitude	75-49-15-E	Latitude	26-55-17-N
Sidereal Time	14-35-19	Date	25/12/1973
Day	Tuesday	Geocentric Latitude	26-45-59-N
Nakshatra	P.Ashadha-1 Qtr.	Time	08:48:02
Lunar Nodes	True	Tithi	Shukla Paksha - Pratipada
Time Zone	+5:30:0 DST	00:00	
Ayanamsa	23-28-56	House System	Placidus

Rashi Chart

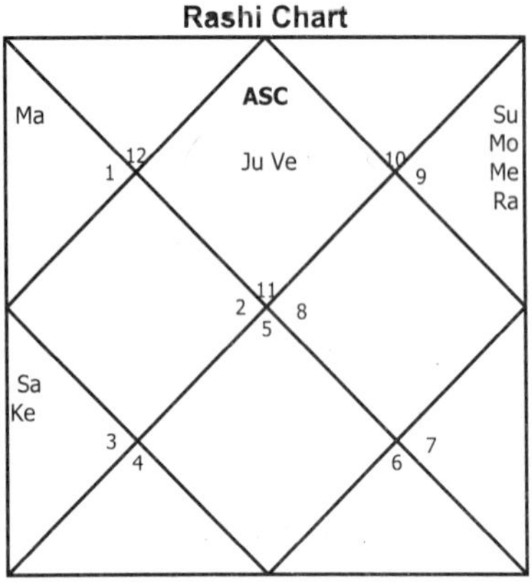

Bhava Chart

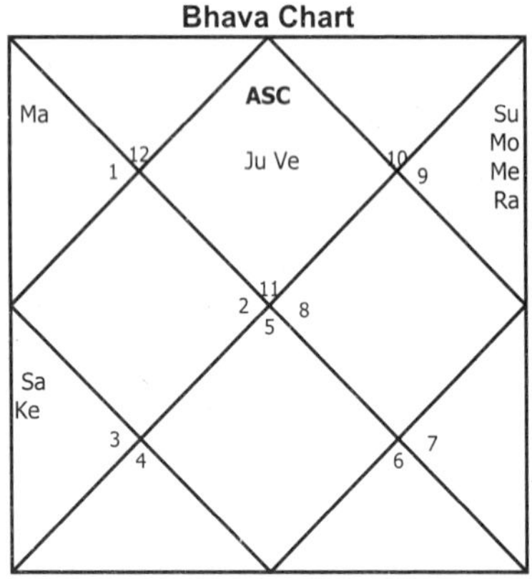

Cusp Chart

II 12-02-35	III 15-45-27 Ma 23-01-10	IV 12-43-32	V 06-37-46 Ke 19-23-13 Sa 21-03-16
Ju 12-38-46 Ve 10-52-52 I 01-50-57			VI 01-24-40
XII 01-24-40			VII 01-50-57
Mo 28-20-21 Su 24-03-03 Ra 22-26-54 Me 21-01-40 XI 06-37-46	X 12-43-32	IX 15-45-27	VIII 12-02-35

Fig. 5.19 Contd......

Planetary Position

Planet	Sign	D-M-S	R L	STL	SL	SSL	Hse	D	S
Sun	Sag	24-03-03	Ju	Ve	Me	Me	11		
Moon	Sag	28-20-21	Ju	Su	Mo	Ve	11	P	
Mars	Ari	23-01-10	Ma	Ve	Sa	Su	3	P	
Mercury	Sag	21-01-40	Ju	Ve	Ju	Ve	11	P	
Jupiter	Aqu	12-38-46	Sa	Ra	Me	Me	1	P	
Venus	Aqu	10-52-52	Sa	Ra	Sa	Me	1	P	
Saturn	Gem	21-03-16	Me	Ju	Ju	Ve	5	P	
Rahu	Sag	22-26-54	Ju	Ve	Sa	Me	11	P	
Ketu	Gem	19-23-13	Me	Ra	Ma	Ju	5	P	

Cuspal Position

Cusp	Sign	D-M-S	R L	STL	SL	SSL	% Arc
Cusp I	Aqu	01-50-57	Sa	Ma	Me	Sa	86.75
Cusp II	Pis	12-02-35	Ju	Sa	Mo	Ve	93.19
Cusp III	Ari	15-45-27	Ma	Ve	Su	Ra	74.25
Cusp IV	Tau	12-43-32	Ve	Mo	Ra	Sa	85.22
Cusp V	Gem	06-37-46	Me	Ma	Mo	Su	33.13
Cusp VI	Can	01-24-40	Mo	Ju	Ra	Ra	25.91
Cusp VII	Leo	01-50-57	Su	Ke	Ve	Ra	82.56
Cusp VIII	Vir	12-02-35	Me	Mo	Ra	Ra	51.35
Cusp IX	Lib	15-45-27	Ve	Ra	Ve	Mo	29.10
Cusp X	Sco	12-43-32	Ma	Sa	Ma	Ve	53.90
Cusp XI	Sag	06-37-46	Ju	Ke	Ra	Me	67.28
Cusp XII	Cap	01-24-40	Sa	Su	Ju	Ju	79.67

The event of death of father happened when Moon was progressing in Sun-Moon-Venus-Sat-Sun.

Dasa and Prana lord is Sun that is a co-ruling planet in 7 which is Badhaka for 9.Sun is in Venus star that appears in 4 and 9. Sun is in Mercury sub that appears in 8 that is 12th from 9. It can be seen that Sun is significator of Maraka and Badhaka houses.

Bhukti lord Moon is in Sun star (7th Badhaka house for 9) and sub of Moon that is the sub sub lord of 9. Thus Moon satisfies all conditions to cause death of father.

Antara lord Venus is in Rahu star that appears in 4 and 9. It is in the sub of Saturn that is the sub sub lord of 4.

Sookshma lord Saturn is the sub sub lord of 4. It is in Venus SS that assumes the role of sub lord because Saturn is in Jupiter star and Jupiter sub. Venus appears in 9. Thus Saturn justifies its role of causing death of father.

Thus the analysis of progressed chart confirms the enactment of the event.

Event of Joining First Job: A native joins first job in the joint period of significators of houses 2, 6 and 10 when transit and progressed ascendant allows the event to happen. It is stated by the native that she joined the first job on 01.06.1997. On this date the native was running the period of Moon-Moon-Rahu-Venus-Mars.

Dasa and Bhukti lord Moon has PS and SSL of 2. Moon is in Venus star and Venus sub and Mercury SS. Venus appears in 10 and Mercury appears in 6 and 11.

Antara lord Rahu represents Jupiter, Ketu, Mars and Mercury. Jupiter is in Moon star (sub sub lord of 2) and sub of Mercury (6 and 11).

Shooksma lord Venus is in Moon star (2) and Saturn sub that is the sub sub lord of 10.

Prana lord Mars Is in Ketu star that represents Mercury (6 and 11), and in sub of Rahu (2, 6 and 10). Since Rahu also appears in 5 this indicates that the job is of temporary nature.

It can be seen that on that date Moon was transiting in Jupiter Sign and Mercury star. Jupiter is in Moon star (2) and Mercury sub (6 and 11) and Saturn SS that is the sub sub lord of 10 and star lord of 11. Mercury is in Ketu star that represents Mercury (6 and 11). Mercury is in the sub of Venus that is the sign lord of 10.

It can be verified that transit supports the event. Let us see if the Progressed ascendant allows the event or not. On this date the Progressed ascendant was co-ruled by Sat-Rahu-Jupiter-Jupiter. All these planets signify 2, 6 and 10.

Let us study the Progressed chart at the time of the happening of the Event. Figure 5.20 represents the Progressed chart.

Fig. 5.20 Progress on 01.06.1997.

Name	Fig 5.20	Place	Amarjain Hospital
Longitude	75-49-15-E	Latitude	26-55-17-N
Sidereal Time	14-35-19	Date	25/12/1973
Day	Tuesday	Geocentric Latitude	26-45-59-N
Nakshatra	P.Ashadha-1 Qtr.	Time	08:48:02
Lunar Nodes	True	Tithi	Shukla Paksha - Pratipada
Time Zone	+5:30:0 DST	00:00	
Ayanamsa	23-28-56	House System	Placidus

Rashi Chart

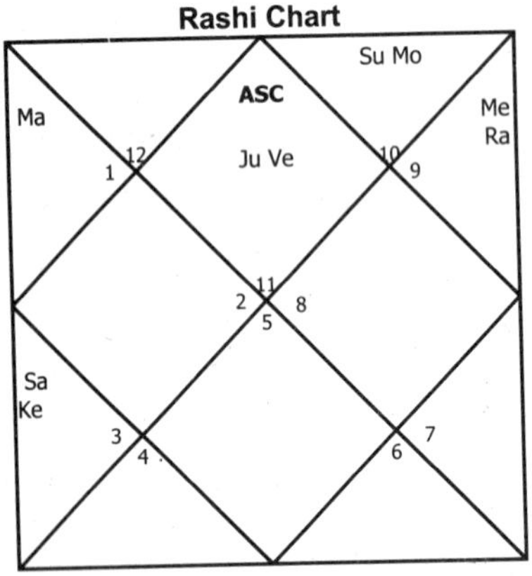

Bhava Chart

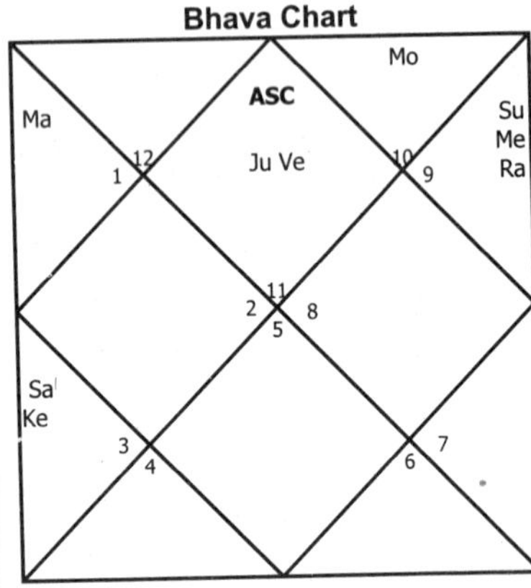

Cusp Chart

II 18-54-00	III 21-33-26 Ma 26-39-15	IV 17-48-26	V 11-36-33 Ke 23-51-13 Sa 25-35-52
Ju 16-41-05 Ve 14-55-10 I 08-49-54			VI 06-58-54
Mo 10-16-23 XII 06-58-54 Su 00-03-47			VII 08-49-54
Ra 26-04-58 Me 24-39-45 XI 11-36-33	X 17-48-26	IX 21-33-26	VIII 18-54-00

Fig. 5.20 Contd......

Planetary Position

Planet	Sign	D-M-S	R L	STL	SL	SSL	Hse	D	S
Sun	Cap	00-03-47	Sa	Su	Ra	Sa	11	P	
Moon	Cap	10-16-23	Sa	Mo	Mo	Ra	12	P	
Mars	Ari	26-39-15	Ma	Ve	Ke	Me	3	P	
Mercury	Sag	24-39-45	Ju	Ve	Me	Ve	11	P	
Jupiter	Aqu	16-41-05	Sa	Ra	Ve	Sa	1	P	
Venus	Aqu	14-55-10	Sa	Ra	Ke	Ju	1	P	
Saturn	Gem	25-35-52	Me	Ju	Me	Sa	5	P	
Rahu	Sag	26-04-58	Ju	Ve	Ke	Su	11	P	
Ketu	Gem	23-51-13	Me	Ju	Sa	Ju	5	P	

Cuspal Position

Cusp	Sign	D-M-S	R L	STL	SL	SSL	% Arc
Cusp I	Aqu	08-49-54	Sa	Ra	Ju	Ju	69.65
Cusp II	Pis	18-54-00	Ju	Me	Ke	Ra	17.47
Cusp III	Ari	21-33-26	Ma	Ve	Ju	Ma	37.29
Cusp IV	Tau	17-48-26	Ve	Mo	Me	Me	10.97
Cusp V	Gem	11-36-33	Me	Ra	Sa	Su	53.47
Cusp VI	Can	06-58-54	Mo	Sa	Me	Ju	79.12
Cusp VII	Leo	08-49-54	Su	Ke	Ju	Mo	11.44
Cusp VIII	Vir	18-54-00	Me	Mo	Me	Ra	23.86
Cusp IX	Lib	21-33-26	Ve	Ju	Ju	Ra	17.28
Cusp X	Sco	17-48-26	Ma	Me	Me	Ra	30.29
Cusp XI	Sag	11-36-33	Ju	Ke	Me	Me	61.58
Cusp XII	Cap	06-58-54	Sa	Su	Me	Sa	93.88

Dasa and Bhukti lord Moon in the Progressed chart is in Moon star and Moon sub and Rahu SS. Moon appears in 6 and Rahu is the sub sub lord of 2 as well as 10.

Antara lord Rahu has PS (exchange of Nakshatra with Venus). It is the sub sub lord of 2 as well as 10. Rahu is in the sub of Ketu that represents Jupiter and Mercury. Mercury appears in 2, 6 and 10.

Thus we see that the Progressed chart clearly justifies the event. Even transit as seen in Progressed chart also supports the event.

The discussion indicates that the chart can be taken as the true chart of the native.

Example 5: A Person provided the following data to one of my students with a request to get a true horoscope.

D.O.B: 14.08.1969, T.O.B: 05.30 hrs. (From memory of mother), P.O.B: Ajmer, Rajasthan, India.

Genitical Connections:

Moon stars of:

Father: Ketu , Mother: Sun/Moon, Elder Sister: Jupiter, Wife: Mars, First Daughter: Saturn, Second Daughter: Moon, Third Daughter: Jupiter

Significant Events:

Marriage: 25.01.2000

First daughter: 11.04.2001 at 10 hrs.

Second Daughter: 14.07.2005 at 02.55 hrs

Third daughter: 04.04.2008

Profession: Heart Specialist

Married life is disturbed.

The student Astrologer took up the job of rectification on 15.07.2011 at 08.08.14 hrs at Noida. The ruling planets at that time were as follows:

RP (Ascendant): Sun-Ketu-Ketu-Saturn-Mercury-Saturn

RP (Moon): Jupiter-Venus-Ketu-Rahu-Sat-Mercury

On that day Rahu represented Mars and Mercury. Ketu represented Venus and Mars.

The chart was rectified by the student following step by step procedure as illustrated in the advanced theory of Birth Time Rectification as stated above.

The chart was cast as per the given data. It was noticed by him that Sun's and Moon's position matches with the ruling planets.

This meant that the chart only needs to be corrected for the correct position of sub and sub sub lords of the ascendant and other cuspal positions to ensure matching of genetical connections and promise of various aspects of life.

The chart was fixed by the student at 05.29.58 hrs. Figure 5.21 is the rectified chart.

Fig. 5.21 Natal Chart

Name	Fig 5.21	Place	Ajmer
Longitude	74-40-0-E	Latitude	26-29-0-N
Sidereal Time	02-27-36	Date	14/8/1969
Day	Thursday	Geocentric Latitude	26-19-48-N
Nakshatra	Magha-2 Qtr.	Time	05:29:58
Lunar Nodes	True	Tithi	Shukla Paksha - Pratipada
Time Zone	+5:30:0	DST	00:00
Ayanamsa	23-25-17	House System	Placidus

Rashi Chart

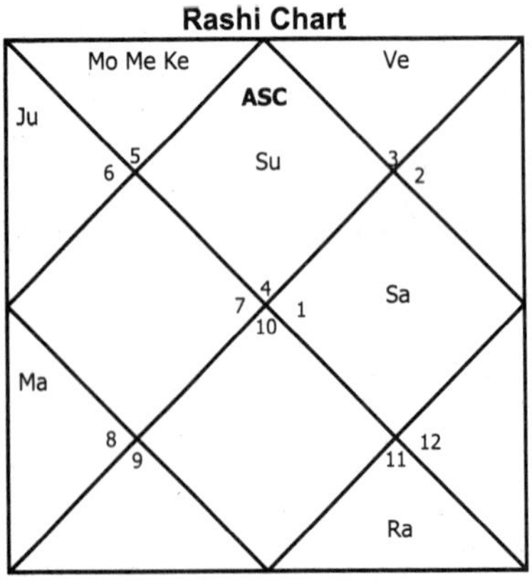

Bhava Chart

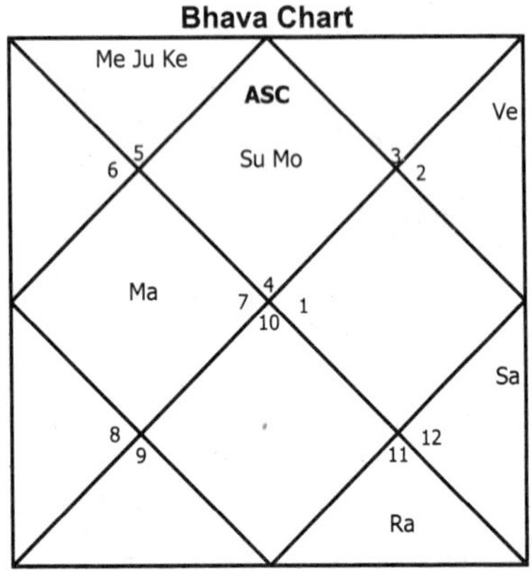

Cusp Chart

IX 13-35-27	Sa 15-28-48 X 15-52-24	XI 18-51-25	Ve 18-54-48 XII 20-16-39
Ra 27-50-11 VIII 14-39-41			I 19-39-17 Su 27-36-25
VII 19-39-17			Mo 06-18-11 II 14-39-41 Me 17-55-53 Ke 27-50-11
VI 20-16-39	V 18-51-25 Ma 16-30-22	IV 15-52-24	Ju 11-19-02 III 13-35-27

Fig. 5.21 Contd......

Planetary Position

Planet	Sign	D-M-S	R L	STL	SL	SSL	Hse	D	S
Sun	Can	27-36-25	Mo	Me	Ju	Ma	1		
Moon	Leo	06-18-11	Su	Ke	Ra	Sa	1		
Mars	Sco	16-30-22	Ma	Sa	Ju	Ra	4	P	
Mercury	Leo	17-55-53	Su	Ve	Ma	Ve	2		
Jupiter	Vir	11-19-02	Me	Mo	Ma	Ju	2		
Venus	Gem	18-54-48	Me	Ra	Mo	Me	11	P	
Saturn	Ari	15-28-48	Ma	Ve	Ve	Ke	9		
T.Rahu	Aqu	27-50-11	Sa	Ju	Ve	Ju	8		
T.Ketu	Leo	27-50-11	Su	Su	Mo	Sa	2		

Cuspal Position

Cusp	Sign	D-M-S	R L	STL	SL	SSL	% Arc
Cusp I	Can	19-39-17	Mo	Me	Ve	Ve	86.81
Cusp II	Leo	14-39-41	Su	Ve	Ve	Ju	67.01
Cusp III	Vir	13-35-27	Me	Mo	Ra	Su	85.38
Cusp IV	Lib	15-52-24	Ve	Ra	Ve	Mo	91.56
Cusp V	Sco	18-51-25	Ma	Me	Ke	Ma	50.18
Cusp VI	Sag	20-16-39	Ju	Ve	Ju	Ju	70.24
Cusp VII	Cap	19-39-17	Sa	Mo	Me	Sa	96.05
Cusp VIII	Aqu	14-39-41	Sa	Ra	Ke	Mo	04.93
Cusp IX	Pis	13-35-27	Ju	Sa	Ra	Sa	42.75
Cusp X	Ari	15-52-24	Ma	Ve	Su	Sa	00.98
Cusp XI	Tau	18-51-25	Ve	Mo	Me	Ra	08.69
Cusp XII	Gem	20-16-39	Me	Ju	Ju	Sa	14.42

Verification of the rectified chart:

Accuracy of Sun, Moon and Ascendant Positions: It can be verified that planets co-ruling Sun, Moon and ascendant are linked with 1, 7 and 10. **It may be remembered that it is not a must that planets should be related to 1, 7 and 10 all simultaneously. Planets may be related to 1 and 7, 7 and 10 like that.**

The native's Moon star is Ketu that is in Sun star. Since Sun is placed in the ascendant it justifies the linkage of the Moon's star with the SS of the ascendant. **Remember planets placed in a Bhava acts as virtual sub sub lords of that Bhava.**

Genetical Connections:

It is stated that the Moon star of the mother could be Sun or Moon. In the chart we find sub sub lord of 4th cusp is Moon.

Fifth cusp sub sub lord is Mars that is in Saturn star which is the Moon star of the first daughter.

Moon star of wife is Mars that is in Saturn star the sub sub lord of 7th cusp. Moon star of the second daughter is Moon that is in Rahu sub. Since Rahu represents Saturn that is the sub sub lord of the 7th cusp we say it justifies the Moon star of the second daughter.

Moon star of elder sister is Jupiter. Sub sub lord of 11th cusp is Rahu that represents Jupiter. More over Venus is placed in the 11th Bhava. Venus is in Rahu star that represents Jupiter.

Moon star of Father is Ketu. The sub sub lord of 9th cusp is Saturn that is in the SS of Ketu.

Promise of Aspects of Life:

Marriage: Sub sub lord of ascendant is Venus that is in Rahu star (sub sub lord of 11) and sub of Moon (star lord of 7 and 11). Sub sub lord of 7th cusp is Saturn that is in Venus star and Venus sub and Ketu SS. We may say that Saturn is in Venus star (placed in 11) and Ketu sub (sub lord of 5). Thus the chart promises marriage.

Promise of Disturbed Married Life: The sub sub lord of the 7th cusp Saturn in addition to its linkages with 11 and 5 also is strongly linked with 2, 4, 10 and 6. This accounts for disturbance in marriage life.

Birth of Children: Sub sub lord of 5th cusp is Mars that has PS. It is in the sub of Jupiter that is the sub sub lord of the second cusp. This indicates that the native has the procreative power to produce children.

Since Mars is in Saturn star that is the sign as well as the sub sub lord of the 7th cusp it indicates that the native can have more than one child.

Promise of Education: Moon is the sub sub lord of the 4th cusp. It is in Ketu star that appears in 8 (serious diseases). Mars has PS and is placed in 4th house and will act as virtual sub sub lord of the 4th cusp. Mars is in Saturn star that is the sub sub lord of the 9th cusp and is also placed in the 9th house. This promises higher education.

Promise of Profession as Heart Specialist: 5th cusp (Heart) sub sub lord is Mars that is in Saturn star which is the sub sub lord of the 10th cusp.

Promise of Execution of Events and Progression: The natal chart sub sub lords of ascendant and the relevant cusp declares the promise of various aspects of life but it is the progressed position of the Ascendant that declares the destined time of the execution of the promised event.

The native took birth in Cancer ascendant. Around 23.10.1982 the ascendant enters in Leo Sign and would remain in Leo till around April, 2011. During the period ascendant progressed in Leo the native got married, produced three children and got higher education. This could happen only if in the chart Sun is linked to those houses which are capable of enacting these events.

Sun in the chart is in Mercury star (1, 2, 3, 5, 7, 11, and 12) and Jupiter sub (2, 6, 9, and 12). Sun promises the execution of marriage (5, 7 and11); disturbance in marriage (7, 2 and 6); birth of first daughter (2, 5 and 11); birth of second daughter (2, 7 and 11); birth of third daughter (2, 9 and 11); higher education (11 and 9).

Verification of Events:

Marriage: The native got married on 25.01.2000 when he was running the period of Moon-Moon-Venus-Saturn-Rahu.

Dasa and Bhukti lord Moon is in Ketu star (2, 5) and Rahu sub (11). It is in the SS of Mars (5). This shows that Moon is not a very strong significator of marriage.

Antara lord Venus is in Rahu star (11) and sub of Moon (7). Venus is in the SS of Mercury (5, 7 and 11).

Sookshama Lord Saturn is the sub sub lord of 7 and is in Venus star and Ketu sub. **When a planet is in the star and sub of the same planet we treat it as a case of bunching and treat the planet as if it is in the star of that planet and**

the sub sub lord of the planet takes upon the role of sub as well as SS.

Venus is placed in 11 and Ketu is the sub lord of 5.

Prana lord Rahu represents Saturn and as stated above allows the marriage event to be enacted.

Figure 5.22 represents the transit position of Planets on the day of marriage.

Figure 5.22 Transit chart 25.01.2000 at 23 hrs.

Planetary Position

Planet	Sign	D-M-S	R L	STL	SL	SSL	Hse	D	S
Sun	Cap	11-12-16	Sa	Mo	Ma	Ra	4		
Moon	Vir	10-46-41	Me	Mo	Mo	Me	12	P	
Mars	Aqu	22-52-27	Sa	Ju	Sa	Ve	6	P	
Mercury	Cap	17-46-08	Sa	Mo	Sa	Ju	4	P	
Jupiter	Ari	03-19-54	Ma	Ke	Su	Sa	7		
Venus	Sag	07-15-45	Ju	Ke	Ra	Su	3	P	
Saturn	Ari	16-37-01	Ma	Ve	Mo	Ju	8		
T.Rahu	Can	09-50-40	Mo	Sa	Ve	Sa	10	P	
T.Ketu	Cap	09-50-40	Sa	Su	Ve	Me	4		

It can be verified that transit supports the enactment of the event. Let us verify the transit position of Jupiter. The planets co-ruling the transit position of Jupiter are Mars-Ketu-Sun-Saturn. Mars is in Saturn star that is the sub sub lord of 7. Mars is in the sub of Jupiter that is in 6, 9 and 12. Thus transit of Jupiter in Aries also hints that the chart needs rectification.

Verification of the event of Marriage from Progressed Chart: Figure 5.23 represents the Progressed chart on the day of Marriage.

Fig. 5.23 Progress on 25.01.2000 at 23 hrs

Name	Fig 5.23	Place	Ajmer
Longitude	74-40-0-E	Latitude	26-29-0-N
Sidereal Time	02-27-36	Date	14/8/1969
Day	Thursday	Geocentric Latitude	26-19-48-N
Nakshatra	Magha-2 Qtr.	Time	05:29:58
Lunar Nodes	True	Tithi	Shukla Paksha - Pratipada
Time Zone	+5:30:0	DST	00:00
Ayanamsa	23-25-17	House System	Placidus

Rashi Chart

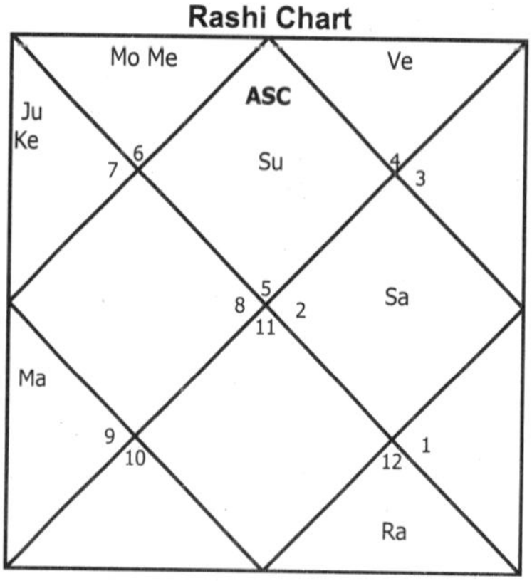

Bhava Chart

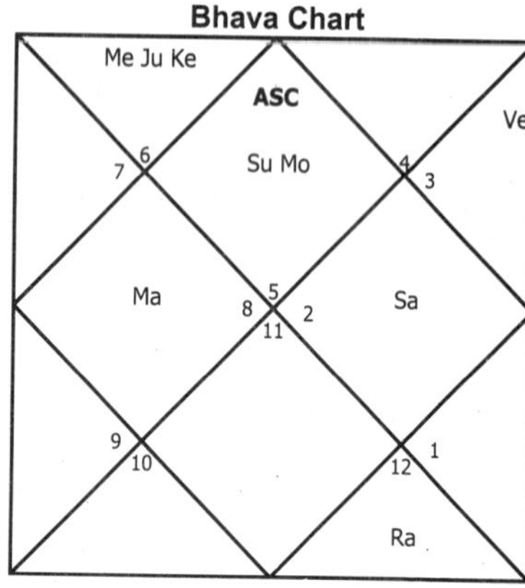

Cusp Chart

Ra 20-28-23 VIII 17-41-51	IX 18-05-50	X 19-40-40 Sa 20-13-33	XI 20-59-39
VII 20-10-23			Ve 12-26-38 XII 21-22-19
VI 21-22-19			I 20-10-23 Su 27-33-08
V 20-59-39 Ma 17-28-50	IV 19-40-40	III 18-05-50 Ju 17-21-40 Ke 12-34-29	Mo 11-00-42 II 17-41-51 Me 25-53-56

Fig. 5.23 Contd......

Planetary Position

Planet	Sign	D-M-S	R L	STL	SL	SSL	Hse	D	S
Sun	Leo	27-33-08	Su	Su	Mo	Ra	1	P	
Moon	Vir	11-00-42	Me	Mo	Mo	Ve	1	P	
Mars	Sag	17-28-50	Ju	Ve	Ma	Ra	4		
Mercury	Vir	25-53-56	Me	Ma	Ra	Mo	2		
Jupiter	Lib	17-21-40	Ve	Ra	Ve	Ke	2	P	
Venus	Can	12-26-38	Mo	Sa	Ma	Sa	11		
Saturn	Tau	20-13-33	Ve	Mo	Ke	Sa	10		
Rahu	Pis	20-28-23	Ju	Me	Ve	Ju	8		
Ketu	Lib	12-34-29	Ve	Ra	Me	Me	2	P	

Cuspal Position

Cusp	Sign	D-M-S	R L	STL	SL	SSL	% Arc
Cusp I	Leo	20-10-23	Su	Ve	Ju	Ju	26.13
Cusp II	Vir	17-41-51	Me	Mo	Sa	Ju	71.44
Cusp III	Lib	18-05-50	Ve	Ra	Su	Ve	87.43
Cusp IV	Sco	19-40-40	Ma	Me	Ve	Ve	93.00
Cusp V	Sag	20-59-39	Ju	Ve	Ju	Ve	03.03
Cusp VI	Cap	21-22-19	Sa	Mo	Ve	Ra	39.39
Cusp VII	Aqu	20-10-23	Sa	Ju	Ju	Ju	73.00
Cusp VIII	Pis	17-41-51	Ju	Me	Me	Ma	78.30
Cusp IX	Ari	18-05-50	Ma	Ve	Ma	Mo	78.46
Cusp X	Tau	19-40-40	Ve	Mo	Ke	Ke	24.47
Cusp XI	Gem	20-59-39	Me	Ju	Ju	Ve	40.53
Cusp XII	Can	21-22-19	Mo	Me	Ve	Me	82.88

We notice that the Progressed ascendant is co-ruled by the planets Sun-Venus-Jupiter –Jupiter. We have already discussed above that Sun allows the enactment of the event of marriage in the natal chart. Venus in the natal chart is placed in 11. It is in Rahu star that is sub sub lord of 11. It is in the sub of Moon that appears in 7. Venus is in the SS of Mercury that appears in 5, 7 and 11. Jupiter is in Moon star that appears in 7. Jupiter is in the sub of Mars that is the sub sub lord of 5. Jupiter is in the SS of Jupiter that is in 6, 9 and 12. Thus we notice that the progressed position of ascendant on the date of marriage does not confirm the accuracy of the chart without any doubt.

Let us study the progressed chart independently. Figure 5.23 represents the Progressed chart. The event of marriage happened when Moon was progressing in Moon star and Moon sub. In the Progressed chart Moon appears in 1, 2, 6, 9, 10 and 12. None of these houses is a relevant house for the event of marriage. This clearly indicates that the chart needs rectification. The student Astrologer had an illusion that the chart fixed by him using the theory of ruling planets is the true chart of the native.

This case study has been presented to let the Astrologers know that the use of ruling planets to fix a correct horoscope requires that the astrologer should be completely focused when he takes the job of rectification. Ruling planets require deft handling by the astrologer. Any lack of concentration can result in erroneous rectification of the chart.

Let us discuss what mistake the student astrologer made in following the step by step approach of rectification.

The student Astrologer should have noticed that the given time of birth is out of memory and the true birth time may not be very close to it. Venus the Sookshma lord of Sun starts at 05.06.16 hrs and ends at 05.32.11 hrs. After this the Sookshama of Sun starts that is also a ruling planet. Sun Sookshma ends at 05.39.56 hrs. Thus the time of birth of the native could be between 05.06.16 and 05.39.56 hrs. The student was advised to re-fix the correct chart using the same ruling planets.

We need to remember that the chart is said to be properly rectified if it justifies the happening of the events not by Dasa period lords or transit but also by progressed charts for the events.

Chapter 6

Rectification of Birth Charts of Twins

A **twin** is one of two offspring produced in the same pregnancy. Twins can either be *identical* (in scientific usage, "monozygotic"), meaning that they develop from one zygote that splits and forms two embryos, or *fraternal* ("dizygotic") because they develop from two separate eggs that are fertilized by two separate sperms. The twin birth rate is about 35 live births per 1000. It becomes imperative for the Astrologers to fix correct position of ascendant and other cuspal positions for twins to ensure that the individual charts satisfy all conditions which we have stated in earlier chapter under the title Advanced techniques of rectification of Birth Chart. In addition we need to look for special conditions that need to be satisfied for Twins charts. These conditions are specified below.

Special Conditions for Twins Charts

One born a little earlier than the other is called elder twin and the other born a little latter is called the younger one. The sub sub lord of each chart should establish link with the Moon star that is common for both. The sub sub lord of ascendant of both may be different to indicate two different persons. Sub sub lord of ascendant and SS arc of ascendant of each twin should indicate the sex of the individual twin.

The sub sub lord of the ascendant of the elder twin should be linked with the third cusp to promise the birth of the younger co-born. Similarly the sub sub lord of 11th cusp should be linked with ascendant to promise the birth of elder co-born.

In the chart of the elder co-born the sub sub lord of the 3rd cusp should be linked with the planet that is the common Moon star for the twins. Similarly the SSL of 11th cusp in the chart of the younger twin should be linked with the planet that is the common Moon star for both the twins.

We will explain the fixation of correct charts of twins through following examples.

Note: Charts in the following examples are cast using True astrology Software version 4.0.3 using Khullar (hourly) Ayanamsa.

Example 1:

"I am one of twins born 5 minutes after my elder sister", said very intelligent and dedicated student of Astrology. The Astrologer was interested in getting his chart rectified using KCIL birth time rectification technique. He furnished details as below:

Find below my details

Self: (Twin-2)

DOB- 30 April 1978, TOB-11.00A.M (IST), POB- Madurai (9N56'08" and 78E7'48), India 5.30 East GMT

Education:

Bachelor of Engineering in Electronics and Instrumentation (1995-1999), MBA in Marketing and IT management (2006-2008), Diploma in Sanskrit

Profession:

1. First Job started as a Trainee Engineer in MNC (tea factory): 07 Mar 2000 to Jan 2001.
2. Second job as Software Engineer (trainee): 07 Mar 2001 to 06 Apr 2002 (resigned)
3. Third job started carrier as Maintenance Engineer in Riyadh (food related factory manufacturer of cheese, chocolate and butter): 25 April 2002 till now.
4. Did export business in India with my friends during 2004 to 2005. It was going good, difficult to manage from foreign countries so we closed.

Marriage: Was celebrated on 21 March 2011 in the morning.

Foreign journeys: 24 Apr 2002 - 9.30 A.M (Mumbai Airport to Riyadh), Bahrain crossing border at night (from Dammam 50E6, 26N25 -3.00 East GMT) on 01 Nov 2005, Singapore and Malaysia tour (from Chennai) (I forget the date 5 or 6) on 05/06 May 2008

Operations: Hernia operation 26 Jun 2006 at Riyadh at around afternoon, next day my mother's elder sister died.

Elder sister: (Twin-1)

DOB: 30 April 1978, TOB: 10.55 A.M (IST), POB: Madurai (9N56′08" and 78E7′48"), India: 5.30 East GMT

Education :

Bachelor of commerce: 1995-1998, MBA: 1998-2000.

Profession:

She worked as a college lecturer. Now she is working in ERP Solution (I don't know the date of joining of post etc.)

Marriage: 13.12.2007

Common for Twin 1 & Twin 2:

Genetical connection:

Moon Stars of:

Mother– Moon, **Father**– Saturn, **Younger sister**– Rahu

Father's Death: On 22 April 2001 in Erode (around 10.00A.M) (77E44, 11N21)

This case study appeared as rectification exercise on Astrology Research forum on 19.12.2008. On 28.12.2008 Mr. A, a very capable astrologer fixed the following time of births for the twins. He followed step by step instructions of BTR using CIL principles.

Twin-1 TOB = 10:56:08. At this time, in ascendant, Gemini sign is rising at 26-19-20.

Twin-2 TOB = 11:02:35. At this time, in ascendant, Gemini sign is rising at 27-47-53.

Twin 2 who is an astrologer of repute raised the following doubts:

1. In twin 2 chart, 4th SSL is Venus and it in star of Sun. Father's death took place in Mercury star. Here Mercury is in Mercury star. Venus and Sun are not relating to Mercury. Am I correct?
2. Similarly in twin 1chart, 4th SSL is Ketu and it denotes Jup and Sat, Mercury is not relating?

3. In twin 2 chart, 10th cusp SSL is Venus who is in star of Sun that appears in cusps 3,5,6,7,10,11,12. Cheese Manufacturing is dairy related so it should link 4th house. Here it is not relating and also food relating so may be it also involves 2nd cups.

Please clarify, if any other way we have to analyze. Your input will facilitate me to learn CIL fast.

To this Mr A replied as follows:

"Mr. Khullar has clearly mentioned in his books that the death of a person happens when Sun and Moon in transit appears in the Star of a planet which should either bear relationship with 8th SSL or its Star Lord. He has also made it clear that the Star lord on the day of death could be a planet which signifies 1 and 8 with respect to 9th Cusp/House (for father). In both charts (Twin 1 & 2) Mercury is in Mercury Star which appears in 4th and 9th Cusp. Thus the Moon's Star Lord on the day of death of father is as per the principle enunciated by Mr. Khullar.

Regarding profession please note that the 10th SSL Venus has PS (Venus in Sun Star and Sun in Venus Star – Exchange on Star Level). Venus is also the 4th SSL which means native's area of work may be related to manufacturing unit. Dairy products are generally related to 6th House (already given in his books). Thus, the chart fully justifies the profession also.

However in February 2011 twin 2 informed the author that he is going to celebrate his marriage on 21.03.2011. Author looked into the chart and found that the event is not justified by the time fixed by CIL follower. It necessitated fixing the correct chart for twin 2 using the advanced techniques of rectification as illustrated in Chapter V.

Figure 6.1 represents the rectified chart. The astrological birth time is fixed as 11.02.07 hrs.

Fig 6.1

Name	Fig 6.1	Place	Madurai
Longitude	78-7-50-E	Latitude	9-56-8-N
Sidereal Time	01-15-53	Date	30/4/1978
Day	Sunday	Geocentric Latitude	09-52-13-N
Nakshatra	Shravana-4 Qtr.	Time	11:02:07
Lunar Nodes	True	Tithi	Krishna Paksha - Asthami
Time Zone	+5:30:0 DST	00:00	
Ayanamsa	23-32-35	House System	Placidus

Rashi Chart

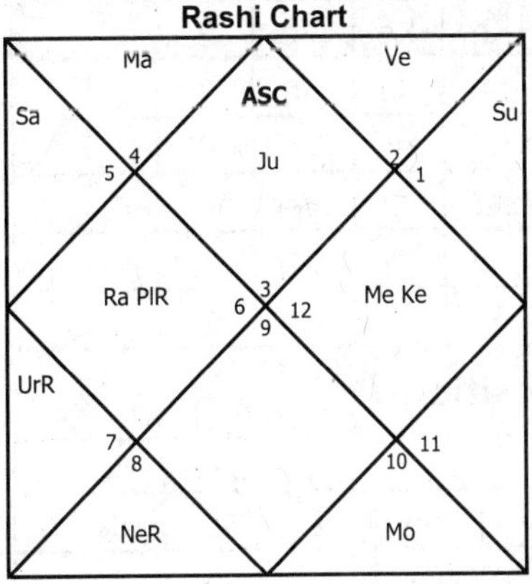

Bhava Chart

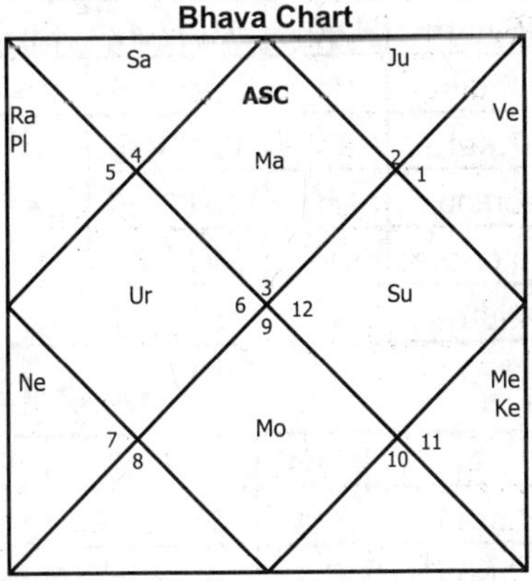

Cusp Chart

X 26-59-46 Me 22-18-00 Ke 11-53-56	Su 15-58-33 XI 28-56-25	Ve 09-59-39 XII 28-56-55	Ju 09-22-12 I 27-41-30
IX 24-45-15			Ma 14-06-34 II 24-48-52
VIII 24-48-52 Mo 20-36-09			Sa 00-07-42 III 24-45-15
VII 27-41-30	VI 28-56-55 NeR 24-21-21	V 28-56-25 UrR 21-03-29	Ra 11-53-56 PlR 21-06-47 IV 26-59-46

Fig. 6.1 Contd......

Planetary Position

Planet	Sign	D-M-S	R L	STL	SL	SSL	Hse	D	S
Sun	Ari	15-58-33	Ma	Ve	Su	Sa	10	P	
Moon	Cap	20-36-09	Sa	Mo	Ve	Ve	7	P	
Mars	Can	14-06-34	Mo	Sa	Ra	Ke	1	P	
Mercury	Pis	22-18-00	Ju	Me	Mo	Mo	9	P	
Jupiter	Gem	09-22-12	Me	Ra	Ju	Me	12	P	
Venus	Tau	09-59-39	Ve	Su	Ve	Ke	11	P	
Saturn	Leo	00-07-42	Su	Ke	Ke	Ve	2	P	
T.Rahu	Vir	11-53-56	Me	Mo	Ra	Ra	3		
T.Ketu	Pis	11-53-56	Ju	Sa	Mo	Ve	9	P	
Uranus	Lib	21-03-29	Ve	Ju	Ju	Ve	4	R	
Neptune	Sco	24-21-21	Ma	Me	Ra	Ra	5	R	
Pluto	Vir	21-06-47	Me	Mo	Ve	Ma	3	R	

Cuspal Position

Cusp	Sign	D-M-S	R L	STL	SL	SSL	% Arc
Cusp I	Gem	27-41-30	Me	Ju	Ve	Ju	02.16
Cusp II	Can	24-48-52	Mo	Me	Ra	Sa	43.13
Cusp III	Leo	24-45-15	Su	Ve	Me	Su	65.15
Cusp IV	Vir	26-59-46	Me	Ma	Ju	Ve	03.73
Cusp V	Lib	28-56-25	Ve	Ju	Su	Ra	34.73
Cusp VI	Sco	28-56-55	Ma	Me	Sa	Ve	86.21
Cusp VII	Sag	27-41-30	Ju	Su	Mo	Ju	23.06
Cusp VIII	Cap	24-48-52	Sa	Ma	Ra	Sa	43.13
Cusp IX	Aqu	24-45-15	Sa	Ju	Me	Mo	49.68
Cusp X	Pis	26-59-46	Ju	Me	Ju	Ve	03.73
Cusp XI	Ari	28-56-25	Ma	Su	Ma	Me	97.07
Cusp XII	Tau	28-56-55	Ve	Ma	Sa	Ve	86.21

Verification of the accuracy of the chart:

Accuracy of Sun, Moon, and Ascendant: The Planets co-ruling the positions of Sun, Moon, and Ascendant justify the necessary conditions of linkages with cusps 1, 7 and 10.

Jupiter is the sub sub lord of the ascendant. It is in Rahu star that represents Moon which is the Moon Star of the native. Male sign rises on the ascendant and sub sub arc of the sub sub lord of the ascendant is in the first half. This justifies the sex of the native.

Promise of Elder Twin: Sub sub lord of 11th cusp is Mercury. Mercury is in Mercury star. Mercury appears in the ascendant. This satisfies the necessary condition. Sub sub lord of 11th cusp also establishes the relationship with the common Moon star of the twins because Mercury is in the sub of Moon.

Promise of Aspects of Life:

Marriage: Sub sub lord of ascendant and 7th cusp is Jupiter that has PS. Jupiter is the star lord of 5 and sub sub lord of 7. Jupiter is in own sub. Jupiter is in Rahu star that represents Mercury and Moon. Moon is the sub lord of 7. Mercury is the sub sub lord of 11. Jupiter is in Jupiter sub which appears in 5 and 7. Thus the chart promises marriage.

Since the sub sub lord of 7th cusp Jupiter is in Rahu star that represents Mercury we may say that Jupiter is in Mercury star that also appears as the star lord of 6 in addition to its appearance as the sub sub lord of the 11. Jupiter is in Jupiter sub which also appears in 4, 10 and 12. These linkages of sub sub lord of the 7th cusp accounts for the delayed marriage.

Genitical Connections: Moon star of mother is Moon that is in the sub of Venus which is the sub sub lord of the 4th cusp. Saturn is the Moon star of father. Saturn is in Ketu star that is placed in 9th cusp. Rahu is placed in the 3rd Bhava and it represents the Moon star of the younger sister.

Promise of Younger Sister: Jupiter the sub sub lord of ascendant is in Rahu star which is placed in 3rd cusp. This satisfies the necessary condition.

Promise of Educational Status: We notice that the 3rd cusp sub sub lord is Sun which is strongly linked with the sub sub lord of the 4th cusp. Third cusp signifies electronics and instrumentation. MBA is signified by the 7th cusp. Sub sub lord of the 7th cusp is Jupiter that is strongly linked with the 9th cusp. Thus the chart justifies the educational prospects of the native. The readers may feel that the sub sub lord of the 4th cusp is not promising higher education. Incidentally if we use True Astrology software version 5 we will notice that the SSSS level of 9th cusp is also ruled by Venus that has PS.

Since the 5th cusp sub sub lord Rahu is in Moon star that is the sub sub lord of the 9th cusp it justifies natives learning the subject of astrology.

Area of Concentration of Professional Activities: Sub sub lord of 10th cusp is Venus that has PS. Notice that Venus is the sub sub lord of 4 (manufacturing unit) and also the sub sub lord of 6 (food items). Thus the chart justifies his profession.

Since Venus is also the sub sub lord of the 12th cusp it promises that the work place may be in a foreign country.

Promise for Foreign Travels: Sub sub lord of ascendant is Jupiter that is linked with 3, 9 and 12. This justifies the native's foreign journeys.

Promise of Hernia Operation: Sub sub lord of the 8th cusp is Saturn that has PS. It is also the sub lord of the 6th cusp. Thus the native is bound to have problems in the lower abdominal region.

Verification of Events:

Marriage of the native: The native celebrated his marriage on 21.03.2011. On the day of marriage the native was running the period of Jup-Mer-Mars-Jup-Moon. Dasa and Sooksma lord is Jupiter which is a strong significator of marriage as stated above. Bhukti lord Mercury is the sub sub lord of 11. Mercury is in Mercury star and Moon sub and Moon sub sub. Moon is the sub lord of 7th cusp. Moon is also placed in 7 with PS. Antara lord Mars has PS and appears in 11. Mars is in the sub of Rahu that is the sub sub lord of the 5th cusp. Since Rahu represents Moon, Mars is considered to be in the sub of Moon which appears in 7.Mars is in the sub sub of Ketu which represents Jupiter (5 and 7). Prana lord Moon is placed in 7 with PS. It is in the sub of Venus that appears in 5 and 11.

Thus the Dasa period lords justify the happening of the event of marriage.

Figure 6.2 represents the transit position of planets on the day of marriage.

Fig. 6.2 Transit on 21.03.2011 at 09 hrs.

Planetary Position

Planet	Sign	D-M-S	R L	STL	SL	SSL	Hse	D	S
Sun	Pis	06-09-54	Ju	Sa	Me	Su	11	P	
Moon	Vir	26-03-56	Me	Ma	Ra	Ma	6		
Mars	Aqu	26-33-42	Sa	Ju	Ve	Ve	11		
Mercury	Pis	24-28-33	Ju	Me	Ra	Ju	12	P	
Jupiter	Pis	18-28-38	Ju	Me	Me	Sa	11		
Venus	Cap	28-37-54	Sa	Ma	Sa	Ke	10	P	
Saturn	Vir	20-55-57	Me	Mo	Ve	Mo	6	R	
T.Rahu	Sag	03-43-19	Ju	Ke	Mo	Mo	8	P	
T.Ketu	Gem	03-43-19	Me	Ma	Ve	Ra	2		

Moon on the day of Marriage was transiting in Mer-Mars-Rahu. All these Planets are strong significators of the event of Marriage. Similarly we can verify the transit of other Planets.

Figure 6.3 represents the progressed chart on the day of marriage. We can notice that the progressed ascendant was co ruled by planets Moon-Mer-Moon-Moon. Both Moon and Mercury are strong significators of the event of marriage in the natal chart. Let us study the progressed chart independently.

Fig. 6.3 Progress on 21.03.2011 at 09.00hrs.

Name	Fig 6.1	Place	Madurai
Longitude	78-7-50-E	Latitude	9-56-8-N
Sidereal Time	01-15-53	Date	30/4/1978
Day	Sunday	Geocentric Latitude	09-52-13-N
Nakshatra	Shravana-4 Qtr.	Time	11:02:07
Lunar Nodes	True	Tithi	Krishna Paksha - Asthami
Time Zone	+5:30:0 DST	00:00	
Ayanamsa	23-32-35	House System	Placidus

Rashi Chart

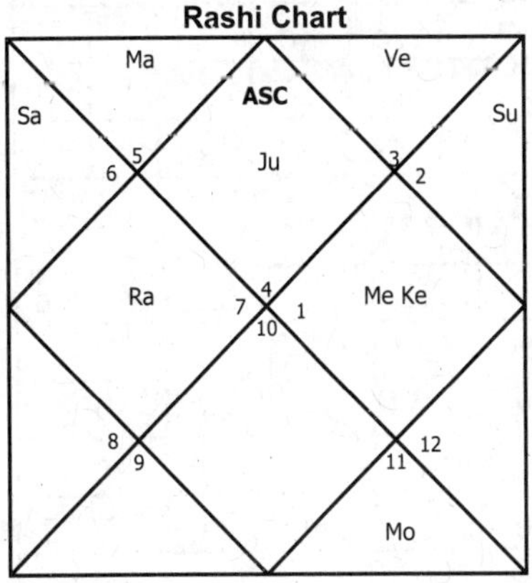

Bhava Chart

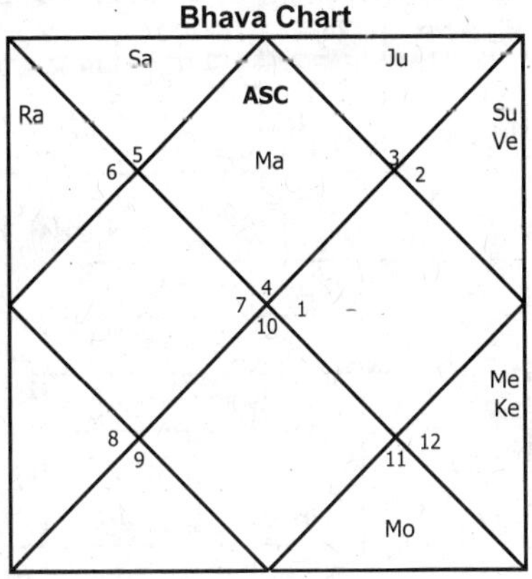

Cusp Chart

IX 22-44-22	Ke 14-43-49 Me 24-02-53 X 24-17-40	XI 24-17-34 Su 24-57-33	Ve 18-26-05 XII 23-09-53
Mo 24-52-04 VIII 21-19-40			Ju 05-06-55 I 22-15-02
VII 22-15-02			Ma 16-49-49 II 21-19-40
VI 23-09-53	V 24-17-34	IV 24-17-40 Ra 19-29-30	Sa 09-54-16 III 22-44-22

Fig. 6.3 Contd......

Planetary Position

Planet	Sign	D-M-S	R L	STL	SL	SSL	Hse	D	S
Sun	Tau	24-57-33	Ve	Ma	Ra	Sa	11		
Moon	Aqu	24-52-04	Sa	Ju	Me	Ma	8	P	
Mars	Leo	16-49-49	Su	Ve	Mo	Sa	1		
Mercury	Ari	24-02-53	Ma	Ve	Me	Me	9	P	
Jupiter	Can	05-06-55	Mo	Sa	Sa	Ra	12		
Venus	Gem	18-26-05	Me	Ra	Mo	Ra	11	P	
Saturn	Vir	09-54-16	Me	Su	Ve	Ke	2		
Rahu	Lib	19-29-30	Ve	Ra	Ma	Sa	3	P	
Ketu	Ari	14-43-49	Ma	Ve	Ve	Ju	9	P	

Cuspal Position

Cusp	Sign	D-M-S	R L	STL	SL	SSL	% Arc
Cusp I	Can	22-15-02	Mo	Me	Mo	Mo	30.60
Cusp II	Leo	21-19-40	Su	Ve	Ju	Su	52.10
Cusp III	Vir	22-44-22	Me	Mo	Su	Mo	70.96
Cusp IV	Lib	24-17-40	Ve	Ju	Me	Ve	08.83
Cusp V	Sco	24-17-34	Ma	Me	Ra	Ra	60.56
Cusp VI	Sag	23-09-53	Ju	Ve	Sa	Mo	35.15
Cusp VII	Cap	22-15-02	Sa	Mo	Ve	Me	09.00
Cusp VIII	Aqu	21-19-40	Sa	Ju	Ju	Mo	46.29
Cusp IX	Pis	22-44-22	Ju	Me	Mo	Sa	25.57
Cusp X	Ari	24-17-40	Ma	Ve	Me	Ke	24.40
Cusp XI	Tau	24-17-34	Ve	Ma	Ra	Ra	60.56
Cusp XII	Gem	23-09-53	Me	Ju	Sa	Mo	98.31

The event of marriage happened when Moon was progressing in Jup-Mer-Mars-Jup-Moon.

Jupiter in the progressed chart is in Saturn star and Saturn sub and Rahu sub sub. Saturn appears in 7 and Rahu is the sub sub lord of 5 and 11. Mercury is in the star of Venus that is placed in 11 and is the sub lord of 7.Mercury is in Mercury sub that is the sub sub lord of 7 and star lord of 5. Mars is in Venus star (7 and 11) and Moon sub (star lord of 7). Moon has PS in the progressed chart. It is the star lord of 7. Moon is in the sub of Mercury that appears in 5 and 7.

Thus we notice that the progressed chart confirms that the event of marriage has taken place as destined.

Marriage of Elder Twin (1): The event of marriage of elder twin took place on 13.12.2007 when the native was running the period of Jup-Sat-Mer-Mer-Jup. Let us see whether the chart of twin 2 promises the execution of the marriage of elder twin or not.

Figure 6.4 represents the native's rotated chart with respect to the 11th cusp.

Fig.6.4 Rotated chart with respect to 11th Cusp as Ascendant

Name	Fig 6.4	Place	Madurai
Longitude	78-7-50-E	Latitude	9-56-8-N
Sidereal Time	01-15-53	Date	30/4/1978
Day	Sunday	Geocentric Latitude	09-52-13-N
Nakshatra	Shravana-4 Qtr.	Time	11:02:07
Lunar Nodes	True	Tithi	Krishna Paksha - Asthami
Time Zone	+5:30:0	DST	00:00
Ayanamsa	23-32-35	House System	Placidus

Rashi Chart

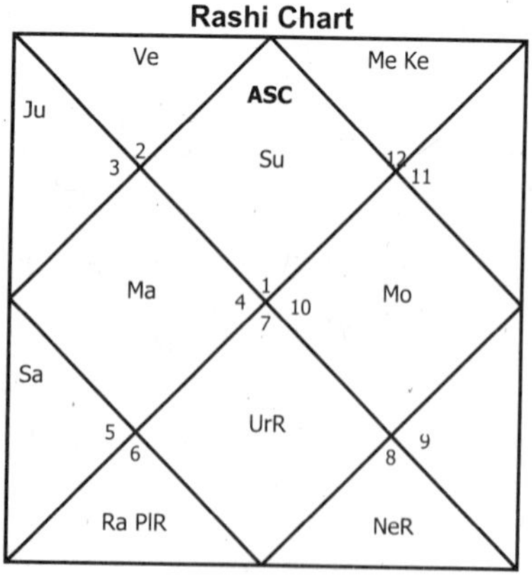

Bhava Chart

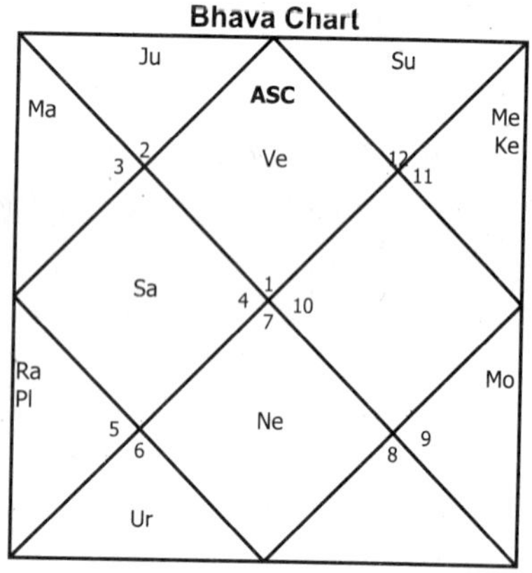

Cusp Chart

XII 26-59-46 Me 22-18-00 Ke 11-53-56	Su 15-58-33 I 28-56-25	Ve 09-59-39 II 28-56-55	Ju 09-22-12 III 27-41-30
XI 24-45-15			Ma 14-06-34 IV 24-48-52
X 24-48-52 Mo 20-36-09			Sa 00-07-42 V 24-45-15
IX 27-41-30	VIII 28-56-55 NeR 24-21-21	VII 28-56-25 UrR 21-03-29	Ra 11-53-56 PlR 21-06-47 VI 26-59-46

Fig. 6.4 Contd......

Planetary Position

Planet	Sign	D-M-S	R L	STL	SL	SSL	Hse	D	S
Sun	Ari	15-58-33	Ma	Ve	Su	Sa	12	P	
Moon	Cap	20-36-09	Sa	Mo	Ve	Ve	9	P	
Mars	Can	14-06-34	Mo	Sa	Ra	Ke	3	P	
Mercury	Pis	22-18-00	Ju	Me	Mo	Mo	11	P	
Jupiter	Gem	09-22-12	Me	Ra	Ju	Me	2	P	
Venus	Tau	09-59-39	Ve	Su	Ve	Ke	1	P	
Saturn	Leo	00-07-42	Su	Ke	Ke	Ve	4	P	
T.Rahu	Vir	11-53-56	Me	Mo	Ra	Ra	5		
T.Ketu	Pis	11-53-56	Ju	Sa	Mo	Ve	11	P	
Uranus	Lib	21-03-29	Ve	Ju	Ju	Ve	6	R	
Neptune	Sco	24-21-21	Ma	Me	Ra	Ra	7	R	
Pluto	Vir	21-06-47	Me	Mo	Ve	Ma	5	R	

Cuspal Position

Cusp	Sign	D-M-S	R L	STL	SL	SSL	% Arc
Cusp I	Ari	28-56-25	Ma	Su	Ma	Me	97.07
Cusp II	Tau	28-56-55	Ve	Ma	Sa	Ve	86.21
Cusp III	Gem	27-41-30	Me	Ju	Ve	Ju	02.16
Cusp IV	Can	24-48-52	Mo	Me	Ra	Sa	43.13
Cusp V	Leo	24-45-15	Su	Ve	Me	Su	65.15
Cusp VI	Vir	26-59-46	Me	Ma	Ju	Ve	03.73
Cusp VII	Lib	28-56-25	Ve	Ju	Su	Ra	34.73
Cusp VIII	Sco	28-56-55	Ma	Me	Sa	Ve	86.21
Cusp IX	Sag	27-41-30	Ju	Su	Mo	Ju	23.06
Cusp X	Cap	24-48-52	Sa	Ma	Ra	Sa	43.13
Cusp XI	Aqu	24-45-15	Sa	Ju	Me	Mo	49.68
Cusp XII	Pis	26-59-46	Ju	Me	Ju	Ve	03.73

Dasa lord and Prana lord Jupiter has PS and signifies 7 and 11. Jupiter is in Rahu star that is the sub sub lord of the 7th cusp and resident of 5th cusp. Jupiter is in Jupiter sub that appears in 7 and 11. Bhukti lord Saturn is in Ketu star and Ketu Sub and Venus sub sub. Ketu is placed in 11 and Venus appears in 5 and 7. Antara and Sookshma lord Mercury is in Mercury star (5 and 11) .It is in the sub of Moon that is the sub sub lord of 11. Since the sub sub lord of 7th cusp is Rahu that represents Mercury we feel that Mercury fully justifies the enactment of the event of marriage of the elder twin.

We can study the progressed chart on the day of the event. Figure 6.5 represents the rotated progressed chart starting with 11th cusp.

Fig. 6.5-Progress chart of 13.12.2007 at 10 hrs.

Name	Fig 6.5	Place	Madurai
Longitude	78-7-50-E	Latitude	9-56-8-N
Sidereal Time	01-15-53	Date	30/4/1978
Day	Sunday	Geocentric Latitude	09-52-13-N
Nakshatra	Shravana-4 Qtr.	Time	11:02:07
Lunar Nodes	True	Tithi	Krishna Paksha - Asthami
Time Zone	+5:30:0	DST	00:00
Ayanamsa	23-32-35	House System	Placidus

Rashi Chart

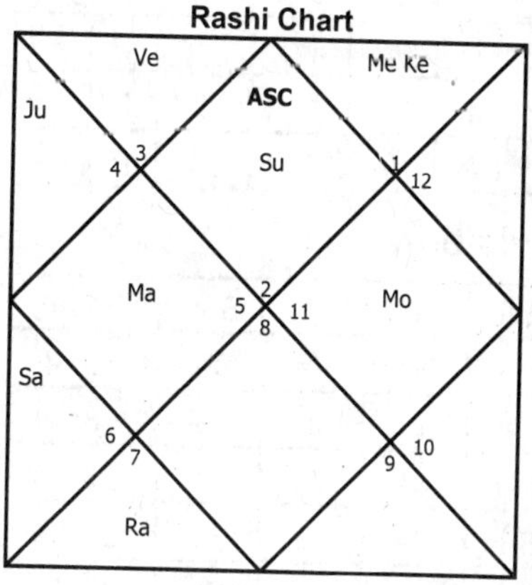

Bhava Chart

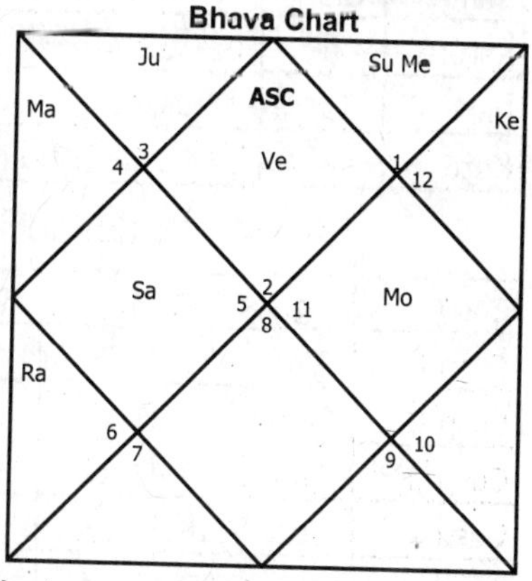

Cusp Chart

XI 19-53-49	Ke 11-05-53 XII 21-35-48 Me 21-52-08	Su 20-06-46 I 21-46-29	Ve 16-00-48 II 20-41-25
Mo 22-08-38 X 18-33-26			Ju 02-43-31 III 19-41-11
IX 19-41-11			Ma 14-39-04 IV 18-33-26
VIII 20-41-25	VII 21-46-29	VI 21-35-48 Ra 17-04-13	Sa 02-38-25 V 19-53-49

Fig. 6.5 Contd......

Planetary Position

Planet	Sign	D-M-S	R L	STL	SL	SSL	Hse	D	S
Sun	Tau	20-06-46	Ve	Mo	Ke	Ju	12		
Moon	Aqu	22-08-38	Sa	Ju	Sa	Me	10		
Mars	Leo	14-39-04	Su	Ve	Ve	Ju	3	P	
Mercury	Ari	21-52-08	Ma	Ve	Ju	Ra	12	P	
Jupiter	Can	02-43-31	Mo	Ju	Ra	Ve	2	P	
Venus	Gem	16-00-48	Me	Ra	Ve	Ma	1	P	
Saturn	Vir	02-38-25	Me	Su	Ju	Ma	4	P	
Rahu	Lib	17-04-13	Ve	Ra	Ve	Me	5	P	
Ketu	Ari	11-05-53	Ma	Ke	Sa	Ra	11	P	

Cuspal Position

Cusp	Sign	D-M-S	R L	STL	SL	SSL	% Arc
Cusp I	Tau	21-46-30	Ve	Mo	Ve	Ju	67.85
Cusp II	Gem	20-41-27	Me	Ju	Ju	Me	68.44
Cusp III	Can	19-41-12	Mo	Me	Ve	Ve	95.43
Cusp IV	Leo	18-33-28	Su	Ve	Ra	Ju	55.04
Cusp V	Vir	19-53-51	Me	Mo	Ke	Mo	26.11
Cusp VI	Lib	21-35-50	Ve	Ju	Ju	Ra	32.30
Cusp VII	Sco	21-46-30	Ma	Me	Su	Ra	91.77
Cusp VIII	Sag	20-41-27	Ju	Ve	Ju	Me	24.32
Cusp IX	Cap	19-41-12	Sa	Mo	Ke	Ke	44.30
Cusp X	Aqu	18-33-28	Sa	Ra	Mo	Ju	82.81
Cusp XI	Pis	19-53-51	Ju	Me	Ve	Mo	44.64
Cusp XII	Ari	21-35-50	Ma	Ve	Ju	Ma	75.92

The event happened when Moon was progressing in Jup-Sat-Mer-Mer-Jup. It can be verified that all these planets are significators of the event of marriage.

Death of Father: The native lost his father on 22.04.2001 at 10 hrs. Death took place in the town Erode in Tamil Nadu, India. On this day native was running the period of Rahu-Venus-Sat-Jup-Sun. Figure 6.6 represents the rotated chart starting with 9th cusp.

Fig. 6.6 Rotated chart of 9th Cusp as Ascendent

Name	Fig 6.6	Place	Madurai
Longitude	78-7-48-E	Latitude	9-56-8-N
Sidereal Time	01-15-53	Date	30/4/1978
Day	Sunday	Geocentric Latitude	09-52-13-N
Nakshatra	Shravana- 4 Qtr.	Time	11:02:07
Lunar Nodes	True	Tithi	Krishna Paksha - Asthami
Time Zone	+5:30:0	DST	00:00
Ayanamsa	23-32-35	House System	Placidus

Rashi Chart

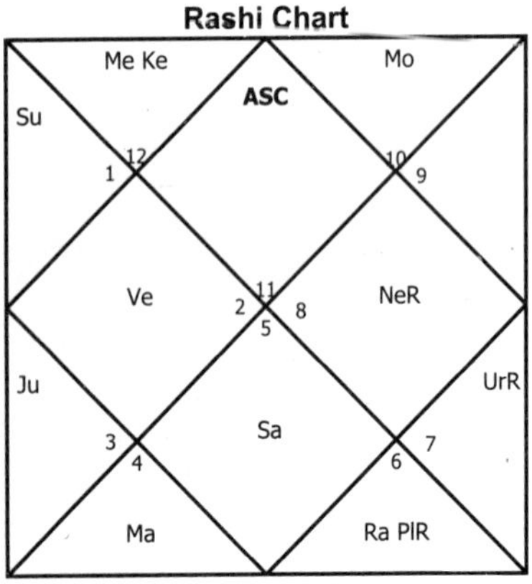

Bhava Chart

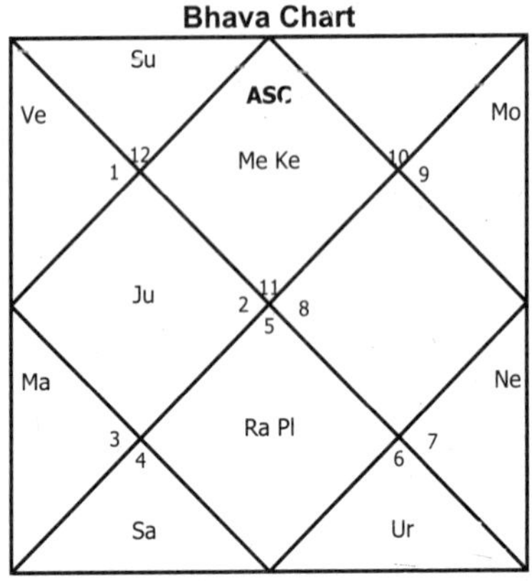

Cusp Chart

II 26-59-44 Me 22-18-00 Ke 11-53-56	Su 15-58-33 III 28-56-23	Ve 09-59-39 IV 28-56-54	Ju 09-22-12 V 27-41-28
I 24-45-13			Ma 14-06-34 VI 24-48-50
XII 24-48-50 Mo 20-36-09			Sa 00-07-42 VII 24-45-13
XI 27-41-28	X 28-56-54 NeR 24-21-21	IX 28-56-23 UrR 21-03-29	Ra 11-53-56 PlR 21-06-47 VIII 26-59-44

Fig. 6.6 Contd......

Planetary Position

Planet	Sign	D-M-S	RL	STL	SL	SSL	Hse	D	S
Sun	Ari	15-58-33	Ma	Ve	Su	Sa	2		P
Moon	Cap	20-36-09	Sa	Mo	Ve	Ve	11		P
Mars	Can	14-06-34	Mo	Sa	Ra	Ke	5		P
Mercury	Pis	22-18-00	Ju	Me	Mo	Mo	1		P
Jupiter	Gem	09-22-12	Me	Ra	Ju	Me	4		P
Venus	Tau	09-59-39	Ve	Su	Ve	Ke	3		P
Saturn	Leo	00-07-42	Su	Ke	Ke	Ve	6		P
T.Rahu	Vir	11-53-56	Me	Mo	Ra	Ra	7		
T.Ketu	Pis	11-53-56	Ju	Sa	Mo	Ve	1		P
Uranus	Lib	21-03-29	Ve	Ju	Ju	Ve	8	R	
Neptune	Sco	24-21-21	Ma	Me	Ra	Ra	9	R	
Pluto	Vir	21-06-47	Me	Mo	Ve	Ma	7	R	

Cuspal Position

Cusp	Sign	D-M-S	RL	STL	SL	SSL	% Arc
Cusp I	Aqu	24-45-13	Sa	Ju	Me	Mo	49.31
Cusp II	Pis	26-59-44	Ju	Me	Ju	Ve	03.53
Cusp III	Ari	28-56-23	Ma	Su	Ma	Me	96.56
Cusp IV	Tau	28-56-54	Ve	Ma	Sa	Ve	86.07
Cusp V	Gem	27-41-28	Me	Ju	Ve	Ju	01.98
Cusp VI	Can	24-48-50	Mo	Me	Ra	Sa	42.96
Cusp VII	Leo	24-45-13	Su	Ve	Me	Su	64.53
Cusp VIII	Vir	26-59-44	Me	Ma	Ju	Ve	03.53
Cusp IX	Lib	28-56-23	Ve	Ju	Su	Ra	34.18
Cusp X	Sco	28-56-54	Ma	Me	Sa	Ve	86.07
Cusp XI	Sag	27-41-28	Ju	Su	Mo	Ju	22.72
Cusp XII	Cap	24-48-50	Sa	Ma	Ra	Sa	42.96

Dasa lord Rahu represents Mercury and Moon those are appearing in the ascendant of father. Rahu is also the sub sub lord of 9th cusp in the rotated chart. Ninth cusp is Badhaka for father. Eighth cusp sub sub lord is Venus. Rahu as Moon is in the sub of Venus. Thus we may say that Dasa lord establishes relationship with the sub sub lord of 8th cusp. Rahu is in Moon star that is the sub sub lord of father's ascendant. Rahu is in Rahu sub and sub sub. Rahu is the sub sub lord of Badhaka. Thus we notice that Dasa lord satisfies all conditions to be the right Markesh Dasa. Bhukti lord Venus is in Sun star (7 and 9 Badhaka) and sub of Venus (2 and 8).

Similarly we can verify that all Dasa period lord planets signify the event of death of father.

On the day of death Moon was transiting in Jup-Mer-Venus-Sat. We may notice that Jup, Venus and Sat appear in Dasa period which caused death of father. Mercury is in Mercury star (1 and 8) and in Moon sub (sub sub lord of ascendant).

On the day of death the progressed ascendant was co-ruled by planets Moon-Sat-Rahu-Moon. Figure 6.7 represents the progressed chart.

Fig. 6.7 Progress Chart of 22.04.2001 at 10 hrs.

Name	Fig. 6.7	Place	Madurai
Longitude	78-7-48-E	Latitude	9-56-8-N
Sidereal Time	01-15-53	Date	30/4/1978
Day	Sunday	Geocentric Latitude	09-52-13-N
Nakshatra	Shravana- 4 Qtr.	Time	11:02:07
Lunar Nodes	True	Tithi	Krishna Paksha - Asthami
Time Zone	+5:30:0	DST	00:00
Ayanamsa	23-32-35	House System	Placidus

Rashi Chart

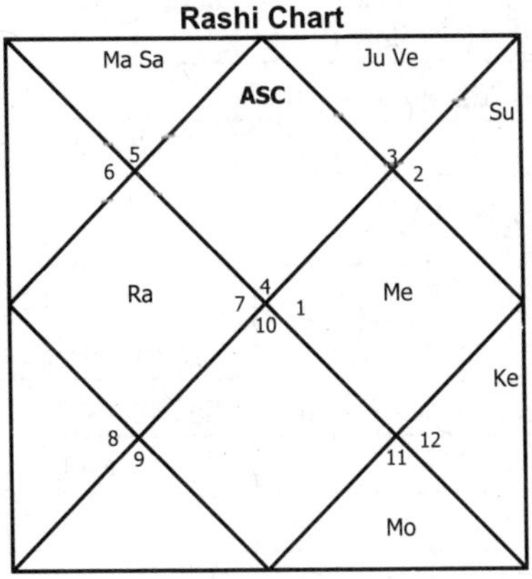

Bhava Chart

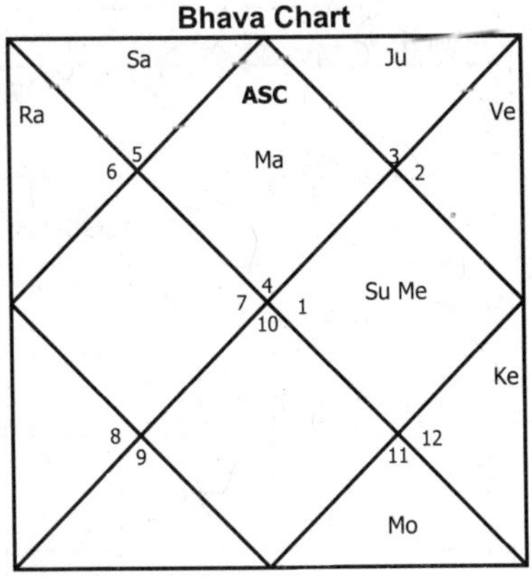

Cusp Chart

Ke 29-21-37 IX 14-18-28	X 16-15-10 Me 17-26-27	Su 11-15-25 XI 16-48-24	Ve 11-05-36 XII 15-51-28 Ju 27-11-24
Mo 16-59-08 VIII 13-10-03			I 14-42-26
VII 14-42-26			Ma 04-26-49 II 13-10-03 Sa 24-01-51
VI 15-51-28	V 16-48-24	IV 16-15-10 Ra 12-09-01	III 14-18-28

Fig. 6.7 Contd......

Planetary Position

Planet	Sign	D-M-S	RL	STL	SL	SSL	Hse	D	S
Sun	Tau	11-15-25	Ve	Mo	Ma	Ra	10		P
Moon	Aqu	16-59-08	Sa	Ra	Ve	Sa	8		
Mars	Leo	04-26-49	Su	Ke	Mo	Me	1		P
Mercury	Ari	17-26-27	Ma	Ve	Ma	Ra	10		
Jupiter	Gem	27-11-24	Me	Ju	Ve	Mo	12		P
Venus	Gem	11-05-36	Me	Ra	Sa	Ke	11		P
Saturn	Leo	24-01-51	Su	Ve	Me	Me	2		P
Rahu	Lib	12-09-01	Ve	Ra	Sa	Ra	3		P
Ketu	Pis	29-21-37	Ju	Me	Sa	Ma	9		

Cuspal Position

Cusp	Sign	D-M-S	RL	STL	SL	SSL	% Arc
Cusp I	Can	14-42-26	Mo	Sa	Ra	Mo	61.07
Cusp II	Leo	13-10-03	Su	Ke	Me	Sa	44.53
Cusp III	Vir	14-18-28	Me	Mo	Ju	Sa	64.59
Cusp IV	Lib	16-15-10	Ve	Ra	Ve	Ra	70.31
Cusp V	Sco	16-48-24	Ma	Me	Me	Me	52.34
Cusp VI	Sag	15-51-28	Ju	Ve	Su	Ju	83.69
Cusp VII	Cap	14-42-26	Sa	Mo	Ju	Ke	46.36
Cusp VIII	Aqu	13-10-03	Sa	Ra	Me	Ve	74.36
Cusp IX	Pis	14-18-28	Ju	Sa	Ra	Ve	40.65
Cusp X	Ari	16-15-10	Ma	Ve	Mo	Mo	33.11
Cusp XI	Tau	16-48-24	Ve	Mo	Sa	Su	30.05
Cusp XII	Gem	15-51-28	Me	Ra	Ve	Mo	83.17

In the natal chart Moon is in Moon Star (sub sub lord of ascendant of father) and Venus sub that is the sub sub lord of 8th cusp. Saturn is in Ketu star ketu sub and Venus sub sub. Ketu is placed in ascendant of father and Venus is the sub sub lord of 8th cusp. Rahu is in Moon Star (sub sub lord of ascendant) and Rahu sub that is the sub sub lord of Badhaka. Thus we find that planets co-ruling the progressed ascendant are strong significators of father's death.

We can study the progressed chart independently. The event of death of father happened when Moon was progressing in Rahu-Venus-Sat-Jup-Sun.

Dasa lord Rahu in the progressed chart is the sub sub lord of 8th cusp. It is in Rahu star and Saturn sub. Rahu appears in 1, 7(Badhaka), 8. Saturn appears in 1 and 7. Thus we see that Dasa lord is a very strong significator of death of father. It satisfies all the conditions for Markesh Dasa. Similarly we can check that all Dasa period planets signify death houses.

Death took place in Mercury star. Sub sub lord of 8th cusp in the progressed chart is Rahu that represents Venus. Since Rahu is placed in Badhaka house we can assume that Venus is placed in Badhaka. Mercury is in Venus star and Mars sub. Mars appears in 2.

From the above discussion we may say that the astrological birth time of the native has been correctly fixed.

Example 2: A learned Astrologer approached the author with the given data and requested for a correct chart as per KCIL theory of birth time rectification.

Male

DOB: 08 March 1946

TOB: 17:30 hrs. or 16.05 hrs.

POB: Mathura (UP), India. Long 77:41:48E, Lat 27:28:21N

Life events

1. The twin sister born after 45 minutes of native's birth died within three months of birth

2.	First job	08.11.1964
3.	Marriage	08.12.1970
4.	Promotion in service	01.07.1972
5.	First child (female)	25.11.1971 at 1245 hrs. Delhi
6.	Daughter's marriage	18.01.1998
7.	Second Daughter	08.11.1974 at 09.30 hrs.
8.	Death of Father	20.04.2003 at about 03.30 hrs.
9.	Death of Mother	29.11.2008 at about 14.30 hrs.

Moon star of:

1.	Wife -	Ket
2.	1st daughter	Mars
3.	2nd Daughter	Sun
4.	3rd daughter	Rahu
5.	Younger sister(Twin)	Sun

Figure 6.8. Shows the chart of the native cast as per given data. Let us first check the accuracy of the chart.

Fig. 6.8 Natal chart at 17.30 hrs

Name	Fig 6.8	Place	Mathura
Longitude	77-41-48-E	Latitude	27-29-21-N
Sidereal Time	04-13-08	Date	08/3/1946
Day	Friday	Geocentric Latitude	27-19-55-N
Nakshatra	Krittika-1 Qtr.	Time	17:30:00.000
Lunar Nodes	True	Tithi	Shukla Paksha - Shasti
Time Zone	+5:30:0 DST	00:00	
Ayanamsa	23-05-40	House System	Placidus

Rashi Chart

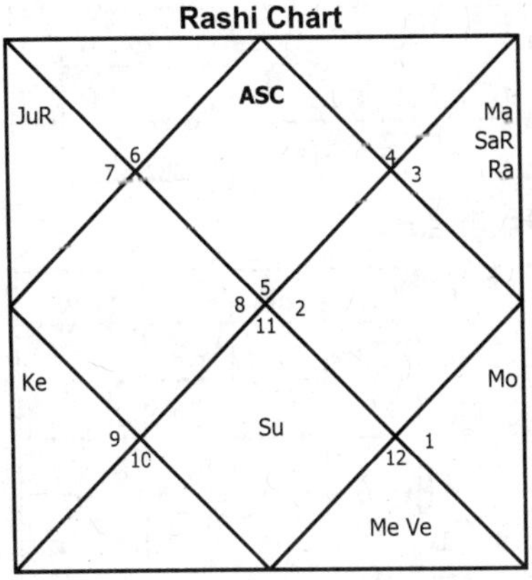

Bhava Chart

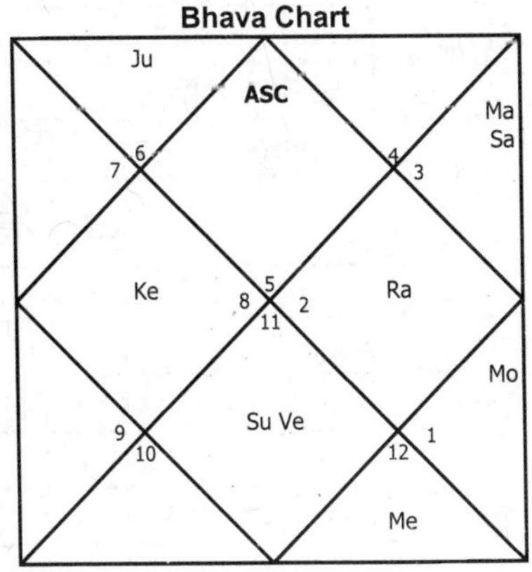

Cusp Chart

Me 12-21-10 VIII 10-01-06 Ve 02-43-46	IX 10-11-56 Mo 27-51-55	X 12-07-11	Ra 02-59-57 XI 13-51-00 Ma 22-15-07 SaR 24-59-24
Su 24-13-40 VII 13-13-30			XII 14-22-59
VI 14-22-59			I 13-13-30
V 13-51-00 Ke 02-59-57	IV 12-07-11	III 10-11-56 JuR 03-17-58	II 10-01-06

Fig. 6.8 Contd......

Planetary Position

Planet	Sign	D-M-S	R L	STL	SL	SSL	SukL	PraL	Hse	D	S
Sun	Aqu	24-13-40	Sa	Ju	Me	Ke	Ju	Ve	7		
Moon	Ari	27-51-55	Ma	Su	Mo	Sa	Ke	Ju	9	P	
Mars	Gem	22-15-07	Me	Ju	Sa	Me	Mo	Me	11	P	
Mercury	Pis	12-21-10	Ju	Sa	Ma	Ju	Mo	Me	8	P	
Jupiter	Lib	03-17-58	Ve	Ma	Ve	Mo	Ve	Su	2	R	P
Venus	Pis	02-43-46	Ju	Ju	Ra	Ve	Ma	Ke	7	P	
Saturn	Gem	24-59-24	Me	Ju	Me	Ra	Ju	Ju	11	R	
T.Rahu	Gem	02-59-57	Me	Ma	Ve	Ve	Me	Ra	10	P	
T.Ketu	Sag	02-59-57	Ju	Ke	Ve	Ke	Me	Sa	4	P	

Cuspal Position

Cusp	Sign	D-M-S	R L	STL	SL	SSL	SukL	PraL	% Arc
Cusp I	Leo	13-13-30	Su	Ke	Me	Sa	Mo	Ke	63.76
Cusp II	Vir	10-01-06	Me	Mo	Mo	Mo	Ra	Sa	19.72
Cusp III	Lib	10-11-56	Ve	Ra	Ju	Ra	Ra	Me	07.96
Cusp IV	Sco	12-07-11	Ma	Sa	Ma	Ma	Ra	Mo	18.95
Cusp V	Sag	13-51-00	Ju	Ve	Ve	Mo	Ra	Sa	18.93
Cusp VI	Cap	14-22-59	Sa	Mo	Ju	Sa	Ju	Me	91.31
Cusp VII	Aqu	13-13-30	Sa	Ra	Me	Ve	Me	Sa	92.63
Cusp VIII	Pis	10-01-06	Ju	Sa	Ve	Me	Su	Ve	41.10
Cusp IX	Ari	10-11-56	Ma	Ke	Sa	Ve	Ma	Ra	31.03
Cusp X	Tau	12-07-11	Ve	Mo	Ra	Ra	Ve	Sa	76.94
Cusp XI	Gem	13-51-00	Me	Ra	Me	Ra	Su	Me	84.60
Cusp XII	Can	14-22-59	Mo	Sa	Ra	Ve	Ju	Ra	63.22

Accuracy of Ascendant: Saturn is the sub sub lord of the ascendant and the Moon star of the native is Sun. There is a relationship between Sun and Saturn because both are in the same star Jupiter.

Genitical Connections: Sub sub lord of the 7th cusp is Venus that is in Jupiter star. Moon's star lord of wife is Ketu that represents Jupiter. Sub sub lord of the 5th cusp is Moon that does not establish any relationship with the Moon's star lord of the first daughter. Similarly we notice that the sub sub lord of the 7th cusp is Venus that does not establish any relation with the Moon star of the second daughter which is Sun. Thus the chart needs rectification.

Promise for younger twin: Sub sub lord of the ascendant is Saturn that is in Jupiter star which appears as sub lord of third cusp. The chart thus satisfies the necessary condition for the birth of the younger co-born.

Moon Star of Twin Sister: The sub sub lord of the 3rd cusp is Rahu that represents Mercury and Mars. Rahu itself does not establish any relationship with Sun the Moon star of the younger co-born. But we can always replace the sub sub lord of a cusp in case of Rahu or Ketu by the planets it represents for the purpose of studying promise. Thus we can assume that 3rd cusp's sub sub lord is Mercury. Sun is in Jupiter star and Mercury sub. Thus the 3rd cusps lord establishes relationship with the common Moon star of the twins.

Verification of Promises:

Marriage: Sub sub lord of ascendant is Saturn that is in Jupiter star and Mercury sub. Jupiter appears in 5 and Mercury appears in 7.Thus the ascendant promises marriage. 7th sub sub lord is Venus that has PS and appears in 7 and 5.Venus is in the sub of Rahu that appears in 7 and 11. Thus the chart promises marriage.

The native got married on 08.12.1970 when the ascendant was progressing in Virgo ruled by Mercury. Marriage could happen only if Mercury in the natal chart is linked with relevant cusps 5, 7 and 11. Mercury in the natal chart is in Saturn star and Mars sub. Saturn appears in 7 and 11. Mars appears in 11. Thus the progressed position of ascendant allows the event to happen.

First child (female): Sub sub lord of 5 is Moon. Moon is in the SS of Saturn that is placed in male Sign Gemini. More over the SS arc of Moon is in first half and male sign rises on the 5th cusp. This promises a male child. Thus this also indicates that the chart needs rectification.

Promise of Death Events: The native lost his mother on 29.11.2008 when the progressed ascendant was in Libra ruled by Venus. If the native had to experience a death event when the progressed ascendant sign lord is Venus then the following two conditions should exist in the natal chart:

Venus should be linked with 12 (loss) and 8 (death).

Venus should be a co ruling planet in the 8th cusp with respect to concerned relative and should be a significator of death of the concerned relation.

In the chart Venus has PS and appears in 8 as well as in 12. Venus is in the sub of Rahu that appears in 12. Thus the chart satisfies the first condition. The second condition is not satisfied because Venus does not appear in 11th cusp even up to SSSS level. 11th cusp is 8th from 4.

Thus the chart needs rectification.

Native lost his mother when he was running Dasa period of Sat-Ketu-Rahu. Dasa lord Saturn is in Jupiter star and Mercury sub. As such Saturn does not appear to have the power to inflict death of mother. This also shows that the chart needs rectification.

From the above analysis it was decided that this cannot be the correct chart of the native.

Let us study the chart at time 18.05hrs. Analysis of this chart indicated that this chart needs micro rectification. Figure 6.9 represents the rectified chart. This chart is cast using the True Astrology software version 5 which provides the position of planets and cusps up to SSSS level. The analysis of the chart for various events is limited to the SS level but fixing the positions of cusp for promise use of SSS and SSSS positions have been accepted.

Fig 6.9 time 18.05.21 hrs. Version 5

Name	Fig 6.9	Place	Mathura
Longitude	77-41-48-E	Latitude	27-29-21-N
Sidereal Time	04-48-35	Date	08/3/1946
Day	Friday	Geocentric Latitude	27-19-55-N
Nakshatra	Krittika-1 Qtr.	Time	18:5:21.000
Lunar Nodes	True	Tithi	Shukla Paksha-Shasti
Time Zone	+5:30:0	DST	00:00
Ayanamsa	23-05-40	House System	Placidus

Rashi Chart

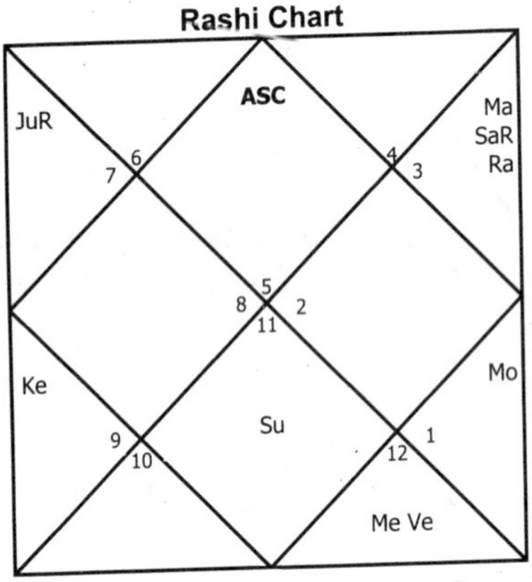

Bhava Chart

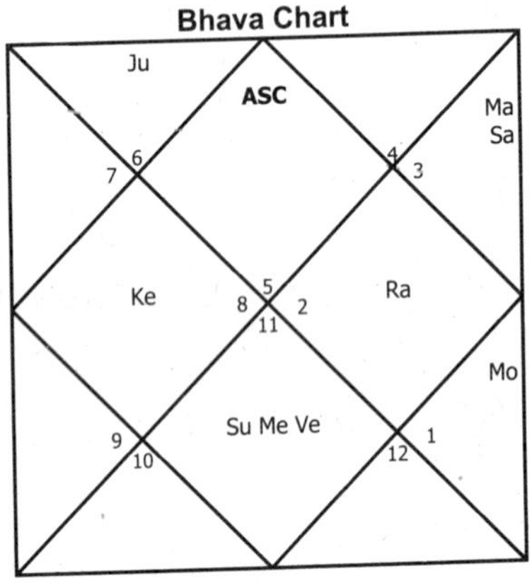

Cusp Chart

VIII 18-24-21 Me 12-22-49 Ve 02-45-36	IX 18-45-43 Mo 28-13-01	X 20-26-29	Ra 02-59-53 XI 21-54-37 Ma 22-15-22 SaR 24-59-22
Su 24-15-09 VII 21-02-26			XII 22-20-52
VI 22-20-52			I 21-02-26
V 21-54-37 Ke 02-59-53	IV 20-26-29	III 18-45-43 JuR 03-17-51	II 18-24-21

Fig. 6.9 Contd......

Planetary Position

Planet	Sign	D-M-S	R L	STL	SL	SSL	SukL	PraL	Hse	D	S
Sun	Aqu	24-15-09	Sa	Ju	Me	Ke	Me	Me	7		
Moon	Ari	28-13-01	Ma	Su	Mo	Ve	Ve	Ra	9	P	
Mars	Gem	22-15-22	Me	Ju	Sa	Me	Mo	Ke	11	P	
Mercury	Pis	12-22-49	Ju	Sa	Ma	Sa	Sa	Me	7	P	
Jupiter	Lib	03-17-51	Ve	Ma	Ve	Mo	Ve	Ve	2	R	P
Venus	Pis	02-45-36	Ju	Ju	Ra	Ve	Ra	Me	7	P	
Saturn	Gem	24-59-22	Me	Ju	Me	Ra	Ju	Ju	11	R	
T.Rahu	Gem	02-59-53	Me	Ma	Ve	Ve	Me	Ra	10	P	
T.Ketu	Sag	02-59-53	Ju	Ke	Ve	Ke	Me	Sa	4	P	

Cuspal Position

Cusp	Sign	D-M-S	R L	STL	SL	SSL	SukL	PraL	% Arc
Cusp I	Leo	21-02-26	Su	Ve	Ju	Ve	Su	Ju	18.68
Cusp II	Vir	18-24-21	Me	Mo	Me	Ve	Sa	Ju	79.48
Cusp III	Lib	18-45-43	Ve	Ra	Mo	Me	Me	Me	01.69
Cusp IV	Sco	20-26-29	Ma	Me	Ve	Ra	Mo	Ve	93.49
Cusp V	Sag	21-54-37	Ju	Ve	Sa	Sa	Sa	Ve	06.36
Cusp VI	Cap	22-20-52	Sa	Mo	Ve	Me	Su	Me	39.85
Cusp VII	Aqu	21-02-26	Sa	Ju	Ju	Ve	Ju	Me	56.18
Cusp VIII	Pis	18-24-21	Ju	Me	Me	Sa	Ve	Me	49.91
Cusp IX	Ari	18-45-43	Ma	Ve	Ra	Sa	Me	Ju	26.57
Cusp X	Tau	20-26-29	Ve	Mo	Ke	Me	Sa	Ra	97.11
Cusp XI	Gem	21-54-37	Me	Ju	Sa	Sa	Ve	Mo	39.60
Cusp XII	Can	22-20-52	Mo	Me	Mo	Ma	Me	Me	50.71

Let us verify the Accuracy of the Chart.

Accuracy of Sun, Moon and Ascendant: It can be seen that the planets co-ruling the positions of Sun, Moon and ascendant relates to the cusps 1, 7 and 10. Sub sub lord of ascendant is Venus that appears to establish no connection with the Moon star Sun as per the conditions stated in the earlier part of this book. However it is experienced that the two planets are said to be related if they are in the same star. In this chart we note that Sun is in Jupiter star and Venus is also in Jupiter star. More over Sun appears in the SSS level in the ascendant and Jupiter appears in the SSSS level.

Promise of younger twin: Sub sub lord of ascendant is Venus that has PS. Venus also appears in the 3rd house. This satisfies the necessary condition for the birth of the younger twin.

Sub sub lord of the 3rd cusp is Mercury that is the sub lord of Moon's star lord Sun. Thus the condition that the sub sub lord of the 3rd cusp should establish link with the common Moon star is also satisfied.

Genetical Connections: It can be verified that the sub sub lord of 5, 7, and 9 establish relationship with the Moon star of first child, second child, wife and third child.

Promise of Aspects of Life:

Marriage: Sub sub lord of ascendant and 7th cusp is Venus that has PS and is placed in 7. Venus also appears in 5. Thus Venus signifies 5 and 7. Venus is in the sub of Rahu that represents Mercury that appears in 7 and 11. Venus is in Jupiter star that appears in 5, 7 & 11. Venus is in the SS of Venus that as stated above appears in 5 and 7. Thus the chart promises the aspect of marriage.

Birth of Children: Sub sub lord of 5th cusp is Saturn that is in Jupiter star (2 and 5) and in Mercury sub (2 and 11). This shows that the native has the necessary procreative power and can produce children.

Since Saturn's star lord Jupiter appears in 7 also this indicates that the native is promised more than one child.

Birth of First Child as Female: We have stated that there is no foolproof method to determine the sex of a child. However we feel that the following two rules if used judicially give fairly correct results. These rules are:

SS arc of the sub sub lord of the fifth cusp (in male charts) decide the sex of the child as per its placement in relevant half. If male sign rises on the 5th cusp then the first half indicates male child. If the female sign rises on the 5th cusp then first half indicates the female child.

If the sub sub lord of the sub sub lord of the 5th cusp is placed in male sign it indicates male child. If it is placed in female sign it indicates female child.

In this chart SS arc of the sub sub lord of the 5th cusp is in first half. Since male sign rises on the 5th cusp it would lead the astrologer to think that the first child should have been male.

Sub sub lord of the 5th cusp is Saturn that is in the SS of Rahu that represents Mercury. Rahu itself is placed in male sign. If we look at the Rashi chart we notice that there are only two planets Mercury and Venus that are placed in female signs. We know that the planet Rahu tries to align itself with the planets it represents if those planets appear in the preceding position. Here Saturn is in the sub of Mercury that is represented by Rahu. Thus we may say that Saturn is in the sub and SS of Mercury that is placed in female sign. This accounts for the birth of the female child.

Promise of Execution of Events and Progression: The natal chart sub sub lords of ascendant and the relevant cusp declares the promise of various aspects of life but it is the progressed position of the ascendant that declares the destined time of the execution of the promised event.

The native was born in Leo ascendant. Progressed ascendant will remain Leo till about 15.02.1956 and then it enters in Virgo. It would have remained in Virgo up to 15.02.1974. According to the concept of progression of ascendant, native could experience all those events which are promised by Mercury as per its signification in the natal chart. During ascendant's progression in Virgo native experienced the death of father, marriage, joined first job. Let us see that Mercury in the natal chart promises these events or not.

Mercury in the natal chart is in Saturn star (5, 6, 7, 8, 9 and 11) and Mars sub (4, 9, 11 and 12. Mercury has PS and it appears in 2, 3, 4, 6, 8, 10, and 12. Mercury signifies 2, 5 and 11.This promises birth of first child.

Linkages with 8 and 12 promises death experience, 5, 7 and 11 (marriage) and 2, 6 and 10 (joining Job).

After 15.02.1974 the native's ascendant progresses to Cancer sign. During the period ascendant progresses in Cancer sign the native will experience all that is promised by the significations of Moon in the natal chart.

Verification of Events:

Birth of First daughter: The native was blessed with first daughter on 25.11.1971 when he was running Dasa period of Rahu-Jupiter-Mercury-Mercury-Venus.

Dasa lord Rahu is In Mars star that is placed in 11. Rahu is in the sub and sub sub of Venus that appears in 2 and 5.

Bhukti lord Jupiter is in Mars star and Venus sub. As stated above Mars appears in 11 and Venus appears in 2 and 5. Jupiter is in the sub sub of Moon that appears in 2.

Antara and Sooksshma lord Mercury is in Saturn star (2 and 5) and in Mars sub (placed in 11 with PS). Mercury is in the sub sub of Saturn (2 and 5).

Prana lord Venus that has PS and signifies 2 and 5 by PS. It is in the sub of Rahu that represents Mercury and Mars. Mercury appears in 2 and 11.

Venus is in Jupiter star that appears in 2, 5 and 11. Thus at stellar level also Venus justifies the enactment of the event.

Fig 6.10 represents the transit position of Planets on that day.

Fig 6.10 Transit Chart 25.11.1971

Name	Fig. 6.10	Place	Delhi
Longitude	77-14-15-E	Latitude	28-33-59-N
Sidereal Time	16-41-54	Date	25/11/1971
Day	Thursday	Geocentric Latitude	28-24-18-N
Nakshatra	Dhanishtha-4 Qtr.	Time	12:48:36.000
Lunar Nodes	True	Tithi	Shukla Paksha - Asthami
Time Zone	+5:30:0	DST	00:00
Ayanamsa	23-27-12	House System	Placidus

Rashi Chart

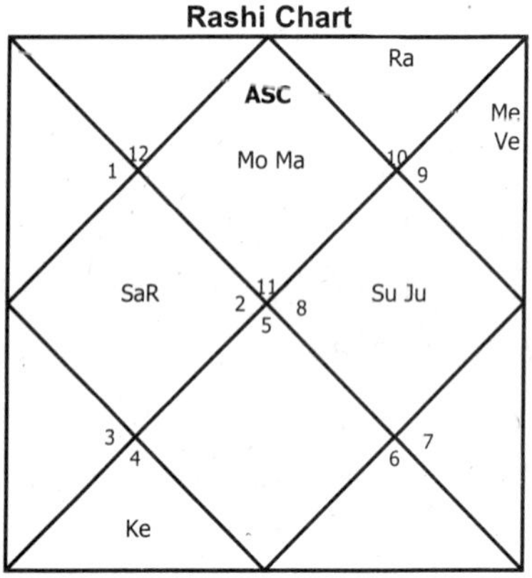

Bhava Chart

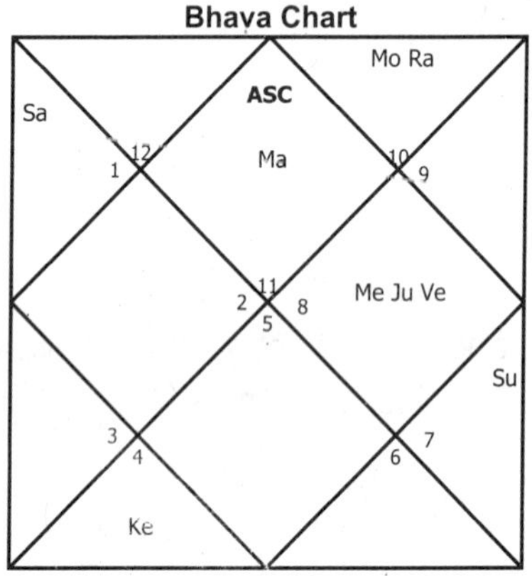

Planetary Position

Planet	Sign	D-M-S	RL	STL	SL	SSL	SukL	PraL	Hse	D	S
Sun	Sco	08-54-22	Ma	Sa	Ve	Ma	Mo	Ve	9		P
Moon	Aqu	03-59-29	Sa	Ma	Ve	Ju	Su	Su	12		
Mars	Aqu	17-03-33	Sa	Ra	Ve	Me	Ke	Sa	1		P
Mercury	Sag	00-43-37	Ju	Ke	Ke	Me	Ma	Ke	10		
Jupiter	Sco	20-37-44	Ma	Me	Ve	Ju	Ve	Ra	10		P
Venus	Sag	01-48-21	Ju	Ke	Ve	Ra	Ve	Ma	10		P
Saturn	Tau	09-37-30	Ve	Su	Ve	Me	Ve	Ve	3	R	P
T.Rahu	Cap	14-02-41	Sa	Mo	Ju	Ju	Ve	Ke	12		
T.Ketu	Can	14-02-41	Mo	Sa	Ra	Me	Sa	Ra	6		

Moon was transiting in Sat-Mars-Venus-Jupiter-Sun-Sun. We have seen above that Jupiter and Venus signifies the relevant houses for the event. Sun in the natal chart is in Jupiter star (2, 5 and 11) and in Mercury sub (2 and 11).Saturn is in Jupiter star (2, 5 and 11) and Mercury sub (2 and 11). Mars is in Jupiter star (2, 5 and 11) and Saturn sub (5 and 11). Thus transit of Moon fully supports the event. Similarly we can verify that transit of other Planets agree with the event.

Figure 6.11 represents the progressed chart for the event of birth of first daughter.

Fig.6.11 Progress Chart of 25.11.1971

Name	Fig 6.11	Place	Mathura
Longitude	77-41-48-E	Latitude	27-29-21-N
Sidereal Time	04-48-35	Date	08/3/1946
Day	Friday	Geocentric Latitude	27-19-55-N
Nakshatra	Krittika-1 Qtr.	Time	18:5:21.000
Lunar Nodes	True	Tithi	Shukla Paksha - Shasti
Time Zone	+5:30:0	DST	00:00
Ayanamsa	23-05-40	House System	Placidus

Rashi Chart

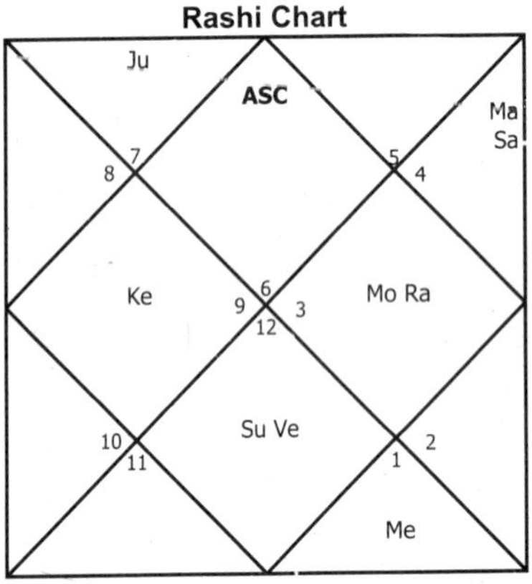

Bhava Chart

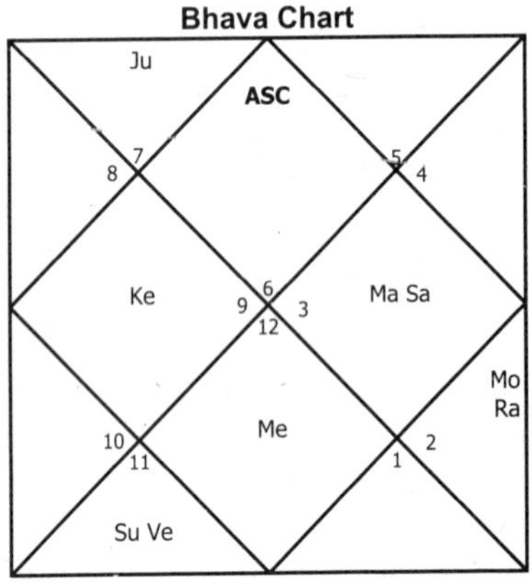

Cusp Chart

VII 25-46-03 Ve 21-23-44 Su 13-44-00	Me 04-58-10 VIII 24-31-16	IX 24-59-03	Mo 09-11-46 Ra 24-49-33 X 26-32-14
VI 28-36-39			Ma 12-03-08 Sa 14-21-15 XI 28-18-26
V 28-18-26			XII 28-36-39
Ke 27-18-49 IV 26-32-14	III 24-59-03	Ju 24-57-25 II 24-31-16	I 25-46-03

Fig. 6.11 Contd......

Planetary Position

Planet	Sign	D-M-S	R L	STL	SL	SSL	Hse	D	S
Sun	Pis	13-44-00	Ju	Sa	Ra	Sa	6		
Moon	Gem	09-11-46	Me	Ra	Ju	Me	9	P	
Mars	Can	12-03-08	Mo	Sa	Mo	Ve	10	P	
Mercury	Ari	04-58-10	Ma	Ke	Ma	Ju	7		
Jupiter	Lib	24-57-25	Ve	Ju	Me	Ra	2	P	
Venus	Pis	21-23-44	Ju	Me	Ve	Me	6	P	
Saturn	Can	14-21-15	Mo	Sa	Ra	Ve	10	P	
Rahu	Gem	24-49-33	Me	Ju	Me	Mo	9		
Ketu	Sag	27-18-49	Ju	Su	Su	Ve	4		

Cuspal Position

Cusp	Sign	D-M-S	R L	STL	SL	SSL	% Arc
Cusp I	Vir	25-46-03	Me	Ma	Ra	Su	39.83
Cusp II	Lib	24-31-16	Ve	Ju	Me	Ve	80.84
Cusp III	Sco	24-59-03	Ma	Me	Ra	Sa	96.78
Cusp IV	Sag	26-32-14	Ju	Ve	Ke	Sa	84.32
Cusp V	Cap	28-18-26	Sa	Ma	Sa	Me	28.10
Cusp VI	Aqu	28-36-39	Sa	Ju	Ve	Me	88.17
Cusp VII	Pis	25-46-03	Ju	Me	Ra	Su	39.83
Cusp VIII	Ari	24-31-16	Ma	Ve	Me	Ve	45.55
Cusp IX	Tau	24-59-03	Ve	Ma	Ra	Sa	96.78
Cusp X	Gem	26-32-14	Me	Ju	Ke	Me	83.32
Cusp XI	Can	28-18-26	Mo	Me	Sa	Me	28.10
Cusp XII	Leo	28-36-39	Su	Su	Ma	Ju	04.25

It can be seen that on 25.11.1971 progressed ascendant was co-ruled by Planets Mercury-Mars-Rahu-Sun. We have seen above that all these Planets are strong significators of the event of birth of first daughter.

Let us study the progresses chart of the event independently.

Dasa lord Rahu is in Jupiter star (placed in 2) and Mercury sub (2, 5, and 11) and in Moon sub-sub (11).

Bhukti lord Jupiter is in Jupiter star (placed in 2) and Mercury sub (2, 5, and 11) and in Rahu sub sub that represents Mercury and Jupiter.

Antara and Sookshma lord Mercury is Ketu star that represents Jupiter. Thus Mercury is as good as in Jupiter star (placed in 2). Mercury is in the sub of Mars that appears in 5.

Prana lord Venus is in Mercury star (sub lord of 2, sub sub lord of 5 and 11). Venus is in the sub of Venus that is the sub sub lord of 2. Venus is in the sub sub of Mercury (2, 5 and 11).

Thus we see that the analysis of progressed chart fully confirms the execution of the event of birth of first daughter.

Death of Father: The native lost his father on 20.04.2003 at 03.30 hrs when he was running the Dasa period of Sat-Sat-Mer-Jup-Ven.

Potential of Dasa and Bhukti Lord Saturn: Saturn appears as sub sub lord of the ascendant of father. Ketu is placed in the 8th Bhava with respect to 9th cusp. Ketu represents Jupiter. Saturn is in Jupiter star (8 and sub lord of Badhaka for 9) and in the sub of Mercury that is the SSS of ascendant of father. Saturn is in the sub sub of Rahu that is the sub sub lord of 8 with respect to 9. Thus the Dasa lord satisfies the necessary conditions to cause death of father.

Antara lord Mercury is in Saturn star (sub sub lord of father's ascendant and sign lord of Badhaka) and Mars sub that appears in 1 and 8. Mercury is in the sub sub of Saturn that appears in Badhaka and 12 from father's ascendant.

Sookshma lord Jupiter is in Mars star (1 and 8 with respect to 9) and Venus sub (sub lord of 8 and sub sub lord of Badhaka with respect to 9).Jupiter is in the sub sub of Moon that appears in 2 and 7 with respect to 9.

Prana lord Venus is in the star of Jupiter that appears in Badhaka. It is in the sub of Rahu that appears in the ascendant and 8th cusp of the father. It can be seen that Venus has PS and strongly signifies the houses of death with respect to 9.

Thus we find that Dasa potential justifies the death of father. It may be noted that on the day of death of father Saturn was transiting in Mer-Mars-Mer-Mars. Mercury is a co-ruling planet in the 8th cusp from 9th. Sub sub lord of 8th cusp from 9th is Rahu that represents Mercury. We have seen above that Mercury has the power to inflict death of father. Thus transit of Saturn fully supports the event.

Figure 6.12 represents the progressed chart of the event of death of father. We notice that the progressed ascendant is co-ruled by planets Ven-Jup-Ketu-Sat. All these planets are strong significators of death of father. Let us study the progressed chart independently.

Fig. 6.12 Progress on 20.04.2003

Name	Fig 6.12	Place	Mathura
Longitude	77-41-48-E	Latitude	27-29-21-N
Sidereal Time	04-48-35	Date	08/3/1946
Day	Friday	Geocentric Latitude	27-19-55-N
Nakshatra	Krittika-1 Qtr.	Time	18:5:21.000
Lunar Nodes	True	Tithi	Shukla Paksha - Shasti
Time Zone	+5:30:0	DST	00:00
Ayanamsa	23-05-40	House System	Placidus

Rashi Chart

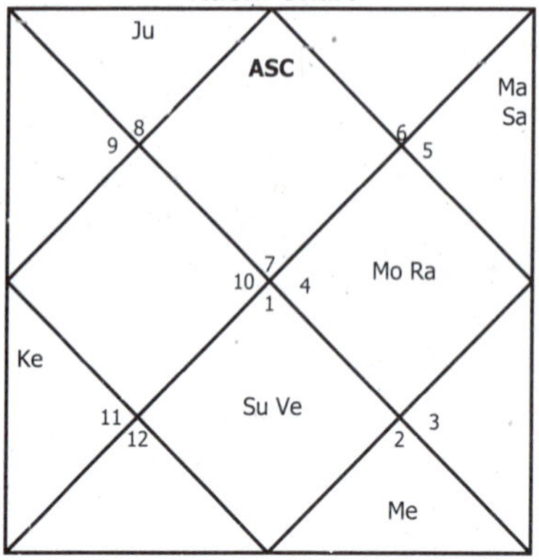

Bhava Chart

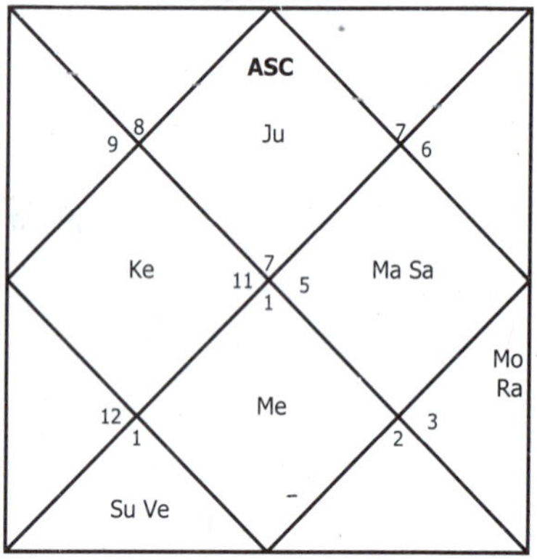

Cusp Chart

V 03-20-13	VI 01-51-23 Su 15-28-44 Ve 22-17-06 VII 26-23-49	Me 11-20-34 VIII 25-54-16	IX 27-42-36
Ke 13-06-12 IV 01-04-38			Mo 03-54-14 Ra 18-23-02
			X 01-04-38 Ma 13-52-54 Sa 16-04-07
III 27-42-36	II 25-54-16 Ju 18-30-26	I 26-23-49 XII 01-51-23	XI 03-20-13

Fig. 6.12 Contd......

Planetary Position

Planet	Sign	D-M-S	R L	STL	SL	SSL	Hse	D	S
Sun	Ari	15-28-44	Ma	Ve	Ve	Ke	6	P	
Moon	Can	03-54-14	Mo	Sa	Sa	Me	9		
Mars	Leo	13-52-54	Su	Ve	Ve	Mo	10	P	
Mercury	Tau	11-20-34	Ve	Mo	Ma	Ju	7		
Jupiter	Sco	18-30-26	Ma	Me	Me	Sa	1	P	
Venus	Ari	22-17-06	Ma	Ve	Sa	Me	6	P	
Saturn	Leo	16-04-07	Su	Ve	Su	Me	10		
Rahu	Can	18-23-02	Mo	Me	Me	Sa	9		
Ketu	Aqu	13-06-12	Sa	Ra	Me	Ve	4	P	

Cuspal Position

Cusp	Sign	D-M-S	R L	STL	SL	SSL	% Arc
Cusp I	Lib	26-23-49	Ve	Ju	Ke	Sa	60.58
Cusp II	Sco	25-54-16	Ma	Me	Ra	Mo	45.93
Cusp III	Sag	27-42-36	Ju	Su	Mo	Ju	35.46
Cusp IV	Aqu	01-04-38	Sa	Ma	Me	Ra	07.94
Cusp V	Pis	03-20-13	Ju	Sa	Sa	Sa	01.11
Cusp VI	Ari	01-51-23	Ma	Ke	Ve	Ra	84.74
Cusp VII	Ari	26-23-49	Ma	Ve	Ke	Ju	64.79
Cusp VIII	Tau	25-54-16	Ve	Ma	Ra	Mo	45.93
Cusp IX	Gem	27-42-36	Me	Ju	Ve	Ju	08.35
Cusp X	Leo	01-04-38	Su	Ke	Ve	Ve	80.82
Cusp XI	Vir	03-20-13	Me	Su	Sa	Me	00.93
Cusp XII	Lib	01-51-23	Ve	Ma	Me	Sa	89.18

Dasa and Bhukti lord Saturn: We notice that Ketu that represents Saturn is placed in the 8th Bhava with respect to 9. Sub sub lord of 8th cusp with respect to 9 is Rahu that represents Moon. Since Moon is in Saturn star we feel that the Dasa lord is related to the sub sub lord of the 8th cusp. Saturn is in Venus star (1) and sub of Sun in 7 (Badhaka for 9). Saturn is in the sub sub of Mercury (8). Thus Saturn justifies the necessary conditions to cause the death of father.

Antara lord Mercury is in Moon star that is placed in the ascendant of father and is also the sub lord of 7 with respect to 9. It is in the sub of Mars that appears in 7, 12, and 8 with respect to 9. Mercury is in the sub sub of Jupiter that is the sub sub lord of 7 with respect to 9.

Sookshma Lord Jupiter is in Mercury star (1 and 8 with respect to 9) and in the sub of Saturn that appears in 8 with respect to 9.

Prana Lord Venus is in Venus star (1 with respect to 9) and Saturn sub that appears in 8 with respect to 9. Venus is in the sub sub of Mercury that appears in 8 with respect to 9.

Thus the progressed chart confirms the execution of the event of death of father.

Heart attack and Angioplasty: The native suffered a mild heart attack on 30.11.2010 around 19 hrs. He had to undergo angioplasty on 01.12.2010 around 01 30 hrs. It may be noted that the native was running the period of Sat-Ven-Jup-Jup-Sat from 14.42.54 hrs of 29.11.2010 to 20.51.05 hrs of 02.12.2010.

Jupiter is a co-ruling Planet in the 5th cusp (heart). It is in Mars star that is placed in 11 (circulatory system) and sub of Venus that appears in 6 (disease). Mars is also the sub sub lord of 12th cusp (hospitalisation).

Prana Lord Saturn is the sub sub lord of the 5th cusp (Heart) and also sub sub lord of 8 (surgery). Saturn is in Jupiter star (5, 8) and in the sub of Mercury that is the sub lord of 8 and star lord of 12. Thus we find Antara, Sookshma and Prana lord justifies the event.

At the time of heart attack Moon was transiting in Mercury sign, Sun star, Mercury sub and Saturn sub sub. All these Planets are related to the houses that are capable to cause the heart disease.

At the time of surgery Moon was transiting in Moon star, Moon sub and Rahu sub sub. In the chart Moon appears in 6 (minor surgery) and 12 (hospitalization). Moon in the chart has PS. Thus we will treat Moon to be in Moon star, Moon Sub and Venus sub sub. Applying the principle of bunching we will say Moon is in Moon star and Venus sub that is the star lord of 5. Thus transit of Moon justifies surgery.

Figure 6.13 represents the progressed chart of the event of surgery. Let us study it independently.

Fig 6.13 Progress on 01.12.2010 at01.30 hrs

Name	Fig 6.13	Place	Mathura
Longitude	77-41-48-E	Latitude	27-29-21-N
Sidereal Time	04-48-35	Date	08/3/1946
Day	Friday	Geocentric Latitude	27-19-55-N
Nakshatra	Krittika-1 Qtr.	Time	18:5:21.000
Lunar Nodes	True	Tithi	Shukla Paksha - Shasti
Time Zone	+5:30:0 DST	00:00	
Ayanamsa	23-05-40	House System	Placidus

Rashi Chart

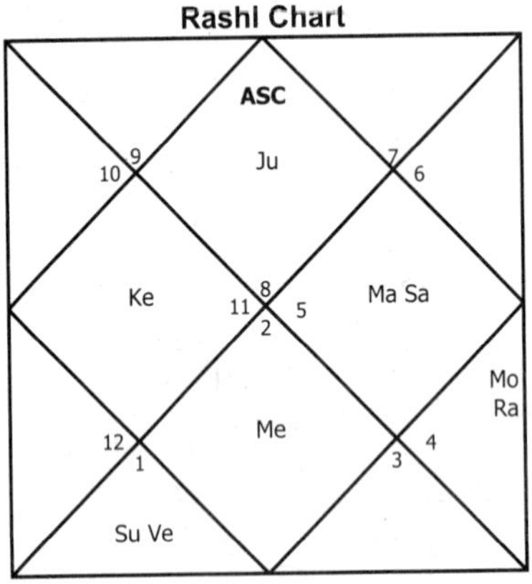

Bhava Chart

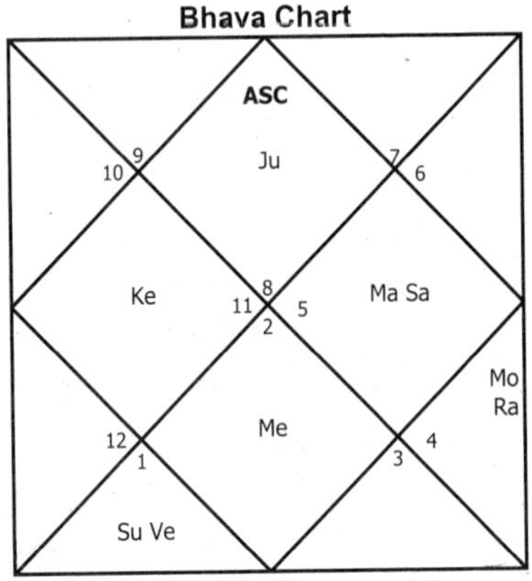

Cusp Chart

V 10-51-07	VI 08-43-17 Su 20-33-23 Ve 28-59-12	VII 02-44-38 Me 21-29-53	VIII 02-34-46
Ke 18-44-42 IV 08-47-44			IX 04-58-28 Mo 09-14-56 Ra 24-21-27
III 04-58-28			X 08-47-44 Ma 18-57-34 Sa 21-08-46
II 02-34-46	Ju 24-28-51 I 02-44-38	XII 08-43-17	XI 10-51-07

Fig. 6.13 Contd......

Planetary Position

Planet	Sign	D-M-S	R L	STL	SL	SSL	Hse	D	S
Sun	Ari	20-33-23	Ma	Ve	Ju	Sa	6	P	
Moon	Can	09-14-56	Mo	Sa	Ve	Ju	9		
Mars	Leo	18-57-34	Su	Ve	Ra	Sa	10	P	
Mercury	Tau	21-29-53	Ve	Mo	Ve	Ra	7		
Jupiter	Sco	24-28-51	Ma	Me	Ra	Ju	1	P	
Venus	Ari	28-59-12	Ma	Su	Ma	Ke	6	P	
Saturn	Leo	21-08-46	Su	Ve	Ju	Ve	10		
Rahu	Can	24-21-27	Mo	Me	Ra	Ra	9		
Ketu	Aqu	18-44-42	Sa	Ra	Mo	Sa	4	P	

Cuspal Position

Cusp	Sign	D-M-S	R L	STL	SL	SSL	% Arc
Cusp I	Sco	02-44-38	Ma	Ju	Ra	Ve	38.16
Cusp II	Sag	02-34-46	Ju	Ke	Ve	Me	07.55
Cusp III	Cap	04-58-28	Sa	Su	Sa	Ju	51.45
Cusp IV	Aqu	08-47-44	Sa	Ra	Ju	Ju	54.36
Cusp V	Pis	10-51-07	Ju	Sa	Su	Ke	05.22
Cusp VI	Ari	08-43-17	Ma	Ke	Ju	Ve	98.47
Cusp VII	Tau	02-44-38	Ve	Su	Ju	Ra	03.95
Cusp VIII	Gem	02-34-46	Me	Ma	Ke	Me	20.73
Cusp IX	Can	04-58-28	Mo	Sa	Sa	Ra	40.47
Cusp X	Leo	08-47-44	Su	Ke	Ju	Su	78.30
Cusp XI	Vir	10-51-07	Me	Mo	Mo	Ke	71.70
Cusp XII	Lib	08-43-17	Ve	Ra	Ju	Ju	23.09

Prana lord Saturn is in Venus star that is placed in 6. It is in the sub of Jupiter that appears in 1 and 5 and 12. Thus we find that progressed chart also confirms the execution of the event.

From the above discussion we can say that the chart cast as per time of birth 18.05.21 hrs is the true chart of the native.

Example 3: An interesting case study was provided on Nov 22, 2008 by Mr Ron Gaunt the administrator of Astrology Research Forum.

"The First of our Interesting Charts (ICs) is the case of female twins born at 6:25 am and 8:00 am 28 March 1869 near Bath in England. The co-ordinates for Bath are 51N23 002W22 and the TZ is UT 00:00.

On 1 May 1889 these twin sisters went out driving. As the bit slipped between the horse's teeth one of the sisters decided to adjust it. The horse bolted when she removed the head piece, and she was killed instantly.

Which sister, the younger or the elder, do you think was killed and why"?

Ron Gaunt

On Nov 23, 2008 the author wrote," The chart can be rectified by setting the ascendant to satisfy necessary conditions. The chart should promise short life and also unnatural death. Third cusp SSL in case of elder twin should also establish link with the Moon star which in this case is Moon.

Dasa potential and transit clearly helps to arrive at the answer. On death day Moon and Sun star needs to be related to the SSL of the 8th cusp".

It was observed by the author that some members were not feeling confidant in fixing the correct charts of the twin sisters. On Nov24, 2008 the author wrote," I have tried to rectify the charts of twin sisters. The Astrological Birth time and ascendant degrees are indicated below:

Elder Twin: TOB 06.23.56 hrs with ascendant Pisces 29.32.03(Khullar Ayanamsa).

Younger Twin TOB: 08.00.21 hrs with ascendant Taurus 11.54.28

Please note that I have used Latitude of Bath as 51N23 05".

Using the rectified charts some members provided correct answer. On Nov26, 2008 Mr Ron Gaunt wrote, "This was a great start to our 'Interesting Charts' Section. Congratulations to all that got the correct answer, which was that it was the younger twin that died. I suspect Mr Khullar made it easier after he posted rectifications for both charts. It shows that even with minimum data, that it is possible to get good rectification".

Let us try to verify the accuracy of the Charts using the concepts of Advanced Techniques of BTR.

Figure 6.14 represents the rectified chart of elder twin. The chart was cast using Khullar Ayanamsa.

Fig. 6.14 on 28.03.1869 at 6.23.56 hrs

Name	TH Fig 614	Place	Bath
Longitude	2-22-0-W	Latitude	51-23-5-N
Sidereal Time	18-37-18	Date	28/3/1869
Day	Sunday	Geocentric Latitude	51-11-49-N
Nakshatra	Hasta-4 Qtr.	Time	06:23:56
Lunar Nodes	True	Tithi	Krishna Paksha - Pratipada
Time Zone	-0:0:0	DST	00:00
Ayanamsa	22-01-15	House System	Placidus

Rashi Chart

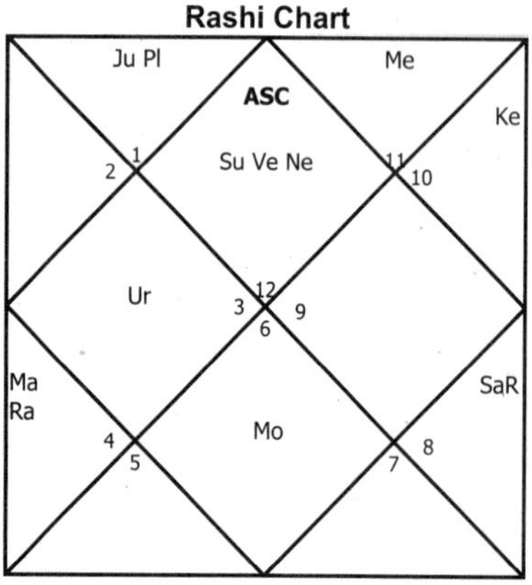

Bhava Chart

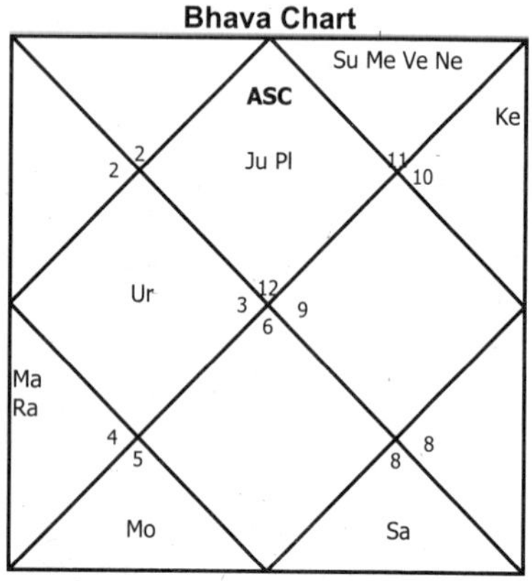

Cusp Chart

I 29-32-03 Ne 24-37-18 Su 15-36-24 Ve 04-40-45	Ju 00-26-59 Pl 23-39-01	II 07-31-10 III 28-48-56	IV 16-32-50 Ur 21-19-24
Me 19-52-07 XII 04-05-57			V 05-55-49 Ma 23-16-52 Ra 23-33-07
Ke 23-33-07 XI 05-55-49			VI 04-05-57
X 16-32-50	IX 28-48-56 SaR 25-08-48 VIII 07-31-10		Mo 20-49-23 VII 29-32-03

Fig. 6.14 Contd......

Planetary Position

Planet	Sign	D-M-S	RL	STL	SL	SSL	Hse	D	S
Sun	Pis	15-36-24	Ju	Sa	Ju	Me	12		P
Moon	Vir	20-49-23	Me	Mo	Ve	Su	6		P
Mars	Can	23-16-52	Mo	Me	Mo	Su	5		
Mercury	Aqu	19-52-07	Sa	Ra	Ma	Ve	12		P
Jupiter	Ari	00-26-59	Ma	Ke	Ke	Ju	1		P
Venus	Pis	04-40-45	Ju	Sa	Sa	Mo	12		P
Saturn	Sco	25-08-48	Ma	Me	Ra	Me	8	R	
T.Rahu	Can	23-33-07	Mo	Me	Ma	Ju	5		P
T.Ketu	Cap	23-33-07	Sa	Ma	Ma	Ju	11		
Uranus	Gem	21-19-24	Me	Ju	Ju	Mo	4		
Neptune	Pis	24-37-18	Ju	Me	Ra	Ju	12		
Pluto	Ari	23-39-01	Ma	Ve	Sa	Ra	1		

Cuspal Position

Cusp	Sign	D-M-S	R L	STL	SL	SSL	% Arc
Cusp I	Pis	29-32-03	Ju	Me	Sa	Ra	41.80
Cusp II	Tau	07-31-10	Ve	Su	Ke	Ju	75.93
Cusp III	Tau	28-48-56	Ve	Ma	Sa	Ve	48.38
Cusp IV	Gem	16-32-50	Me	Ra	Ve	Ju	65.90
Cusp V	Can	05-55-49	Mo	Sa	Me	Ve	34.29
Cusp VI	Leo	04-05-57	Su	Ke	Mo	Ju	73.22
Cusp VII	Vir	29-32-03	Me	Ma	Sa	Ra	41.80
Cusp VIII	Sco	07-31-10	Ma	Sa	Ke	Su	28.66
Cusp IX	Sco	28-48-56	Ma	Me	Sa	Ve	48.38
Cusp X	Sag	16-32-50	Ju	Ve	Mo	Ju	00.56
Cusp XI	Cap	05-55-49	Sa	Su	Me	Mo	20.35
Cusp XII	Aqu	04-05-57	Sa	Ma	Ve	Sa	01.88

Accuracy of the Positions of Sun, Moon and Ascendant: It can be verified that the planets co-ruling the positions of Sun, Moon and ascendant are related to 1, 7 and 10. Sub sub lord of ascendant is Rahu that represents Moon and Mercury. We can always replace the sub sub lord of a cusp in case of Rahu or Ketu by the planets it represents when we are checking the promise of some aspect of life from that cusp. We can thus assume that Moon is the sub sub lord of ascendant. Thus the sub sub lord of ascendant establishes relationship with the Moon's star lord which is Moon.

Promise of Younger co-born: Sub sub lord of ascendant is Rahu that has PS. It is in the sub of Mars that appears in 3. Sub sub lord of 3rd cusp is Venus. Moon the star lord of Moon is in the sub of Venus. Thus 3rd sub sub lord establishes relationship with the common Moon star Lord.

Promise of Longevity: Short, medium or long life of the native is declared by analyzing the relationship which the 1, 3 and 8 houses sub sub lords make with Maraka and Badhakasthana.

Short Life (i.e. up to 33 Years): If the sub sub lords of 1, 3 and 8 houses become the fruitful significators of 2nd and 7th and Badhaka house the life of the native is short.

Long Life (beyond 66 Years): If the sub sub lords of 1, 3 and 8 houses become significators of 1, 3, 5, 8, 9 (not for fixed ascendant's), and 11 (not for Moveable ascendants), the native is destined to live long.

Medium Span of Life (i.e. between 33 to 66 years): If the SS lords of 1, 3 and 8 houses become significators of both Maraka houses as well as houses of Longevity, the native is destined to have medium span of life.

In this chart we find that sub sub lord of ascendant is Rahu that is in Mercury star that appears in 1, 4, 5, 7, 9, 11 and 12. Rahu is in the sub of Mars that appears in 3, 7, 8 & 9. It is placed in 5 but it has no PS. Thus the sub sub lord does not promise short life.

Promise of Unnatural Death: For unnatural death the following conditions should exist in the chart.

1. Eighth Cusp sub sub lord should be significator of 8th and 12th house.
2. Eighth cusp sub sub lord and its star lord should be in cardinal and violent signs Aries, Taurus, Scorpio, Leo, Sagittarius or Capricorn.
3. Ascendant sub sub lord should also be connected with 8 and 12 houses to promise unnatural death.

Sub sub lord of 8th cusp in this chart is Sun that is in Pisces which is not a violent sign. However Sun is in Saturn star that is placed in Scorpio which is a violent sign. Saturn appears in 1, 8 and 12. Thus 8th sub sub lord does indicate the possibility of unnatural death.

Let us see what is promised by the sub sub lord of ascendant. Rahu is in Mercury star which is placed in 12 and Rahu is in the sub of Mars that appears in 8.

We may say that the chart does promise unnatural death. But the native cannot meet death on 01.05.1889 because chart does not promise short life. More over on that date the native was running Dasa of Rahu that represents Moon. Rahu Dasa becomes Markesh only if Rahu as Rahu and the planets which Rahu represents simultaneously show the power to inflict death. Here Moon has no power to cause the death of the native.

This indicates the accuracy of the chart because the elder twin did not meet death on 01.05.1889.

Figure 6.15 represents the chart of the younger twin. Let us check the accuracy of this chart.

Fig. 6.15 at 08.00.21 hrs

Name	Fig 6.15	Place	Bath
Longitude	2-22-0-W	Latitude	51-23-05-N
Sidereal Time	20-13-59	Date	28/3/1869
Day	Sunday	Geocentric Latitude	51-11-49-N
Nakshatra	Hasta-4 Qtr.	Time	08:00:21
Lunar Nodes	True	Tithi	Krishna Paksha - Pratipada
Time Zone	-0:0:0	DST	00:00
Ayanamsa	22-01-15	House System	Placidus

Rashi Chart

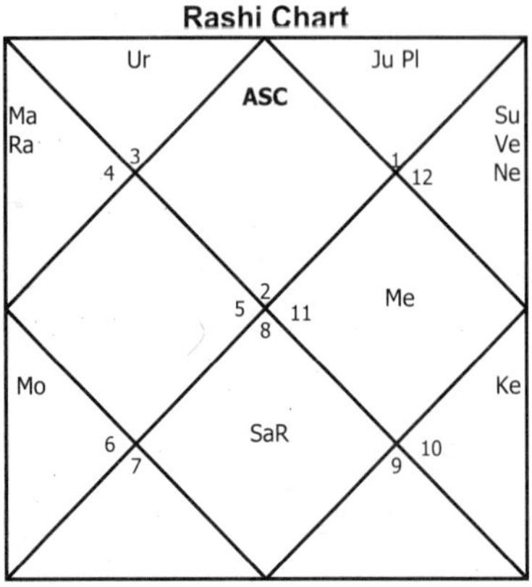

Bhava Chart

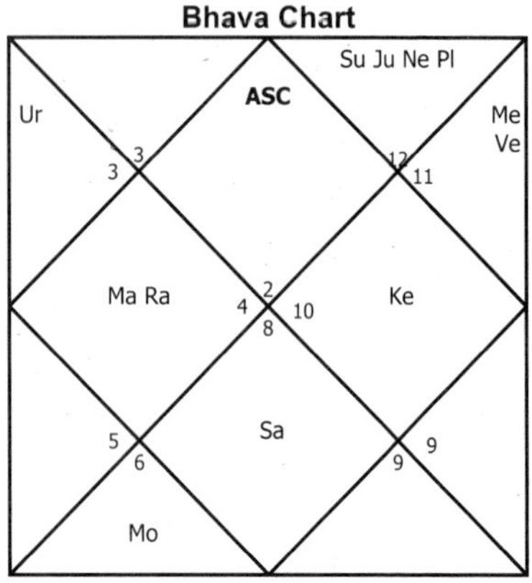

Cusp Chart

Ne 24-37-27 Su 15-40-22 XII 13-55-31 Ve 04-45-44	Ju 00-27-56 Pl 23-39-05	I 11-54-28	II 03-33-20 III 20-52-49 Ur 21-19-25
Me 19-57-34 XI 03-40-03			IV 09-14-31 Ma 23-16-57 Ra 23-32-36
Ke 23-32-36 X 09-14-31			V 03-40-03
IX 20-52-49 VIII 03-33-20	SaR 25-08-47 VII 11-54-28		VI 13-55-31 Mo 21-50-03

Fig. 6.15 Contd......

Planetary Position

Planet	Sign	D-M-S	R L	STL	SL	SSL	Hse	D	S
Sun	Pis	15-40-22	Ju	Sa	Ju	Ke	12	P	
Moon	Vir	21-50-03	Me	Mo	Ve	Ju	6	P	
Mars	Can	23-16-57	Mo	Me	Mo	Su	4		
Mercury	Aqu	19-57-34	Sa	Ra	Ma	Mo	11	P	
Jupiter	Ari	00-27-56	Ma	Ke	Ke	Ju	12	P	
Venus	Pis	04-45-44	Ju	Sa	Sa	Ma	11	P	
Saturn	Sco	25-08-47	Ma	Me	Ra	Me	7	R	
T.Rahu	Can	23-32-36	Mo	Me	Ma	Ju	4	P	
T.Ketu	Cap	23-32-36	Sa	Ma	Ma	Ju	10		
Uranus	Gem	21-19-25	Me	Ju	Ju	Mo	3		
Neptune	Pis	24-37-27	Ju	Me	Ra	Ju	12		
Pluto	Ari	23-39-05	Ma	Ve	Sa	Ra	12		

Cuspal Position

Cusp	Sign	D-M-S	R L	STL	SL	SSL	% Arc
Cusp I	Tau	11-54-28	Ve	Mo	Ra	Ra	06.26
Cusp II	Gem	03-33-20	Me	Ma	Ve	Ra	27.79
Cusp III	Gem	20-52-49	Me	Ju	Ju	Ve	02.14
Cusp IV	Can	09-14-31	Mo	Sa	Ve	Ju	00.45
Cusp V	Leo	03-40-03	Su	Ke	Mo	Mo	00.97
Cusp VI	Vir	13-55-31	Me	Mo	Ju	Ju	15.36
Cusp VII	Sco	11-54-28	Ma	Sa	Mo	Ve	20.15
Cusp VIII	Sag	03-33-20	Ju	Ke	Su	Ve	00.03
Cusp IX	Sag	20-52-49	Ju	Ve	Ju	Me	99.58
Cusp X	Cap	09-14-31	Sa	Su	Ve	Sa	10.91
Cusp XI	Aqu	03-40-03	Sa	Ma	Ve	Ra	61.38
Cusp XII	Pis	13-55-31	Ju	Sa	Ra	Me	54.03

Accuracy of Sun, Moon and Ascendant: It can be verified that planets co ruling the positions of Sun, Moon and ascendant satisfies the necessary conditions. Sub sub lord of ascendant is Rahu that represents Moon. Thus the sub sub lord of ascendant establishes relationship with the Moon's star lord.

11th cusp sub sub lord is Rahu that represents Moon. Thus the sub sub lord of 11th cusp establishes relationship with the common Moon star lord of twins.

Rahu has PS. As such sub sub lord of 11th cusp is linked with the ascendant. This promises birth of younger co born.

Promise of Longevity: Sub sub lord of ascendant is Rahu that is in Mercury star. Mercury appears as sub sub lord of 9 (Badhaka) and Sign lord of 2 Maraka). Rahu is in the sub of Mars that appears in 7 (Maraka). Thus the sub sub lord of ascendant is a fruitful significator of Maraka and Badhaka houses.

Sub sub lord of 3rd and 8th cusp is Venus that has PS. Venus appears in 2, 7 and 9. Venus is in the sub of Saturn and SS of Mars. Both Saturn and Mars appear in 7 and 2. Thus Venus is a fruitful significator of Maraka and Badhaka houses.

Above discussion clearly reveals that the native's life span is short.

Promise of unnatural Death: Sub sub lord of 8th cusp is Venus that is placed in Pisces but Venus is in Saturn star that is placed in violent sign Scorpio. Venus has PS and as such it signifies 8.It is in the sub of Saturn that appears in 12. Thus 8th sub sub lord indicates the possibility of unnatural death.

Note: Kindly note as stated above Rahu the dasa lord along with the planet which Rahu represents (Moon & Mercury) in this case should simultaneously show the power to inflict death. Here Rahu does not operate 8th cusp.

Sub sub lord of ascendant is Rahu that represents Mercury and Moon. It may be observed that both Rahu and Mercury signify 12 and Moon strongly signify 1 and 8. This not only indicates unnatural death but also points out that the native himself may become cause of her death.

Verification of the Event of Death: The native died on 01.05.1889 in the morning when she was running Dasa period of Rahu-Venus-Venus-Mercury-Venus. All these planets have the potential to cause the death of the native. It is worth noting that the Prana lord is Venus that is the sub sub lord of the 8th cusp. Thus it accounts for unnatural death as discussed above.

Let us check whether the progressed chart confirms the event or not. Figure 6.16 represents the progressed chart for the event of death.

Fig. 6.16 Progress on 01.05.1889

Name	Fig 6.15	Place	Bath
Longitude	2-22-0-W	Latitude	51-23-5-N
Sidereal Time	20-13-59	Date	28/3/1869
Day	Sunday	Geocentric Latitude	51-11-49-N
Nakshatra	Hasta-4 Qtr.	Time	08:00:21
Lunar Nodes	True	Tithi	Krishna Paksha - Pratipada
Time Zone	-0:0:0	DST	00:00
Ayanamsa	22-01-15	House System	Placidus

Rashi Chart

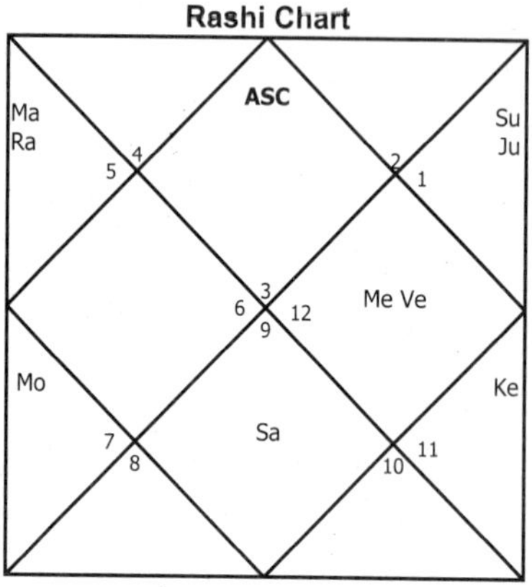

Bhava Chart

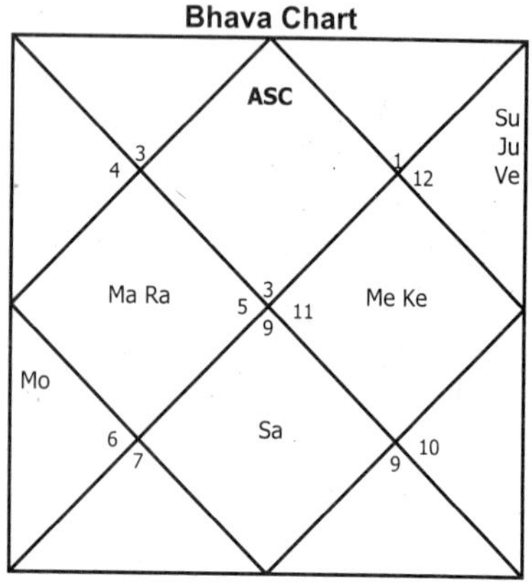

Cusp Chart

Ve 19-07-16 XI 07-26-29 Me 06-10-02	Su 03-11-40 Ju 22-13-31 XII 24-49-25		I 10-01-04 II 26-21-59
Ke 16-26-49 X 05-22-26			III 13-35-41
IX 13-35-41			IV 05-22-26 Ma 16-21-09 Ra 16-34-26
VIII 26-21-59 Sa 17-56-12 VII 10-01-04		VI 24-49-25 Mo 15-31-57	V 07-26-29

Fig. 6.16 Contd......

Planetary Position

Planet	Sign	D-M-S	R L	STL	SL	SSL	Hse	D	S
Sun	Ari	03-11-40	Ma	Ke	Su	Ra	11	P	
Moon	Lib	15-31-57	Ve	Ra	Ve	Ve	5	P	
Mars	Leo	16-21-09	Su	Ve	Mo	Ma	4	P	
Mercury	Pis	06-10-02	Ju	Sa	Me	Su	10		
Jupiter	Ari	22-13-31	Ma	Ve	Sa	Me	11	P	
Venus	Pis	19-07-16	Ju	Me	Ke	Sa	11		
Saturn	Sag	17-56-12	Ju	Ve	Ma	Ve	7		
Rahu	Leo	16-34-26	Su	Ve	Mo	Ju	4		
Ketu	Aqu	16-26-49	Sa	Ra	Ve	Ju	10	P	

Cuspal Position

Cusp	Sign	D-M-S	R L	STL	SL	SSL	% Arc
Cusp I	Gem	10-01-04	Me	Ra	Ju	Mo	62.04
Cusp II	Gem	26-21-59	Me	Ju	Ke	Sa	35.90
Cusp III	Can	13-35-41	Mo	Sa	Ra	Sa	43.93
Cusp IV	Leo	05-22-26	Su	Ke	Ma	Ve	39.88
Cusp V	Vir	07-26-29	Me	Su	Ke	Ju	00.63
Cusp VI	Lib	24-49-25	Ve	Ju	Me	Mo	93.76
Cusp VII	Sag	10-01-04	Ju	Ke	Sa	Ke	41.55
Cusp VIII	Sag	26-21-59	Ju	Ve	Ke	Ju	35.49
Cusp IX	Cap	13-35-41	Sa	Mo	Ra	Su	89.12
Cusp X	Aqu	05-22-26	Sa	Ma	Su	Me	66.50
Cusp XI	Pis	07-26-29	Ju	Sa	Ke	Ve	48.36
Cusp XII	Ari	24-49-25	Ma	Ve	Me	Mo	23.17

The native's death took place when Moon was progressing in Rahu-Vens-Venus-Mercury-Venus.

Rahu in the progressed chart is in Venus star that is the star lord of 8. Rahu is in the sub of Moon that is the sub sub lord of 1. Rahu is in the SS of Jupiter that is sub sub lord of 8 and star lord of 2 and Sign lord of 7.

Venus is in the star of Mercury that appears in 1. Venus is in the sub of Ketu that is sub sub lord of 7 (Badhaka) and sub lord of 8.

Mercury is in the star of Saturn that is placed in 7 (Maraka and Badhaka) and sub of Mercury that appears in 1 and 2.

Thus we find that the event is confirmed by the analysis of progressed chart.

We may say that the chart was correctly rectified.

Index